Get the eBook FREE!

(PDF, ePub, Kindle, and liveBook all included)

We believe that once you buy a book from us, you should be able to read it in any format we have available. To get electronic versions of this book at no additional cost to you, purchase and then register this book at the Manning website.

Go to https://www.manning.com/freebook and follow the instructions to complete your pBook registration.

That's it!
Thanks from Manning!

Ensemble Methods
for Machine Learning

Ensemble Methods
for Machine Learning

GAUTAM KUNAPULI

MANNING
SHELTER ISLAND

Manning Publications Co.
20 Baldwin Road
PO Box 761
Shelter Island, NY 11964

Development editors:	Katherine Olstein and Karen Miller
Technical development editor:	Alain Couniot
Review editor:	Mihaela Batinic
Production editor:	Kathleen Rossland
Copy editor:	Julie McNamee
Proofreader:	Katie Tennant
Technical proofreader:	Manish Jain
Typesetter and cover designer:	Marija Tudor

ISBN 9781617297137
Printed in the United States of America

To my cousin Bhima,
who inspired me to board a plane and go far away from home,
who made grad school look glamorous (it wasn't, but was worth it),
without whose example, my own journey would have been very different,
and this book would probably not exist.
Wish you were here.

contents

preface

Once upon a time, I was a graduate student, adrift and rudderless in an ocean of unfulfilling research directions and uncertain futures. Then I stumbled upon a remarkable article titled "Support Vector Machines: Hype or Hallelujah?" This being the early 2000s, support vector machines (SVMs) were, of course, the preeminent machine-learning technique of the time.

In the article, the authors (one of whom would later become my PhD advisor) took a rather reductionist approach to explaining the considerably complex topic of SVMs, interleaving intuition and geometry with theory and application. The article made a powerful impression on me, at once igniting a lifelong fascination with machine learning and an obsession with understanding how such methods work under the hood. Indeed, the title of the first chapter pays homage to that paper that had so profound an influence over my life.

Much like SVMs then, ensemble methods are widely considered a preeminent machine-learning technique today. But what many people don't realize is that some ensemble method or another has always been considered state of the art over the decades: bagging in the 1990s, random forests and boosting in the 2000s, gradient boosting in the 2010s, and XGBoost in the 2020s. In the ever-mutable world of the best machine-learning models, ensemble methods, it seems, are indeed worth the hype.

I've been fortunate to spend a good deal of the past decade training many kinds of ensemble models, making industry applications out of them, and writing academic research papers on them. In this book, I try to showcase as many of these ensemble methods as possible: some that you've definitely heard of and some new ones that you should really hear about.

This book was never intended to be just a tutorial with step-by-step instructions and cut-and-paste code (although you can use it that way, too). There are dozens of such fantastic tutorials on the web, and they can get you going on your data set in an instant. Instead, I talk about each new method using an immersive approach inspired by that first machine-learning paper I ever read and refined in college classrooms during my time as a graduate lecturer.

I've always felt that to understand a technical topic deeply, it helps to strip it down, take it apart, and try to put it back together again. I adopt the same approach in this book: we'll take ensemble methods apart and (re)create them ourselves. We'll tweak them and poke them to see how they change. And, in doing so, we'll see exactly what makes them tick!

I hope this book will be helpful in demystifying those technical and algorithmic details and get you into the ensemble mindset, be it for your class project, Kaggle competition, or production-quality application.

acknowledgments

I never thought that a book on ensemble methods would itself turn into an ensemble effort of family and friends, colleagues, and collaborators, all of whom had a lot to do with this book, from conception to completion.

To Brian Sawyer, who let me pitch the idea of this book, for believing in this project, for being patient, and for keeping me on track: thank you for giving me this opportunity to do this thing that I've always wanted to do.

To my first development editor, Katherine Olstein, second development editor, Karen Miller, and technical development editor, Alain Couniot: I had a vision for what this book would look like when I started, and you helped make it better. Thank you for the hours and days of meticulous reviews, for your eagle-eyed edits, and for challenging me always to be a better writer. Your efforts have much to do with the final quality of this book.

To Manish Jain: thank you for painstakingly proofreading the code line by line. To Marija Tudor: thank you for designing this absolutely fantastic cover (which I still think is the best part of this book), for making it orange at my request, and for typesetting it from cover to cover. To the proofing and production team at Manning: thank you for your exceptional craft—this book looks perfect—review editor Mihaela Batinic, production editor Kathleen Rossland, copy editor Julie McNamee, and proofreader Katie Tennant.

To my reviewers, Al Krinker, Alain Lompo, Biswanath Chowdhury, Chetan Saran Mehra, Eric Platon, Gustavo A. Patino, Joaquin Beltran, Lucian Mircea Sasu, Manish Jain, McHugson Chambers, Ninoslav Cerkez, Noah Flynn, Oliver Korten, Or Golan, Peter V. Henstock, Philip Best, Sergio Govoni, Simon Seyag, Stephen John Warnett, Subhash Talluri, Todd Cook, and Xiangbo Mao: thank you for your fabulous feedback and some truly terrific insights and comments. I tried to take in all of your advice (I really did), and much of it has worked its way into the book.

To the readers who read the book during early access and who left many comments, corrections, and words of encouragement—you know who you are—thank you for the support!

To my mentors, Kristin Bennett, Jong-Shi Pang, Jude Shavlik, Sriraam Natarajan, and Maneesh Singh, who have each shaped my thinking profoundly at different stages of my journey as a student, postdoc, professor, and professional: thank you for teaching me how to think in machine learning, how to speak machine learning, and how to build with machine learning. Much of your wisdom and many of your lessons endure in this book. And Kristin, I hope you like the title of the first chapter.

To Jenny and Guilherme de Oliveira, for your friendship over the years, but especially during the great pandemic, when much of this book was written: thank you for keeping me sane. I will always treasure our afternoons and evenings in that summer and fall of 2020, tucked away in your little backyard, our pod and sanctuary.

To my parents, Vijaya and Shivakumar, and my brother, Anupam: thank you for always believing in me, and for always supporting me, even from tens of thousands of miles away. I know you're proud of me. This book is finally finished, and now we can do all those other things we're always talking about . . . until I start writing the next one, anyway.

To my wife, best friend, and biggest champion, Kristine: you've been an inexhaustible source of comfort and encouragement, especially when things got tough. Thank you for bouncing ideas with me, for proofreading with me, for the tea and snacks, for the Gus, for sacrificing all those weekends (and, sometimes, weeknights) when I was writing. Thank you for hanging in there with me, for always being there for me, and for never once doubting that I could do this. I love you!

about this book

There has never been a better time to learn about ensemble methods. The models covered in this book fall into three broad categories:

- *Foundational ensemble methods*—The classics that everyone has heard of, including historical ensemble techniques such as bagging, random forests, and AdaBoost
- *State-of-the-art ensemble methods*—The tried and tested powerhouses of the modern ensemble era that form the core of many real-world, in-production prediction, recommendation, and search systems
- *Emerging ensemble methods*—The latest methods fresh out of the research foundries to handle new needs and emerging priorities such as explainability and interpretability

Each chapter will introduce a different ensembling technique, using a three-pronged approach. First, you'll learn the *intuition* behind each ensemble method by visualizing step by step how learning actually takes place. Second, you'll *implement* a basic version of each ensemble method yourself to fully understand the algorithmic nuts and bolts. Third, you'll learn how to *apply* powerful ensemble libraries and tools practically.

Most chapters also come with their own case study on real-world data, drawn from applications such as handwritten digit prediction, recommendation systems, sentiment analysis, demand forecasting, and others. These case studies tackle several real-world issues where appropriate, including preprocessing and feature engineering, hyperparameter selection, efficient training techniques, and effective model evaluation.

Who should read this book

This book is intended for a broad audience:

- Data scientists who are interested in using ensemble methods to get the best out of their data for real-world applications

- MLOps and DataOps engineers who are building, evaluating, and deploying ensemble-based, production-ready applications and pipelines
- Students of data science and machine learning who want to use this book as a learning resource or as a practical reference to supplement textbooks
- Kagglers and data science enthusiasts who can use this book as an entry point into learning about the endless modeling possibilities with ensemble methods

This book is *not* an introduction to machine learning and data science. This book assumes that you have some basic working knowledge of machine learning and that you've used or played around with at least one fundamental learning technique (e.g., decision trees).

A basic working knowledge of Python is also assumed. Examples, visualizations, and chapter case studies all use Python and Jupyter Notebooks. Knowledge of other commonly used Python packages such as NumPy (for mathematical computations), pandas (for data manipulation), and Matplotlib (for visualization) is useful, but not necessary. In fact, you can learn how to use these packages through the examples and case studies.

How this book is organized: A road map

This book is organized into nine chapters in three parts. Part 1 is a gentle introduction to ensemble methods, part 2 introduces and explains several essential ensemble methods, and part 3 covers advanced topics.

Part 1, "The basics of ensembles," introduces ensemble methods and why you should care about them. This part also contains a road map of ensemble methods covered in the rest of the book:

- Chapter 1 discusses ensemble methods and basic ensemble terminology. It also introduces the fit-versus-complexity tradeoff (or the bias-variance tradeoff, as it's more formally called). You'll build your very first ensemble in this chapter.

Part 2, "Essential ensemble methods," covers several important families of ensemble methods, many of which are considered "essential" and are widely used in real-world applications. In each chapter, you'll learn how to implement different ensemble methods from scratch, how they work, and how to apply them to real-world problems:

- Chapter 2 begins our journey with parallel ensemble methods, specifically, parallel homogeneous ensembles. Ensemble methods covered include bagging, random forests, pasting, random subspaces, random patches, and Extra Trees.
- Chapter 3 continues the journey with more parallel ensembles, but the focus in this chapter is on parallel heterogeneous ensembles. Ensemble methods covered include combining base models by majority voting, combining by weighting, prediction fusion with Dempster-Shafer, and meta-learning by stacking.
- Chapter 4 introduces another family of ensemble methods—sequential adaptive ensembles—in particular, the fundamental concept of boosting many weak

models into one powerful model. Ensemble methods covered include Ada-Boost and LogitBoost.

- Chapter 5 builds on the foundational concepts of boosting and covers another fundamental sequential ensemble method, gradient boosting, which combines gradient descent with boosting. This chapter discusses how we can train gradient-boosting ensembles with scikit-learn and LightGBM.
- Chapter 6 continues to explore sequential ensemble methods with Newton boosting, an efficient and effective extension of gradient boosting that combines Newton's descent with boosting. This chapter discusses how we can train Newton boosting ensembles with XGBoost.

Part 3, "Ensembles in the wild: Adapting ensemble methods to your data," shows you how to apply ensemble methods to many scenarios, including data sets with continuous and count-valued labels and data sets with categorical features. You'll also learn how to interpret your ensembles and explain their predictions:

- Chapter 7 shows how we can train ensembles for different types of regression problems and generalized linear models, where training labels are continuous- or count-valued. Parallel and sequential ensembles for linear regression, Poisson regression, gamma regression, and Tweedie regression are covered.
- Chapter 8 identifies challenges in learning with nonnumeric features, specifically, categorical features, and encoding schemes that will help us train effective ensembles for this kind of data. This chapter also discusses two important practical issues: data leakage and prediction shift. Finally, we'll see how to overcome these issues with ordered boosting and CatBoost.
- Chapter 9 covers the newly emerging and very important topic of explainable AI from the perspective of ensemble methods. This chapter introduces the notion of explainability and why it's important. Several common black-box explainability methods are also discussed, including permutation feature importance, partial dependence plots, surrogate methods, Locally Interpretable Model-Agnostic Explanation, Shapley values, and SHapley Additive exPlanations. The glass-box ensemble method, explainable boosting machines, and the InterpretML package are also introduced.
- The epilogue concludes our journey with additional topics for further exploration and reading.

While most of the chapters in the book can reasonably be read in a standalone manner, chapters 7, 8, and 9 build on part 2 of the book.

About the code

All the code and examples in this book are written in Python 3. The code is organized into Jupyter Notebooks and is available in an online GitHub repository (https://github .com/gkunapuli/ensemble-methods-notebooks) and for download from the Manning website (www.manning.com/books/ensemble-methods-for-machine-learning). You can get executable snippets of code from the liveBook (online) version of this book at https://livebook.manning.com/book/ensemble-methods-for-machine-learning.

Several Python scientific and visualization libraries are also used, including NumPy (https://numpy.org/), SciPy (https://scipy.org/), pandas (https://pandas.pydata .org/), and Matplotlib (https://matplotlib.org/). The code also uses several Python machine-learning and ensemble-method libraries, including scikit-learn (https:// scikit-learn.org/stable/), LightGBM (https://lightgbm.readthedocs.io/), XGBoost (https://xgboost.readthedocs.io/), CatBoost (https://catboost.ai/), and InterpretML (https://interpret.ml/).

This book contains many examples of source code both in numbered listings and in line with normal text. In both cases, source code is formatted in a `fixed-width font like this` to separate it from ordinary text. In many cases, the original source code has been reformatted; we've added line breaks and reworked indentation to accommodate the available page space in the book. Additionally, comments in the source code have often been removed from the listings when the code is described in the text. Code annotations accompany many of the listings, highlighting important concepts.

liveBook discussion forum

Purchase of *Ensemble Methods for Machine Learning* includes free access to liveBook, Manning's online reading platform. Using liveBook's exclusive discussion features, you can attach comments to the book globally or to specific sections or paragraphs. It's a snap to make notes for yourself, ask and answer technical questions, and receive help from the author and other users. To access the forum, go to https://livebook .manning.com/book/ensemble-methods-for-machine-learning/discussion. You can also learn more about Manning's forums and the rules of conduct at https://livebook .manning.com/discussion.

Manning's commitment to our readers is to provide a venue where a meaningful dialogue between individual readers and between readers and the author can take place. It's not a commitment to any specific amount of participation on the part of the author, whose contribution to the forum remains voluntary (and unpaid). We suggest you try asking the author some challenging questions lest his interest stray! The forum and the archives of previous discussions will be accessible from the publisher's website as long as the book is in print.

about the author

 **GAUTAM KUNAPULI** has more than 15 years of experience in both academia and the machine-learning industry. His work focuses on human-in-the-loop learning, knowledge-based and advice-taking learning algorithms, and scalable learning for difficult machine-learning problems. Gautam has developed several novel algorithms for diverse application domains, including social network analysis, text and natural language processing, computer vision, behavior mining, educational data mining, insurance and financial analytics, and biomedical applications. He has also published papers exploring ensemble methods in relational domains and with imbalanced data.

about the cover illustration

The figure on the cover of *Ensemble Methods for Machine Learning* is "Huonv ou Musiciene Chinoise," or "Huonv or Chinese musician," from a collection by Jacques Grasset de Saint-Sauveur, published in 1788. Each illustration is finely drawn and colored by hand.

In those days, it was easy to identify where people lived and what their trade or station in life was just by their dress. Manning celebrates the inventiveness and initiative of the computer business with book covers based on the rich diversity of regional culture centuries ago, brought back to life by pictures from collections such as this one.

Part 1

The basics of ensembles

Y**ou've** probably heard a lot about "random forests," "XGBoost," or "gradient boosting." Someone always seems to be using one or another of these to build cool applications or win Kaggle competitions. Have you ever wondered what this fuss is all about?

The fuss, it turns out, is all about *ensemble methods*, a powerful machine-learning paradigm that has found its way into all kinds of applications in health care, finance, insurance, recommendation systems, search, and a lot of other areas.

This book will introduce you to the wide world of ensemble methods, and this part will get you going. To paraphrase the incomparable Julie Andrews from *The Sound of Music,*

Let's start at the very beginning,
A very good place to start.
When you read, you begin with A-B-C.
When you ensemble, you begin with fit-versus-complexity.

The first part of this book will gently introduce ensemble methods with a bit of intuition and a bit of theory on fit versus complexity (or the bias-variance tradeoff, as it's more formally called). You'll then build your very first ensemble from scratch.

When you're finished with this part of the book, you'll understand why ensemble models are often better than individual models and why you should care about them.

Ensemble methods: Hype or hallelujah?

This chapter covers

- Defining and framing the ensemble learning problem
- Motivating the need for ensembles in different applications
- Understanding how ensembles handle fit versus complexity
- Implementing our first ensemble with ensemble diversity and model aggregation

In October 2006, Netflix announced a $1 million prize for the team that could improve movie recommendations by 10% via Netflix's own proprietary recommendation system, CineMatch. The Netflix Grand Prize was one of the first-ever open data science competitions and attracted tens of thousands of teams.

The training set consisted of 100 million ratings that 480,000 users had given to 17,000 movies. Within three weeks, 40 teams had already beaten CineMatch's results. By September 2007, more than 40,000 teams had entered the contest, and a team from AT&T Labs took the 2007 Progress Prize by improving upon CineMatch by 8.42%.

As the competition progressed with the 10% mark remaining elusive, a curious phenomenon emerged among the competitors. Teams began to collaborate and share knowledge about effective feature engineering, algorithms, and techniques. Inevitably, they began combining their models, blending individual approaches into powerful and sophisticated ensembles of many models. These ensembles combined the best of various diverse models and features, and they proved to be far more effective than any individual model.

In June 2009, nearly two years after the contest began, BellKor's Pragmatic Chaos, a merger of three different teams, edged out another merged team, The Ensemble (which was a merger of more than 30 teams!), to improve on the baseline by 10% and take the $1 million prize. Just "edged out" is a bit of an understatement as BellKor's Pragmatic Chaos managed to submit their final models barely 20 minutes before The Ensemble got their models in (http://mng.bz/K08O). In the end, both teams achieved a final performance improvement of 10.06%.

While the Netflix competition captured the imagination of data scientists, machine learners, and casual data science enthusiasts worldwide, its lasting legacy has been to establish ensemble methods as a powerful way to build practical and robust models for large-scale, real-world applications. Among the individual algorithms used are several that have become staples of collaborative filtering and recommendation systems today: k-nearest neighbors, matrix factorization, and restricted Boltzmann machines. However, Andreas Töscher and Michael Jahrer of BigChaos, co-winners of the Netflix prize, summed up[1] their keys to success:

> *During the nearly 3 years of the Netflix competition, there were two main factors which improved the overall accuracy: the quality of the individual algorithms and the ensemble idea. . . . The ensemble idea was part of the competition from the beginning and evolved over time. In the beginning, we used different models with different parametrization and a linear blending. . . . [Eventually] the linear blend was replaced by a nonlinear one.*

In the years since, the use of ensemble methods has exploded, and they have emerged as a state-of-the-art technology for machine learning.

The next two sections provide a gentle introduction to what ensemble methods are, why they work, and where they are applied. Then, we'll look at a subtle but important challenge prevalent in all machine-learning algorithms: the *fit versus complexity tradeoff*.

Finally, we jump into training our very first ensemble method for a hands-on view of how ensemble methods overcome this fit versus complexity tradeoff and improve overall performance. Along the way, you'll become familiar with several key terms that form the lexicon of ensemble methods and will be used throughout the book.

---

[1] Andreas Töscher, Michael Jahrer, and Robert M. Bell, "The BigChaos Solution to the Netflix Grand Prize," (http://mng.bz/9V4r).

1.1 Ensemble methods: The wisdom of the crowds

What exactly is an ensemble method? Let's get an intuitive idea of ensemble methods and how they work by considering the allegorical case of Dr. Randy Forrest. We can then go on to frame the ensemble learning problem.

Dr. Randy Forrest is a famed and successful diagnostician, much like his idol Dr. Gregory House of TV fame. His success, however, is due not only to his exceeding politeness (unlike his cynical and curmudgeonly idol) but also his rather unusual approach to diagnosis.

You see, Dr. Forrest works at a teaching hospital and commands the respect of a large number of doctors-in-training. Dr. Forrest has taken care to assemble a team with a *diversity of skills* (this is pretty important, and we'll see why shortly). His residents excel at different specializations: one is good at cardiology (heart), another at pulmonology (lungs), yet another at neurology (nervous system), and so on. All in all, the group is a rather diversely skillful bunch, each with their own strengths.

Every time Dr. Forrest gets a new case, he solicits the opinions of his residents and collects possible diagnoses from all of them (see figure 1.1). He then democratically selects the final diagnosis as the *most common one* from among all those proposed.

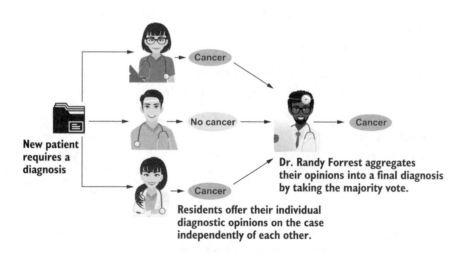

Figure 1.1 The diagnostic procedure followed by Dr. Randy Forrest every time he gets a new case is to ask all of his residents their opinions of the case. His residents offer their diagnoses: either the patient does or does not have cancer. Dr. Forrest then selects the majority answer as the final diagnosis put forth by his team.

Dr. Forrest embodies a diagnostic *ensemble*: he aggregates his residents' diagnoses into a single diagnosis representative of the collective wisdom of his team. As it turns out, Dr. Forrest is right more often than any individual resident because he knows that his residents are pretty smart, and a large number of pretty smart residents are unlikely to *all* make the same mistake. Here, Dr. Forrest relies on the power of *model aggregating* or *model averaging*: he knows that the average answer is most likely going to be a good one.

Still, how does Dr. Forrest know that *all* his residents aren't wrong? He can't know that for sure, of course. However, he has guarded against this undesirable outcome all the same. Remember that his residents all have diverse specializations. Because of their diverse backgrounds, training, specialization, and skills, it's possible, but highly unlikely, that all his residents are wrong. Here, Dr. Forrest relies on the power of *ensemble diversity*, or the diversity of the individual components of his ensemble.

Dr. Randy Forrest, of course, is an ensemble method, and his residents (who are in training) are the machine-learning algorithms that make up the ensemble. The secrets to his success, and indeed the success of ensemble methods as well, are

- *Ensemble diversity*—He has a variety of opinions to choose from.
- *Model aggregation*—He can combine those opinions into a single final opinion.

Any collection of machine-learning algorithms can be used to build an ensemble, which is, literally, a group of machine learners. But why do they work? James Surowiecki, in *The Wisdom of Crowds*, describes human ensembles or wise crowds thus:

> *If you ask a large enough group of diverse and independent people to make a prediction or estimate a probability, the average of those answers will cancel out errors in individual estimation. Each person's guess, you might say, has two components: information and errors. Subtract the errors, and you're left with the information.*

This is also precisely the intuition behind ensembles of learners: it's possible to build a wise machine-learning ensemble by aggregating individual learners.

Ensemble methods

Formally, an *ensemble method* is a machine-learning algorithm that aims to improve predictive performance on a task by aggregating the predictions of multiple estimators or models. In this manner, an ensemble method learns a *meta-estimator*.

The key to success with ensemble methods is ensemble diversity, also known by alternate terms such as model complementarity or model orthogonality. Informally, ensemble diversity refers to the fact that individual ensemble components, or machine-learning models, are different from each other. Training such ensembles of diverse individual models is a key challenge in ensemble learning, and different ensemble methods achieve this in different ways.

1.2   *Why you should care about ensemble learning*

What can you do with ensemble methods? Are they really just hype, or are they hallelujah? As we see in this section, they can be used to train and deploy robust and effective predictive models for many different applications.

One palpable success of ensemble methods is their domination of data science competitions (alongside deep learning), where they have been generally successful on different types of machine-learning tasks and application areas.

Anthony Goldbloom, CEO of Kaggle, revealed in 2015 that the three most successful algorithms for structured problems were XGBoost, random forest, and gradient boosting, all ensemble methods. Indeed, the most popular way to tackle data science competitions these days is to combine feature engineering with ensemble methods. Structured data is generally organized in tables, relational databases, and other formats most of us are familiar with, and ensemble methods have proven to be very successful on this type of data.

Unstructured data, in contrast, doesn't always have a tabular structure. Images, audio, video, waveform, and text data are typically unstructured, and deep learning approaches—including automated feature generation—have been very successful on these types of data. While we focus on structured data for most of this book, ensemble methods can be combined with deep learning for unstructured problems as well.

Beyond competitions, ensemble methods drive data science in several areas, including financial and business analytics, medicine and health care, cybersecurity, education, manufacturing, recommendation systems, entertainment, and many more.

In 2018, Olson et al.[2] conducted a comprehensive analysis of 14 popular machine-learning algorithms and their variants. They ranked each algorithm's performance on 165 classification benchmark data sets. Their goal was to emulate the standard machine-learning pipeline to provide advice on how to select a machine-learning algorithm.

These comprehensive results are compiled into figure 1.2. Each row shows how often one model outperforms other models across all 165 data sets. For example, XGBoost beats gradient boosting on 34 of 165 benchmark data sets (first row, second column), while gradient boosting beats XGBoost on 12 of 165 benchmark data sets (second row, first column). Their performance is very similar on the remaining 119 of 165 data sets, meaning both models perform equally well on 119 data sets.

In contrast, XGBoost beats multinomial naïve Bayes (MNB) on 157 of 165 data sets (first row, last column), while MNB only beats XGBoost on 2 of 165 data sets (last row, first column) and can only match XGBoost on 6 of 165 data sets!

In general, ensemble methods (1: XGBoost, 2: gradient boosting, 3: Extra Trees, 4: random forests, 8: AdaBoost) outperformed other methods handily. These results demonstrate exactly why ensemble methods (specifically, tree-based ensembles) are considered state of the art.

If your goal is to develop state-of-the-art analytics from your data, or to eke out better performance and improve models you already have, this book is for you. If your goal is to start competing more effectively in data science competitions for fame and

---

[2] Randal S. Olson, William La Cava, Zairah Mustahsan, Akshay Varik, and Jason H. Moore, *Data-driven Advice for Applying Machine Learning to Bioinformatics Problems*, Pacific Symposium on Machine Learning (2018); arXiv preprint: https://arxiv.org/abs/1708.05070.

How often one model outperforms another model (on 165 data sets)

Wins \ Losses	XGBoost	Gradient Boosting	Extra Trees	Random Forest	Kernel SVM	Decision Tree	K-Nearest Neighbor	AdaBoost	Logistic Regression	Linear SVM	Passive Aggressive	Bernoulli Naïve Bayes	Gaussian Naïve Bayes	Multinominal Naïve Bayes
XGBoost	0	34	51	48	74	124	130	132	128	129	139	151	158	157
Gradient Boosting	12	0	40	37	67	116	115	129	122	124	137	149	159	156
Extra Trees	22	28	0	27	59	107	128	116	116	121	133	146	159	157
Random Forest	16	20	28	0	59	105	120	118	118	122	133	143	158	154
Kernel SVM	21	24	27	34	0	83	111	101	102	111	128	138	154	151
Decision Tree	1	2	4	0	26	0	72	81	85	87	99	119	137	137
K-Nearest Neighbor	4	9	3	4	8	49	0	72	70	72	90	119	140	137
AdaBoost	0	3	11	9	15	35	55	0	58	60	73	98	131	126
Logistic Regression	6	7	10	10	6	42	55	58	0	25	82	93	132	139
Linear SVM	5	6	8	9	3	38	47	52	6	0	68	88	132	137
Passive Aggressive	1	3	5	9	1	35	40	51	15	19	0	85	129	124
Bernoulli Naïve Bayes	0	1	1	1	5	17	29	27	24	28	38	0	99	107
Gaussian Naïve Bayes	1	0	0	1	5	15	7	16	14	14	18	39	0	77
Multinominal Naïve Bayes	2	2	2	2	1	10	10	22	1	3	8	25	66	0

Figure 1.2   Which machine-learning algorithm should I use for my data set? The performance of several different machine-learning algorithms, relative to each other on 165 benchmark data sets, is shown here. The final trained models are ranked (top-to-bottom, left-to-right) based on their performance on all benchmark data sets in relation to all other methods. In their evaluation, Olson et al. consider two methods to have the same performance on a data set if their prediction accuracies are within 1% of each other. This figure was reproduced using the codebase and comprehensive experimental results compiled by the authors into a publicly available GitHub repository (https://github.com/rhiever/sklearn -benchmarks) and includes the authors' evaluation of XGBoost as well.

fortune or to just improve your data science skills, this book is also for you. If you're excited about adding powerful ensemble methods to your machine-learning arsenal, this book is definitely for you.

To drive home this point, we'll build our first ensemble method: a *simple model combination ensemble.* Before we do, let's dive into the tradeoff between fit and complexity that most machine-learning methods have to grapple with, as it will help us understand why ensemble methods are so effective.

1.3   *Fit vs. complexity in individual models*

In this section, we look at two popular machine-learning methods: decision trees and support vector machines (SVMs). As we do so, we'll explore how their fitting and predictive behavior changes as they learn increasingly complex models. This section also serves as a refresher of the training and evaluation practices we usually follow during modeling.

Machine-learning tasks are typically

- *Supervised learning tasks*—These have a data set of *labeled examples*, where data has been annotated. For example, in cancer diagnoses, each example will be an individual patient, with label/annotation "has cancer" or "does not have cancer." Labels can be 0–1 (binary classification), categorical (multiclass classification), or continuous (regression).

- *Unsupervised learning tasks*—These have a data set of *unlabeled examples*, where the data lacks annotations. This includes tasks such as grouping examples together by some notion of "similarity" (clustering) or identifying anomalous data that doesn't fit the expected pattern (anomaly detection).

We'll create a simple, synthetically generated, supervised regression data set to illustrate the key challenge in training machine-learning models and to motivate the need for ensemble methods. With this data set, we'll train increasingly complex machine-learning models that fit and eventually overfit the data during training. As we'll see, overfitting during training doesn't necessarily produce models that generalize better.

1.3.1   *Regression with decision trees*

One of the most popular machine-learning models is the decision tree,[3] which can be used for classification as well as regression tasks. A decision tree is made up of decision nodes and leaf nodes, and each decision node tests the current example for a specific condition.

For example, in figure 1.3, we use a decision-tree classifier for a binary classification task over a data set with two features, x_1 and x_2. The first node tests each input example to see if the second feature $x_2 > 5$ and then funnels the example to the right or left branch of the decision tree depending on the result. This continues until the input example reaches a leaf node; at this point, the prediction corresponding to the leaf node is returned. For classification tasks, the leaf value is a class label, whereas for regression tasks, the leaf returns a regression value.

A decision tree of depth 1 is called a *decision stump* and is the simplest possible tree. A decision stump contains a single decision node and two leaf nodes. A *shallow decision tree* (say, depth 2 or 3) will have a small number of decision nodes and leaf nodes and is a simple model. Consequently, it can only represent simple functions.

---

[3] For more details about learning with decision trees, see chapters 3 (classification) and 9 (regression) of *Machine Learning in Action* by Peter Harrington (Manning, 2012).

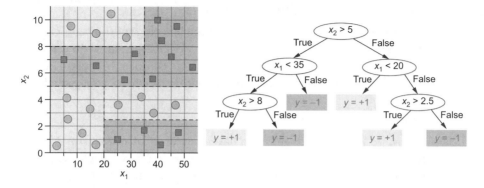

Figure 1.3 Decision trees partition the feature space into axis-parallel rectangles. When used for classification, the tree checks for conditions on the features in the decision nodes, funneling the example to the left or right after each test. Ultimately, the example filters down to a leaf node, which will give its classification label. The partition of the feature space according to this decision tree is shown on the left.

On the other hand, a deeper decision tree is a more complex model with many more decision nodes and leaf nodes. A deeper decision tree, thus, can represent richer and more complex functions.

FIT VS. COMPLEXITY IN DECISION TREES

We'll explore such tradeoffs between model fit and representation complexity in the context of a synthetic data set called *Friedman-1*, originally created by Jerome Friedman in 1991 to explore how well his new multivariate adaptive regression splines (MARS) algorithm was fitting high-dimensional data.

This data set was carefully generated to evaluate a regression method's ability to only pick up true feature dependencies in the data set and ignore others. More specifically, the data set is generated to have 15 randomly generated features of which only the first 5 features are relevant to the target variable:

$$y = 10 \sin{(\pi x_1 x_2)} + 20 \left(x_3 - \frac{1}{2}\right)^2 + 10x_4 + 5x_5 + \text{Gaussian Noise}(0, \sigma)$$

scikit-learn contains a built-in function that we can use to generate as much data in this scheme as possible:

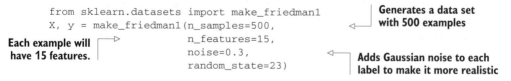

We'll randomly split the data set into a training set (with 67% of the data) and a test set (with 33% of the data) in order to illustrate the effects of the complexity versus fit more clearly.

TIP During modeling, we often have to split the data into a training and a test set. How big should these sets be? If the fraction of the data that makes up the training set is too small, the model won't have enough data to train. If the fraction of the data that makes up the test set is too small, there will be higher variation in our generalization estimates of how well the model performs on future data. A good rule of thumb for medium to large data sets (known as the Pareto principle) is to start with an 80%–20% train-test split. Another good rule for small data sets is to use the leave-one-out approach, where a single example is left out each time for evaluation, and the overall training and evaluation process is repeated for every example.

For different depths d = 1 to 10, we train a tree on the training set and evaluate it on the test set. When we look at the training errors and the test errors across different depths, we can identify the depth of the "best tree." We characterize "best" in terms of an *evaluation metric*. For regression problems, there are several evaluation metrics: mean squared error (MSE), mean absolute deviation (MAD), coefficient of determination, and so on.

We'll use the coefficient of determination, also known as the R^2 *score*, which measures the proportion of the variance in the labels (y) that is predictable from the features (x).

Coefficient of determination

The coefficient of determination (R^2) is a measure of regression performance. R^2 is the proportion of variance in the true labels that is predictable from the features. R^2 depends on two quantities: (1) the total variance in the true labels, or *total sum of squares* (TSS); and (2) the MSE, or the *residual sum of squares* (RSS) between the true and predicted labels. We have $R^2 = 1 - RSS / TSS$. A perfect model will have zero prediction error, or $RSS = 0$ and its corresponding $R^2 = 1$. Really good models have R^2 values close to 1. A really bad model will have high prediction error and high RSS. This means that for really bad models, we can have negative R^2.

One last thing to note is that we are splitting the data into a training set and test set *randomly*, which means that it's possible to get very lucky or very unlucky in our split. To avoid the influence of randomness, we repeat our experiment $K = 5$ times and average the results across the runs. Why 5? This choice is often somewhat arbitrary, and you'll have to decide whether you want less variation in the test errors (large values of K) or less computation time (small values of K).

The pseudocode for our experiment is as follows:

```
for run = 1:5
    (Xtrn, ytrn), (Xtst, ytst) = split data (X), labels (y) into
                            training & test subsets randomly
    for depth d = 1:10
        tree[d] = train decision tree of depth d on the
                    training subset (Xtrn, ytrn)
        train_scores[run, d] = compute R2 score of tree[d] on the
```

```
                              training set (Xtrn, ytrn)
          test_scores[run, d]  = compute R2 score of tree[d] on the
                              test set (Xtst, ytst)
mean_train_score = average train_scores across runs
mean_test_score = average test_scores across runs
```

The following code snippet does precisely this, and then it plots the training and test scores. Rather than explicitly implement the preceding pseudocode, the following code uses the scikit-learn function `sklearn.model_selection.ShuffleSplit` to automatically split the data into five different training and test subsets, and it uses `sklearn.model_selection.validation_curve` to determine R^2 scores for varying decision tree depths:

```
import numpy as np
from sklearn.tree import DecisionTreeRegressor
from sklearn.model_selection import ShuffleSplit
from sklearn.model_selection import validation_curve

subsets = ShuffleSplit(n_splits=5, test_size=0.33,
                       random_state=23)

model = DecisionTreeRegressor()
trn_scores, tst_scores = validation_curve(model, X, y,
                                     param_name='max_depth',
                                     param_range=range(1, 11),
                                     cv=subsets, scoring='r2')
mean_train_score = np.mean(trn_scores, axis=1)
mean_test_score = np.mean(tst_scores, axis=1)
```

Sets up five different random splits of the data into train and test sets

For each split, trains decision trees of depths from 1 to 10 and then evaluates on the test set

Remember, our ultimate goal is to build a machine-learning model that *generalizes* well, that is, a model that performs well on *future, unseen data*. Our first instinct then, will be to train a model that achieves the smallest training error. Such models will typically be quite complex in order to fit as many training examples as possible. After all, a complex model will likely fit our training data well and have a small training error. It is natural to presume that a model that achieves the smallest training error should also generalize well in the future and predict unseen examples equally well.

Now, let's look at the training and test scores in figure 1.4 to see if this is the case. Remember that an R^2 score close to 1 indicates a very good regression model, and scores further away from 1 indicate worse models.

Deeper decision trees are more complex and have greater representational power, so it's not surprising to see that deeper trees fit the training data better. This is clear from figure 1.4: as tree depth (model complexity) increases, the training score approaches $R^2 = 1$. Thus, more complex models achieve better fits on the training data.

What is surprising, however, is that the *test* R^2 score doesn't similarly keep increasing with complexity. In fact, beyond `max_depth=4`, test scores remain fairly consistent. This suggests that a tree of depth 8 might fit the training data better than a tree of depth 4, but both trees will perform roughly identically when they try to generalize and predict on new data!

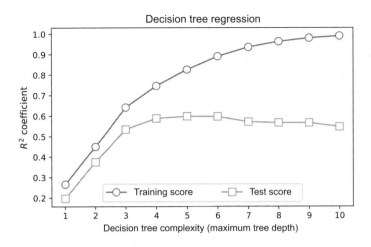

Figure 1.4   Comparing decision trees of different depths on the Friedman-1 regression data set using R^2 as the evaluation metric. Higher R^2 scores mean that the model achieves lower error and fits the data better. An R^2 score close to 1 means that the model achieves nearly zero error. It's possible to fit the training data nearly perfectly with very deep decision trees, but such overly complex models actually overfit the training data and don't generalize well to future data, as evidenced by the test scores.

As decision trees become deeper, they get more complex and achieve lower training errors. However, their ability to generalize to future data (estimated by test scores) doesn't keep decreasing. This is a rather counterintuitive result: the model with the best fit on the training set isn't necessarily the best model for predictions when deployed in the real world.

It's tempting to argue that we got unlucky when we partitioned the training and test sets randomly. However, we ran our experiment with five different random partitions and averaged the results to avoid this. To be sure, however, let's repeat this experiment with another well-known machine-learning method: support vector regression.[4]

1.3.2   *Regression with support vector machines*

Like decision trees, support vector machines (SVMs) are a great off-the-shelf baseline modeling approach, and most packages come with a robust implementation of SVMs. You may have used SVMs for classification, where it's possible to learn nonlinear models of considerable complexity using kernels such as the radial basis function (RBF) kernel, or the polynomial kernel. SVMs have also been adapted for regression, and as in the classification case, they try to find a model that trades off between regularization and fit during training. Specifically, SVM training tries to find a model to minimize

$$\underbrace{\text{regularization}}_{\textbf{measures model flatness}} + \text{C} \cdot \overset{\overset{\textbf{measures model fit}}{\uparrow}}{\text{loss}}$$

---

[4] For more details on SVMs for classification, see chapter 6 of *Machine Learning in Action* by Peter Harrington (Manning, 2012). For SVMs for regression, see "A Tutorial on Support Vector Regression" by Alex J. Smola and Bernhard Scholköpf (*Statistics and Computing*, 2004), as well as the documentation pages of `sklearn.SVM.SVR()`.

The regularization term measures the flatness of the model: the more it is minimized, the more linear and less complex the learned model is. The loss term measures the fit to the training data through a *loss function* (typically, MSE): the more it is minimized, the better the fit to the training data. The *regularization* parameter C trades off between these two competing objectives:

- A small value of C means the model will focus more on regularization and simplicity, and less on training error, which causes the model to have higher training error and *underfit.*
- A large value of C means the model will focus more on training error and learn more complex models, which causes the model to have lower training errors and possibly *overfit.*

We can see the effect of increasing the value of C on the learned models in figure 1.5. In particular, we can visualize the tradeoff between fit and complexity.

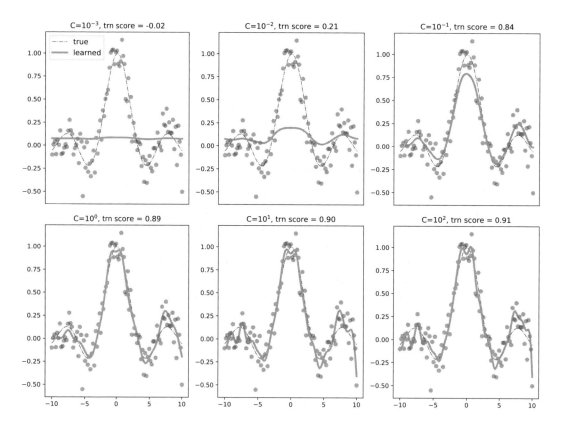

Figure 1.5 Support vector machine with an RBF kernel, with kernel parameter gamma = 0.75. Small values of *C* result in more linear (flatter) and less complex models that underfit the data, while large values of *C* result in more nonlinear (curvier) and more complex models that overfit the data. Selecting a good value for *C* is critically important in training a good SVM model.

CAUTION SVMs identify support vectors, a smaller working set of training examples that the model depends on. Counting the number of support vectors isn't an effective way to measure model complexity as small values of C restrict the model more, forcing it to use more support vectors in the final model.

Fit vs. complexity in support vector machines

Much like `max_depth` in `DecisionTreeRegressor()`, the parameter `C` in support vector regression, `SVR()`, can be tuned to obtain models with different behaviors. Again, we're faced with the same question: which is the best model? To answer this, we can repeat the same experiment as with decision trees:

```
from sklearn.svm import SVR

model = SVR(kernel='rbf', gamma=0.1)
trn_scores, tst_scores = validation_curve(model, X, y.ravel(),
                                          param_name='C',
                                          param_range=np.logspace(-2, 4, 7),
                                          cv=subsets, scoring='r2')

mean_train_score = np.mean(trn_scores, axis=1)
mean_test_score = np.mean(tst_scores, axis=1)
```

In this code snippet, we train an SVM with a three-degree polynomial kernel. We try seven values of C—10^{-3}, 10^{-2}, 10^{-1}, 1, 10, 10^2, and 10^3—and visualize the train and test scores, as before, in figure 1.6.

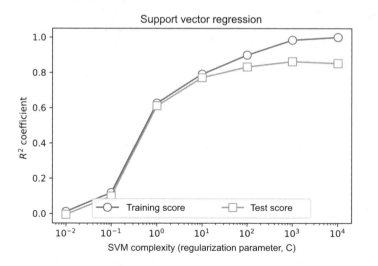

Figure 1.6 Comparing SVM regressors of different complexities on the Friedman-1 regression data set using R^2 as the evaluation metric. As with decision trees, highly complex models (corresponding to higher C values) appear to achieve fantastic fit on the training data, but they don't actually generalize as well. This means that as C increases, so does the possibility of overfitting.

Again, rather counterintuitively, the model with the best fit on the training set isn't necessarily the best model for predictions when deployed in the real world. Every machine-learning algorithm, in fact, exhibits this behavior:

- Overly simple models tend to not fit the training data properly and tend to generalize poorly on future data; a model that is performing poorly on training and test data is *underfitting*.
- Overly complex models can achieve very low training errors but tend to generalize poorly on future data too; a model that is performing very well on training data, but poorly on test data is *overfitting*.
- The best models trade off between complexity and fit, sacrificing a little bit of each during training so that they can generalize most effectively when deployed.

As we'll see in the next section, ensemble methods are an effective way of tackling the problem of fit versus complexity.

The bias-variance tradeoff

What we've informally discussed so far as the fit versus complexity tradeoff is more formally known as the *bias-variance tradeoff*. The *bias* of a model is the error arising from the effect of modeling assumptions (such as a preference for simpler models). The *variance* of a model is the error arising from sensitivity to small variations in the data set.

Highly complex models (low bias) will overfit the data and be more sensitive to noise (high variance), while simpler models (high bias) will underfit the data and be less sensitive to noise (low variance). This tradeoff is inherent in every machine-learning algorithm. Ensemble methods seek to overcome this problem by combining several low-bias models to reduce their variance or combining several low-variance models to reduce their bias.

1.4   *Our first ensemble*

In this section, we'll overcome the fit versus complexity problems of individual models by training our first ensemble. Recall from the allegorical Dr. Forrest that an effective ensemble performs model aggregation on a set of component models, as follows:

- We train a set of *base estimators* (also known as *base learners*) using diverse base-learning algorithms on the same data set. That is, we count on the significant variations in each learning algorithm to produce a diverse set of base estimators.
- For a regression problem (e.g., the Friedman-1 data introduced in the previous section), the predictions of individual base estimators are continuous. We can aggregate the results into one final ensemble prediction by *simple averaging* of the individual predictions.

We use the following regression algorithms to produce base estimators from our data set: kernel ridge regression, support vector regression, decision-tree regression, k-nearest neighbor regression, Gaussian processes, and multilayer perceptrons (neural networks).

Once we have the trained models, we use each one to make individual predictions and then aggregate the individual predictions into a final prediction, as shown in figure 1.7.

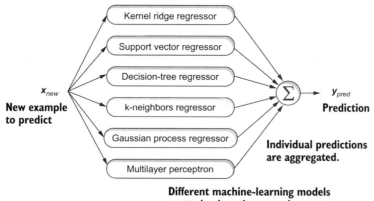

Figure 1.7 **Our first ensemble method ensembles the predictions of six different regression models by averaging them. This simple ensemble illustrates two key principles of ensembling: (1) model diversity, achieved in this case by using six different base machine-learning models; and (2) model aggregation, achieved in this case by simple averaging across predictions.**

The code for training individual base estimators is shown in the following listing.

Listing 1.1 **Training diverse base estimators**

```
from sklearn.model_selection import train_test_split
from sklearn.datasets import make_friedman1

X, y = make_friedman1(n_samples=500, n_features=15,
                noise=0.3, random_state=23)
Xtrn, Xtst, ytrn, ytst = train_test_split(
                        X, y, test_size=0.25)

from sklearn.kernel_ridge import KernelRidge
from sklearn.svm import SVR
from sklearn.tree import DecisionTreeRegressor
from sklearn.neighbors import KNeighborsRegressor
from sklearn.gaussian_process import GaussianProcessRegressor
from sklearn.neural_network import MLPRegressor

estimators = {'krr': KernelRidge(kernel='rbf',
                        gamma=0.25),
          'svr': SVR(gamma=0.5),
          'dtr': DecisionTreeRegressor(max_depth=3),
```

Generates a synthetic Friedman-1 data set with 500 examples and 15 features

Splits into a training set (with 75% of the data) and a test set (with the remaining 25%)

Initializes hyperparameters of each individual base estimator

```
                  'knn': KNeighborsRegressor(n_neighbors=4),
                  'gpr': GaussianProcessRegressor(alpha=0.1),
                  'mlp': MLPRegressor(alpha=25, max_iter=10000)}
```

```
for name, estimator in estimators.items():          Trains the individual
    estimator = estimator.fit(Xtrn, ytrn)  ◁────┘    base estimators
```

We have now trained six diverse base estimators using six different base-learning algorithms. Given new data, we can aggregate the individual predictions into a final prediction as shown in the following listing.

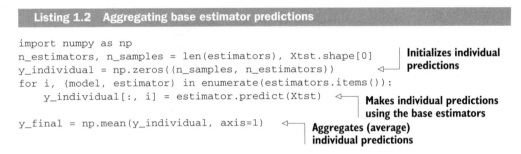

Listing 1.2   Aggregating base estimator predictions

```
import numpy as np
n_estimators, n_samples = len(estimators), Xtst.shape[0]        Initializes individual
y_individual = np.zeros((n_samples, n_estimators))   ◁────┘     predictions
for i, (model, estimator) in enumerate(estimators.items()):
    y_individual[:, i] = estimator.predict(Xtst)  ◁──┐   Makes individual predictions
                                                     │   using the base estimators
y_final = np.mean(y_individual, axis=1)  ◁──┐   Aggregates (average)
                                            │   individual predictions
```

One way to understand the benefits of ensembling is if we look at all possible combinations of models for predictions. That is, we look at the performance of one model at a time, then all possible ensembles of two models (there are 15 such combinations), then all possible ensembles of three models (there are 20 such combinations), and so on. For ensemble sizes 1 to 6, we plot the test set performances of all these ensemble combinations in figure 1.8.

As we aggregate more and more models, we see that the ensembles generalize increasingly better. The most striking result of our experiment, though, is that the performance of the ensemble of all six estimators is often better than the performances of each individual estimator.

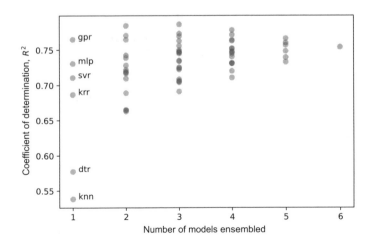

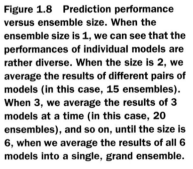

Figure 1.8   **Prediction performance versus ensemble size. When the ensemble size is 1, we can see that the performances of individual models are rather diverse. When the size is 2, we average the results of different pairs of models (in this case, 15 ensembles). When 3, we average the results of 3 models at a time (in this case, 20 ensembles), and so on, until the size is 6, when we average the results of all 6 models into a single, grand ensemble.**

Finally, what of fit versus complexity? It's difficult to characterize the complexity of the ensemble, as different types of estimators in our ensemble have different complexities. However, we can characterize the *variance* of the ensemble.

Recall that variance of an estimator reflects its sensitivity to the data. A high variance estimator is highly sensitive and less robust, often because it's overfitting. In figure 1.9, we show the variance of the ensembles from figure 1.8, which is the width of the band.

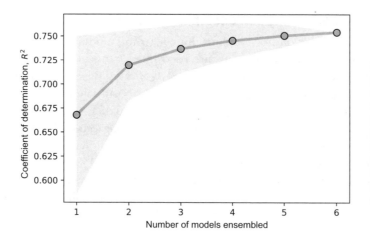

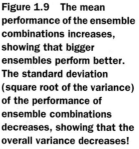

Figure 1.9 **The mean performance of the ensemble combinations increases, showing that bigger ensembles perform better. The standard deviation (square root of the variance) of the performance of ensemble combinations decreases, showing that the overall variance decreases!**

As ensemble size increases, the variance of the ensemble decreases! This is a consequence of model aggregation or averaging. We know that averaging "smooths out the rough edges." In the case of our ensemble, averaging individual predictions smooths out mistakes made by individual base estimators, replacing them instead with the wisdom of the ensemble: from many, one. The overall ensemble is more robust to mistakes and, unsurprisingly, generalizes better than any single base estimator.

Each component estimator in the ensemble is an individual, like one of Dr. Forrest's residents, and each makes predictions based on its own experiences (introduced during learning). At prediction time, when we have six individuals, we'll have six predictions, or six opinions. For "easy examples," the individuals will mostly agree. For "difficult examples," the individuals will differ among each other but, on average, are more likely to be closer to the correct answer.[5]

---

[5] There are cases when this breaks down. In the UK version of *Who Wants To Be A Millionaire?*, a contestant successfully made it as far as £125,000 (or about $160,000), when he was asked which novel begins with the words: "3 May. Bistritz. Left Munich at 8:35 PM." After using the 50/50 lifeline, he was left with only two choices: *Tinker Tailor Soldier Spy* and *Dracula*. Knowing he could lose £93,000 if he got it wrong, he asked the studio audience. In response, 81% of the audience voted for *Tinker Tailor Soldier Spy*. The audience was overwhelmingly confident and—unfortunately for the contestant—overwhelmingly wrong. As you'll see in the book, we look to avoid this situation by making certain assumptions about the "audience," which, in our case, is the base estimators.

In this simple scenario, we trained six "diverse" models by using six different learning algorithms. Ensemble diversity is critical to the success of the ensemble as it ensures that the individual estimators are different from each other and don't all make the same mistakes.

As we'll see over and over again in each chapter, different ensemble methods take different approaches to train diverse ensembles. Before we end this chapter, let's take a look at a broad classification of various ensembling techniques, many of which will be covered in the next few chapters.

1.5   *Terminology and taxonomy for ensemble methods*

All ensembles are composed of individual machine-learning models called *base models, base learners,* or *base estimators* (these terms are used interchangeably throughout the book) and are trained using *base machine-learning algorithms.* Base models are often described in terms of their complexity. Base models that are sufficiently complex (e.g., a deep decision tree) and have "good" prediction performance (e.g., accuracy over 80% for a binary classification task) are typically known as *strong learners* or *strong models.*

In contrast, base models that are pretty simple (e.g., a shallow decision tree) and achieve barely acceptable performance (e.g., accuracy around 51% for a binary classification task) are known as *weak learners* or *weak models.* More formally, a weak learner only has to do slightly better than random chance, or 50% for a binary classification task. As we'll see shortly, ensemble methods use either weak learners or strong learners as base models.

More broadly, ensemble methods can be classified into two types depending on how they are trained: *parallel* and *sequential ensembles.* This is the taxonomy we'll adopt in this book as it gives us a neat way of grouping the vast number of ensemble methods out there (see figure 1.10).

Parallel ensemble methods, as the name suggests, train each component base model *independently* of the others, which means that they can be trained in parallel. Parallel ensembles are often constructed out of strong learners and can further be categorized into the following:

- *Homogeneous parallel ensembles*—All the base learners are of the same type (e.g., all decision trees) and trained using the same base-learning algorithm. Several well-known ensemble methods, such as bagging, random forests, and extremely randomized trees (Extra Trees), are parallel ensemble methods. These are covered in chapter 2.
- *Heterogeneous parallel ensembles*—The base learners are trained using different base-learning algorithms. Meta-learning by stacking is a well-known exemplar of this type of ensembling technique. These are covered in chapter 3.

Sequential ensemble methods, unlike parallel ensemble methods, exploit the dependence of base learners. More specifically, during training, sequential ensembles train a new base learner in such a manner that it minimizes mistakes made by the base learner trained in the previous step. These methods construct ensembles sequentially

PARALLEL HOMOGENEOUS ENSEMBLES
Use many strong learners, or complex models, trained using the same base machine-learning algorithm. Ensemble diversity is created from a single algorithm with random data or feature sampling for training each base model.

Ensembles in this family: bagging, random forests, pasting, random subspaces, random patches, extremely randomized trees (Extra Trees)

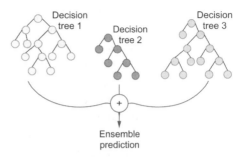

PARALLEL HETEROGENEOUS ENSEMBLES
Also use many strong learners, but each trained using a different base machine-learning algorithm. Ensemble diversity is created by using multiple training algorithms on the same data set and combining learners with different types of prediction aggregation.

Ensembles in this family: majority voting, entropy-based prediction weighting, Dempster-Shafer prediction fusion, meta-learning for stacking and blending.

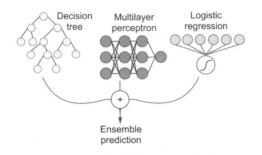

SEQUENTIAL ADAPTIVE BOOSTING ENSEMBLES
Use many weak learners, or simple models, trained in a stage-wise, sequential manner. Each successive model is trained to fix the mistakes made by the previously trained model, allowing the ensemble to adapt during training. The predictions of a large number of weak models are boosted into a strong model!

Ensembles in this family: AdaBoost, LogitBoost

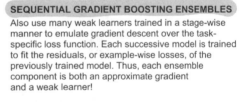

SEQUENTIAL GRADIENT BOOSTING ENSEMBLES
Also use many weak learners trained in a stage-wise manner to emulate gradient descent over the task-specific loss function. Each successive model is trained to fit the residuals, or example-wise losses, of the previously trained model. Thus, each ensemble component is both an approximate gradient and a weak learner!

Ensembles in this family: gradient boosting and LightGBM, Newton boosting and XGBoost, ordered boosting and CatBoost, explainable boosting models

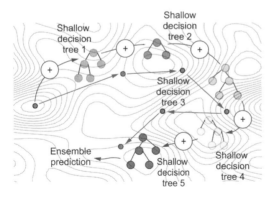

Figure 1.10 A taxonomy of ensemble methods covered in this book

in stages and often use weak learners as base models. They can also be further categorized into the following:

- *Adaptive boosting ensembles*—Also called vanilla boosting, these ensembles train successive base learners by reweighting examples adaptively to fix mistakes in previous iterations. AdaBoost, the granddaddy of all the boosting methods, is an example of this type of ensemble method. These are covered in chapter 4.

- *Gradient-boosting ensembles*—These ensembles extend and generalize the idea of adaptive boosting and aim to mimic gradient descent, which is often used under the hood to actually train machine-learning models. Some of the most powerful modern ensemble learning packages implement some form of gradient boosting (LightGBM, chapter 5), Newton boosting (XGBoost, chapter 6), or ordered boosting (CatBoost, chapter 8).

Summary

- Ensemble learning aims to improve predictive performance by training multiple models and combining them into a meta-estimator. The component models of an ensemble are called base estimators or base learners.
- Ensemble methods use the power of "the wisdom of crowds," which relies on the principle that the collective opinion of a group is more effective than any single individual in the group.
- Ensemble methods are widely used in several application areas, including financial and business analytics, medicine and health care, cybersecurity, education, manufacturing, recommendation systems, entertainment, and many more.
- Most machine-learning algorithms contend with a fit versus complexity (also called bias-variance) tradeoff, which affects their ability to generalize well to future data. Ensemble methods use multiple component models to overcome this tradeoff.
- An effective ensemble requires two key ingredients: (1) ensemble diversity and (2) model aggregation for the final predictions.

Part 2

Essential ensemble methods

This part of the book will introduce several "essential" ensemble methods. In each chapter you'll learn how to (1) implement a basic version of an ensemble method from scratch to gain an under-the-hood understanding; (2) visualize, step-by-step, how learning actually takes place; and (3) use sophisticated, off-the-shelf implementations to ultimately get the best out of your models.

Chapters 2 and 3 cover different types of well-known parallel ensemble methods, including bagging, random forests, stacking, and their variants. Chapter 4 introduces a fundamental sequential ensembling technique called boosting, as well as another well-known ensemble method called AdaBoost (and its variants).

Chapters 5 and 6 are all about gradient boosting, the ensembling technique that is all the rage at the time of this writing and is widely considered state-of-the-art. Chapter 5 covers the fundamentals and inner workings of gradient-boosting. You'll also learn how to get started with LightGBM, a powerful gradient-boosting framework with which you can build scalable and effective gradient boosting applications. Chapter 6 covers an important variant of gradient boosting called Newton boosting. You'll also learn how to get started with XGBoost, another well-known and powerful gradient-boosting framework.

This part of the book mostly covers applications of ensemble methods for classification tasks using tree-based ensembles. Once finished with this part of the book, you'll have a deeper and broader understanding of many ensembling techniques, including why they work and what their limitations are.

Homogeneous parallel ensembles: Bagging and random forests

2

This chapter covers

- Training homogeneous parallel ensembles
- Implementing and understanding bagging
- Implementing and understanding how random forests work
- Training variants with pasting, random subspaces, random patches, and Extra Trees
- Using bagging and random forests in practice

In chapter 1, we introduced ensemble learning and created our first rudimentary ensemble. To recap, an ensemble method relies on the notion of "wisdom of the crowd": the *combined* answer of many models is often better than any one individual answer. We begin our journey into ensemble learning methods in earnest with parallel ensemble methods. We begin with this type of ensemble method because, conceptually, parallel ensemble methods are easy to understand and implement.

Parallel ensemble methods, as the name suggests, train each component base estimator independently of the others, which means that they can be trained in parallel. As we'll see, parallel ensemble methods can be further distinguished as homogeneous and heterogeneous parallel ensembles depending on the kind of learning algorithms they use.

In this chapter, you'll learn about homogeneous parallel ensembles, whose component models are all trained using the same machine-learning algorithm. This is in contrast to heterogeneous parallel ensembles (covered in the next chapter), whose component models are trained using different machine-learning algorithms. The class of homogeneous parallel ensemble methods includes two popular machine-learning methods, one or both of which you might have come across and even used before: *bagging* and *random forests*.

Recall that the two key components of an ensemble method are ensemble diversity and model aggregation. Because homogeneous ensemble methods use the same learning algorithm on the same data set, you may wonder how they can generate a set of diverse base estimators. They do this through *random sampling* of either the training examples (as bagging does), features (as some variants of bagging do), or both (as random forests do).

Some of the algorithms introduced in this chapter, such as random forests, are widely used in medical and bioinformatics applications. In fact, random forests are still a strong off-the-shelf baseline algorithm to try on a new data set, owing to its efficiency (it can be parallelized or distributed easily over multiple processors).

We'll begin with the most basic parallel homogeneous ensemble: bagging. Once you understand how bagging achieves ensemble diversity through sampling, we'll look at the most powerful variant of bagging: random forests.

You'll also learn about other variants of bagging (pasting, random subspaces, random patches) and random forests (Extra Trees). These variants are often effective for big data or in applications with high-dimensional data.

2.1 Parallel ensembles

First, we concretely define the notion of a parallel ensemble. This will help us put the algorithms in this chapter and the next into a single context, so that we can easily see both their similarities and differences.

Recall Dr. Randy Forrest, our ensemble diagnostician from chapter 1. Every time Dr. Forrest gets a new case, he solicits the opinions of all his residents. He then determines the final diagnosis from among those proposed by his residents (figure 2.1, top). Dr. Forrest's diagnostic technique is successful for two reasons:

- He has assembled a *diverse* set of residents, with different medical specializations, which means they each think differently about a case. This works out well for Dr. Forrest as it puts several different perspectives on the table for him to consider.
- He *aggregates* the *independent* opinions of his residents into one final diagnosis. Here, he is democratic and selects the majority opinion. However, he can also aggregate his residents' opinions in other ways. For instance, he can weight the opinions of his more experienced residents higher. This reflects that he trusts some residents more than others, based on factors such as experience or skill, which means they are right more often than other residents on the team.

Dr. Forrest and his residents are a parallel ensemble (figure 2.1, bottom). Each resident in the preceding example is a component base estimator (or base learner) that we have to train. Base estimators can be trained using different base algorithms (leading to heterogeneous ensembles) or the same base algorithm (leading to homogeneous ensembles).

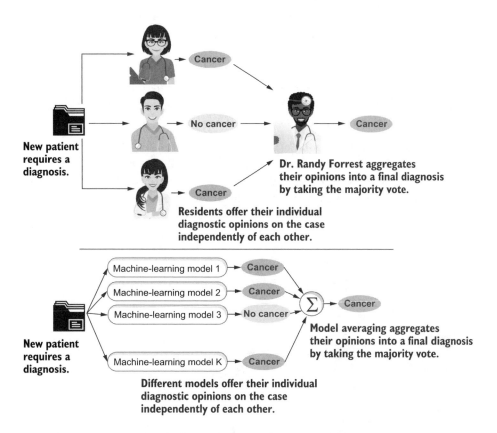

Figure 2.1   Dr. Randy Forrest's diagnostic process is an analogy of a parallel ensemble method.

If we want to put together an effective ensemble similar to Dr. Forrest's, we have to address two problems:

- How do we create a set of base estimators with diverse opinions from a single data set? That is, how can we ensure ensemble diversity during training?
- How can we aggregate decisions, or predictions, of each individual base estimator into a final prediction? That is, how can we perform model aggregation during prediction?

You'll see exactly how to do both in the next section.

2.2   *Bagging: Bootstrap aggregating*

Bagging, short for *bootstrap aggregating*, was introduced by Leo Breiman in 1996. The name refers to how bagging achieves ensemble diversity (through bootstrap sampling) and performs ensemble prediction (through model aggregating).

Bagging is the most basic homogeneous parallel ensemble method we can construct. Understanding bagging will be helpful in understanding the other ensemble methods in this chapter. These methods further enhance the basic bagging approach in different ways: to improve either ensemble diversity or overall computational efficiency.

Bagging uses the *same* base machine-learning algorithm to train base estimators. So how can we get multiple base estimators from a single data set and a single learning algorithm, let alone diversity? This comes by training base estimators on *replicates of the data set*. Bagging consists of two steps, as illustrated in figure 2.2:

1 During training, bootstrap sampling, or sampling with replacement, is used to generate replicates of the training data set that are different from each other but drawn from the original data set. This ensures that base learners trained on each of the replicates are also different from each other.

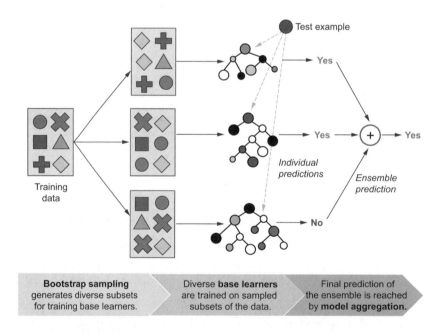

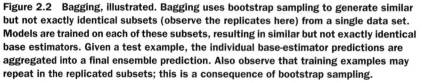

Figure 2.2   Bagging, illustrated. Bagging uses bootstrap sampling to generate similar but not exactly identical subsets (observe the replicates here) from a single data set. Models are trained on each of these subsets, resulting in similar but not exactly identical base estimators. Given a test example, the individual base-estimator predictions are aggregated into a final ensemble prediction. Also observe that training examples may repeat in the replicated subsets; this is a consequence of bootstrap sampling.

2 During prediction, model aggregation is used to combine the predictions of the individual base learners into one ensemble prediction. For classification tasks, we can combine individual predictions using majority voting. For regression tasks, we can combine individual predictions using simple averaging.

2.2.1 Intuition: Resampling and model aggregation

The key challenge for ensemble diversity is that we need to create (and use) different base estimators using the same learning algorithm and the same data set. We'll now see how to (1) generate replicates of the data set, which, in turn, can be used to train base estimators; and (2) combine predictions of base estimators.

BOOTSTRAP SAMPLING: SAMPLING WITH REPLACEMENT

We'll use random sampling to easily generate smaller subsets from the original data set. To generate same-size replicates of the data set, we'll need to perform *sampling with replacement*, otherwise known as bootstrap sampling.

When sampling with replacement, some objects that were already sampled have a chance to be sampled a second time (or even a third, or fourth, etc.) because they were replaced. In fact, some objects may be sampled many times, while some objects may never be sampled. Sampling with replacement is illustrated in figure 2.3, where we see that allowing replacement after sampling leads to repeats.

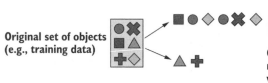
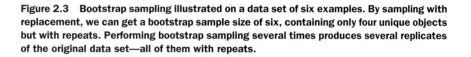

Original set of objects (e.g., training data)

Bootstrap sample: Sampling with replacement allows some objects to be selected more than once.

Out-of-bag sample: Sampling with replacement means some objects will not be selected even once.

Figure 2.3 Bootstrap sampling illustrated on a data set of six examples. By sampling with replacement, we can get a bootstrap sample size of six, containing only four unique objects but with repeats. Performing bootstrap sampling several times produces several replicates of the original data set—all of them with repeats.

Thus, bootstrap sampling naturally partitions a data set into two sets: a bootstrap sample (with training examples that were sampled at least once) and an *out-of-bag (OOB) sample* (with training examples that were never sampled even once).

We can use each bootstrap sample for training a different base estimator. Because different bootstrap samples will contain different examples repeating a different number of times, each base estimator will turn out to be somewhat different from the others.

THE OUT-OF-BAG SAMPLE

Just throwing away the OOB sample seems rather wasteful. However, if we train a base estimator on the bootstrap sample, the OOB sample is *held out* and never seen by the base estimator during learning. Sound familiar?

The OOB sample is effectively a *held-out test set* and can be used to evaluate the ensemble without the need for a separate validation set or even a cross-validation procedure. This is great because it allows us to utilize data more efficiently during training. The error estimate computed using OOB instances is called the *OOB error* or the *OOB score*.

It's very easy to generate bootstrap samples with replacement using `numpy.random .choice`. Suppose we have a data set with 50 training examples (say, patient records with unique IDs from 0 to 49). We can generate a bootstrap sample, also of size 50 (same size as the original data set), for training (`replace=True` to sample with replacement):

```
import numpy as np
bag = np.random.choice(range(0, 50), size=50, replace=True)
np.sort(bag)
```

This produces the following output:

```
array([ 1,  3,  4,  6,  7,  8,  9, 11, 12, 12, 14, 14, 15, 15, 21, 21, 21,
       24, 24, 25, 25, 26, 26, 29, 29, 31, 32, 32, 33, 33, 34, 34, 35, 35,
       37, 37, 39, 39, 40, 43, 43, 44, 46, 46, 48, 48, 48, 49, 49, 49])
```

Can you spot the repeats in this bootstrap sample? This bootstrap sample now serves as one replicate of the original data set and can be used for training. The corresponding OOB sample is all the examples *not* in the bootstrap sample:

```
oob = np.setdiff1d(range(0, 50), bag)
oob
```

This produces the following output:

```
array([ 0,  2,  5, 10, 13, 16, 17, 18, 19, 20, 22, 23, 27, 28, 30, 36, 38,
       41, 42, 45, 47])
```

It's easy to verify that there is no overlap between the bootstrap subset and the OOB subset. This means that the OOB sample can be used as a "test set." To summarize: after one round of bootstrap sampling, we get one bootstrap sample (for training a base estimator) and a corresponding OOB sample (to evaluate *that* base estimator).

> **NOTE** Sampling with replacement drops certain items but, more importantly, replicates other items. When applied to a data set, bootstrap sampling can be used to create training sets with replicates. You can think of these replicates as *weighted training examples*. For instance, if a particular example is replicated four times in the bootstrap sample, when used for training a base estimator, these four replicates will be equivalent to using a single training example with a weight of 4. In this manner, different random bootstrap samples are effectively randomly sampled and weighted training sets.

When we repeat this step many times, we'll have trained several base estimators and will also have estimated their individual generalization performances through individual OOB errors. The averaged OOB error is a good estimate of the performance of the overall ensemble.

0.632 bootstrap

When sampling with replacement, the bootstrap sample will contain roughly 63.2% of the data set, while the OOB sample will contain the other 36.8% of the data set. We can show this by computing the probabilities of a data point being sampled. If our data set has n training examples, the probability of picking one particular data point x in the bootstrap sample is $\frac{1}{n}$. The probability of not picking x in the bootstrap sample (i.e., picking x in the OOB sample) is $1 - \frac{1}{n}$.

For n data points, the overall probability of being selected in the OOB sample is

$$\left(1 - \left(\frac{1}{n}\right)\right)^n \approx e^{-1} = 0.368$$

(for sufficiently large n). Thus, each OOB sample will contain (approximately) 36.8% of the training examples, and the corresponding bootstrap sample will contain (approximately) the remaining 63.2% of the instances.

MODEL AGGREGATION

Bootstrap sampling generates diverse replicates of the data set, which allows us to train diverse models independently of each other. Once trained, we can use this ensemble for prediction. The key is to combine their sometimes-differing opinions into a single final answer.

We've seen two examples of model aggregation: majority voting and model averaging. For classification tasks, majority voting is used to aggregate predictions of individual base learners. The majority vote is also known as the *statistical mode*. The mode is simply the most frequently occurring element and is a statistic similar to the mean or the median.

We can think of model aggregation as averaging: it smooths out imperfections among the chorus and produces a single answer reflective of the majority. If we have a set of robust base estimators, model aggregation will smooth out mistakes made by individual estimators.

Ensemble methods use a variety of aggregation techniques depending on the task, including majority vote, mean, weighted mean, combination functions, and even another machine-learning model! In this chapter, we'll stick to majority voting as our aggregator. We'll explore some other aggregation techniques for classification in chapter 3.

2.2.2 *Implementing bagging*

We can implement our own version of bagging easily. This illustrates the simplicity of bagging and provides a general template for how other ensemble methods in this chapter work. Each base estimator in our bagging ensemble is trained *independently* using the following steps:

1 Generate a bootstrap sample from the original data set.
2 Fit a base estimator to the bootstrap sample.

Here, "independently" means that the training stage of each individual base estimator takes place without consideration of what is going on with the other base estimators.

We use decision trees as base estimators; the maximum depth can be set using the `max_depth` parameter. We'll need two other parameters: `n_estimators`, which is the ensemble size, and `max_samples`, which is the size of the bootstrap subset, that is, the number of training examples to sample (with replacement) per estimator.

Our naïve implementation trains each base decision tree sequentially, as shown in listing 2.1. If it takes 10 seconds to train a single decision tree, and we're training an ensemble of 100 trees, it will take our implementation 10 s × 100 = 1,000 s of total training time.

Listing 2.1   Bagging with decision trees: training

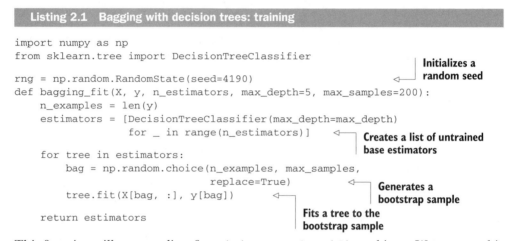

```
import numpy as np
from sklearn.tree import DecisionTreeClassifier

rng = np.random.RandomState(seed=4190)
def bagging_fit(X, y, n_estimators, max_depth=5, max_samples=200):
    n_examples = len(y)
    estimators = [DecisionTreeClassifier(max_depth=max_depth)
                  for _ in range(n_estimators)]

    for tree in estimators:
        bag = np.random.choice(n_examples, max_samples,
                               replace=True)
        tree.fit(X[bag, :], y[bag])

    return estimators
```

Initializes a random seed

Creates a list of untrained base estimators

Generates a bootstrap sample

Fits a tree to the bootstrap sample

This function will return a list of `DecisionTreeClassifier` objects. We can use this ensemble for prediction, which is implemented in the following listing.

Listing 2.2   Bagging with decision trees: prediction

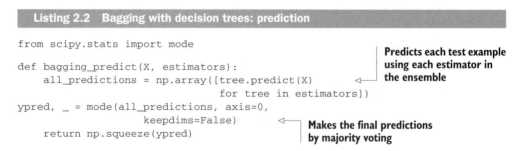

```
from scipy.stats import mode

def bagging_predict(X, estimators):
    all_predictions = np.array([tree.predict(X)
                                for tree in estimators])
ypred, _ = mode(all_predictions, axis=0,
                keepdims=False)
    return np.squeeze(ypred)
```

Predicts each test example using each estimator in the ensemble

Makes the final predictions by majority voting

We can test our implementation on 2D data and visualize the results, as shown in the following snippet. Our bagging ensemble has 500 decision trees, each of depth 12 and trained on bootstrap samples of size 300.

```
from sklearn.datasets import make_moons
from sklearn.model_selection import train_test_split
from sklearn.metrics import accuracy_score

X, y = make_moons(n_samples=300, noise=.25,
                  random_state=rng)
```

Creates a 2D data set

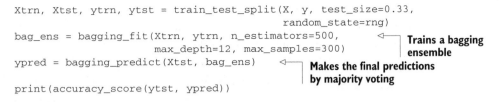

```
Xtrn, Xtst, ytrn, ytst = train_test_split(X, y, test_size=0.33,
                                   random_state=rng)
bag_ens = bagging_fit(Xtrn, ytrn, n_estimators=500,          Trains a bagging
                      max_depth=12, max_samples=300)          ensemble
ypred = bagging_predict(Xtst, bag_ens)          Makes the final predictions
                                                 by majority voting
print(accuracy_score(ytst, ypred))
```

This snippet produces the following output:

```
0.898989898989899
```

Our bagging implementation achieves a test set accuracy of 89.90%. We can now see what a bagged ensemble looks like, compared to a single tree, which achieves a test set accuracy of 83.84% (figure 2.4).

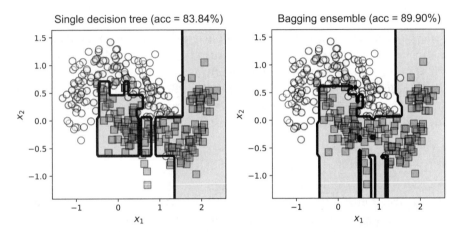

Figure 2.4   A single decision tree (left) overfits the training set and can be sensitive to outliers. A bagging ensemble (right) smooths out the overfitting effects and misclassifications of several such base estimators and often returns a robust answer.

Bagging can learn fairly complex and nonlinear decision boundaries. Even if individual decision trees (and, generally, base estimators) are sensitive to outliers, the ensemble of base learners will smooth out individual variations and be more robust.

This smoothing behavior of bagging is due to model aggregation. When we have many highly nonlinear classifiers, each trained on a slightly different replicate of the training data, each may overfit, but they don't all overfit the same way. More importantly, aggregating leads to smoothing, which effectively reduces the effect of overfitting! Thus, when we aggregate predictions, it smooths out the errors, improving the ensemble performance! Much like an orchestra, the final result is a smooth symphony that can easily overcome the mistakes of any individual musician in it.

2.2.3   *Bagging with scikit-learn*

Now that we're armed with an under-the-hood understanding of how bagging works, let's look at how to use scikit-learn's `BaggingClassifier` package, as shown in the following listing. scikit-learn's implementation provides additional functionality, including support for parallelization, the ability to use other base-learning algorithms beyond decision trees, and—most importantly—OOB evaluation.

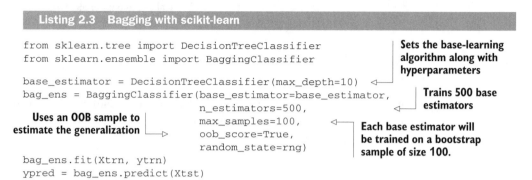

Listing 2.3   Bagging with scikit-learn

```
from sklearn.tree import DecisionTreeClassifier
from sklearn.ensemble import BaggingClassifier

base_estimator = DecisionTreeClassifier(max_depth=10)
bag_ens = BaggingClassifier(base_estimator=base_estimator,
                            n_estimators=500,
                            max_samples=100,
                            oob_score=True,
                            random_state=rng)
bag_ens.fit(Xtrn, ytrn)
ypred = bag_ens.predict(Xtst)
```

Annotations:
- **Sets the base-learning algorithm along with hyperparameters**
- **Trains 500 base estimators**
- **Each base estimator will be trained on a bootstrap sample of size 100.**
- **Uses an OOB sample to estimate the generalization**

`BaggingClassifier` supports OOB evaluation and will return OOB accuracy if we set `oob_score=True`. Recall that for each bootstrap sample, we also have a corresponding OOB sample that contains all the data points that weren't selected during sampling.

Thus, each OOB sample is a surrogate for "future data" because it isn't used to train the corresponding base estimator. After training, we can query the learned model to obtain the OOB score:

```
bag_ens.oob_score_
0.9658792650918635
```

The OOB score is an estimate of the bagging ensemble's predictive (generalization) performance (here, 96.6%). In addition to the OOB samples, we've also held out a test set. We compute another estimate of this model's generalization on the test set:

```
accuracy_score(ytst, ypred)
0.9521276595744681
```

The test accuracy is 95.2%, which is pretty close to the OOB score. We used decision trees of maximum depth 10 as base estimators. Deeper decision trees are more complex, which allows them to fit (and even overfit) the training data.

> **TIP** Bagging is most effective with complex and nonlinear classifiers that tend to overfit the data. Such complex, overfitting models are *unstable*, that is, highly sensitive to small variations in the training data. To see why, consider that individual decision trees in a bagged ensemble have roughly the same complexity. However, due to bootstrap sampling, they have been trained on different replicates of the data set and overfit differently. Put another way, they all overfit by roughly the same amount, but in different places. Bagging works best with such models because its model aggregation reduces overfitting, ultimately leading to a more robust and stable ensemble.

We can visualize the smoothing behavior of `BaggingClassifier` by comparing its decision boundary to its component base `DecisionTreeClassifiers`, as shown in figure 2.5.

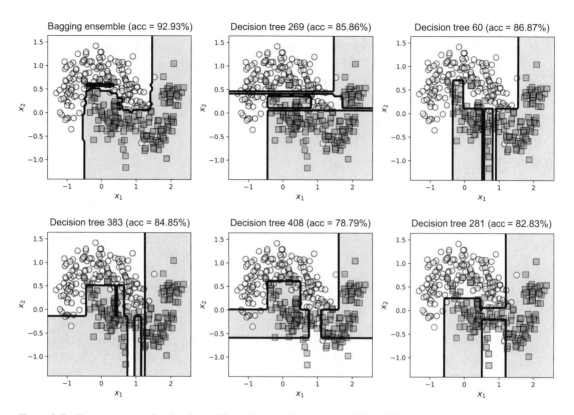

Figure 2.5 Bootstrap sampling leads to different base estimators overfitting differently, while model aggregation averages out individual mistakes and produces smoother decision boundaries.

2.2.4 Faster training with parallelization

Bagging is a parallel ensemble algorithm as it trains each base learner independently of other base learners. This means that training bagging ensembles can be parallelized if you have access to computing resources such as multiple cores or clusters.

BaggingClassifier supports the speedup of both training and prediction through the n_jobs parameter. By default, this parameter is set to 1, and bagging will run on one CPU and train models one at a time, sequentially.

Alternatively, you can specify the number of concurrent processes Bagging-Classifier should use by setting n_jobs. If n_jobs is set to –1, then all available CPUs will be used for training, with one ensemble trained per CPU. This, of course, allows training to proceed faster as more models are trained simultaneously and in parallel.

```
bag_ens = BaggingClassifier(base_estimator=DecisionTreeClassifier(),
                            n_estimators=100, max_samples=100,
                            oob_score=True, n_jobs=-1)
```

If n_jobs is set to –1, BaggingClassifier uses all available CPUs.

Figure 2.6 compares the training efficiency of bagging trained with 1 CPU (n_jobs=1) with multiple CPUs (n_jobs=-1) on a machine with six cores. This comparison shows that bagging can be effectively parallelized and training times significantly reduced if we have access to sufficient computational resources.

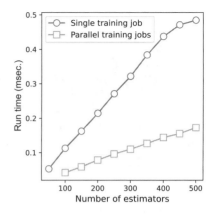

Figure 2.6 Bagging can be parallelized to increase training efficiency.

2.3 Random forests

We've seen how bagging uses random sampling with replacement, or bootstrap sampling, for ensemble diversity. Now, let's look at random forests, a special extension of bagging that introduces additional randomization to further promote ensemble diversity.

Until the emergence of gradient boosting (see chapters 5 and 6), random forests were state of the art and were widely utilized. They are still a popular go-to method for many applications, especially in bioinformatics. Random forests can be an excellent off-the-shelf baseline for your data, as they are computationally efficient to train. They can also rank data features by importance, which makes them particularly suited for high-dimensional data analysis.

2.3.1 Randomized decision trees

"Random forest" specifically refers to an ensemble of randomized decision trees constructed using bagging. Random forests perform bootstrap sampling to generate a training subset (exactly like bagging), and then use randomized decision trees as base estimators.

Randomized decision trees are trained using a modified decision-tree learning algorithm, which introduces randomness when growing our trees. This additional source of randomness increases ensemble diversity and generally leads to better predictive performance.

The key difference between a standard decision tree and a randomized decision tree is how a decision node is constructed. In standard decision-tree construction, *all available features* are evaluated exhaustively to identify the best feature to split on. Because decision-tree learning is a greedy algorithm, it will choose the highest-scoring features to split on.

When bagging, this exhaustive enumeration (combined with greedy learning) means that it's often possible that the same small number of dominant features are repeatedly used in different trees. This makes the ensemble less diverse.

To overcome this limitation of standard decision-tree learning, random forests introduce an additional element of randomness into tree learning. Specifically, instead of considering *all* the features to identify the best split, a random subset of features is evaluated to identify the best feature to split on.

Thus, random forests use a modified tree learning algorithm, which first randomly samples features before creating a decision node. The resulting tree is a *randomized decision tree*, which is a new type of base estimator.

As you'll see, random forests essentially extend bagging by using randomized decision trees as base estimators. Thus, random forests contain two types of randomization: (1) bootstrap sampling, similar to bagging; and (2) random feature sampling for learning randomized decision trees.

EXAMPLE: RANDOMIZATION IN TREE LEARNING

Consider tree learning on a data set with six features (here, $\{f_1, f_2, f_3, f_4, f_5, f_6\}$). In standard tree learning, all six features are evaluated, and the best splitting feature is identified (say, f_3).

In randomized decision-tree learning, we first randomly sample a subset of features (say, f_2, f_4, f_5} and then choose the best from among them (which is, say, f_5). This means that the feature f_3 is no longer available at this stage of tree learning. Thus, randomization has inherently forced tree learning to split on a different feature. The impact of randomization on the choice of the next best split during tree learning is illustrated in figure 2.7.

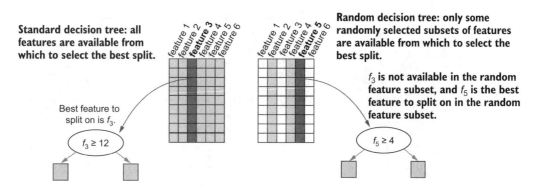

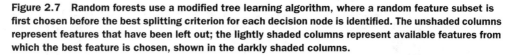

Figure 2.7 Random forests use a modified tree learning algorithm, where a random feature subset is first chosen before the best splitting criterion for each decision node is identified. The unshaded columns represent features that have been left out; the lightly shaded columns represent available features from which the best feature is chosen, shown in the darkly shaded columns.

Ultimately, this randomization occurs every time a decision node is constructed. Thus, even if we use the same data set, we'll obtain a different randomized tree each time we train. When randomized tree learning (with a random sampling of features) is combined with bootstrap sampling (with a random sampling of training examples), we obtain an ensemble of randomized decision trees, known as a *random decision forest* or simply random forest.

The random forest ensemble will be more diverse than bagging, which only performs bootstrap sampling. Next, we'll see how to use random forests in practice.

2.3.2   *Random forests with scikit-learn*

scikit-learn provides an efficient implementation of random forests that also supports OOB estimation and parallelization. Because random forests are specialized to use decision trees as base learners, `RandomForestClassifier` also takes `DecisionTree-Classifier` parameters such as `max_leaf_nodes` and `max_depth` to control tree complexity. The following listing demonstrates how to call `RandomForestClassifier`.

Listing 2.4   Random forests with scikit-learn

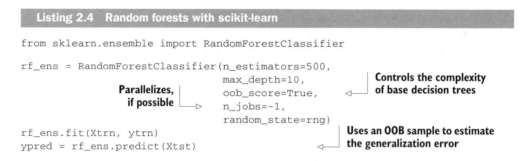

```
from sklearn.ensemble import RandomForestClassifier

rf_ens = RandomForestClassifier(n_estimators=500,
                                max_depth=10,
                                oob_score=True,
                                n_jobs=-1,
                                random_state=rng)
rf_ens.fit(Xtrn, ytrn)
ypred = rf_ens.predict(Xtst)
```

Parallelizes, if possible

Controls the complexity of base decision trees

Uses an OOB sample to estimate the generalization error

Figure 2.8 illustrates a random forest classifier, along with several component base estimators.

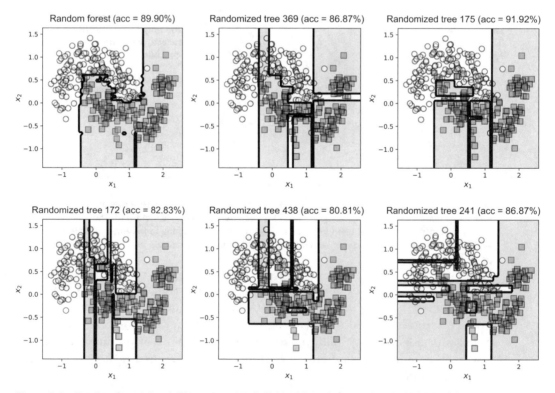

Figure 2.8   Random forest (top left) compared to individual base learners (randomized decision trees). Much like bagging, the random forest ensemble also produces a smooth and stable decision boundary. Also observe the effect of randomization on the individual trees, which are far spikier than regular decision trees.

2.3.3   *Feature importances*

One benefit of using random forests is that they also provide a natural mechanism for scoring features based on their importance. This means that we can rank features to identify the most important ones and drop less effective features, thus performing feature selection!

> **Feature selection**
>
> *Feature selection*, also known as *variable subset selection*, is a procedure for identifying the most influential or relevant data features/attributes. Feature selection is an important step of the modeling process, especially for high-dimensional data.
>
> Dropping the least-relevant features often improves generalization performance and minimizes overfitting. It also often improves the computational efficiency of training. These concerns are consequences of the *curse of dimensionality*, where a large number of features can inhibit a model's ability to generalize effectively.
>
> See *The Art of Feature Engineering: Essentials for Machine Learning* by Pablo Duboue (Cambridge University Press, 2020) to learn more about feature selection and engineering.

We can obtain feature importances for the simple 2D data set with the query `rf_ens.feature_importances_`:

```
for i, score in enumerate(rf_ens.feature_importances_):
    print('Feature x{0}: {1:6.5f}'.format(i, score))
```

This produces the following output:

```
Feature x0: 0.50072
Feature x1: 0.49928
```

The feature scores for the simple two-dimensional data set suggest that both features are roughly equally important. In the case study toward the end of the chapter, we'll compute and visualize the feature importances for a data set from a real task: breast cancer diagnosis. We'll also revisit and delve deeper into the topic of feature importances in chapter 9.

Note that feature importances sum to 1 and are effectively *feature weights*. Less important features have lower weights and can often be dropped without significantly affecting the overall quality of the final model, while improving training and prediction times.

> **Feature importances with correlated features**
>
> If two features are strongly correlated or dependent, then, intuitively, we know that it's sufficient to use either one of them in the model. However, the *order* in which the features are used can affect feature importance. For instance, when classifying abalone (sea snails), the features `size` and `weight` are highly correlated (unsurprising,

(continued)

since bigger snails will be heavier). This means that including them in a decision tree will add roughly the same amount of information and cause the overall error (or entropy) to decrease by roughly the same amount. Thus, we expect that their mean error decrease scores will be the same.

However, say we select `weight` first as a splitting variable. Adding this feature to the tree removes information contained in both `size` and `weight` features. This means that the feature importance of `size` is reduced because any decrease in error that we could have had by including `size` in our model was already previously decreased by including `weight`. Thus, correlated features can sometimes be assigned imbalanced feature importances. Random feature selection mitigates this problem a little, but not consistently.

In general, you must proceed with caution when interpreting feature importances in the presence of feature correlations so that you don't miss the whole story in the data.

2.4   *More homogeneous parallel ensembles*

We've seen two important parallel homogeneous ensemble methods: bagging and random forests. Let's now explore a few variants that were developed for large data sets (e.g., recommendation systems) or high-dimensional data (e.g., image or text databases). These include bagging variants such as pasting, random subspaces and random patches, and an extreme random forest variant called Extra Trees. All these methods introduce randomization in different ways to ensure ensemble diversity.

2.4.1   *Pasting*

Bagging uses bootstrap sampling, or sampling with replacement. If, instead, we sample subsets for training *without replacement*, we have a variant of bagging known as *pasting*. Pasting was designed for very large data sets, where sampling with replacement isn't necessary. Instead, because training full models on data sets of such scale is difficult, pasting aims to take small pieces of the data by sampling without replacement.

Pasting exploits the fact that sampling without replacement with a very large data set can inherently generate diverse data subsets, which in turn leads to ensemble diversity. Pasting also ensures that each training subsample is a small piece of the overall data set and can be used to train a base learner efficiently.

Model aggregation is still used to make a final ensemble prediction. However, since each base learner is trained on small pieces of the large data set, we can view model aggregation as *pasting the predictions* of the base learners together for a final prediction.

> **TIP**   `BaggingClassifier` can easily be extended to perform pasting by setting `bootstrap=False` and making it subsample small subsets for training by setting `max_samples` to a small fraction, say `max_samples=0.05`.

2.4.2 Random subspaces and random patches

We can make the base learners even more diverse by randomly sampling the features (see figure 2.9) as well. Instead of sampling training examples, if we generate subsets by sampling features (with or without replacement), we obtain a variant of bagging called *random subspaces*.

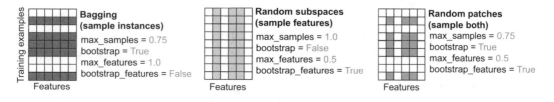

Figure 2.9 **Bagging compared to random subspaces and random patches. The unshaded rows and columns represent training examples and features, respectively, that have been left out.**

`BaggingClassifier` supports bootstrap sampling of features through two parameters: `bootstrap_features` (default: `False`) and `max_features` (default: `1.0`, or all the features), which are analogous to the parameters `bootstrap` (default: `False`) and `max_samples` for sampling training examples, respectively. To implement random subspaces, we randomly sample features only:

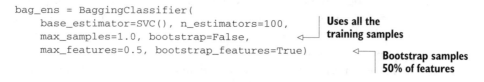

If we randomly sample *both* training examples and features (with or without replacement), we obtain a variant of bagging called *random patches*:

Note that in the preceding examples, the base estimator is the support vector classifier, `sklearn.svm.SVC`. In general, random subspaces and random patches can be applied to any base learner to improve estimator diversity.

> **TIP** In practice, these variants of bagging can be especially effective for big data. For example, because random subspaces and random patches sample features, they can be used to train base estimators more efficiently for data with lots of features, such as image data. Alternatively, because pasting performs

sampling without replacement, it can be used to train base estimators more efficiently when you have a big data set with a lot of training instances.

The key difference between random forests and bagging variants, such as random subspaces and random patches, is where the feature sampling occurs. Random forests exclusively use randomized decision trees as base estimators. Specifically, they perform feature sampling *inside* the tree learning algorithm each time they grow the tree with a decision node.

Random subspaces and random patches, on the other hand, aren't restricted to tree learning and can use any learning algorithm as a base estimator. They randomly sample features once *outside* before calling the base-learning algorithm for each base estimator.

2.4.3   *Extra Trees*

Extremely randomized trees take the idea of randomized decision trees to the extreme by selecting not just the splitting variable from a random subset of features (see figure 2.9) but also the splitting threshold! To understand this more clearly, recall that every node in a decision tree tests a condition of the form "is $f_k < threshold$?" where f_k is the kth feature, and *threshold* is the split value (see section 2.3.1).

Standard decision-tree learning looks at *all the features* to determine the best f_k and then looks at all the values of that feature to determine the threshold. Randomized decision-tree learning looks at a *random subset of features* to determine the best f_k and then looks at all the values of that feature to determine the threshold.

Extremely randomized decision-tree learning also looks at a random subset of features to determine the best f_k. But to be even more efficient, it selects a random splitting threshold. Note that extremely randomized decision trees are yet another type of base learner used for ensembling.

This extreme randomization is so effective, in fact, that we can construct an ensemble of extremely randomized trees directly from the original data set *without* bootstrap sampling! This means that we can construct an Extra Trees ensemble very efficiently.

> **TIP**   In practice, Extra Trees ensembles are well suited for high-dimensional data sets with a large number of continuous features.

scikit-learn provides an `ExtraTreesClassifier` that supports OOB estimation and parallelization, much like `BaggingClassifier` and `RandomForestClassifier`. Note that Extra Trees typically *do not* perform bootstrap sampling (`bootstrap=False`, by default), as we're able to achieve base-estimator diversity through extreme randomization.

> **CAUTION**   scikit-learn provides two very similarly named classes: `sklearn.tree.ExtraTreeClassifier` and `sklearn.ensemble.ExtraTreesClassifier`. The `tree.ExtraTreeClassifier` class is a base-learning algorithm and should be used for learning individual models or as a base estimator with ensemble methods. `ensemble.ExtraTreesClassifier` is the ensemble method discussed in this section. The difference is in the singular usage of

"Extra Tree" (`ExtraTreeClassifier` is the base learner) versus the plural usage "Extra Trees" (`ExtraTreesClassifier` is the ensemble method).

2.5   Case study: Breast cancer diagnosis

Our first case study explores a medical decision-making task: breast cancer diagnosis. We'll see how to use scikit-learn's homogeneous parallel ensemble modules in practice. Specifically, we'll train and evaluate the performance of three homogeneous parallel algorithms, each characterized by increasing randomness: bagging with decision trees, random forests, and Extra Trees.

Doctors make many decisions regarding patient care every day: tasks such as diagnosis (what disease does the patient have?), prognosis (how will their disease progress?), treatment planning (how should the disease be treated?), to name a few. They make these decisions based on a patient's health records, medical history, family history, test results, and so on.

The specific data set we'll use is the Wisconsin Diagnostic Breast Cancer (WDBC) data set, a common benchmark data set in machine learning. Since 1993, the WDBC data has been used to benchmark the performance of dozens of machine-learning algorithms.

The machine-learning task is to train a classification model that can diagnose patients with breast cancer. By modern standards and in the era of big data, this is a small data set, but it's perfectly suited to show the ensemble methods we've seen so far in action.

2.5.1   Loading and preprocessing

The WDBC data set was originally created by applying feature extraction techniques on patient biopsy medical images. More concretely, for each patient, the data describes the size and texture of the cell nuclei of cells extracted during biopsy.

WDBC is available in scikit-learn and can be loaded as shown in figure 2.10. In addition, we also create a `RandomState` so that we can generate randomization in a reproducible manner:

```
from sklearn.datasets import load_breast_cancer
dataset = load_breast_cancer()
X, y = dataset['data'], dataset['target']
rng=np.random.RandomState(seed=4190)
```

index	mean radius	mean texture	mean perimeter	mean area	mean smoothness	mean compactness	mean concavity	diagnosis
0	216	11.89	18.35	77.32	432.2	0.09363	0.11540	0.06636	1
1	30	18.63	25.11	124.80	1088.0	0.10640	0.18870	0.23190	0
2	445	11.99	24.89	77.61	441.3	0.10300	0.09218	0.05441	1
3	496	12.65	18.17	82.69	485.6	0.10760	0.13340	0.08017	1
4	469	11.62	18.18	76.38	408.8	0.11750	0.14830	0.10200	1

Figure 2.10   The WDBC data set consists of 569 training examples, each described by 30 features. A few of the 30 features for a small subset of patients, along with each patient's *diagnosis* (training label), are shown here. `diagnosis=1` indicates `malignant`, and `diagnosis=0` indicates `benign`.

2.5.2   *Bagging, random forests, and Extra Trees*

Once we've preprocessed our data set, we'll train and evaluate bagging with decision trees, random forests, and Extra Trees to answer the following questions:

- How does the ensemble performance change with ensemble size? That is, what happens when our ensembles get bigger and bigger?
- How does the ensemble performance change with base learner complexity? That is, what happens when our individual base estimators become more and more complex?

In this case study, since all three ensemble methods considered use decision trees as base estimators, one "measure" of complexity is tree depth, with deeper trees being more complex.

ENSEMBLE SIZE VS. ENSEMBLE PERFORMANCE

First, let's look at how training and testing performance change with ensemble size by comparing the behavior of the three algorithms as the parameter n_estimators increases. As always, we follow good machine-learning practices and split the data set into a training set and a hold-out test set randomly. Our goal will be to learn a diagnostic model on the training set and evaluate how well that diagnostic model does using the test set.

Recall that because the test set is held out during training, the test error is generally a useful estimate of how well we'll do on future data, that is, generalize. However, because we don't want our learning and evaluation to be at the mercy of randomness, we'll repeat this experiment 20 times and average the results. In the following listing, we'll see how the ensemble size influences model performance.

Listing 2.5   Training and test errors with increasing ensemble size

```
max_leaf_nodes = 8
n_runs = 20
n_estimator_range = range(2, 20, 1)
```
◁ Every base decision tree in every ensemble will have at most eight leaf nodes.

```
bag_trn_error = \
    np.zeros((n_runs, len(n_estimator_range)))
rf_trn_error = \
    np.zeros((n_runs, len(n_estimator_range)))
xt_trn_error = \
    np.zeros((n_runs, len(n_estimator_range)))
```
Initializes arrays to store training errors

```
bag_tst_error = \
    np.zeros((n_runs, len(n_estimator_range)))
rf_tst_error = \
    np.zeros((n_runs, len(n_estimator_range)))
xt_tst_error =
    np.zeros((n_runs, len(n_estimator_range)))
```
Initializes arrays to store test errors

```
for run in range(0, n_runs):
    X_trn, X_tst, y_trn, y_tst = train_test_split(
                    X, y, test_size=0.25, random_state=rng)
```
Performs 20 runs, each with a different split of train/test data

```
for j, n_estimators in enumerate(n_estimator_range):

    tree = DecisionTreeClassifier(                      Trains and evaluates bagging
            max_leaf_nodes=max_leaf_nodes)              for this run and iteration
    bag = BaggingClassifier(base_estimator=tree,
                            n_estimators=n_estimators,
                            max_samples=0.5, n_jobs=-1,
                            random_state=rng)
    bag.fit(X_trn, y_trn)
    bag_trn_error[run, j] = 1 - accuracy_score(y_trn, bag.predict(X_trn))
    bag_tst_error[run, j] = 1 - accuracy_score(y_tst, bag.predict(X_tst))

    rf = RandomForestClassifier(
            max_leaf_nodes=max_leaf_nodes, n_estimators=n_estimators,
            n_jobs=-1, random_state=rng)


    rf.fit(X_trn, y_trn)
    rf_trn_error[run, j] = 1 - accuracy_score(y_trn, rf.predict(X_trn))
    rf_tst_error[run, j] = 1 - accuracy_score(y_tst, rf.predict(X_tst))

    xt = ExtraTreesClassifier(
            max_leaf_nodes=max_leaf_nodes, n_estimators=n_estimators,
            bootstrap=True, n_jobs=-1, random_state=rng)


    xt.fit(X_trn, y_trn)
    xt_trn_error[run, j] = 1 - accuracy_score(y_trn, xt.predict(X_trn))
    xt_tst_error[run, j] = 1 - accuracy_score(y_tst, xt.predict(X_tst))
```

Trains and evaluates random forests for this run and iteration

Trains and evaluates Extra Trees for this run and iteration

We can now visualize the averaged training and test errors on the WDBC data set, as shown in figure 2.11. As expected, the training error for all the approaches decreases steadily as the number of estimators increases. The test error also decreases with ensemble size and then stabilizes. As the test error is an estimate of the generalization error, our experiment confirms our intuition about the performance of these ensemble methods in practice.

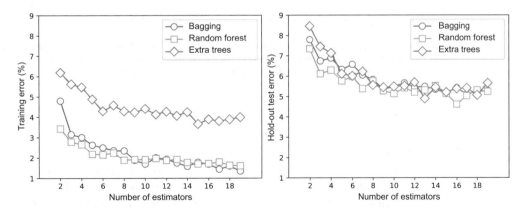

Figure 2.11 Training and test performance of bagging, random forest, and Extra Trees as ensemble size increases. Bagging used decision trees as the base estimator, random forest used randomized decision trees, and Extra Trees used extremely randomized trees.

Finally, all three approaches greatly outperform single decision trees (where the plot begins). This shows that, in practice, even if single decision trees are unstable, ensembles of decision trees are robust and can generalize well.

BASE LEARNER COMPLEXITY VS. ENSEMBLE PERFORMANCE

Next, we compare the behavior of the three algorithms as the complexity of the base learners increases (figure 2.12). There are several ways to control the complexity of the base decision trees: maximum depth, maximum number of leaf nodes, impurity criteria, and so on. Here, we compare the performance of the three ensemble methods with complexity of each base learner determined by `max_leaf_nodes`.

This comparison can be performed in a manner similar to the previous one. To allow each ensemble method to use increasingly complex base learners, we can steadily increase the number of in `max_leaf_nodes` for each base decision tree. That is, in each of `BaggingClassifier`, `RandomForestClassifier`, and `ExtraTrees-Classifier`, we set `max_leaf_nodes` = 2, 4, 8, 16, and 32, in turn, through the following parameter:

```
base_estimator=DecisionTreeClassifier(max_leaf_nodes=32)
```

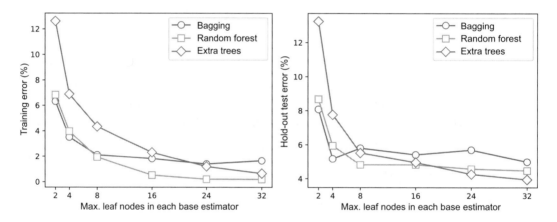

Figure 2.12 Training and test performance of bagging, random forest, and Extra Trees as base learner complexity increases. Bagging used decision trees as the base estimator, random forest used randomized decision trees, and Extra Trees used extremely randomized trees.

Recall that highly complex trees are inherently unstable and sensitive to small perturbations in the data. This means that, in general, if we increase the complexity of the base learners, we'll need a lot more of them to successfully reduce the variability of the ensemble overall. Here, however, we've fixed `n_estimators=10`.

One key consideration in determining the depth of the base decision trees is computational efficiency. Training deeper and deeper trees will take more and more time without producing a significant improvement in predictive performance. For instance, base decision trees of depths 24 and 32 perform roughly similarly.

2.5.3 *Feature importances with random forests*

Finally, let's see how we can use feature importances to identify the most predictive features for breast cancer diagnosis using the random forest ensemble. Such analysis adds *interpretability* to the model and can be very helpful in communicating and explaining such models to domain experts such as doctors.

FEATURE IMPORTANCES FROM LABEL CORRELATIONS

First, let's peek into the data set to see if we can discover some interesting relationships among the features and the diagnosis. This type of analysis is typical when we get a new data set, as we try to learn more about it. Here, our analysis will try to identify which features are most correlated with each other and with the diagnosis (label), so that we can check if random forests can do something similar. In the following listing, we use the pandas and seaborn packages to visualize feature and label correlations.

> **Listing 2.6 Visualizing correlations between features and labels**

```
import pandas as pd
import seaborn as sea
                                          Converts the data into
                                          a pandas DataFrame
df = pd.DataFrame(data=dataset['data'],
                  columns=dataset['feature_names'])
df['diagnosis'] = dataset['target']

fig, ax = plt.subplots(nrows=1, ncols=1, figsize=(8, 8))
cor = np.abs(df.corr())
sea.heatmap(cor, annot=False, cbar=False, cmap=plt.cm.Greys, ax=ax)
fig.tight_layout()
                              Computes and plots the
                              correlation between some selected
                              features and the label (diagnosis)
```

The output of this listing is shown in figure 2.13. Several features are highly correlated with each other, for example, mean radius, mean perimeter, and mean area. Several features are also highly correlated with the label, that is, the diagnosis as benign or malignant. Let's identify the 10 features most correlated with the diagnosis label:

```
label_corr = cor.iloc[:, -1]
label_corr.sort_values(ascending=False)[1:11]
```

This produces the following ranking of the top-10 features:

```
worst concave points    0.793566
worst perimeter         0.782914
mean concave points     0.776614
worst radius            0.776454
mean perimeter          0.742636
worst area              0.733825
mean radius             0.730029
mean area               0.708984
mean concavity          0.696360
worst concavity         0.659610
```

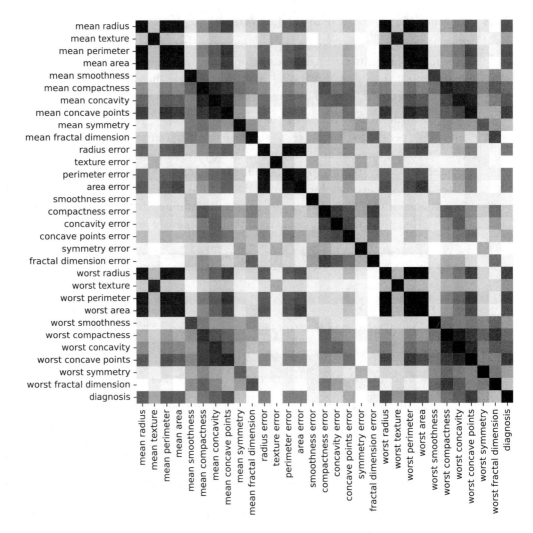

Figure 2.13 Absolute feature correlations between all 30 features and the label (diagnosis)

Thus, our correlation analysis tells us that these 10 features are the most highly correlated with the diagnosis; that is, these features are likely most helpful in breast cancer diagnosis.

Keep in mind that correlation isn't always a reliable means of identifying effective variables, especially if there are highly nonlinear relationships between features and labels. However, it's often a reasonable guideline as long as we're aware of its limitations.

FEATURE IMPORTANCES USING RANDOM FORESTS

Random forests can also provide feature importances, as illustrated in the following listing.

Listing 2.7 Feature importances in the WDBC data set using random forests

```
X_trn, X_tst, y_trn, y_tst = train_test_split(X, y, test_size=0.15)
n_features = X_trn.shape[1]

rf = RandomForestClassifier(max_leaf_nodes=24,          ⟵  Trains a random
                            n_estimators=50, n_jobs=-1)      forest ensemble
rf.fit(X_trn, y_trn)
err = 1 - accuracy_score(y_tst, rf.predict(X_tst))
print('Prediction Error = {0:4.2f}%'.format(err*100))

importance_threshold = 0.02
for i, (feature, importance) in enumerate(zip(dataset['feature_names'],
                                              rf.feature_importances_)):

    if importance > importance_threshold:
        print('[{0}] {1} (score={2:4.3f})'.
            format(i, feature, importance))
```

Sets an importance threshold wherein all the features above the threshold are important

Prints the "important" features, that is, those above the importance threshold

Listing 2.7 depends on an `importance_threshold`, which is set to `0.02` here. Typically, such a threshold is set by inspection such that we get a target feature set, or using a separate validation set to identify important features so that overall performance doesn't degrade.

For the WDBC data set, the random forest identifies the following features as being important. Observe that a considerable overlap exists between important features identified by correlation analysis and random forests, though their relative rankings are different:

```
[2] mean perimeter (score=0.055)
[3] mean area (score=0.065)
[6] mean concavity (score=0.071)
[7] mean concave points (score=0.138)
[13] area error (score=0.065)
[20] worst radius (score=0.080)
[21] worst texture (score=0.023)
[22] worst perimeter (score=0.067)
[23] worst area (score=0.131)
[26] worst concavity (score=0.029)
[27] worst concave points (score=0.149)
```

Finally, the feature importances identified by the random forest ensemble are visualized in figure 2.14.

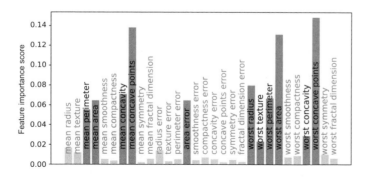

Figure 2.14 The random forest ensemble can score features by their importance. This allows us to perform feature selection by only using features with the highest scores.

CAUTION   Note that feature importances will often change between runs owing to randomization during tree construction. Note also that if two features are highly correlated, random forests will often distribute the feature importance between them, leading to their overall weights appearing smaller than they actually are. There are other, more robust ways to compute feature importances for the purposes of ensemble interpretability, which we'll explore in chapter 9.

Summary

- Parallel homogeneous ensembles promote ensemble diversity through randomization: random sampling of training examples and of features, or even introducing randomization in the base-learning algorithm.
- Bagging is a simple ensemble method that relies on (1) bootstrap sampling (or sampling with replacement) to generate diverse replicates of the data set and training diverse models, and (2) model aggregation to produce an ensemble prediction from a set of individual base learner predictions.
- Bagging and its variants work best with any unstable estimators (unpruned decision trees, support vector machines [SVMs], deep neural networks, etc.), which are models of higher complexity and/or nonlinearity.
- Random forest refers to a variant of bagging specifically designed to use randomized decision trees as base learners. Increasing randomness increases ensemble diversity considerably, allowing the ensemble to decrease the variability and smooth out predictions.
- Pasting, a variant of bagging, samples training examples without replacement and can be effective on data sets with a very large number of training examples.
- Other variants of bagging, such as random subspaces (sampling features) and random patches (sampling both features and training examples), can be effective on data sets with high dimensionality.
- Extra Trees is another bagging-like ensemble method that is specifically designed to use extremely randomized trees as base learners. However, Extra Trees doesn't use bootstrap sampling as additional randomization helps in generating ensemble diversity.
- Random forests provide feature importances to rank the most important features from a predictive standpoint.

Heterogeneous parallel ensembles: Combining strong learners

3

This chapter covers

- Combining base-learning models by performance-based weighting
- Combining base-learning models with meta-learning by stacking and blending
- Avoiding overfitting by ensembling with cross validation
- Exploring a large-scale, real-world, text-mining case study with heterogeneous ensembles

In the previous chapter, we introduced two parallel ensemble methods: bagging and random forests. These methods (and their variants) train *homogeneous ensembles*, where every base estimator is trained using the same base-learning algorithm. For example, in bagging classification, all the base estimators are decision-tree classifiers.

In this chapter, we continue exploring parallel ensemble methods, but this time focusing on *heterogeneous ensembles*. Heterogeneous ensemble methods use different base-learning algorithms to directly ensure ensemble diversity. For example, a heterogeneous ensemble can consist of three base estimators: a decision tree, a support vector machine (SVM), and an artificial neural network (ANN). These base estimators are still trained independently of each other.

The earliest heterogeneous ensemble methods, such as stacking, were developed as far back as 1992. However, these methods really came to the fore during the Netflix Prize competition in the mid-2000s. The top three teams, including the one that eventually won the $1 million prize, were ensemble teams, and their solutions were a complex blend of hundreds of different base models. This success was a striking and very public demonstration of the effectiveness of many of the methods we'll be discussing in this chapter.

Inspired by this success, stacking and blending have become widely popular. With sufficient base-estimator diversity, these algorithms can often boost performance on your data set and serve as powerful ensembling tools in any data analyst's arsenal.

Another reason for their popularity is that they can easily combine existing models, which allows us to use previously trained models as base estimators. For example, say you and a friend were working independently on a data set for a Kaggle competition. You trained an SVM, while your friend trained a logistic regression model. While your individual models are doing okay, you both figure that you may do better if you put your heads (and models) together. You build a heterogeneous ensemble with these existing models without having to train them all over again. All you need to figure out is a way to combine your two models. Heterogeneous ensembles come in two flavors, depending on how they combine individual base-estimator predictions into a final prediction (see figure 3.1):

- *Weighting methods*—These methods assign individual base-estimator predictions a weight that corresponds to their strength. Better base estimators are assigned higher weights and influence the overall final prediction more. The predictions

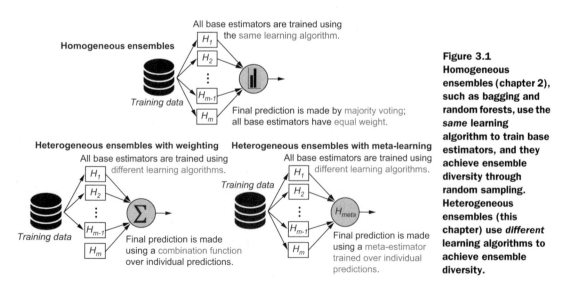

Figure 3.1 Homogeneous ensembles (chapter 2), such as bagging and random forests, use the *same* learning algorithm to train base estimators, and they achieve ensemble diversity through random sampling. Heterogeneous ensembles (this chapter) use *different* learning algorithms to achieve ensemble diversity.

of individual base estimators are fed into a predetermined combination function, which makes the final predictions.

- *Meta-learning methods*—These methods use a learning algorithm to combine the predictions of base estimators; the predictions of individual base estimators are treated as metadata and passed to a second-level meta-learner, which is trained to make final predictions.

We begin by introducing weighting methods, which combine classifiers by weighting the contribution of each one based on how effective it is.

3.1 Base estimators for heterogeneous ensembles

In this section, we'll set up a learning framework for fitting heterogeneous base estimators and getting predictions from them. This is the first step in building heterogeneous ensembles for any application and corresponds to training the individual base estimators H_1, H_2, ..., H_m at the bottom of figure 3.1, shown previously.

We'll train our base estimators using a simple 2D data set so we can explicitly visualize the decision boundaries and behavior of each base estimator as well as the diversity of the estimators. Once trained, we can construct a heterogeneous ensemble using a weighting method (section 3.2) or a meta-learning method (section 3.3):

```
from sklearn.datasets import make_moons
from sklearn.model_selection import train_test_split
X, y = make_moons(600, noise=0.25, random_state=13)
X, Xval, y, yval = train_test_split(X, y,
                                    test_size=0.25)
Xtrn, Xtst, ytrn, ytst = train_test_split(X, y,
                                          test_size=0.25)
```

Sets aside 25% of the data for validation

Sets aside a further 25% of the data for hold-out testing

This code snippet generates 600 synthetic training examples equally distributed into two classes, which are visualized in figure 3.2 as circles and squares.

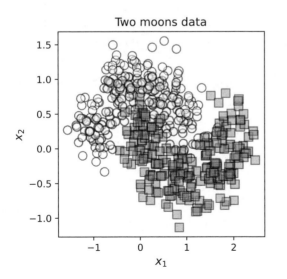

Figure 3.2 **Synthetic data set with two classes: 300 examples each in Class 0 (circles) and Class 1 (squares)**

3.1.1   Fitting base estimators

Our first task is to train the individual base estimators. Unlike homogeneous ensembles, we can use any number of different learning algorithms and parameter settings to train base estimators. The key is to ensure that we choose learning algorithms that are different enough to produce a diverse collection of estimators. The more diverse our set of base estimators, the better the resulting ensemble will be. For this scenario, we use six popular machine-learning algorithms, all of which are available in scikit-learn: `DecisionTreeClassifier`, `SVC`, `GaussianProcessClassifier`, `KNeighborsClassifier`, `RandomForestClassifier`, and `GaussianNB` (see figure 3.3).

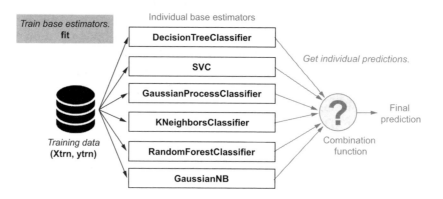

Figure 3.3   Fitting six base estimators using scikit-learn

The following listing initializes the six base estimators shown in figure 3.3 and trains them. Note the individual parameter settings used to initialize each base estimator (e.g., `max_depth=5` for `DecisionTreeClassifier` or `n_neighbors=3` for `KNeighborsClassifier`). In practice, these parameters have to be chosen carefully. For this simple data set, we can guess or just use the default parameter recommendations.

Listing 3.1   Fitting different base estimators

```
from sklearn.tree import DecisionTreeClassifier
from sklearn.svm import SVC
from sklearn.neighbors import KNeighborsClassifier
from sklearn.gaussian_process import GaussianProcessClassifier
from sklearn.gaussian_process.kernels import RBF
from sklearn.ensemble import RandomForestClassifier
from sklearn.naive_bayes import GaussianNB

estimators = [                                                    Initializes several base-
    ('dt', DecisionTreeClassifier (max_depth=5)),         ◁───    learning algorithms
    ('svm', SVC(gamma=1.0, C=1.0, probability=True)),
```

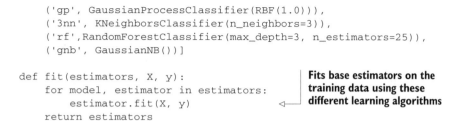

```
    ('gp', GaussianProcessClassifier(RBF(1.0))),
    ('3nn', KNeighborsClassifier(n_neighbors=3)),
    ('rf',RandomForestClassifier(max_depth=3, n_estimators=25)),
    ('gnb', GaussianNB())]
```

```
def fit(estimators, X, y):
    for model, estimator in estimators:
        estimator.fit(X, y)
    return estimators
```

Fits base estimators on the training data using these different learning algorithms

We train our base estimators on the training data:

```
estimators = fit(estimators, Xtrn, ytrn)
```

Once trained, we can also visualize how each base estimator behaves on our data set. It appears we were able to produce some pretty decently diverse base estimators.

Aside from ensemble diversity, one other aspect that is immediately apparent from the visualization of individual base estimators is that they all don't perform equally well on a held-out test set. In figure 3.4, 3-nearest neighbor (3nn) has the best test set performance, while Gaussian naïve Bayes (gnb) has the worst.

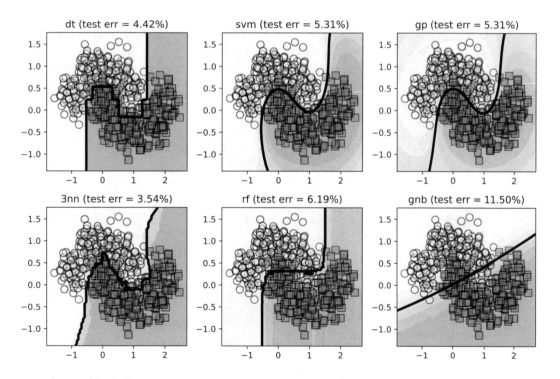

Figure 3.4 Base estimators in our heterogeneous ensemble. Each base estimator was trained using a different learning algorithm, which generally leads to a diverse ensemble.

For instance, `DecisionTreeClassifier` (dt) produces classifiers that partition the feature space into decision regions using axis-parallel boundaries (because each decision node in the tree splits on a single variable). Alternatively, the svm classifier `SVC` uses a radial basis function (RBF) kernel, which leads to smoother decision boundaries. Thus, while both learning algorithms can learn nonlinear classifiers, they are nonlinear in different ways.

Kernel methods

An SVM is an example of a *kernel method*, which is a type of machine-learning algorithm that can use kernel functions. A kernel function can efficiently measure the similarity between two data points implicitly in a high-dimensional space without explicitly transforming the data into that space. A linear estimator can be turned into a nonlinear estimator by replacing inner product computations with a kernel function. Commonly used kernels include the polynomial kernel and the Gaussian (also known as the RBF) kernel. For details, see chapter 12 of *The Elements of Statistical Learning: Data Mining, Inference, and Prediction*, 2nd ed., by Trevor Hastie, Robert Tibshirani, and Jerome Friedman (Springer, 2016).

3.1.2 Individual predictions of base estimators

Given test data to predict (`Xtst`), we can get the predictions of each test example using each base estimator. In our scenario, given that we have six base estimators, each test example will have six predictions, one corresponding to each base estimator (see figure 3.5).

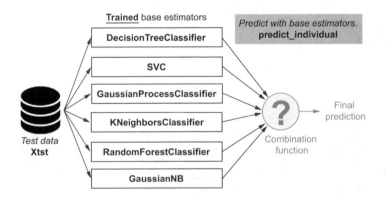

Figure 3.5   Individual predictions of a test set with the six trained base estimators in scikit-learn

Our task now is to collect the predictions of each test example by each trained base estimator into an array. In listing 3.2, the variable `y` is the structure that holds the predictions and is of size `n_samples * n_estimators`. That is, the entry `y[15, 1]` will be the prediction of the 2nd classifier (SVC) on the 16th test example (remember that indices in Python begin from 0).

Listing 3.2 Individual predictions of base estimators

```
import numpy as np                                        The flag "proba" allows us
                                                          to predict labels or
def predict_individual(X, estimators, proba=False):  ◄── probability over the labels.
    n_estimators = len(estimators)
    n_samples = X.shape[0]
                                                               If true, predicts the
    y = np.zeros((n_samples, n_estimators))                    probability of Class 1
    for i, (model, estimator) in enumerate(estimators):        (returns a float point
        if proba:                                              probability value
            y[:, i] = estimator.predict_proba(X)[:, 1]  ◄──    between 0 and 1)
        else:
            y[:, i] = estimator.predict(X)   ◄──   Otherwise, directly predicts Class 1
    return y                                        (returns an integer class label 0 or 1)
```

Observe that our function `predict_individual` has the flag `proba`. When we set `proba=False`, `predict_individual` returns the predicted labels according to each estimator. The predicted labels take the values $y_{pred} = 0$ or $y_{pred} = 1$, which tells us the estimator has predicted that the example belongs to Class 0 or Class 1, respectively.

When we set `proba=True`, however, each estimator will return the class prediction probabilities instead via each base estimator's `predict_proba()` function:

```
y[:, i] = estimator.predict_proba(X)[:, 1]
```

> **Note**
> Most classifiers in scikit-learn can return the probability of a label rather than the label directly. Some of them, such as SVC, should be explicitly told to do so (notice that we set `probability=True` when initializing SVC), while others are natural probabilistic classifiers and can represent and reason over class probabilities. These probabilities represent each base estimator's *confidence* in its prediction.

We can use this function to predict the test examples:

```
y_individual = predict_individual(Xtst, estimators, proba=False)
```

This produces the following output:

```
[[0. 0. 0. 0. 0. 0.]
 [1. 1. 1. 1. 1. 1.]
 [1. 1. 1. 1. 1. 1.]
 ...
 [0. 0. 0. 0. 0. 0.]
 [1. 1. 1. 1. 1. 1.]
 [0. 0. 0. 0. 0. 0.]]
```

Each row contains six predictions, and each one corresponds to the prediction of each base estimator. We sanity check our predictions: Xtst has 113 test examples, and y_individual has six predictions for each of them, which gives us a 113×6 array of predictions.

When proba=True, predict_individual returns the probability that an example belongs to Class 1, which we denote with $P(y_{pred} = 1)$. For two-class (binary) classification problems such as this one, the probability that the example belongs to Class 0 is simply $1 - P(y_{pred} = 1)$ because the example can only belong to one or the other, and probabilities over all possibilities sum to 1. We compute them as follows:

```
y_individual = predict_individual(Xtst, estimators, proba=True)
```

This produces the following output:

```
array([[0.  , 0.01, 0.08, 0.  , 0.04, 0.01],
       [1.  , 0.99, 0.92, 1.  , 0.92, 0.97],
       [0.98, 0.89, 0.76, 1.  , 0.89, 0.95],
       ...,
       [0.  , 0.03, 0.15, 0.  , 0.11, 0.07],
       [1.  , 0.97, 0.87, 1.  , 0.72, 0.62],
       [0.  , 0.  , 0.05, 0.  , 0.1 , 0.12]])
```

In the third row of this output, the third entry is 0.76, which indicates that our third base estimator, the GaussianProcessClassifier, is 76% confident that the third test example belongs to Class 1. On the other hand, the first entry in the third row is 0.98, which means that the DecisionTreeClassifier is 98% confident that the first test example belongs to Class 1.

Such prediction probabilities are often called *soft predictions.* Soft predictions can be converted to hard (0–1) predictions by simply picking the class label with the highest probability; in this example, according to the GaussianProcessClassifier, the hard prediction would be $y = 0$ because $P(y = 0) > P(y = 1)$.

For the purpose of building a heterogeneous ensemble, we can either use the predictions directly or use their probabilities. Using the latter typically produces a smoother output.

> **CAUTION**   The prediction function just discussed is specifically written for two-class, that is, binary classification, problems. It can be extended to multiclass problems if care is taken to store the prediction probabilities for each class. That is, for multiclass problems, you'll need to store the individual prediction probabilities in an array of size n_samples * n_estimators * n_classes.

We've now set up the basic infrastructure necessary to create a heterogeneous ensemble. We've trained six classifiers, and we have a function that gives us their individual predictions on a new example. Of course, the last and most important step is how we combine these individual predictions: by weighting or by meta-learning.

3.2 *Combining predictions by weighting*

What do weighting methods aim to do? Let's return to the performance of the 3nn and the gnb classifiers on our simple 2D data set (see figure 3.6). Imagine we were trying to build a very simple heterogeneous classifier using these two classifiers as base estimators.

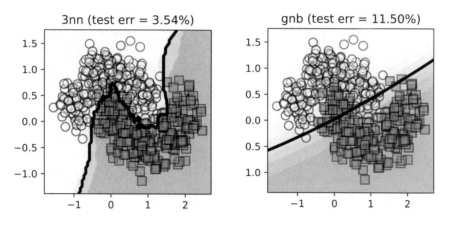

Figure 3.6 Two base estimators can have very different behaviors on the same data set. A weighting strategy should reflect their performance by weighting better-performing classifiers higher.

Let's say we compare the behavior of these two classifiers using test error as our evaluation metric. The test error can be evaluated using the examples in `Xtst`, which was held out during training; this gives us a good estimate of how the models will behave on future, unseen data.

The 3nn classifier has a test error rate of 3.54%, while gnb has a test error rate of 11.5%. Intuitively, we would trust the 3nn classifier more *on this* data set than the gnb classifier. However, this doesn't mean that gnb is useless and should be discarded. For many examples, it can reinforce the decision made by 3nn. What we don't want it to do is contradict 3nn when it isn't confident of its predictions.

This notion of base-estimator confidence can be captured by assigning weights. When we're looking to assign weights to base classifiers, we should do so in a manner consistent with this intuition, such that the final prediction is influenced more by the stronger classifiers and less by the weaker classifiers.

Say we're given a new data point x, and the individual predictions are y_{3nn} and y_{gnb}. A simple way to combine them would be to weight them based on their performance. The test set accuracy of 3nn is $a_{3nn} = 1 - 0.0354 = 0.9646$, and the test set accuracy of gnb $a_{gnb} = 1 - 0.115 = 0.885$. The final prediction can be computed as follows:

$$y = \underbrace{\frac{\alpha_{3nn}}{\alpha_{3nn} + \alpha_{gnb}}}_{w_{3nn}} \cdot y_{3nn} + \underbrace{\frac{\alpha_{gnb}}{\alpha_{3nn} + \alpha_{gnb}}}_{w_{gnb}} \cdot y_{gnb}$$

The estimator weights w_{3nn} and w_{gnb} are proportional to their respective accuracies, and the higher accuracy classifier will have the higher weight. In this example, we have $w_{3nn} = 0.522$ and $w_{gnb} = 0.478$. We've combined the two base estimators using a simple linear combination function (technically, a convex combination, since all the weights are positive and sum to 1).

Let's continue with the task of classifying our 2D two-moons data set and explore various weighting and combination strategies. This will typically consist of two steps (see figure 3.7):

1   Assign weights (w_{clf}) to each classifier (clf) in some way, reflecting its importance.

2   Combine the weighted predictions ($w_{clf} \cdot y_{clf}$) using a combination function h_c.

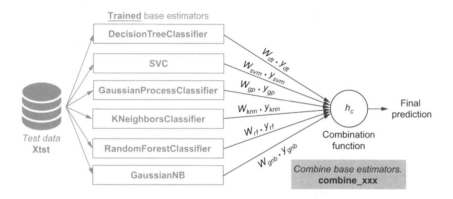

Figure 3.7   Each base classifier is assigned an importance weight that reflects how much its opinion contributes to the final decision. Weighted decisions of each base classifier are combined using a combination function.

We now look at several such strategies that generalize this intuition for both predictions and prediction probabilities. Many of these strategies are very easy to implement and commonly used in fusing predictions from multiple models.

3.2.1   *Majority vote*

You're already familiar with one type of weighted combination from the previous chapter: the majority vote. We briefly revisit majority vote here to show that it's just one of many combination schemes and to put it into the general framework of combination methods.

Majority voting can be viewed as a weighted combination scheme in which each base estimator is assigned an equal weight; that is, if we have m base estimators, each base estimator has a weight of $w_{clf} = \frac{1}{m}$. The (weighted) predictions of the individual base estimators are combined using the majority vote.

Like bagging, this strategy can be extended to heterogeneous ensembles as well. In the general combination scheme presented in figure 3.8, to implement this weighting strategy, we set $w_{clf} = \frac{1}{m}$ and h_c = majority vote, which is the statistical mode.

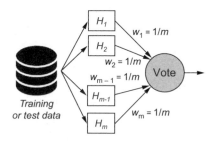

Training or test data

Figure 3.8 Combining by majority voting. Bagging can be viewed as a simple weighting method applied to a homogeneous ensemble. All classifiers have equal weights, and the combination function is the majority vote. We can adopt the majority voting strategy for heterogeneous ensembles as well.

The following listing combines the individual predictions `y_individual` from a heterogeneous set of base estimators using majority voting. Note that because the weights of the base estimators are all equal, we don't explicitly compute them.

Listing 3.3 Combining predictions using majority vote

```
from scipy.stats import mode

def combine_using_majority_vote(X, estimators):
    y_individual = predict_individual(X, estimators, proba=False)
    y_final = mode(y_individual, axis=1, keepdims=False)
    return y_final[0].reshape(-1, )
```

Reshapes the vector to ensure it returns one prediction per example

We can use this function to make predictions on the test data set, `Xtst`, using our previously trained base estimators:

```
from sklearn.metrics import accuracy_score
ypred = combine_using_majority_vote(Xtst, estimators)
tst_err = 1 - accuracy_score(ytst, ypred)
```

This produces the following test error:

```
0.06194690265486724
```

This weighting strategy produces a heterogeneous ensemble with a test error of 6.19%.

3.2.2 Accuracy weighting

Recall our motivating example at the start of this section, where we were trying to build a very simple heterogeneous classifier using 3nn and gnb as base estimators. In that example, our intuitive ensembling strategy was to weight each estimator by its performance, specifically, the accuracy score. That was a very simple example of accuracy weighting.

Here, we generalize this procedure to more than two estimators, as in figure 3.8. To get *unbiased performance estimates* for the base classifiers, we'll use a *validation set*.

WHY DO WE NEED A VALIDATION SET?

When we generated our data set, we partitioned it into a training set, a validation set, and a hold-out test set. The three subsets are mutually exclusive; that is, they don't have any overlapping examples. So, which of these three should we use to obtain unbiased estimates of the performance of each individual base classifier?

It's always good machine-learning practice to *not* reuse the training set for performance estimates because we've already seen this data, so the performance estimate will be biased. This is like seeing a previously assigned homework problem on your final exam. It doesn't really tell the professor that you're performing well because you've learned the concept; it just shows that you're good at that specific problem. In the same way, using training data to estimate performance doesn't tell us if a classifier can generalize well; it just tells us how well it does on examples it's already seen. To get an effective and unbiased estimate, we'll need to evaluate performance on data that the model has never seen before.

We can get unbiased estimates using either the validation set or the hold-out test set. However, the test set will often be used to evaluate the *final model performance*, that is, the performance of the *overall ensemble*.

Here, we're interested in estimating the performance of *each base classifier*. For this reason, we'll use the validation set to obtain unbiased estimates of each base classifier's performance: accuracy.

ACCURACY WEIGHTS USING A VALIDATION SET

Once we've trained each base classifier (clf), we evaluate its performance on a validation set. Let α_t be the validation accuracy of the tth classifier, H_t. The weight of each base classifier is then computed as follows:

$$w_t = \frac{\alpha_t}{\sum_{t=1}^{m} \alpha_t}$$

The denominator is a normalization term: the sum of all the individual validation accuracies. This computation ensures that a classifier's weight is proportional to its accuracy and that all the weights sum to 1.

Given a new example to predict *x*, we can get the predictions of the individual classifiers, y_t (using `predict_individual`). Now, the final prediction can be computed as a weighted sum of the individual predictions:

$$y_{final} = w_1 \cdot y_1 + w_2 \cdot y_2 + \cdots + w_m \cdot y_m = \sum_{t=1}^{m} w_t \cdot y_t$$

This procedure is illustrated in figure 3.9.

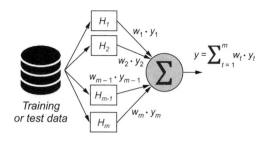

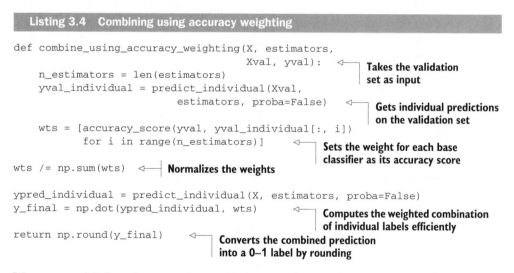

Figure 3.9 Combining by performance weighting. Each classifier is assigned a weight proportional to its accuracy. The final prediction is computed as a weighted combination of the individual predictions.

Listing 3.4 implements the combination by accuracy weighting. Note that while the individual classifier predictions will have values of 0 or 1, the overall final prediction will be a real number between 0 and 1, as the weights are fractions. This fractional prediction can be converted to a 0–1 final prediction easily by thresholding the weighted predictions on 0.5.

For example, a combined prediction of y_final=0.75 will be converted to y_final=1 (because 0.75 > the 0.5 threshold), while a combined prediction of y_final=0.33 will be converted to y_final=0 (because 0.33 < the 0.5 threshold). Ties, while extremely rare, can be broken arbitrarily.

Listing 3.4   Combining using accuracy weighting

```
def combine_using_accuracy_weighting(X, estimators,
                                     Xval, yval):     ◁──  Takes the validation
    n_estimators = len(estimators)                         set as input
    yval_individual = predict_individual(Xval,
                        estimators, proba=False)    ◁──  Gets individual predictions
                                                          on the validation set
    wts = [accuracy_score(yval, yval_individual[:, i])
           for i in range(n_estimators)]      ◁──  Sets the weight for each base
                                                    classifier as its accuracy score
wts /= np.sum(wts)   ◁──  Normalizes the weights

ypred_individual = predict_individual(X, estimators, proba=False)
y_final = np.dot(ypred_individual, wts)      ◁──  Computes the weighted combination
                                                  of individual labels efficiently
return np.round(y_final)     ◁──  Converts the combined prediction
                                  into a 0–1 label by rounding
```

We can use this function to make predictions on the test data set, Xtst, using our previously trained base estimators:

```
ypred = combine_using_accuracy_weighting(Xtst, estimators, Xval, yval)
tst_err = 1 - accuracy_score(ytst, ypred)
```

This produces the following output:

```
0.03539823008849563
```

This weighting strategy produces a heterogeneous ensemble with a test error of 3.54%.

3.2.3   *Entropy weighting*

The entropy weighting approach is another performance-based weighting approach, except that it uses entropy as the evaluation metric to judge the value of each base estimator. Entropy is a measure of *uncertainty* or impurity in a set; a more disorderly set will have higher entropy.

> **Entropy**
>
> Entropy, or *information entropy* to be precise, was originally devised by Claude Shannon to quantify the "amount of information" conveyed by a variable. This is determined by two factors: (1) the number of distinct values the variable can take, and (2) the uncertainty associated with each value.
>
> Consider that three patients—Ana, Bob, and Cam—are in the doctor's office awaiting the doctor's diagnosis of a disease. Ana is told with 90% confidence that she is healthy (i.e., 10% chance she is sick). Bob is told with 95% confidence that he is ill (i.e., 5% chance he is healthy). Cam is told that his test results are inconclusive (i.e., 50%/50%).
>
> Ana has received good news and there is little uncertainty in her diagnosis. Even though Bob has received bad news, there is little uncertainty in his diagnosis as well. Cam's situation has the highest uncertainty: he has received neither good nor bad news and is in for more tests.
>
> Entropy quantifies this notion of uncertainty across various outcomes. Entropy-based measures are commonly used during decision-tree learning to greedily identify the best variables to split on and are used as loss functions in deep neural networks.

Instead of using accuracy to weight classifiers, we can use entropy. However, because lower entropies are desirable, we need to ensure that base classifier weights are *inversely proportional* to their corresponding entropies.

COMPUTING ENTROPY OVER PREDICTIONS

Let's say that we have a test example, and an ensemble of 10 base estimators returned a vector of predicted labels: [1, 1, 1, 0, 0, 1, 1, 1, 0, 0]. This set has six predictions of $y = 1$ and four predictions of $y = 0$. These *label counts* can be equivalently expressed as *label probabilities*: the probability of predicting $y = 1$ is $P(y = 1) = \frac{6}{10} = 0.6$, and the probability of predicting $y = 0$ is $P(y = 0) = \frac{4}{10} = 0.4$. With these label probabilities, we can compute the entropy over this set of base estimator predictions as

$$E = -P(y = 0) \log_2 P(y = 0) - P(y = 1) \log_2 P(y = 1)$$

In this case, we'll have $E = -0.4 \log 0.4 - 0.6 \log 0.6 = 0.971$.

Alternatively, consider that a second test example, where the 10 base estimators returned a vector of predicted labels: [1, 1, 1, 1, 0, 1, 1, 1, 1, 1]. This set has nine predictions of $y = 1$ and one prediction of $y = 0$. The *label probabilities* in this case are $P(y = 1) = \frac{9}{10} = 0.9$ and $P(y = 0) = \frac{1}{10} = 0.1$. The entropy in this case will be $E = -0.1 \log 0.1 - 0.9 \log 0.9 = 0.469$. This set of predictions has a lower entropy because it's *purer* (mostly all predictions are $y = 1$). Another way of viewing this is to say that the 10 base estimators are less uncertain about the predictions on the second example. The following listing can be used to compute the entropy of a set of discrete values.

Listing 3.5 Computing entropy

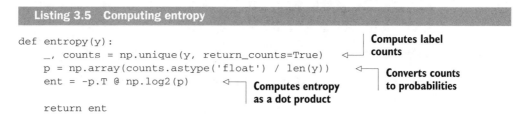

```
def entropy(y):                                          Computes label
    _, counts = np.unique(y, return_counts=True)         counts
    p = np.array(counts.astype('float') / len(y))        Converts counts
    ent = -p.T @ np.log2(p)          Computes entropy     to probabilities
                                     as a dot product
    return ent
```

Entropy weighting with a validation set

Let E_t be the validation entropy of the tth classifier, H_t. The weight of each base classifier is

$$w_t = \frac{\frac{1}{E_t}}{\sum_{t=1}^{m}\left(\frac{1}{E_t}\right)}$$

There are two key differences between entropy weighting and accuracy weighting:

- The accuracy of a base classifier is computed using both the true labels `ytrue` and the predicted labels `ypred`. In this manner, the accuracy metric measures how well a classifier performs. A classifier with high accuracy is better.
- The entropy of a base classifier is computed using only the predicted labels `ypred`, and the entropy metric measures how uncertain a classifier is about its predictions. A classifier with low entropy (uncertainty) is better. Thus, individual base classifier weights are inversely proportional to their corresponding entropies.

As with accuracy weighting, the final predictions need to be thresholded at 0.5. The following listing implements combining with entropy weighting.

Listing 3.6 Combining using entropy weighting

```
def combine_using_entropy_weighting(X, estimators,       Takes only the
                                    Xval):               validation examples
    n_estimators = len(estimators)
    yval_individual = predict_individual(Xval,           Gets individual predictions
                      estimators, proba=False)           on the validation set

    wts = [1/entropy(yval_individual[:, i])              Sets the weight for each base
           for i in range(n_estimators)]                 classifier as its inverse entropy
    wts /= np.sum(wts)        Normalizes the weights

    ypred_individual = predict_individual(X, estimators, proba=False)
    y_final = np.dot(ypred_individual, wts)              Computes the weighted combination
                                                         of individual labels efficiently
    return np.round(y_final)         Returns the
                                     rounded predictions
```

We can use this function to make predictions on the test data set, `Xtst`, using our previously trained base estimators:

```
ypred = combine_using_entropy_weighting(Xtst, estimators, Xval)
tst_err = 1 - accuracy_score(ytst, ypred)
```

This produces the following output:

```
0.03539823008849563
```

This weighting strategy produces a heterogeneous ensemble with a test error of 3.54%.

3.2.4 *Dempster-Shafer combination*

The methods we've seen so far combine predictions of individual base estimators directly (notice that we've set the flag `proba=False` when calling `predict_individual`). When we set `proba=True` in `predict_individual`, each classifier returns its individual estimate of the probability of belonging to Class 1. That is, when `proba=True`, instead of returning $y_{pred} = 0$ or $y_{pred} = 1$, each estimator will return $P(y_{pred} = 1)$.

This probability reflects a classifier's belief in what the prediction should be and offers a more nuanced view of the predictions. While the methods described in this section can also work with probabilities, the Dempster-Shafer theory (DST) method is another way to fuse these base-estimator beliefs into an overall final belief, or prediction probability.

DST FOR LABEL FUSION

DST is a generalization of probability theory that supports reasoning under uncertainty and with incomplete knowledge. While the foundations of DST are beyond the scope of this book, the theory itself provides a way to fuse beliefs and evidence from multiple sources into a single belief.

DST uses a number between 0 and 1 to indicate belief in a proposition, such as "the test example x belongs to Class 1." This number is known as a *basic probability assignment* (BPA) and expresses the certainty that the text example x belongs to Class 1. BPA values closer to 1 characterize decisions made with more certainty. The BPA allows us to translate an estimator's confidence into a belief about the true label.

Let's say a 3nn classifier is used to classify a test example x, and it returns $P(y_{pred} = 1 \mid 3nn) = 0.75$. Now, gnb is also used to classify the same test example and returns $P(y_{pred} = 1 \mid gnb) = 0.6$. According to DST, we can compute the BPA for the proposition "test example x belongs to Class 1 according to both 3nn and gnb." We do this by fusing their individual prediction probabilities:

$$BPA(y_{pred} = 1|3nn, gnb) = 1 - \left(1 - P\left(y_{pred} = 1|3nn\right)\right) \cdot \left(1 - P\left(y_{pred} = 1|gnb\right)\right)$$
$$= 1 - (1 - 0.75) \cdot (1 - 0.6) = 0.9$$

We can also compute the BPA for the proposition "test example x belongs to Class 0 according to both 3nn and gnb":

$$BPA\left(y_{pred} = 0|3nn, gnb\right) = 1 - \left(1 - P\left(y_{pred} = 0|3nn\right)\right) \cdot \left(1 - P\left(y_{pred} - 0|gnb\right)\right)$$
$$= 1 - (1 - 0.25) \cdot (1 - 0.4) = 0.55$$

Based on these scores, we're more certain that the test example x belongs to Class 1. The BPAs can be thought of as certainty scores, with which we can compute our final belief of belonging to Class 0 or Class 1.

The BPAs are used to compute beliefs. The unnormalized beliefs (denoted Bel) that "test example x belongs to Class 1" are computed as

$$Bel\left(y_{pred} = 1\right) = \frac{BPA(y_{pred} = 1)}{1 - BPA(y_{pred} = 1)} = \frac{0.9}{0.1} = 9,$$

$$Bel(y_{pred} = 0) = \frac{BPA(y_{pred} = 0)}{1 - BPA(y_{pred} = 0)} = \frac{0.55}{0.45} = 1.22.$$

These unnormalized beliefs can be normalized using the normalization factor $Z = Bel(y_{pred} = 1) + Bel(y_{pred} = 0) + 1$, to give us $Bel(y_{pred} = 1) = 0.80$ and $Bel(y_{pred} = 0) = 0.11$. Finally, we can use these beliefs to get the final prediction: the class with the highest belief. For this test example, the DST method produces a final prediction of $y_{pred} = 1$.

COMBINING USING DST

The following listing implements this approach.

Listing 3.7 Combining using Dempster-Shafer

```
def combine_using_Dempster_Schafer(X, estimators):
    p_individual = predict_individual(X,              Gets individual predictions
                    estimators, proba=True)    ◁——┘   on the validation set
    bpa0 = 1.0 - np.prod(p_individual, axis=1)
    bpa1 = 1.0 - np.prod(1 - p_individual, axis=1)
                                                      Stacks the beliefs for Class 0
    belief = np.vstack([bpa0 / (1 - bpa0),            and Class 1 side by side for
                    bpa1 / (1 - bpa1)]).T   ◁——┘      every test example
    y_final = np.argmax(belief, axis=1)   ◁——  Selects the final label as the
    return y_final                             class with the highest belief
```

We can use this function to make predictions on the test data set, `Xtst`, using our previously trained base estimators:

```
ypred = combine_using_Dempster_Schafer(Xtst, estimators)
tst_err = 1 - accuracy_score(ytst, ypred)
```

This produces the following output:

```
0.053097345132743334
```

This output means that DST achieved 5.31% accuracy.

We've seen four methods of combining predictions into one final prediction. Two use the predictions directly, while two use prediction probabilities. We can visualize the decision boundaries produced by these weighting methods, as shown in figure 3.10.

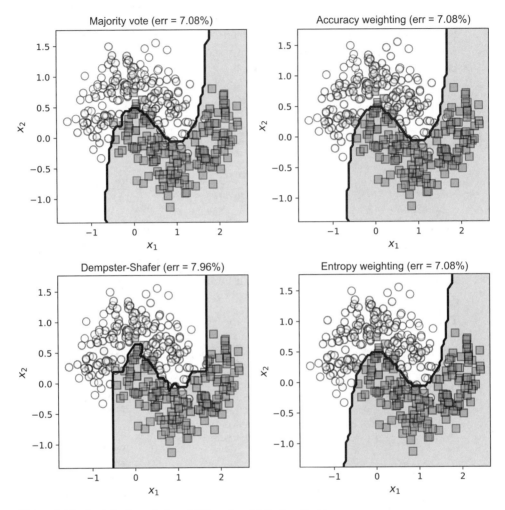

Figure 3.10 Decision boundaries of different weighting methods

3.3   Combining predictions by meta-learning

In the previous section, we saw one approach to constructing heterogeneous ensembles of classifiers: weighting. We weighted each classifier by its performance and used a *predetermined combination function* to combine predictions of each classifier. In doing so, we had to carefully design the combination function to reflect our performance priorities.

Now, we'll look at another approach to constructing heterogeneous ensembles: meta-learning. Instead of carefully designing a combination function to combine predictions, we'll *train a combination function* over individual predictions. That is, the predictions of the base estimators are given as inputs to a second-level learning algorithm. Thus, rather than designing one ourselves, we'll train a second-level *meta-classification function*.

Meta-learning methods have been widely and successfully applied to a variety of tasks in chemometrics analysis, recommendation systems, text classification, and spam filtering. For recommendation systems, meta-learning methods of stacking and blending were brought to prominence after they were used by several top teams during the Netflix prize competition.

3.3.1   Stacking

Stacking is the most common meta-learning method and gets its name because it stacks a second classifier on top of its base estimators. The general stacking procedure has two steps:

1   Level 1: Fit base estimators on the training data. This step is the same as before and aims to create a diverse, heterogeneous set of base classifiers.
2   Level 2: Construct a new data set from the predictions of the base classifiers, which become *meta-features*. Meta-features can either be the predictions or the probability of predictions.

Let's return to our example, where we construct a simple heterogeneous ensemble from a 3nn classifier and a gnb classifier on our 2D synthetic data set. After training the classifiers (3nn and gnb), we create new features, called *meta-features from classifications*, of these two classifiers (see figure 3.11).

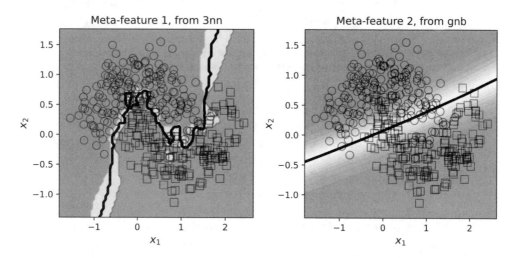

Figure 3.11   The probability of prediction of each training example according to 3nn and gnb are used as meta-features for a new classifier. Data points in darker regions indicate high-confidence predictions. Each training example now has two meta-features, one each from 3nn and gnb.

Since we have two base classifiers, we can use each one to generate one meta-feature in our meta-example. Here we use the prediction probabilities of 3nn and gnb as meta-features. Thus, for each training example, say x_i, we obtain two meta features: y_{3nn}^i and y_{gnb}^i, which are the prediction probabilities of x_i according to 3nn and gnb, respectively.

These meta-features become metadata for a second-level classifier. Contrast this stacking approach to combination by weighting. For both approaches, we obtain individual predictions using the function `predict_individual`. For combination by weighting, we use these predictions directly in some *predetermined combination function*. In stacking, we use these predictions as a new training set *to train a combination function*.

Stacking can use any number of level-1 base estimators. Our goal, as always, will be to ensure that there is sufficient diversity among these base estimators. Figure 3.12 shows the stacking schematic for the six popular algorithms we've used previously to explore combining by weighting: `DecisionTreeClassifier`, `SVC`, `GaussianProcess Classifier`, `KNeighborsClassifier`, `RandomForestClassifier`, and `GaussianNB`.

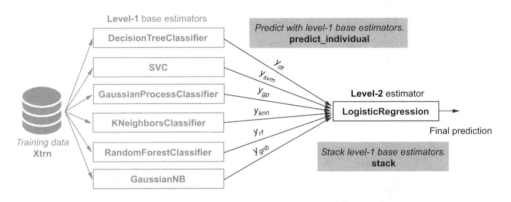

Figure 3.12   Stacking with six level-1 base estimators produces a metadata set of six meta-features that can be used to train a level-2 meta-classifier (here, logistic regression).

The level-2 estimator here can be trained using any base-learning algorithm. Historically, linear models such as linear regression and logistic regression have been used. An ensembling method that uses such linear models in the second level is called *linear stacking*. Linear stacking is generally popular because it's fast: learning linear models is generally computationally efficient, even for large data sets. Often, linear stacking can also be an effective exploratory step in analyzing your data set.

However, stacking can also employ powerful nonlinear classifiers in its second level, including SVMs and ANNs. This allows the ensemble to combine meta-features in complex ways, though at the expense of interpretability inherent in linear models.

NOTE   scikit-learn (v1.0 and above) contains `StackingClassifier` and `StackingRegressor`, which can be used directly for training. In the following subsections, we implement our own stacking algorithms to understand the finer details of how meta-learning works under the hood.

Let's revisit the task of classifying our 2D two-moons data set. We'll implement a linear stacking procedure, which consists of the following steps: (1) train individual base estimators (level 1), (2a) construct meta-features, and (2b) train a linear regression model (level 2).

We've already developed most of the framework we need to quickly implement linear stacking. We can train individual base estimators using `fit` (refer to listing 3.1) and obtain meta-features from `predict_individual` (refer to listing 3.2). The following listing uses these functions to fit a stacking model with any level-2 estimator. Since the level-2 estimator uses generated features or meta-features, it's also called a *meta-estimator*.

> **Listing 3.8 Stacking with a second-level estimator**

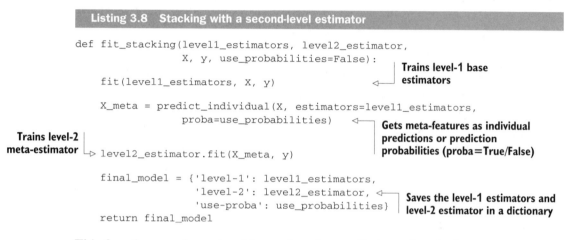

This function can learn by either using the predictions directly (`use_probabilities=False`) or by using the prediction probabilities (`use_probabilities=True`), as shown in figure 3.13.

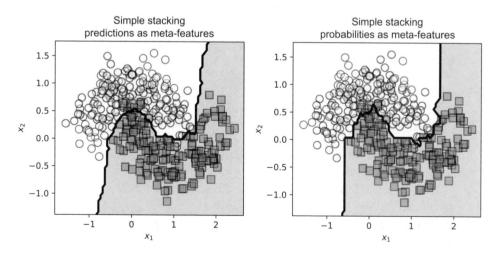

Figure 3.13 Final models produced by stacking with logistic regression using either predictions (left) or prediction probabilities (right) as meta-features

The level-2 estimator here can be any classification model. Logistic regression is a common choice, which leads the ensemble to stack level-1 predictions using a linear model.

A nonlinear model can also be used as a level-2 estimator. In general, any learning algorithm can be used to train a `level2_estimator` over the meta-features. A learning algorithm such as an SVM with RBF kernels or an ANN can learn powerful nonlinear models at the second level and potentially improve performance even more.

Prediction proceeds in two steps:

1 For each test example, get the meta-features using the trained level-1 estimators and create a corresponding test meta-example.
2 For each meta-example, get the final prediction using the level-2 estimator.

Making predictions with a stacked model can also be implemented easily, as shown in listing 3.9.

Listing 3.9 Making predictions with a stacked model

```
def predict_stacking(X, stacked_model):
    level1_estimators = stacked_model['level-1']       Gets level-1 base
    use_probabilities = stacked_model['use-proba']     estimators

    X_meta = predict_individual(X, estimators=level1_estimators,
                 proba=use_probabilities)              Gets meta-features using
                                                       the level-1 base estimators
    level2_estimator = stacked_model['level-2']
    y = level2_estimator.predict(X_meta)               Gets level-2 estimator and uses
                                                       it to make the final predictions
    return y                                           on the meta-features
```

In the following example, we use the same six base estimators from the previous section in level 1 and logistic regression as the level-2 meta-estimator:

```
from sklearn.linear_model import LogisticRegression
meta_estimator = LogisticRegression(C=1.0, solver='lbfgs')
stacking_model = fit_stacking(estimators, meta_estimator,
                              Xtrn, ytrn, use_probabilities=True)
ypred = predict_stacking(Xtst, stacking_model)
tst_err = 1 - accuracy_score(ytst, ypred)
```

This produces the following output:

```
0.06194690265486724
```

In the preceding snippet, we used the prediction probabilities as meta-features. This linear stacking model obtains a test error of 6.19%.

This simple stacking procedure is often effective. However, it does suffer from one significant drawback: overfitting, especially in the presence of noisy data. The effects of overfitting can be observed in figure 3.14. In the case of stacking, the overfitting occurs because we used the same data set to train all the base estimators.

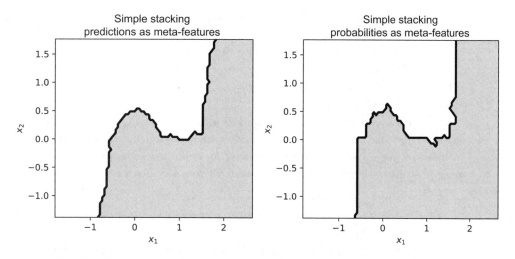

Figure 3.14 **Stacking can overfit the data. There is evidence of overfitting here: the decision boundaries are highly jagged where the classifiers have attempted to fit individual, noisy examples.**

To guard against overfitting, we can incorporate *k-fold cross validation* (CV) such that each base estimator isn't trained on the exact same data set. You may have previously encountered and used CV for parameter selection and model evaluation.

Here, we use CV to partition the data set into subsets so that different base estimators are trained on different subsets. This often leads to more diversity and robustness, while decreasing the chances of overfitting.

3.3.2 Stacking with cross validation

CV is a model validation and evaluation procedure that is commonly employed to simulate out-of-sample testing, tune model hyperparameters, and test the effectiveness of machine-learning models. The prefix "k-fold" is used to describe the number of subsets we'll be partitioning our data set into. For example, in 5-fold CV, data is (often randomly) partitioned into five nonoverlapping subsets. This gives rise to five folds, or combinations, of these subsets for training and validation, as shown in figure 3.15.

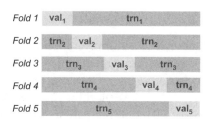

Figure 3.15 **k-fold CV (here, *k*=5) generates *k* different splits of the data set into a training set and a validation set. This simulates out-of-sample validation during training.**

More concretely, in 5-fold CV, let's say the data set D is partitioned into five subsets: D_1, D_2, D_3, D_4, and D_5. These subsets are disjointed, that is, any example in the data set appears in only one of the subsets. The third fold will comprise the training set $trn_3 = \{D_1, D_2, D_4, D_5\}$ (all subsets *except* D_3) and the validation set $val_3 = \{D_3\}$ (*only* D_3). This fold allows us to train and validate one model. Overall, 5-fold CV will allow us to train and validate five models.

In our case, we'll use the cross-validation procedure slightly differently in order to ensure robustness of our level-2 estimator. Instead of using the validation sets val_k for evaluation, we'll use them for generating meta-features for the level-2 estimator. The precise steps for combining stacking with CV are as follows:

1 Randomly split the data into k equal-sized subsets.
2 Train k models for each base estimator using the training data from the corresponding kth fold, trn_k.
3 Generate k sets of meta-examples from each trained base estimator using the validation data from the corresponding kth fold, val_k.
4 Retrain each level-1 base estimator on the full data set.

The first three steps of this procedure are illustrated in figure 3.16.

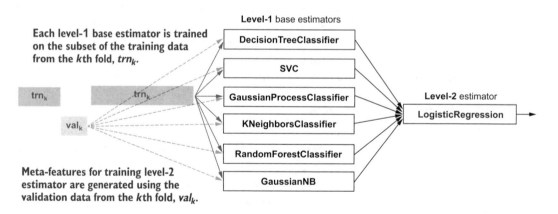

Figure 3.16 Stacking with k-fold CV. *k* versions of each level-1 base estimator are trained using the training sets within each fold, and *k* subsets of meta-examples are generated from the validation sets in each fold for the level-2 estimator.

A key part of stacking with CV is to split the data set into training and validation sets for each fold. scikit-learn contains many utilities to perform precisely this, and the one we'll use is called `model_selection.StratifiedKFold`. The `StratifiedKFold` class is a variation of the `model_selection.KFold` class that returns *stratified folds*. This means that the folds preserve the class distributions in the data set when generating folds.

For example, if the ratio of positive examples to negative examples in our data set is 2:1, `StratifiedKFold` will ensure that this ratio is preserved in the folds as well. Finally, it should be noted that rather than creating multiple copies of the data set for each fold (which is very wasteful in terms of storage), `StratifiedKFold` actually returns indices of the data points in the training and validation subsets of each fold. The following listing demonstrates how to perform stacking with cross validation.

Listing 3.10 Stacking with cross validation

```
from sklearn.model_selection import StratifiedKFold

def fit_stacking_with_CV(level1_estimators, level2_estimator,
                         X, y, n_folds=5, use_probabilities=False):
    n_samples = X.shape[0]
    n_estimators = len(level1_estimators)
    X_meta = np.zeros((n_samples, n_estimators))        Initializes the
                                                        metadata matrix

    splitter = StratifiedKFold(n_splits=n_folds, shuffle=True)

    for trn, val in splitter.split(X, y):
        level1_estimators = fit(level1_estimators, X[trn, :], y[trn])
        X_meta[val, :] = predict_individual(X[val, :],
                                            estimators=level1_estimators,
                                            proba=use_probabilities)

        level2_estimator.fit(X_meta, y)

        level1_estimators = fit(level1_estimators, X, y)

    final_model = {'level-1': level1_estimators,
                   'level-2': level2_estimator,
                   'use-proba': use_probabilities}

    return final_model
```

Trains level-2 meta-estimator

Trains level-1 estimators and then makes meta-features for the level-2 estimator with individual predictions

Saves the level-1 estimators and level-2 estimator in a dictionary

We can use this function to train a stacking model with CV:

```
stacking_model = fit_stacking_with_CV(estimators, meta_estimator,
                                      Xtrn, ytrn,
                                      n_folds=5, use_probabilities=True)
ypred = predict_stacking(Xtst, stacking_model)
tst_err = 1 - accuracy_score(ytst, ypred)
```

This produces the following output:

```
0.053097345132743334
```

With CV, stacking obtains a test error of 5.31%. As before, we can visualize our stacked model, as shown in figure 3.17. We see that the decision boundary is smoother, less jagged, and less prone to overfitting overall.

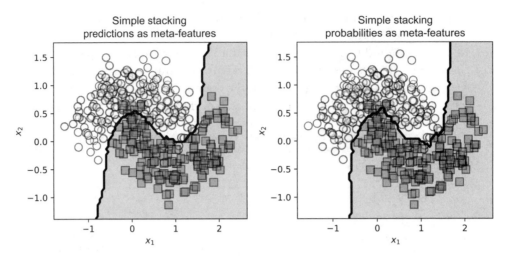

Figure 3.17   Stacking with CV is more robust to overfitting.

TIP   In our example scenario, we have six base estimators; if we choose to perform stacking with 5-fold CV, we'll have to train $6 \times 5 = 30$ models totally. Each base estimator is trained on a $\frac{k-1}{k}$ fraction of the data set. For smaller data sets, the corresponding increase in training time is modest, and is often well worth the cost. For larger data sets, this training time can be significant. If a full cross-validation-based stacking model is too prohibitively expensive to train, then it's usually sufficient to hold out a single validation set, rather than several cross-validation subsets. This procedure is known as *blending*.

We can now see meta-learning in action on a large-scale, real-world classification task with our next case study: sentiment analysis.

3.4   *Case study: Sentiment analysis*

Sentiment analysis is a natural language processing (NLP) task widely used to identify and analyze opinion in text. In its simplest form, it's mainly concerned with identifying the *effect* or the *polarity* of opinion as positive, neutral, or negative. Such "voice of the customer" analytics are a key part of brand monitoring, customer service, and market research.

This case study explores a supervised sentiment analysis task for movie reviews. The data set we'll use is the Large Movie Review Dataset, which was originally collected and curated from IMDB.com for NLP research by a group at Stanford University.[1] It's a large, publicly available data set that has become a text-mining/machine-

---

[1]   Andrew L. Maas, Raymond E. Daly, Peter T. Pham, Dan Huang, Andrew Y. Ng, and Christopher Potts, "Learning Word Vectors for Sentiment Analysis," 2011, http://mng.bz/nJRe.

learning benchmark over the past few years and has also featured in several Kaggle competitions (www.kaggle.com/c/word2vec-nlp-tutorial).

The data set contains 50,000 movie reviews split into training (25,000) and test (25,000) sets. Each review is also associated with a numerical rating from 1 to 10. This data set, however, only considers strongly opinionated labels, that is, reviews that are strongly positive about a movie (7–10) or strongly negative about a movie (1–4). These labels are condensed into binary sentiment polarity labels: strongly positive sentiment (Class 1) and strongly negative sentiment (Class 0). Here's an example of a positive review (label = 1) from the data set:

> *What a delightful movie. The characters were not only lively but alive, mirroring real every day life and strife within a family. Each character brought a unique personality to the story that the audience could easily associate with someone they know within their own family or circle of close friends.*

And here's an example of a negative review (label = 0):

> *This is the worst sequel on the face of the world of movies. Once again it doesn't make since. The killer still kills for fun. But this time he is killing people that are making a movie about what happened in the first movie. Which means that it's the stupidest movie ever. Don't watch this. If you value the one precious hour during this movie then don't watch it.*

Note the misspelling of "sense" as "since" above. Real-world text data can be highly noisy due to such spelling, grammatical, and linguistic idiosyncrasies, which makes these problems very challenging for machine learning. To begin, download and unzip this data set.

3.4.1 Preprocessing

The data set is preprocessed to bring each review from an unstructured, free-text form to a structured, vector representation. Put another way, preprocessing aims to bring this corpus (collection) of text files into a *term-document matrix* representation.

This usually involves steps such as removing special symbols, tokenization (chopping it up into tokens, typically individual words), lemmatization (recognizing different usages of the same word, e.g., organize, organizes, organizing), and count vectorization (counting the words that appear in each document). The last step produces a *bag-of-words* (BoW) representation of the corpus. In our case, each row (example) of the data set will be a review, and each column (feature) will be a word.

The example in figure 3.18 illustrates this representation when the sentence "this is a terrible terrible movie" is converted to a BoW representation with the vocabulary consisting of the words {this, is, a, brilliant, terrible, movie}.

Since the word "brilliant" doesn't occur in the review, its count is 0, while most of the other entries are 1 corresponding to the fact that they appear once in the review. This reviewer apparently thought the movie was doubly terrible—captured in our count features as the entry for the feature "terrible" is 2.

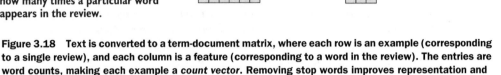

Each review is vectorized into a bag-of-words representation, which becomes a row in the term-document matrix.

Each column is a unique word that appears in the vocabulary.

Stop words, or common words, are often removed to improve performance.

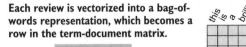

This is a terrible terrible movie

Each entry in the row is a count of how many times a particular word appears in the review.

Figure 3.18   Text is converted to a term-document matrix, where each row is an example (corresponding to a single review), and each column is a feature (corresponding to a word in the review). The entries are word counts, making each example a *count vector*. Removing stop words improves representation and often also improves performance.

Fortunately, this data set has already been preprocessed by count vectorization. These preprocessed term-document count features, our data set, can be found in /train/ labeledBow.feat and /test/labeledBow.feat. Both the train and test sets are of size $25,000 \times 89,527$. Thus, there are about 90,000 features (i.e., words), meaning that the entire set of reviews used about 90,000 unique words. We preprocess the data further with two additional steps, as discussed in the following subsections.

STOP-WORD REMOVAL

This step aims to remove common words such as "the," "is," "a," and "an." Traditionally, stop-word removal can reduce the dimensionality of the data (to make processing faster) and can improve classification performance. This is because words like "the" are often not really informative for information retrieval and text-mining tasks.

> **WARNING**   Care should be taken with certain stop words such as "not," as this common word significantly affects the underlying semantics and sentiment. For example, if we don't account for negation and apply stop-word removal on the sentence "not a good movie," we get "good movie," which completely changes the sentiment. Here, we don't selectively account for such stop words, and we rely on the strength of other expressive words, such as "awful," "brilliant," and "mediocre," to capture sentiment. However, performance on your own data set can be improved by careful feature engineering based on an understanding of the vocabulary as well as how pruning (or maybe even augmenting) it will affect your task.

The Natural Language Toolkit (NLTK) is a powerful Python package that provides many tools for NLP. In listing 3.11, we use NLTK's standard stop-word removal tool. The entire vocabulary for the IMDB data set is available in the file imdb.vocab, sorted by their frequency, from most common to least common.

We can directly apply stop-word removal on this set of features to identify which words we'll keep. In addition, we only keep the 5,000 most common words in order for our running time to be more manageable.

Listing 3.11 Dropping stop words from the vocabulary

```
import nltk
import numpy as np

def prune_vocabulary(data_path, max_features=5000):
    with open('{0}/imdb.vocab'.format(data_path), 'r', encoding='utf8') \
        as vocab_file:
        vocabulary = vocab_file.read().splitlines()        ◁── Loads the
                                                               vocabulary file
    nltk.download('stopwords')

    stopwords = set(                                   ┐ Converts the list of stop words
        nltk.corpus.stopwords.words("english"))    ◁──┘ to a set for faster processing


    to_keep = [True if word not in stopwords       ┐ Removes stop words
                    else False for word in vocabulary]  ◁──┘ from the vocabulary
    feature_ind = np.where(to_keep)[0]
                                               ┐ Keeps the top
    return feature_ind[:max_features]       ◁──┘ 5,000 words
```

TF-IDF TRANSFORMATION

Our second preprocessing step converts the count features to *term frequency-inverse document frequency* (TF-IDF) features. TF-IDF represents a statistic that weights each feature in a document (in our case, a single review) relative to how often it appears in that document as well as how often it appears in the entire corpus (in our case, all the reviews).

Intuitively, TF-IDF weights words by how often they appear in a document and also adjusts for how often they appear overall, and accounts for the fact that some words are generally used more often than others. We can use scikit-learn's preprocessing toolbox to convert our count features to TF-IDF features using the `TfidfTransformer`. Listing 3.12 creates and saves training and test sets, each of which comprises 25,000 reviews × 5,000 TF-IDF features.

Listing 3.12 Extracting TF-IDF features and saving the data set

```
import h5py
from sklearn.datasets import load_svmlight_files
from scipy.sparse import csr_matrix as sp
from sklearn.feature_extraction.text import TfidfTransformer
                                                             ┐ Loads train
def preprocess_and_save(data_path, feature_ind):           │ and test data
    data_files = ['{0}/{1}/labeledBow.feat'.format(data_path, data_set)
                for data_set in ['train', 'test']]   ◁──────┘
```

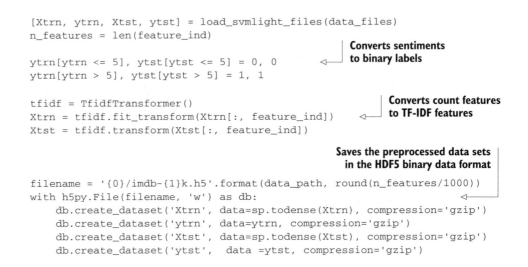

```
[Xtrn, ytrn, Xtst, ytst] = load_svmlight_files(data_files)
n_features = len(feature_ind)

ytrn[ytrn <= 5], ytst[ytst <= 5] = 0, 0
ytrn[ytrn > 5], ytst[ytst > 5] = 1, 1

tfidf = TfidfTransformer()
Xtrn = tfidf.fit_transform(Xtrn[:, feature_ind])
Xtst = tfidf.transform(Xtst[:, feature_ind])

filename = '{0}/imdb-{1}k.h5'.format(data_path, round(n_features/1000))
with h5py.File(filename, 'w') as db:
    db.create_dataset('Xtrn', data=sp.todense(Xtrn), compression='gzip')
    db.create_dataset('ytrn', data=ytrn, compression='gzip')
    db.create_dataset('Xtst', data=sp.todense(Xtst), compression='gzip')
    db.create_dataset('ytst',  data =ytst, compression='gzip')
```

Converts sentiments to binary labels

Converts count features to TF-IDF features

Saves the preprocessed data sets in the HDF5 binary data format

3.4.2   *Dimensionality reduction*

We continue to process the data with dimensionality reduction, which aims to represent the data more compactly. The main purpose of applying dimensionality reduction is to avoid the "curse of dimensionality," where algorithm performance deteriorates as the dimensionality of the data increases.

We adopt the popular dimensionality reduction approach of *principal components analysis* (PCA), which aims to compress and embed the data into a lower-dimensional feature space in a manner that preserves as much of the variability (measured using standard deviation or variance) as possible. This ensures that we're able to extract a lower-dimensional representation without too much loss of information.

This data set contains thousands of examples as well as features, which means that applying PCA to the entire data set will likely be highly computationally intensive and very slow. To avoid loading the entire data set into memory and to process the data more efficiently, we perform incremental PCA (IPCA) instead.

IPCA breaks the data set down into chunks that can be easily loaded into memory. Note, however, that while this chunking reduces the number of samples (rows) loaded into memory substantially, it still loads all the features (columns) for each row.

scikit-learn provides the class `sklearn.decomposition.IncrementalPCA`, which is far more memory efficient. The following listing performs PCA to reduce the dimension of the data to 500 dimensions.

Listing 3.13   Performing dimensionality reduction using IPCA

```
from sklearn.decomposition import IncrementalPCA

def transform_sentiment_data(data_path, n_features=5000, n_components=500):
    db = h5py.File('{0}/imdb-{1}k.h5'.format(
            data_path, round(n_features/1000)), 'r')
```

Loads preprocessed train and test data

```
pca = IncrementalPCA(n_components=n_components)
chunk_size = 1000
n_samples = db['Xtrn'].shape[0]
for i in range(0, n_samples // chunk_size):
    pca.partial_fit(db['Xtrn'][i*chunk_size:(i+1) * chunk_size])

Xtrn = pca.transform(db['Xtrn'])
Xtst = pca.transform(db['Xtst'])

with h5py.File('{0}/imdb-{1}k-pca{2}.h5'.format(data_path,
        round(n_features/1000), n_components), 'w') as db2:
    db2.create_dataset('Xtrn', data=Xtrn, compression='gzip')
    db2.create_dataset('ytrn', data=db['ytrn'], compression='gzip')
    db2.create_dataset('Xtst', data=Xtst, compression='gzip')
    db2.create_dataset('ytst', data=db['ytst'],
                        compression='gzip')
```

Applies IPCA to the data in manageable chunks

Reduces the dimension of both the train and test examples

Saves the preprocessed data sets in the HDF5 binary data format

Note that `IncrementalPCA` is fit using *only* the training set. Recall that the test data must *always* be held out and should only be used to provide an accurate estimate of how our pipeline will generalize to future, unseen data. This means that we can't use the test data during any part of preprocessing or training and can only use it for evaluation.

3.4.3 Blending classifiers

Our goal now is to train a heterogeneous ensemble with meta-learning. Specifically, we'll ensemble several base estimators by blending them. Recall that blending is a variant of stacking, where, instead of using CV, we use a single validation set.

First, we load the data using the following function:

```
def load_sentiment_data(data_path,n_features=5000, n_components=1000):

    with h5py.File('{0}/imdb-{1}k-pca{2}.h5'.format(data_path,
                round(n_features/1000), n_components), 'r') as db:
        Xtrn = np.array(db.get('Xtrn'))
        ytrn = np.array(db.get('ytrn'))
        Xtst = np.array(db.get('Xtst'))
        ytst = np.array(db.get('ytst'))

    return Xtrn, ytrn, Xtst, ytst
```

Next, we use five base estimators: `RandomForestClassifier` with 100 randomized decision trees, `ExtraTreesClassifier` with 100 extremely randomized trees, Logistic Regression, Bernoulli naïve Bayes (`BernoulliNB`), and a linear SVM trained with stochastic gradient descent (`SGDClassifier`):

```
from sklearn.ensemble import RandomForestClassifier, ExtraTreesClassifier
from sklearn.linear_model import LogisticRegression, SGDClassifier
from sklearn.naive_bayes import BernoulliNB

estimators = [('rf', RandomForestClassifier(n_estimators=100, n_jobs=-1)),
              ('xt', ExtraTreesClassifier(n_estimators=100, n_jobs=-1)),
```

```
('lr', LogisticRegression(C=0.01, solver='lbfgs')),
('bnb', BernoulliNB()),
('svm', SGDClassifier(loss='hinge', penalty='l2', alpha=0.01,
                      n_jobs=-1, max_iter=10, tol=None))]
```

The Bernoulli naïve Bayes classifier learns linear models but is especially effective for count-based data arising from text-mining tasks such as ours. Logistic regression and SVM with `SGDClassifier` both learn linear models. Random forests and Extra Trees are two homogeneous ensembles that produce highly nonlinear classifiers using decision trees as base estimators. This is a diverse set of base estimators, containing a good mix of linear and nonlinear classifiers.

To blend these base estimators into a heterogeneous ensemble with meta-learning, we use the following procedure:

1 Split the training data into a training set (`Xtrn`, `ytrn`) with 80% of the data and a validation set (`Xval`, `yval`) with the remaining 20% of the data.
2 Train each of the level-1 `estimators` on the training set (`Xtrn`, `ytrn`).
3 Generate meta-features `Xmeta` with the trained estimators using `Xval`.
4 Augment the validation data with the meta-features: [`Xval`, `Xmeta`]; this augmented validation set will have 500 original features + 5 meta-features.
5 Train the level-2 estimator with the augmented validation set ([`Xval`, `Xmeta`], `yval`).

The key to our combining-by-meta-learning procedure is meta-feature augmentation: we augment the validation set with the meta-features produced by the base estimators.

This leaves one final decision: the choice of the level-2 estimator. Previously, we used simple linear classifiers. For this classification task, we use a neural network.

Neural networks and deep learning

Neural networks are one of the oldest machine-learning algorithms. There has been a significant resurgence of interest in neural networks, especially deep neural networks, owing to their widespread success in many applications.

For a quick refresher on neural networks and deep learning, see chapter 2 of *Probabilistic Deep Learning with Python, Keras, and TensorFlow Probability* by Oliver Dürr, Beate Sick, and Elvis Murina (Manning, 2020).

We'll use a shallow neural network as our level-2 estimator. This will produce a highly nonlinear meta-estimator that can combine the predictions of the level-1 classifiers:

```
from sklearn.neural_network import MLPClassifier
meta_estimator = MLPClassifier(hidden_layer_sizes=(128, 64, 32),
                               alpha=0.001)
```

The following listing implements our strategy.

Listing 3.14   Blending models with a validation set

```python
from sklearn.model_selection import train_test_split

def blend_models(level1_estimators, level2_estimator,
                 X, y , use_probabilities=False):
    Xtrn, Xval, ytrn, yval = train_test_split(X, y,
                                 test_size=0.2)

    n_estimators = len(level1_estimators)
    n_samples = len(yval)
    Xmeta = np.zeros((n_samples, n_estimators))
    for i, (model, estimator) in
        enumerate(level1_estimators):
        estimator.fit(Xtrn, ytrn)
        Xmeta[:, i] = estimator.predict(Xval)

    Xmeta = np.hstack([Xval, Xmeta])

    level2_estimator.fit(Xmeta, yval)

    final_model = {'level-1': level1_estimators,
                   'level-2': level2_estimator,
                   'use-proba': use_probabilities}

    return final_model
```

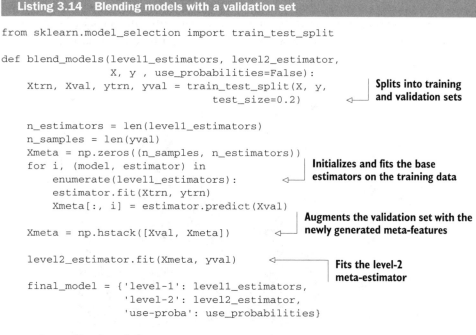

Splits into training and validation sets

Initializes and fits the base estimators on the training data

Augments the validation set with the newly generated meta-features

Fits the level-2 meta-estimator

We can now fit a heterogeneous ensemble on the training data:

```python
stacked_model = blend_models(estimators, meta_estimator, Xtrn, ytrn)
```

Then, we evaluate it on both the training and test data to compute the training and test error. First, we compute the training error with

```python
ypred = predict_stacking(Xtrn, stacked_model)
trn_err = (1 - accuracy_score(ytrn, ypred)) * 100
print(trn_err)
```

which gives us a training error of 7.84%:

```
7.8359999999999985
```

Next, we compute the test error with

```python
ypred = predict_stacking(Xtst, stacked_model)
tst_err = (1 - accuracy_score(ytst, ypred)) * 100
print(tst_err)
```

which gives us a test error of 17.2%:

```
17.196
```

So how well did we actually do? Did our ensembling procedure help at all? To answer these questions, we compare the performance of the ensemble to the performance of each base estimator in the ensemble.

Figure 3.19 shows the training and test errors of the individual base estimators as well as the stacking/blending ensemble. Some individual classifiers achieve a training error of 0%, which means they are likely overfitting the training data. This affects their performance as evidenced by the test error.

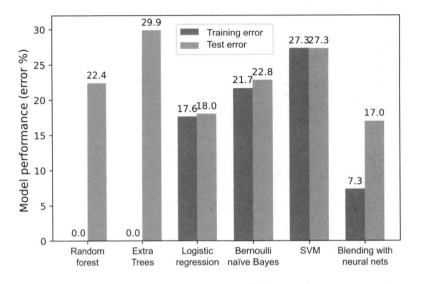

Figure 3.19   Comparing the performance of each individual base classifier with the meta-classifier ensemble. Stacking/blending improves classification performance by ensembling diverse base classifiers.

Overall, stacking/blending these heterogeneous models produces a test error of 17.2%, which is better than all the other models. In particular, let's compare this result to logistic regression with a test error of 18%. Recall that the test set contains 25,000 examples, which means that our stacked model classifies (approximately) another 200 examples correctly!

On the whole, the performance of the heterogeneous ensemble is better than a lot of the base estimators that contribute to it. This is an example of how heterogeneous ensembles can improve the overall performance of the underlying individual base estimators.

TIP   Remember that any linear or nonlinear classifier can be used as a meta-estimator. Common choices include decision trees, kernel SVMs, and even other ensembles!

Summary

- Heterogeneous ensemble methods promote ensemble diversity through heterogeneity; that is, they use different base-learning algorithms to train the base estimators.

- Weighting methods assign individual base-estimator predictions a weight that corresponds to their performance; better base estimators are assigned higher weights and influence the overall final prediction more.

- Weighting methods use a predefined combination function to combine the weighted predictions of the individual base estimators. Linear combination functions (e.g., weighted sum) are often effective and easy to interpret. Nonlinear combination functions can also be used, though the added complexity may lead to overfitting.

- Meta-learning methods learn a combination function from the data, in contrast to weighting methods, where we have to make one up ourselves.

- Meta-learning methods create multiple layers of estimators. The most common meta-learning method is stacking, so called because it literally stacks learning algorithms in a pyramid-like learning scheme.

- Simple stacking creates two levels of estimators. The base estimators are trained in the first level, and their outputs are used to train a second-level estimator called a meta-estimator. More complex stacking models with many more levels of estimators are possible.

- Stacking can often overfit, especially in the presence of noisy data. To avoid overfitting, stacking is combined with cross validation (CV) to ensure that different base estimators see different subsets of the data set for increased ensemble diversity.

- Stacking with CV, though it reduces overfitting, can also be computationally intensive, leading to long training times. To speed up training while guarding against overfitting, a single validation set can be used. This procedure is known as blending.

- Any machine-learning algorithm can be used as a meta-estimator in stacking. Logistic regression is the most common and leads to linear models. Nonlinear models, obviously, have greater representative power, but they are also at a greater risk for overfitting.

- Both weighting and meta-learning approaches can use either the base-estimator predictions directly or the prediction probabilities. The latter typically leads to a smoother, more nuanced model.

Sequential ensembles: Adaptive boosting

The ensembling strategies we've seen thus far have been parallel ensembles. These include homogeneous ensembles such as bagging and random forests (where the same base-learning algorithm is used to train base estimators) and heterogeneous ensemble methods such as stacking (where different base-learning algorithms are used to train base estimators).

Now, we'll explore a new family of ensemble methods: sequential ensembles. Unlike parallel ensembles, which exploit the *independence* of each base estimator, sequential ensembles exploit the *dependence* of base estimators. More specifically, during learning, sequential ensembles train a new base estimator in such a manner that it minimizes mistakes made by the base estimator trained in the previous step.

The first sequential ensemble method we'll investigate is *boosting*. Boosting aims to combine *weak learners*, or simple base estimators. Put another way, boosting literally aims to boost the performance of a collection of weak learners.

This is in contrast to algorithms such as bagging, which combine complex base estimators, also known as *strong learners*. Boosting commonly refers to AdaBoost, or *adaptive boosting*. This approach was introduced by Freund and Schapire in 1995,[1] for which they eventually won the prestigious Gödel Prize for outstanding papers in theoretical computer science.

Since 1995, boosting has emerged as a core machine-learning method. Boosting is surprisingly simple to implement, computationally efficient, and can be used with a wide variety of base-learning algorithms. Prior to the reemergence of deep learning in the mid-2010s, boosting was widely applied to computer vision tasks such as object classification and natural language processing tasks such as text filtering.

For most of this chapter, we focus on AdaBoost, a popular boosting algorithm that is also quite illustrative of the general framework of sequential ensemble methods. Other boosting algorithms can be derived by changing aspects of this framework, such as the loss function. Such variants are usually not available in packages and must be implemented. We also implement one such variant: LogitBoost.

4.1 Sequential ensembles of weak learners

There are two key differences between parallel and sequential ensembles:

- Base estimators in parallel ensembles can usually be trained independently, while in sequential ensembles, the base estimator in the current iteration depends on the base estimator in the previous iteration. This is shown in figure 4.1, where (in iteration t) the behavior of base estimator M_{t-1} influences the sample S_t, and the next model M_t.
- Base estimators in parallel ensembles are typically strong learners, while in sequential ensembles, they are weak learners. Sequential ensembles aim to combine several weak learners into one strong learner.

Intuitively, we can think of strong learners as professionals: highly confident people who are independent and sure about their answers. Weak learners, on the other hand, are like amateurs: not so confident and unsure about their answers. How can we get a bunch of not-so-confident amateurs to come together? By boosting them, of course. Before we see how exactly, let's characterize what weak learners are.

WEAK LEARNERS

While the precise definition of the strength of learners is rooted in machine-learning theory, for our purposes, a strong learner is a good model (or estimator). In contrast,

---

[1] Yoav Freund and Robert E. Schapire. "A decision-theoretic generalization of on-line learning and an application to boosting," *Journal of Computer and System Sciences*, 55(1):119–139, 1997.

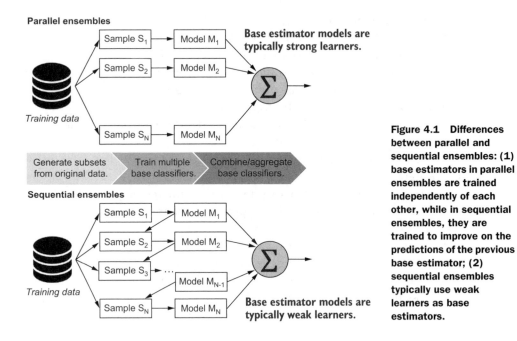

Figure 4.1   Differences between parallel and sequential ensembles: (1) base estimators in parallel ensembles are trained independently of each other, while in sequential ensembles, they are trained to improve on the predictions of the previous base estimator; (2) sequential ensembles typically use weak learners as base estimators.

a weak learner is a very simple model that doesn't perform that well. The only requirement of a weak learner (for binary classification) is that it performs better than random guessing. Put another way, its accuracy needs to be only slightly better than 50%. Decision trees are often used as base estimators for sequential ensembles. Boosting algorithms typically use decision stumps, or decision trees of depth 1 (see figure 4.2).

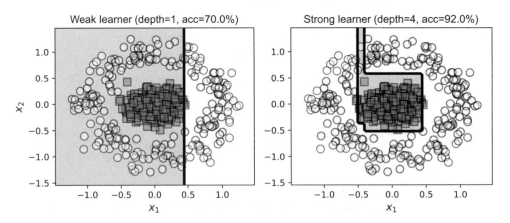

Figure 4.2   Decision stumps (trees of depth 1, left) are commonly used as weak learners in sequential ensemble methods such as boosting. As tree depth increases, a decision stump grows into a decision tree, becoming a stronger classifier, and its performance improves. However, it isn't possible to arbitrarily increase the strength of classifiers as they will begin to overfit during training, which decreases their prediction performance when deployed.

Sequential ensemble methods such as boosting aim to combine several weak learners into a single strong learner. These methods literally "boost" weak learners into a strong learner.

> **TIP** A weak learner is a simple classifier that is easy and efficient to train, but generally performs much worse than a strong learner (though better than random guessing). Sequential ensembles are generally agnostic to the underlying base-learning algorithms, meaning that you can use any classification algorithm as a weak learner. In practice, weak learners, such as shallow decision trees and shallow neural networks, are common.

Recall Dr. Randy Forrest's ensemble of interns from chapters 1 and 2. In a parallel ensemble of knowledgeable medical personnel, each intern can be considered a strong learner. To understand how different the philosophy of sequential ensembles is, we turn to Freund and Schapire, who describe boosting as "a committee of blockheads that can somehow arrive at highly reasoned decisions."[2]

This would be akin to Dr. Randy Forrest sending away his interns and deciding to crowdsource medical diagnoses instead. While this is certainly a far-fetched (and unreliable) strategy for diagnosing a patient, it turns out that "garnering wisdom from a council of fools"[3] works surprisingly well in machine learning. This is the underlying motivation for sequential ensembles of weak learners.

4.2 AdaBoost: Adaptive boosting

In this section, we begin with an important sequential ensemble: AdaBoost. AdaBoost is simple to implement and computationally efficient to use. As long as the performance of each weak learner in AdaBoost is slightly better than random guessing, the final model converges to a strong learner. However, beyond applications, understanding how AdaBoost works is also key to understanding two state-of-the-art sequential ensemble methods we'll look at in the next couple of chapters: gradient boosting and Newton boosting.

A brief history of boosting

The origins of boosting lie in computational learning theory, when learning theorists Leslie Valiant and Michael Kearns posed the following question in 1988: Can one boost a weak learner to a strong learner? This question was answered affirmatively two years later by Rob Schapire in his now landmark paper, "The Strength of Weak Learnability."

The earliest boosting algorithms were limited because weak learners didn't adapt to fix the mistakes made by weak learners trained in previous iterations. Freund and

---

[2] Ibid.
[3] Ibid.

(continued)

Schapire's AdaBoost, or *adaptive boosting* algorithm, proposed in 1994, ultimately addressed these limitations. Their original algorithm endures to this day and has been widely applied in several application domains, including text mining, computer vision, and medical informatics.

4.2.1 Intuition: Learning with weighted examples

AdaBoost is an adaptive algorithm: at every iteration, it trains a new base estimator that fixes the mistakes made by the previous base estimator. Thus, it needs some way to ensure that the base-learning algorithm prioritizes misclassified training examples. AdaBoost does this by maintaining *weights over individual training examples.* Intuitively, weights reflect the relative importance of training examples. Misclassified examples have higher weights, while correctly classified examples have lower weights.

When we train the next base estimator sequentially, the weights will allow the learning algorithm to prioritize (and hopefully fix) mistakes from the previous iteration. This is the adaptive component of AdaBoost, which ultimately leads to a powerful ensemble.

> **NOTE** All machine-learning frameworks use *loss functions* (and, in some cases, *likelihood functions*) to characterize performance, and training is essentially the process of finding the best-fitting model according to the loss function. Loss functions can either treat all training examples equally (by weighting them all exactly the same) or focus on some specific examples (by assigning higher weights to specific examples to reflect their increased priority). When implementing ensemble methods that use weights on training examples, care must be taken to ensure that the base-learning algorithm can actually use these weights. Most weighted classification algorithms use modified loss functions to prioritize correct classification of examples with higher weights.

Let's visualize the first few iterations of boosting. Each iteration performs the same steps:

1. Train a weak learner (here, a decision stump) that learns a model to ensure that training examples with higher weights are prioritized.
2. Update the weights of the training examples such that misclassified examples are assigned higher weights; the worse the error, the higher the weight.

Initially (iteration $t - 1$), all examples are initialized with *equal weights.* The decision stump trained in iteration 1 (figure 4.3) is a simple, axis-parallel classifier with an error rate of 15%. The misclassified points are plotted larger than the correctly classified points.

The next decision stump (in iteration 2, as shown in figure 4.4) to be trained must correctly classify the examples misclassified by the previous decision stump (in iteration 1). Thus, mistakes are weighted higher, which enables the decision-tree algorithm to prioritize them during learning.

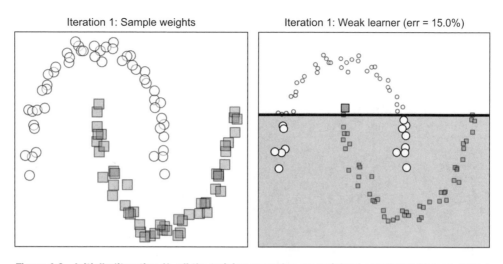

Figure 4.3   Initially (iteration 1), all the training examples are weighted equally (and hence plotted with the same size on the left). The decision stump learned on this data set is shown on the right. The correctly classified examples are plotted with smaller markers compared to the misclassified examples, which are plotted with larger markers.

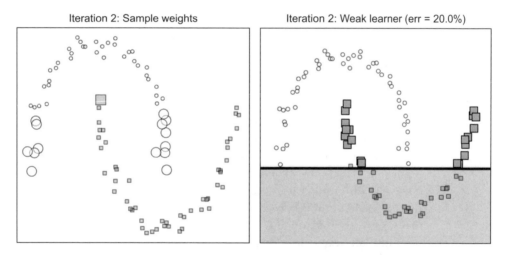

Figure 4.4   At the start of iteration 2, training examples misclassified in iteration 1 (shown with larger markers in figure 4.3, right) are assigned higher weights. This is visualized on the left, where each example's size is proportional to its weight. Since weighted examples have higher priority, the new decision stump in the sequence (right) ensures that these are now correctly classified. Observe that the new decision stump on the right correctly classifies most of the misclassified examples (shown larger) on the left.

The decision stump trained in the second iteration does indeed correctly classify the training examples with higher weights, though it makes mistakes of its own. In iteration 3, a third decision stump can be trained that aims to rectify these mistakes (see figure 4.5).

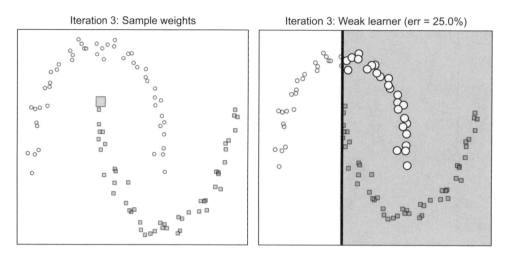

Figure 4.5   At the start of iteration 3, training examples misclassified in iteration 2 (shown with larger markers in figure 4.4, right) are assigned higher weights. Note that misclassified points also have different weights. The new decision stump in the sequence trained in this iteration (right) ensures that these are now correctly classified.

After three iterations, we can combine the three individual weak learners into a strong learner, shown in figure 4.6. Following are some useful points to note:

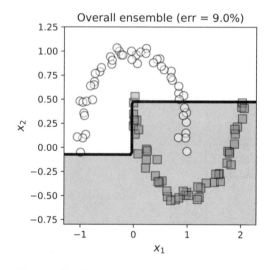

Figure 4.6   The three weak decision stumps shown in the previous figures can be boosted into a stronger ensemble.

- Observe the weak estimators trained in the three iterations. They are all different from each other and classify the problem in diversely different ways. Recall that at each iteration, base estimators are trained on the same training set but with *different weights*. Reweighting allows Ada-Boost to train a different base estimator at each iteration, one that is often different from an estimator trained at the previous iterations. Thus, *adaptive reweighting*, or updating adaptively, promotes ensemble diversity.

- The resulting ensemble of weak (and linear) decision stumps is stronger (and nonlinear). More precisely, each base estimator had training error rates of 15%, 20%, and 25%, respectively, while their ensemble has an error rate of 9%.

As noted earlier, this boosting algorithm earns its name from boosting the performance of weak learners into a more powerful and complex ensemble, a strong learner.

4.2.2 Implementing AdaBoost

First, we'll implement our own version of AdaBoost. As we do so, we'll keep the following key properties of AdaBoost in mind:

- AdaBoost uses decision stumps as base estimators, which can be trained extremely quickly, even with a large number of features. Decision stumps are *weak learners*. Contrast this to bagging, which uses deeper decision trees, that is, strong learners.
- AdaBoost keeps track of *weights on individual training examples*. This allows AdaBoost to ensure ensemble diversity by *reweighting* training examples. We saw how reweighting helped AdaBoost learn different base estimators in the visualizations in the previous subsection. Contrast this to bagging and random forests, which use resampling of training examples.
- AdaBoost keeps track of *weights on individual base estimators*. This is similar to combination methods, which weight each classifier differently.

AdaBoost is fairly straightforward to implement. The basic algorithmic outline at the *t*th iteration can be described by the following steps:

1. Train a weak learner $h_t(x)$ using the weighted training examples, (x_i, y_i, D_i).
2. Compute the training error ϵ_t of the weak learner $h_t(x)$.
3. Compute the weight of the weak learner α_t that depends on ϵ_t.
4. Update the weights of the training examples, as follows:
   - Increase the weight of misclassified examples by $D_i e^{\alpha_t}$.
   - Decrease the weight of misclassified examples by $\frac{D_i}{e^{\alpha_t}}$.

At the end of *T* iterations, we have weak learners h_t along with the corresponding weak learner weight α_t. The overall classifier after *t* iterations is just a weighted ensemble:

$$H(x) = \sum_{t=1}^{T} \alpha_t h_t(x)$$

This form is a *weighted linear combination of base estimators*, similar to the linear combinations used by parallel ensembles we've seen previously, such as bagging, combination methods, or stacking. The main difference from those methods is that the base estimators used by AdaBoost are weak learners. Now, we need to answer two key questions:

- How do we update the weights on the training examples, D_i?
- How do we compute the weight of each base estimator, α_t?

AdaBoost uses the same intuition as the combination methods we've seen previously in chapter 3. Recall that weights are computed to reflect base estimator *performance*: base estimators with better performance (say, accuracy) should have higher weights than those with worse performance.

WEAK LEARNER WEIGHTS

At each iteration t, we train a base estimator $h_t(x)$. Each base estimator (which is also a weak learner) has a corresponding weight α_t that depends on its training error. The training error ϵ_t of $h_t(x)$ is a simple and immediate measure of its performance. Ada-Boost computes the weight of estimator $h_t(x)$ as follows:

$$\alpha_t = \frac{1}{2} \log \left(\frac{1 - \epsilon_t}{\epsilon_t} \right)$$

Why this particular formulation? Let's look at the relationship between α_t and the error ϵ_t by visualizing how α_t changes with increasing error ϵ_t (figure 4.7). Recall our intuition: better-performing base estimators (those with lower errors) must be weighted higher so that their contribution to the ensemble prediction is higher.

Conversely, the weakest learners perform the worst. Sometimes, they are barely better than random guessing. Put another way, in a binary classification problem, the weakest learners are only slightly better than flipping a coin to decide the answer.

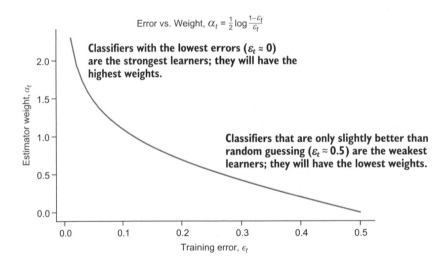

Figure 4.7 AdaBoost assigns stronger learners (which have lower training errors) higher weights, and assigns weaker learners (which have higher training errors) lower weights.

Concretely, the weakest learners have error rates only slightly better than 0.5 (or 50%). These weakest learners have the lowest weights, $\alpha_t \approx 0$. The strongest learners achieve training errors close to 0.0 (or 0%). These learners have the highest weights.

TRAINING EXAMPLE WEIGHTS

The base estimator weight (α_t) can also be used to update the weights of each training example. AdaBoost updates example weights as

$$D_i^{t+1} = D_i^t \cdot \begin{cases} e^{\alpha_t}, \text{ if misclassified}, \\ e^{-\alpha_t}, \text{ if correctly classified}. \end{cases}$$

When examples are correctly classified, the new weight is decreased by e^{α_t}: $D_i^{t+1} = \frac{D_i^t}{e^{\alpha_t}}$. Stronger base estimators will decrease the weight more because they are more confident in their correct classification. Similarly, when examples are misclassified, the new weight is increased by e^{α_t}: $D_i^{t+1} = D_i^t \cdot e^{\alpha_t}$.

In this manner, AdaBoost ensures that misclassified training examples receive higher weights, which will then be better classified in the next iteration, t+1. For example, let's say we have two training examples x_1 and x_2, both with weights $D_1^t = D_2^t = 0.75$. The current weak learner h_t has weight $\alpha_t = 1.5$. Let's say x_1 is correctly classified by h_t; hence, its weight should decrease by a factor of e^{α_t}. The new weight for the next iteration t+1 will be $D_1^{t+1} = \frac{D_1}{e^{\alpha_t}} = \frac{0.75}{e^{1.5}} = 0.17$.

Conversely, if x_1 is misclassified by h_t, its weight should increase by a factor of e^{α_t}. The new weight will be $D_2^{t+1} = D_2 \cdot e^{\alpha_t} = 0.75 \cdot e^{1.5} = 3.36$. This is illustrated in figure 4.8.

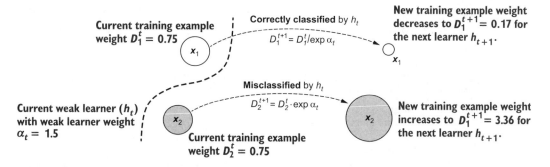

Figure 4.8 In iteration t, two training examples, x_1 and x_2, have the same weights. x_1 is correctly classified, while x_2 is misclassified by the current base estimator h_t. As the goal in the next iteration is to learn a classifier h_{t+1} that fixes the mistakes of h_t, AdaBoost increases the weight of the misclassified example x_2, while decreasing the weight of the correctly classified example x_1. This allows the base-learning algorithm to prioritize x_2 during training in iteration t+1.

TRAINING WITH ADABOOST

The AdaBoost algorithm is easy to implement. The following listing shows training for boosting.

Listing 4.1 Training an ensemble of weak learners using AdaBoost

```
from sklearn.tree import DecisionTreeClassifier
from sklearn.metrics import accuracy_score
import numpy as np

def fit_boosting(X, y, n_estimators=10):
    n_samples, n_features = X.shape
```

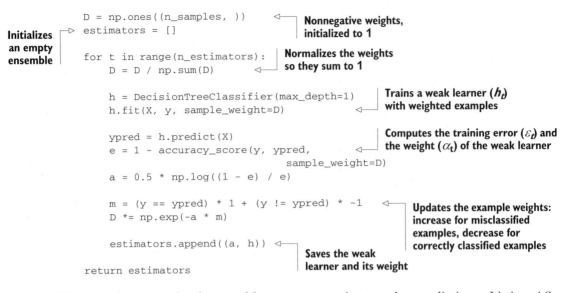

Once we have a trained ensemble, we can use it to make predictions. Listing 4.2 shows how to predict new test examples using the boosted ensemble. Observe that this is identical to making predictions with other weighted ensemble methods such as stacking.

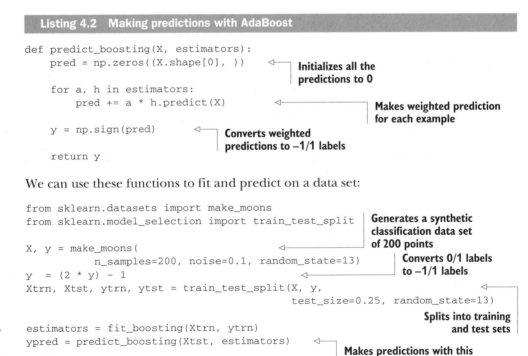

We can use these functions to fit and predict on a data set:

```
from sklearn.datasets import make_moons
from sklearn.model_selection import train_test_split

X, y = make_moons(
        n_samples=200, noise=0.1, random_state=13)
y = (2 * y) - 1
Xtrn, Xtst, ytrn, ytst = train_test_split(X, y,
                              test_size=0.25, random_state=13)

estimators = fit_boosting(Xtrn, ytrn)
ypred = predict_boosting(Xtst, estimators)
```

Generates a synthetic classification data set of 200 points

Converts 0/1 labels to −1/1 labels

Splits into training and test sets

Trains an AdaBoost model using listing 4.1

Makes predictions with this AdaBoost using listing 4.2

How did we do? We can compute the overall test set accuracy of our model:

```
from sklearn.metrics import accuracy_score
tst_err = 1 - accuracy_score(ytst, ypred)
print(tst_err)
```

This produces the following output:

```
0.020000000000000018
```

The test error of the ensemble learned by our implementation using 10 weak stumps is 2%.

Training labels for binary classification: 0/1 or –1/1?

The boosting algorithm we've implemented requires negative examples and positive examples to be labeled –1 and 1, respectively. The function `make_moons` creates labels *y* with negative examples labeled 0 and positive examples labeled 1, respectively. We manually convert them from 0 and 1 to –1 and 1, respectively, with $y_{converted} = 2 \cdot y_{original} - 1$.

Abstractly, labels for each class in a binary classification task can be anything we like, as long as the labels are helpful in clearly distinguishing between the two classes. Mathematically, this choice depends on the loss function. If using the cross-entropy loss, for example, the classes need to be 0 and 1 for the loss function to work correctly. In contrast, if using the hinge loss in SVMs, the classes need to be –1 and 1.

AdaBoost uses the exponential loss (more on this in section 4.5), and requires class labels to be –1 and 1 for the subsequent training to be mathematically sound and convergent.

Luckily for us, we don't have to worry about this when using most machine-learning packages such as scikit-learn as they automatically preprocess a variety of training labels to what the underlying training algorithm needs.

We visualize the performance of AdaBoost as the number of base estimators increases in figure 4.9. As we add more and more weak learners into the mix, the overall ensemble is increasingly boosted into a stronger, more complex, and more nonlinear classifier.

While AdaBoost is generally more resistant to overfitting, like many other classifiers, overtraining a boosting algorithm can also result in overfitting, especially in the presence of noise. We'll see how do deal with such situations in section 4.3.

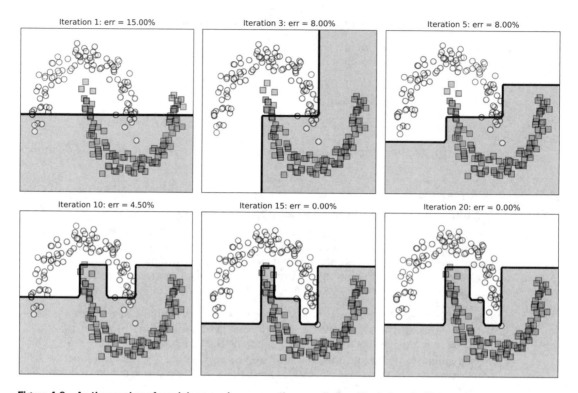

Figure 4.9 As the number of weak learners increases, the overall classifier is boosted into a strong model, which becomes increasingly nonlinear and is able to fit (and possibly overfit) the training data.

4.2.3 *AdaBoost with scikit-learn*

Now that we understand the intuition of how the AdaBoost classification algorithm works, we can look at how to use scikit-learn's `AdaBoostClassifier` package. scikit-learn's implementation provides additional functionality, including support for multiclass classification, as well as other base-learning algorithms beyond decision trees.

The `AdaBoostClassifier` package takes the following three important arguments for binary and multiclass classification tasks:

- `base_estimator`—The base-learning algorithm AdaBoost uses to train weak learners. In our implementation, we used decision stumps. However, it's possible to use other weak learners such as shallow decision trees, shallow artificial neural networks, and stochastic gradient descent–based classifiers.

- `n_estimators`—The number of weak learners that will be trained sequentially by AdaBoost.

- `learning_rate`—An additional parameter that progressively shrinks the contribution of each successive weak learner trained for the ensemble.

  - Smaller values of `learning_rate` make the weak learner weights α_t smaller. Smaller α_t means the variation in the example weights D_i decreases, and there are less-diverse weak learners. Larger values of `learning_rate` have the opposite effect and increase diversity in weak learners.

The `learning_rate` parameter has a natural interplay and tradeoff with `n_estimators`. Increasing n_estimators (essentially, the number of iterations since we train one estimator per iteration) can lead to the training example weights D_i to keep growing. The unconstrained growth of example weights can be controlled by the `learning_rate`.

The following example illustrates `AdaBoostClassifier` in action on a binary classification data set. First, we load the breast cancer data and split into training and test sets:

```
from sklearn.datasets import load_breast_cancer
from sklearn.model_selection import train_test_split
X, y = load_breast_cancer(return_X_y=True)
Xtrn, Xtst, ytrn, ytst = train_test_split(X, y,
                                test_size=0.25, random_state=13)
```

We'll use shallow decision trees of depth 2 as base estimators for training:

```
from sklearn.ensemble import AdaBoostClassifier
shallow_tree = DecisionTreeClassifier(max_depth=2)
ensemble = AdaBoostClassifier(base_estimator=shallow_tree,
                         n_estimators=20, learning_rate=0.75)
ensemble.fit(Xtrn, ytrn)
```

After training, we can use the boosted ensemble to make predictions on the test set:
```
ypred = ensemble.predict(Xtst)

err = 1 - accuracy_score(ytst, ypred)
print(err)
```

AdaBoost achieves a test error rate of 5.59% on the breast cancer data set:

```
0.05594405594405594
```

MULTICLASS CLASSIFICATION

scikit-learn's `AdaBoostClassifier` also supports multiclass classification, where data belongs to more than two classes. This is because scikit-learn contains the multiclass implementation of AdaBoost called Stagewise Additive Modeling using Multiclass Exponential loss, or SAMME. SAMME is a generalization of Freund and Schapire's adaptive boosting algorithm (implemented in section 4.2.2) from two to multiple classes. In addition to SAMME, `AdaBoostClassifier` also provides a variant called SAMME.R. The key difference between these two algorithms is that SAMME.R handles real-valued predictions from base-estimator algorithms (i.e., class probabilities), whereas vanilla SAMME handles discrete predictions (i.e., class labels).

Does this sound familiar? Recall from chapter 3 that there are two types of combination functions: those that use the predicted class labels directly, and those that can use predicted class probabilities. This is precisely the difference between SAMME and SAMME.R as well.

The following example illustrates `AdaBoostClassifier` in action on a multiclass classification data set called iris, where the classification task is to distinguish between three species of iris based on the sizes of their petals and sepals. First, we load the iris data and split that data into training and test sets:

```
from sklearn.datasets import load_iris
from sklearn.utils.multiclass import unique_labels
X, y = load_iris(return_X_y=True)
Xtrn, Xtst, ytrn, ytst = train_test_split(X, y,
                                    test_size=0.25, random_state=13)
```

We check that this data set has three different labels with `unique_labels(y)`, which produces `array([0, 1, 2])`, meaning that this is a three-class classification problem. As before, we can train and evaluate AdaBoost on this multiclass data set:

```
ensemble = AdaBoostClassifier(base_estimator=shallow_tree,
                              n_estimators=20,
                              learning_rate=0.75, algorithm='SAMME.R')
ensemble.fit(Xtrn, ytrn)
ypred = ensemble.predict(Xtst)
err = 1 - accuracy_score(ytst, ypred)
print(err)
```

AdaBoost achieves a test error of 7.89% on the three-class iris data set:

```
0.07894736842105265
```

4.3   *AdaBoost in practice*

In this chapter, we look at some practical challenges we can expect to encounter when using AdaBoost and strategies to ensure that we train robust models. AdaBoost's adaptive procedure makes it susceptible to *outliers*, or data points that are extremely noisy. In this section, we'll see examples of how this problem can affect the robustness of AdaBoost and what we can do to mitigate it.

At the core of AdaBoost is its ability to adapt to mistakes made by previous weak learners. This adaptive property, however, can also be a disadvantage when outliers are present.

Outliers

Outliers are extremely noisy data points that are often the result of measurement or input errors and are prevalent in real data to varying degrees. Standard preprocessing techniques such as normalization often simply rescale the data and don't remove outliers, which allows them to continue to affect algorithm performance. This can be addressed by preprocessing the data to specifically detect and remove outliers.

For some tasks (e.g., detecting network cyberattacks), the very thing we need to detect and classify (a cyberattack) will be an outlier, also called an anomaly, and extremely rare. In such situations, the goal of our learning task will itself be anomaly detection.

AdaBoost is especially susceptible to outliers. Outliers are often misclassified by weak learners. Recall that AdaBoost increases the weight of misclassified examples, so the weight assigned to outliers continues to increase. When the next weak learner is trained, it does one of the following:

- Continues to misclassify the outlier, in which case AdaBoost will increase its weight further, which, in turn, causes succeeding weak learners to misclassify, fail, and keep growing its weight.
- Correctly classifies the outlier, in which case AdaBoost has just overfit the data, as illustrated in figure 4.10.

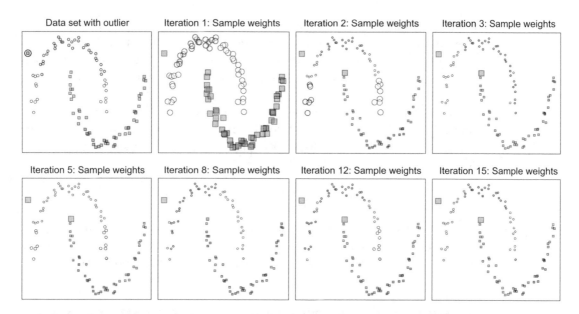

Figure 4.10   Consider a data set with an outlier (circled, top left). In iteration 1, it has the same weight as all the examples. As AdaBoost continues to sequentially train new weak learners, the weights of other data points eventually decrease as they are correctly classified. The weight of the outlier continues to increase, ultimately resulting in overfitting.

Outliers force AdaBoost to spend a disproportionate amount of effort on training examples that are noisy. Put another way, outliers tend to confound AdaBoost and make it less robust.

4.3.1   *Learning rate*

Now, let's look at ways to train robust models with AdaBoost. The first aspect we can control is *learning rate*, which adjusts the contribution of each estimator to the ensemble. For example, a learning rate of 0.75 tells AdaBoost to decrease the overall contribution of each base estimator by a factor of 0.75. When there are outliers, a high learning rate will cause their influence to grow proportionally quickly, which can absolutely kill the performance of your model. Therefore, one way to mitigate the effect of outliners is to lower the learning rate.

As lowering the learning rate shrinks the contribution of each base estimator, controlling the learning rate is also known as *shrinkage* and is a form of model regularization to minimize overfitting. Concretely, at iteration t, the ensemble F_t is updated to F_{t+1} as

$$F_{t+1}(x) = F_t(x) + \eta \cdot \alpha_t \cdot h_t(x)$$

Here, α_t is the weight of weak learner h_t computed by AdaBoost, and η is the learning rate. The learning rate is a user-defined learning parameter that lies in the range $0 < \eta \le 1$.

A slower learning rate means that it will often take more iterations (and consequently, more base estimators) to build an effective ensemble. More iterations also mean more computational effort and longer training times. Often, however, slower learning rates may produce a robust model that generalizes better and may well be worth the effort.

An effective way to select the best learning rate is with a validation set or cross validation (CV). Listing 4.3 uses 10-fold CV to identify the best learning rate in the range `[0.1, 0.2, …, 1.0]`. We can observe the effectiveness of shrinkage on the breast cancer data:

```
from sklearn.datasets import load_breast_cancer
X, y = load_breast_cancer(return_X_y=True)
```

We use stratified k-fold CV, as we did with stacking. Recall that *stratified* means the folds are created in such a way that the class distribution is preserved across the folds. This also helps with imbalanced data sets, as stratification ensures that data from all classes is represented.

Listing 4.3 Cross validation to select the best learning rate

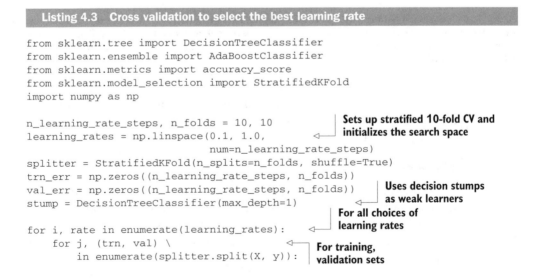

```
from sklearn.tree import DecisionTreeClassifier
from sklearn.ensemble import AdaBoostClassifier
from sklearn.metrics import accuracy_score
from sklearn.model_selection import StratifiedKFold
import numpy as np

n_learning_rate_steps, n_folds = 10, 10          Sets up stratified 10-fold CV and
learning_rates = np.linspace(0.1, 1.0,           initializes the search space
                    num=n_learning_rate_steps)
splitter = StratifiedKFold(n_splits=n_folds, shuffle=True)
trn_err = np.zeros((n_learning_rate_steps, n_folds))
val_err = np.zeros((n_learning_rate_steps, n_folds))     Uses decision stumps
stump = DecisionTreeClassifier(max_depth=1)              as weak learners

                                                 For all choices of
for i, rate in enumerate(learning_rates):        learning rates
    for j, (trn, val) \
        in enumerate(splitter.split(X, y)):      For training,
                                                 validation sets
```

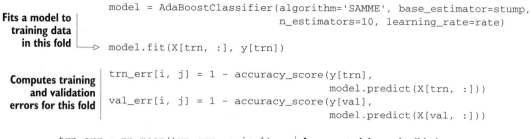

Fits a model to training data in this fold

```
model = AdaBoostClassifier(algorithm='SAMME', base_estimator=stump,
                           n_estimators=10, learning_rate=rate)
model.fit(X[trn, :], y[trn])
```

Computes training and validation errors for this fold

```
trn_err[i, j] = 1 - accuracy_score(y[trn],
                                   model.predict(X[trn, :]))
val_err[i, j] = 1 - accuracy_score(y[val],
                                   model.predict(X[val, :]))
```

```
trn_err = np.mean(trn_err, axis=1)
val_err = np.mean(val_err, axis=1)
```

Averages training and validation errors across the folds

We plot the results of this parameter search in figure 4.11, which shows how the training and validation errors change as the learning rate increases. The number of base learners is fixed to 10. While the average training error continues to decrease with increasing learning rate, the best average validation error is achieved for `learning_rate=0.8`.

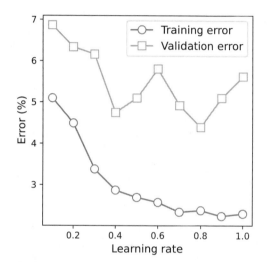

Figure 4.11 Average training and validation errors for different learning rates. The validation error for `learning_rate=0.6` is lowest, and, in fact, lower than the default `learning_rate=1.0`.

4.3.2 *Early stopping and pruning*

Besides the `learning_rate`, the other important consideration for practical boosting is the number of base learners, `n_estimators`. It might be tempting to try to build an ensemble with a very large number of weak learners, but this doesn't always translate to the best generalization performance. In fact, we often can achieve roughly the same performance with fewer base estimators than we think we might need. Identifying the least number of base estimators to build an effective ensemble is known as *early stopping*. Maintaining fewer base estimators can help control overfitting. Additionally, early stopping can also decrease training time as we end up having to train fewer base estimators. Listing 4.4 uses a CV procedure identical to the one in listing 4.3 to identify the best number of estimators. The learning rate here is fixed to 1.0.

Listing 4.4   Cross validation to select the best number of weak learners

```
n_estimator_steps, n_folds = 5, 10

number_of_stumps = np.arange(5, 50, n_estimator_steps)
splitter = StratifiedKFold(n_splits=n_folds, shuffle=True)
```

Sets up stratified 10-fold CV and initializes the search space

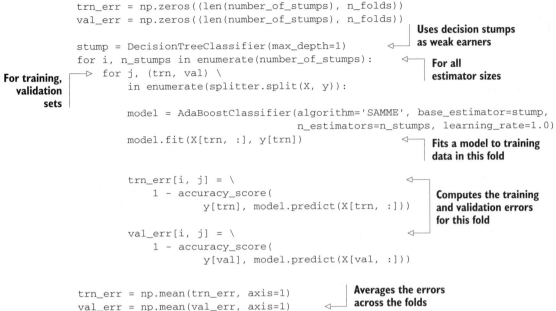

```
trn_err = np.zeros((len(number_of_stumps), n_folds))
val_err = np.zeros((len(number_of_stumps), n_folds))

stump = DecisionTreeClassifier(max_depth=1)
for i, n_stumps in enumerate(number_of_stumps):
    for j, (trn, val) \
        in enumerate(splitter.split(X, y)):

        model = AdaBoostClassifier(algorithm='SAMME', base_estimator=stump,
                                   n_estimators=n_stumps, learning_rate=1.0)
        model.fit(X[trn, :], y[trn])

        trn_err[i, j] = \
            1 - accuracy_score(
                    y[trn], model.predict(X[trn, :]))

        val_err[i, j] = \
            1 - accuracy_score(
                    y[val], model.predict(X[val, :]))

trn_err = np.mean(trn_err, axis=1)
val_err = np.mean(val_err, axis=1)
```

Uses decision stumps as weak earners

For all estimator sizes

For training, validation sets

Fits a model to training data in this fold

Computes the training and validation errors for this fold

Averages the errors across the folds

The results of this search for the best number of estimators are shown in figure 4.12. The average validation error suggests that it's sufficient to use as few as 30 decision trees to achieve good predictive performance on this data set. In practice, we can stop training early once the performance on the validation set reaches an acceptable level.

Early stopping is also known as *pre-pruning*, as we terminate training before fitting a large number of base estimators and often leads to faster training times. If we aren't concerned about training time but want to be more judicious in selecting the number of base estimators, we can also consider *post-pruning*. Post-pruning means that we train a very large ensemble and then drop the worst base estimators.

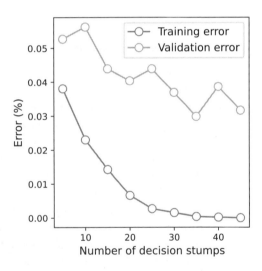

Figure 4.12   Average training and validation errors for different numbers of base estimators (decision stumps, in this case). The validation error for `n_estimators=20` is lowest.

For AdaBoost, post-pruning drops all weak learners whose weights (α_t) are below a certain threshold. We can access the individual weak learners as well as their weights after training an `AdaBoostClassifier` through the fields `model.estimators_` and `model.estimator_weights_`. To prune the contribution of the least-significant weak learners (those whose weight is below a certain `threshold`), we can simply set their weights to zero:

```
model.estimator_weights_[model.estimator_weights_ <= threshold] = 0.0
```

As before, CV can be used to select a good threshold. Always remember that there is typically a tradeoff between AdaBoost's `learning_rate` and `n_estimators` parameters. Lower learning rates typically require more iterations (hence, more weak learners), while higher learning rates require fewer iterations (and fewer weak learners).

To be most effective, the best values of these parameters should be identified using grid search combined with CV. An example of this is shown in the case study, which we look at in the next section.

> ### Outlier detection and removal
>
> While the procedures described here are generally effective on noisy data sets, training examples with high amounts of noise (i.e., outliers) can still cause significant problems. In such cases, it's often advisable to preprocess the data set to remove these outliers entirely.

4.4   Case study: Handwritten digit classification

One of the earliest machine-learning applications is on handwritten digit classification. In fact, this task has been studied so extensively since the early 1990s that we might consider it the "Hello World!" of object recognition.

This task originated with the US Postal Service's attempts to automate digit recognition to accelerate mail processing by rapidly identifying ZIP codes. Since then, several different handwritten data sets have been created and are widely used to benchmark and evaluate various machine-learning algorithms.

In this case study, we'll use scikit-learn's digits data set to illustrate the effectiveness of AdaBoost. The data set consists of 1,797 scanned images of handwritten digits from 0 to 9. Each digit is associated with a unique label, which makes this a 10-class classification problem. There are roughly 180 digits per class. We can load the data set directly from scikit-learn:

```
from sklearn.datasets import load_digits
X, y = load_digits(return_X_y=True)
```

The digits themselves are represented as 16 x 16 normalized grayscale bitmaps (see figure 4.13), which, when flattened, results in a 64-dimensional (64D) vector for each handwritten digit. The training set comprises 1,797 examples × 64 features.

Figure 4.13   A snapshot of the digits data set used in this case study

4.4.1 Dimensionality reduction with t-SNE

While AdaBoost can effectively handle the dimensionality of the digits data set (64 features), we'll (rather aggressively) look to reduce the dimensionality to 2. The main reason for this is to be able to visualize the data as well as the models learned by Ada-Boost.

We'll use a nonlinear dimensionality reduction technique known as t-distributed stochastic neighbor embedding (t-SNE). t-SNE is a highly effective preprocessing technique for the digits data set and extracts an embedding in a 2D space.

T-SNE

Stochastic neighbor embedding, as its name suggests, uses neighborhood information to construct a lower dimensional embedding. Specifically, it exploits the similarity between two examples: x_i and x_j. In our case, x_i and x_j are two example digits from the data set and are 64D. The similarity between two digits can be measured as

$$\text{sim}(x_i, x_j) = \exp\left(-\frac{\|x_i - x_j\|^2}{2\sigma_i^2}\right)$$

where $\|x_i - x_j\|^2$ is the squared distance between x_i and x_j, and σ_i^2 is a similarity parameter. You may have seen this form of a similarity function in other areas of machine learning, especially in the context of support vector machines, where it's known as the radial basis function (RBF) kernel or the Gaussian kernel.

The similarity between x_i and x_j can be converted to a probability $p_{j|i}$ that x_j is a neighbor of x_i. The probability is just a normalized similarity measure, where we normalize by the sum of similarities of all points in the data set x_k with x_i:

$$p_{j|i} = \frac{\text{sim}(x_i, x_j)}{\text{sum of sim}(x_i, x_k) \text{ for all data points}} = \frac{\exp\left(-\frac{\|x_i - x_j\|^2}{2\sigma_i^2}\right)}{\sum_{k \neq i} \exp\left(-\frac{\|x_i - x_k\|^2}{2\sigma_i^2}\right)}$$

Let's say that the 2D embedding of these two digits is given by z_i and z_j. Then, it's natural to expect that two similar digits x_i and x_j will continue to be neighbors even embedding into z_i and z_j, respectively. The probability of z_j being a neighbor of z_i can be measured similarly:

$$q_{j|i} = \frac{\text{sim}(z_i, z_j)}{\text{sum of sim}(z_i, z_k) \text{ for all data points}} = \frac{\exp\|z_i - z_j\|^2}{\sum_{k \neq i} \exp(-\|z_i - z_k\|^2)}$$

Here, we assume that the variance in the exponential distribution in the 2D (z-space) is $1/2$. Then, we can identify the embeddings of all the points by ensuring that $q_{j|i}$, the probabilities in the 2D embedding space (z-space) are well-aligned with $p_{j|i}$ in the 64D original digit space (x-space). Mathematically, this is achieved by minimizing the

KL-divergence (a statistical measure of the difference or distance) between the distributions $q_{j|i}$ and $p_{j|i}$. With scikit-learn, the embeddings can be computed very easily:

```
from sklearn.manifold import TSNE
Xemb = TSNE(n_components=2, init='pca').fit_transform(X)
```

Figure 4.14 shows what this data set looks like when embedded into a 2D space.

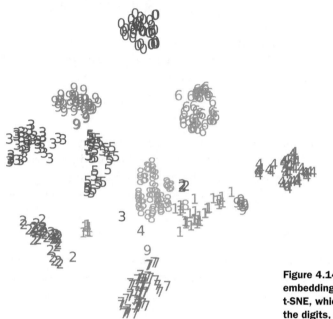

Figure 4.14   Visualization of the 2D embedding of the digits data set produced by t-SNE, which is able to embed and separate the digits, effectively clustering them

TRAIN-TEST SPLIT

As always, it's important to hold aside a part of the training data for evaluation and to quantify the predictive performance of our models on future data. We split the lower-dimensional data `Xemb` and the labels into training and test sets:

```
from sklearn.model_selection import train_test_split
Xtrn, Xtst, ytrn, ytst = train_test_split(Xemb, y,
                                           test_size=0.2,
                                           stratify=y,
                                           random_state=13)
```

Observe the use of `stratify=y` to ensure that the ratios of the different digits in train and test sets are identical.

4.4.2   Boosting

We'll now train an AdaBoost model for this digit classification task. Recall from our earlier discussion that AdaBoost requires us to first choose the type of base estimator. We continue to use decision stumps, as follows:

```
from sklearn.tree import DecisionTreeClassifier
from sklearn.ensemble import AdaBoostClassifier

stump = DecisionTreeClassifier(max_depth=2)
ensemble = AdaBoostClassifier(algorithm='SAMME', base_estimator=stump)
```

In the previous section, we saw how to use CV for selecting the best value of `learning_rate` and `n_estimators` individually. In practice, we have to identify the *best combination* of `learning_rate` and `n_estimators`. For this, we'll employ a combination of k-fold CV and grid search.

The basic idea is to consider different combinations of `learning_rate` and `n_estimators` and evaluate what their performance would be like via CV. First, we select various parameter values we want to explore:

```
parameters_to_search = {'n_estimators': [200, 300, 400, 500],
                        'learning_rate': [0.6, 0.8, 1.0]}
```

Next, we make a scoring function to evaluate the performance of each parameter combination. For this task, we use the *balanced accuracy score*, which is essentially just the accuracy score weighted by each class. This scoring criterion is effective for multiclass classification problems such as this one, and also for imbalanced data sets:

```
from sklearn.metrics import balanced_accuracy_score, make_scorer
scorer = make_scorer(balanced_accuracy_score, greater_is_better=True)
```

Now, we set up and run the grid search to identify the best parameter combination with the `GridSearchCV` class. Several arguments to `GridSearchCV` are of interest to us. Parameter `cv=5` specifies 5-fold CV, and `n_jobs=-1` specifies that the job should use all available cores for parallel processing (see chapter 2):

```
from sklearn.model_selection import GridSearchCV
search = GridSearchCV(ensemble, param_grid=parameters_to_search,
                      scoring=scorer, cv=5, n_jobs=-1, refit=True)
search.fit(Xtrn, ytrn)
```

The final parameter in `GridSearchCV` is set to `refit=True`. This tells `GridSearchCV` to train a final model using all the available training data, using the best parameter combination it has identified.

> **TIP** For many data sets, it may not be computationally efficient to exhaustively explore and validate all possible hyperparameter choices with `GridSearchCV`. For such cases, it may be more computationally efficient to use `RandomizedSearchCV`, which samples a much smaller subset of hyperparameter combinations to validate.

After training, we can look up the scores for every parameter combination and even pull out the best results:

```
best_combo = search.cv_results_['params'][search.best_index_]
best_score = search.best_score_
```

```
print('The best parameter settings are {0}, with score = \
    {1}.'.format(best_combo, best_score))
```

These results print the following:

```
The best parameter settings are {'learning_rate': 0.6, 'n_estimators': 200},
    with score = 0. 0.9826321839080459.
```

The best model is also available (because we set `refit=True`). Note that this model is trained using the `best_combo` parameters, using the entire training data (`Xtrn`, `ytrn`) by `GridSearchCV`. This model is available in `search.best_estimator_` and can be used for making predictions on the test data:

```
ypred = search.best_estimator_.predict(Xtst)
```

How well did this model do? We can first look at the classification report:

```
from sklearn.metrics import classification_report
print('Classification report:\n{0}\n'.format(
    classification_report(ytst, ypred)))
```

The classification report contains class-wise performance metrics, including precision and recall for each digit. Precision is the fraction of true positives among anything that was predicted as positive, including false positives. It's computed as *TP / (TP + FP)*, where *TP* is the number of true positives and *FP* is the number of false positives.

Recall is the fraction of true positives among everything that was supposed to be predicted as positive, including false negatives. It's computed as *TP / (TP + FN)*, where *FN* is the number of false negatives. The classification report is as follows:

```
Classification report:
            precision    recall  f1-score   support

         0       1.00      0.97      0.99        36
         1       1.00      1.00      1.00        37
         2       1.00      0.97      0.99        35
         3       1.00      1.00      1.00        37
         4       0.97      1.00      0.99        36
         5       0.72      1.00      0.84        36
         6       1.00      1.00      1.00        36
         7       1.00      1.00      1.00        36
         8       0.95      1.00      0.97        35
         9       1.00      0.58      0.74        36

  accuracy                           0.95       360
 macro avg       0.96      0.95      0.95       360
weighted avg     0.96      0.95      0.95       360
```

AdaBoost does quite well on most digits. It seems that it struggles a bit with 5s and 9s, which both have lower F1 scores. We can also look at the *confusion matrix*, which will give us a good idea which letters are being confounded with others:

```
from sklearn.metrics import confusion_matrix
print("Confusion matrix: \n {0}".format(confusion_matrix(ytst, ypred)))
```

The confusion matrix allows us to visualize how the model performed on each class:

```
[[35  0  0  0  1  0  0  0  0  0]
 [ 0 37  0  0  0  0  0  0  0  0]
 [ 0  0 34  0  0  0  0  0  1  0]
 [ 0  0  0 37  0  0  0  0  0  0]
 [ 0  0  0  0 36  0  0  0  0  0]
 [ 0  0  0  0  0 36  0  0  0  0]
 [ 0  0  0  0  0  0 36  0  0  0]
 [ 0  0  0  0  0  0  0 36  0  0]
 [ 0  0  0  0  0  0  0  0 35  0]
 [ 0  0  0  0  0 14  0  0  1 21]]
```

Each row of the confusion matrix corresponds to the true labels (digits to 0 to 9), and each column corresponds to the predicted labels. The $(9, 5)$ entry in the confusion matrix (tenth row, sixth column, as we begin indexing from 0) indicates that several 9s are misclassified as 5s by AdaBoost. Finally, we can plot the decision boundaries of the trained AdaBoost model, shown in figure 4.15.

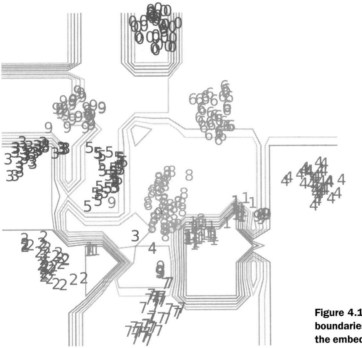

Figure 4.15   The decision boundaries learned by AdaBoost on the embeddings of the digits data set

This case study illustrates how AdaBoost can boost the performance of weak learners into a powerful strong learner that can achieve good performance on a complex task. Before we end the chapter, let's look at another adaptive boosting algorithm, Logit-Boost.

4.5   LogitBoost: Boosting with the logistic loss

We now move on to a second boosting algorithm called logistic boosting (LogitBoost). The development of LogitBoost was motivated by the desire to bring loss functions from established classification models (e.g., logistic regression) into the AdaBoost framework. In this manner, the general boosting framework can be applied to specific classification settings to train boosted ensembles with properties similar to those classifiers.

4.5.1   Logistic vs. exponential loss functions

Recall from section 4.2.2 that AdaBoost updates weights α_t of weak learners with the following:

$$\alpha_t = \frac{1}{2} \log \left(\frac{1 - \epsilon_t}{\epsilon_t} \right)$$

Where does this weighting scheme come from? This expression is a consequence of the fact that AdaBoost optimizes the exponential loss. In particular, AdaBoost optimizes the exponential loss of an example (x,y) with respect to a weak learner $h_t(x)$ as given by

$$L(x; \alpha_t) = \exp(-\alpha_t \cdot y \cdot h_t(x))$$

where y is the true label, and $h_t(x)$ is the prediction made by the weak learner h_t.

Can we use other loss functions to derive variants of AdaBoost? We absolutely can! LogitBoost is essentially an AdaBoost-like ensemble method whose weighting scheme uses a different loss function. It's just that when we change the underlying loss function, we also need to make some other small tweaks to get the overall approach to work.

LogitBoost differs from AdaBoost in three important ways. First, LogitBoost optimizes the logistic loss:

$$L(x; \alpha_t) = \log(1 + \exp(-\alpha_t \cdot y \cdot h_t(x)))$$

You may have seen the logistic loss in other machine-learning formulations, most notably logistic regression. The logistic loss penalizes mistakes differently than the exponential loss (see figure 4.16).

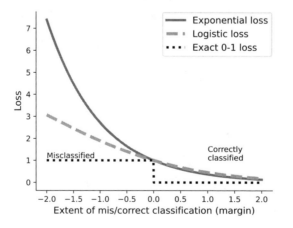

Figure 4.16   Comparing the exponential loss and the logistic loss functions

The exact 0–1 loss (also known as the misclassification loss) is an idealized loss function that returns 0 for correctly classified examples and 1 for misclassified examples. However, this loss is difficult to optimize as it's not continuous. To build feasible machine-learning algorithms, different methods use different surrogates, such as the exponential and logistic losses.

The exponential loss function and the logistic loss function both penalize correctly classified examples similarly. Training examples that are correctly classified with greater confidence have corresponding losses close to zero. The exponential loss penalizes misclassified examples far more harshly than the logistic loss, which makes it more susceptible to outliers and noise. The logistic loss is more measured.

4.5.2   *Regression as a weak learning algorithm for classification*

The second key difference is that AdaBoost works with predictions, while LogitBoost works with prediction probabilities. More precisely, AdaBoost works with the predictions of the overall ensemble $F(x)$, while LogitBoost works with prediction probabilities, $P(x)$.

The probability of predicting a training example x as a positive example is given by

$$P(y = 1|x) = \frac{1}{1 + e^{-F(x)}}$$

while the probability of predicting x as a negative example is given by $P(y = 0 \mid x) = 1 - P(y = 1 \mid x)$. This fact directly influences our choice of base estimator.

The third key difference is that because AdaBoost works directly with discrete predictions (–1 or 1, for negative and positive examples), it uses any classification algorithm as the base-learning algorithm. LogitBoost, instead, works with continuous prediction probabilities. Consequently, it uses *any regression algorithm* as the base-learning algorithm.

4.5.3   *Implementing LogitBoost*

Putting all of these together, the LogitBoost algorithm performs the following steps within each iteration. The probability $P(y_i = 1 \mid x_i)$ is abbreviated P_i in the following:

1. Compute the working response, or how much the prediction probability differs from the true label:

$$z_i = \frac{y_i - P_i}{P_i(1 - P_i)}$$

2. Update the example weights, $D_i = P_i(1 - P_i)$
3. Train a weak regression stump $h_t(x)$ on the weighted examples (x_i, z_i, D_i)
4. Update the ensemble, $F_{t+1}(x) = F_t(x) + h_t(x)$
5. Update the example probabilities

$$P_i = \frac{1}{1 + e^{-F_{t+1}(x)}}$$

As we can see from step 4, LogitBoost, like AdaBoost, is an *additive ensemble*. This means that LogitBoost ensembles base estimators and combines their predictions additively. Furthermore, any weak regressor can be used in step 3, where we use regression stumps, which are shallow regression trees. The LogitBoost algorithm is also easy to implement, as shown in the following listing.

Listing 4.5   LogitBoost for classification

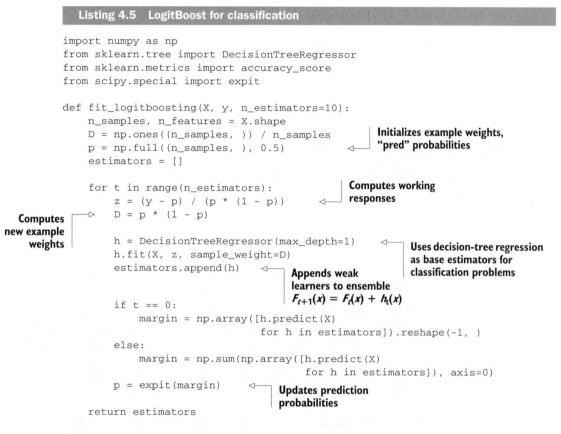

```python
import numpy as np
from sklearn.tree import DecisionTreeRegressor
from sklearn.metrics import accuracy_score
from scipy.special import expit

def fit_logitboosting(X, y, n_estimators=10):
    n_samples, n_features = X.shape
    D = np.ones((n_samples, )) / n_samples
    p = np.full((n_samples, ), 0.5)
    estimators = []

    for t in range(n_estimators):
        z = (y - p) / (p * (1 - p))
        D = p * (1 - p)

        h = DecisionTreeRegressor(max_depth=1)
        h.fit(X, z, sample_weight=D)
        estimators.append(h)

        if t == 0:
            margin = np.array([h.predict(X)
                            for h in estimators]).reshape(-1, )
        else:
            margin = np.sum(np.array([h.predict(X)
                            for h in estimators]), axis=0)
        p = expit(margin)
    return estimators
```

Initializes example weights, "pred" probabilities

Computes working responses

Computes new example weights

Uses decision-tree regression as base estimators for classification problems

Appends weak learners to ensemble $F_{t+1}(x) = F_t(x) + h_t(x)$

Updates prediction probabilities

The `predict_boosting` function described in listing 4.2 can be used to make predictions with the LogitBoost ensembles as well and is implemented in listing 4.6.

However, LogitBoost requires training labels to be in 0/1 form while AdaBoost requires them to be in –1/1 form. Thus, we modify that function slightly to return 0/1 labels.

Listing 4.6   LogitBoost for prediction

```python
def predict_logit_boosting(X, estimators):
    pred = np.zeros((X.shape[0], ))

    for h in estimators:
        pred += h.predict(X)
```

```
y = (np.sign(pred) + 1) / 2

return y
```

◁─┐ **Converts –1/1**
   predictions to 0/1

As with AdaBoost, we can visualize how the ensemble trained by LogitBoost evolves over several iterations in figure 4.17. Contrast this figure with the earlier figure 4.9, which shows the evolution of the ensemble trained by AdaBoost over several iterations.

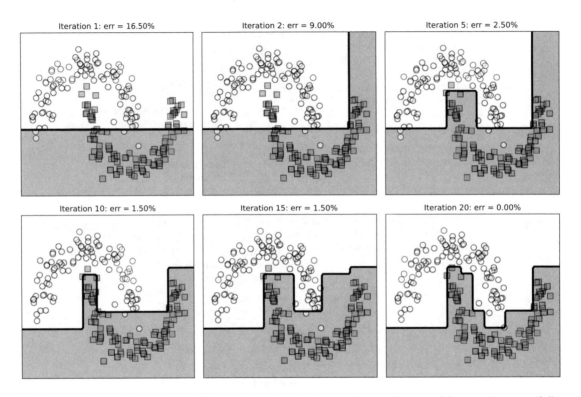

Figure 4.17   LogitBoost uses decision-tree regression to train regression stumps as weak learners to sequentially optimize the logistic loss.

We've now seen two boosting algorithms that handle two different loss functions. Is there a way to generalize boosting to different loss functions and for different tasks such as regression?

The answer to this question is an emphatic yes, as long as the loss function is differentiable (and you can compute its gradient). This is the intuition behind *gradient boosting*, which we'll look into in the next two chapters.

Summary

- Adaptive boosting (AdaBoost) is a sequential ensemble algorithm that uses weak learners as base estimators.

- In classification, a weak learner is a simple model that performs only slightly better than random guessing, that is, 50% accuracy. Decision stumps and shallow decision trees are examples of weak learners.

- AdaBoost maintains and updates weights over training examples. It uses reweighting both to prioritize misclassified examples and to promote ensemble diversity.

- AdaBoost is also an additive ensemble in that it makes final predictions through weighted additive (linear) combinations of the predictions of its base estimators.

- AdaBoost is generally robust to overfitting as it ensembles several weak learners. However, AdaBoost is sensitive to outliers owing to its adaptive reweighting strategy, which repeatedly increases the weight of outliers over iterations.

- The performance of AdaBoost can be improved by finding a good tradeoff between the learning rate and number of base estimators.

- Cross validation with grid search is commonly deployed to identify the best parameter tradeoff between learning rate and number of estimators.

- Under the hood, AdaBoost optimizes the exponential loss function.

- LogitBoost is another boosting algorithm that optimizes the logistic loss function. It differs from AdaBoost in two other ways: (1) by working with prediction probabilities, and (2) by using any classification algorithm as the base-learning algorithm.

5

Sequential ensembles: Gradient boosting

This chapter covers

- Using gradient descent to optimize loss functions for training models
- Implementing gradient boosting
- Training histogram gradient-boosting models efficiently
- Gradient boosting with the LightGBM framework
- Avoiding overfitting with LightGBM
- Using custom loss function with LightGBM

The previous chapter introduced boosting, where we train weak learners sequentially and "boost" them into a strong ensemble model. An important sequential ensemble method introduced in chapter 4 is adaptive boosting (AdaBoost).

AdaBoost is a foundational boosting model that trains a new weak learner to fix the misclassifications of the previous weak learner. It does this by maintaining and adaptively updating weights on training examples. These weights reflect the extent of misclassification and indicate priority training examples to the base-learning algorithm.

In this chapter, we look at an alternative to weights on training examples to convey misclassification information to a base-learning algorithm for boosting: loss function gradients. Recall that we use loss functions to measure how well a model fits each training example in the data set. The gradient of the loss function for a single example is called the *residual* and, as we'll see shortly, captures the deviation between true and predicted labels. This error, or residual, of course, measures the amount of misclassification.

In contrast to AdaBoost, which uses weights as a surrogate for residuals, gradient boosting uses these residuals directly! Thus, gradient boosting is another sequential ensemble method that aims to train weak learners over residuals (i.e., gradients).

The framework of gradient boosting can be applied to any loss function, which means that any classification, regression, or ranking problem can be "boosted" using weak learners. This flexibility has been a key reason for the emergence and ubiquity of gradient boosting as a state-of-the-art ensemble approach. Several powerful packages and implementations of gradient boosting are available (LightGBM, CatBoost, XGBoost) and provide the ability to train models on big data efficiently via parallel computing and GPUs.

This chapter is organized as follows. To gain a deeper understanding of gradient boosting, we need a deeper understanding of gradient descent. So, we kick off the chapter with an example of gradient descent that can be used to train a machine-learning model (section 5.1).

Section 5.2 aims to provide intuition for learning with residuals, which is at the heart of gradient boosting. Then, we implement our own version of gradient boosting and walk through it to understand how it combines gradient descent and boosting at every step to train a sequential ensemble. This section also introduces histogram-based gradient boosting, which essentially bins the training data to significantly accelerate tree learning and allows for scaling to larger data sets.

Section 5.3 introduces LightGBM, a free and open source gradient-boosting package and important tool for building and deploying real-world machine learning applications. In section 5.4, we see how to avoid overfitting with strategies such as early stopping and adapting the learning rate to train effective models with LightGBM and how to extend LightGBM to custom loss functions.

All of this leads us to a demonstration of how to use gradient boosting in a real-world task: document retrieval, which will be the focus of our chapter-concluding case study (section 5.5). Document retrieval, which is a form of information retrieval, is a key task in many applications and one we've all used at some time or another (e.g., web search engines).

To understand gradient boosting, we first have to understand gradient descent, a simple yet effective approach that is widely used for training many machine-learning algorithms. This will help us contextualize the role gradient descent plays inside gradient boosting, both conceptually and algorithmically.

5.1   *Gradient descent for minimization*

We now delve into gradient descent, an optimization approach at the heart of many training algorithms. Understanding gradient descent will allow us to understand how the gradient-boosting framework ingeniously combines this optimization procedure with ensemble learning. Optimization, or the search for the "best," is at the heart of many applications. Indeed, the search for the best model is at the heart of all machine learning.

> **NOTE** Learning problems are often cast as optimization problems. For example, training is essentially finding the best-fitting model given the data. If the notion of "best" is characterized by a loss function, then training is cast as a minimization problem because the best model corresponds to the lowest loss. Alternately, if the notion of "best" is characterized by a likelihood function, then training is cast as a maximization problem because the best model corresponds to the highest likelihood (or probability). Unless specified, we'll characterize model quality or fit using loss functions, which will require us to perform minimization.

Loss functions explicitly measure the fit of a model on a data set. Most often, we measure loss with respect to the true labels, by quantifying the error between the predicted and true labels. Thus, the best model will have the lowest error, or loss.

You may be familiar with loss functions such as cross entropy (for classification) or mean squared error (for regression). We'll revisit cross entropy in section 5.4.3 and mean squared error in chapter 7. Given a loss function, training is the search for the optimal model that minimizes the loss, as illustrated in figure 5.1.

One example of such a search you may be familiar with is a grid search for parameter selection during training of, say, decision trees. With grid search, we choose among many modeling choices: number of leaves, maximum tree depth, and so on systematically and exhaustively over a grid of parameters.

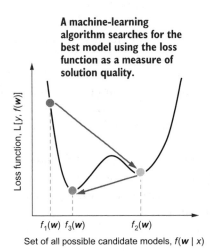

A machine-learning algorithm searches for the best model using the loss function as a measure of solution quality.

Loss function, $L[y, f(w)]$

$f_1(w)$ $f_3(w)$ $f_2(w)$

Set of all possible candidate models, $f(w \mid x)$

Figure 5.1   An optimization procedure for finding the best model. Machine-learning algorithms search for the best model among all possible candidate models. The notion of "best" is quantified by the loss function, which evaluates the quality of a selected candidate using the labels and the data. Thus, machine-learning algorithms are essentially optimization procedures. Here, the optimization procedure sequentially identifies increasingly better models f_1, f_2, and the final model, f_3.

Another, more effective optimization technique is gradient descent, which uses first derivative information, or gradients, to guide our search. In this section, we look at two examples of gradient descent. The first is a simple illustrative example to understand and visualize the basics of how gradient descent works. The second example demonstrates how gradient descent can be used on an actual loss function with data to train a machine-learning model.

5.1.1 Gradient descent with an illustrative example

We'll use the Branin function, a commonly used example function, to illustrate how gradient descent works, before moving on to a more concrete case grounded in machine learning (section 5.1.2). The Branin function is a function of two variables (w_1 and w_2), defined as

$$f(w_1, w_2) = a \left(w_2 - b w_1^2 + c w_1 - r \right)^2 + s(1 - t)\cos(w_1) + s$$

where $a = 1$, $b = \frac{5.1}{4\pi^2}$, $c = \frac{5}{\pi}$, $r = 6$, $s = 10$, and $t = \frac{1}{8\pi}$ are fixed constants, which we won't worry about. We can visualize this function by plotting a 3D plot of w_1 versus w_2 versus $f(w_1, w_2)$. Figure 5.2 illustrates the 3D surface plot as well as the contour plot (i.e., the surface plot viewed from above).

Visualization of the Branin function shows us that it takes the smallest values at four different locations, which are called local minimizers, or minima. So how can we identify these local minima? There's always the brute-force approach: we can make a

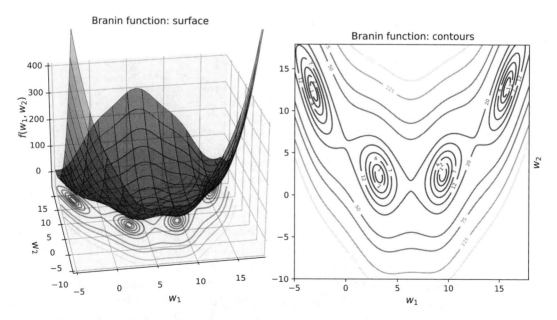

Figure 5.2 The surface plot (left) and contour plot (right) of the Branin function. We can visually verify that this function has four minima, which are the centers of the elliptical regions in the contour plot.

grid over the variables w_1 and w_2 and evaluate $f(w_1, w_2)$ at every possible combination exhaustively. However, there are several problems with this. First, how coarse or fine should our grid be? If our grid is too coarse, we may miss the minimizer in our search. If our grid is too fine, then we'll have a very large number of grid points to search over, making our optimization procedure very slow.

Second, and more worrying, this approach ignores all the extra information inherent in the function itself, which could be quite helpful in guiding our search. For instance, the first derivatives, or the rates of change of $f(w_1, w_2)$ with respect to w_1 and w_2, can be very helpful.

UNDERSTANDING AND IMPLEMENTING GRADIENT DESCENT

The first derivative information is known as the gradient of $f(w_1, w_2)$ and is a measure of the (local) slope of the function surface. More importantly, the gradient points in the direction of steepest ascent; that is, moving in the direction of steepest ascent will lead us to bigger values of $f(w_1, w_2)$.

If we want to use gradient information to find the minimizers, then we have to travel in the opposite direction of the gradient! This is precisely the simple, yet highly effective principle behind gradient descent: keep going in the direction of the negative gradient, and you'll end up at a (local) minimizer.

We can formalize this intuition in the following pseudocode, which describes the steps of gradient descent. As shown, gradient descent is an iterative procedure that steadily moves toward a local minimizer by moving in the direction of steepest descent, that is, the negative gradient:

```
initialize: w_old = some initial guess, converged=False
while not converged:
1. compute the direction (d) as negative gradient at w_old and normalize
     to unit length
2. compute the step length using line search (distance, α)
3. update the solution: w_new = w_old + distance * direction = w_old + α · d
4. if change between w_new and w_old is below some specified tolerance:
     converged=True, so break
5. else set w_new = w_old, get ready for the next iteration
```

The gradient descent procedure is fairly straightforward. First, we initialize our solution (and call it w_{old}); this can be a random initialization or perhaps a more sophisticated guess. Starting from this initial guess, we compute the negative gradient, which tells us which direction we want to go.

Next, we compute a step length, which tells us the distance or how far we want to go in the direction of the negative gradient. Computing the step length is important, as it ensures that we don't overshoot our solution.

The step length computation is another optimization problem, where we want to identify a scalar $\alpha > 0$ such that traveling along the gradient g for a distance of α produces the biggest decrease in the loss function. Formally, this is known as a *line search problem* and is often used to efficiently select step lengths during optimization.

NOTE Many optimization packages and tools (e.g., `scipy.optimize` used in this chapter) provide exact and approximate line search functions that can be used to identify step lengths. Alternately, step length can also be set according to some predetermined strategy, often for efficiency. In machine learning, the step length is often called the *learning rate* and is represented by the Greek letter eta (η).

With a direction and distance, we can take this step and update our solution guess to $\mathbf{w}_{\text{new}}$. Once we get there, we check for convergence. There are several tests for convergence; here, we assume convergence if the solution doesn't change much between consecutive iterations. If converged, then we've found a local minimizer. If not, then we iterate again from $\mathbf{w}_{\text{new}}$. The following listing shows how to perform gradient descent.

Listing 5.1 Gradient descent

```python
import numpy as np
from scipy.optimize import line_search

def gradient_descent(f, g, x_init,              # Gradient descent requires a
                     max_iter=100, args=()):    # function f and its gradient g.
    converged = False                           # Initializes gradient descent
    n_iter = 0                                  # to "not converged"

    x_old, x_new = np.array(x_init), None
    descent_path = np.full((max_iter + 1, 2), fill_value=np.nan)
    descent_path[n_iter] = x_old

    while not converged:
        n_iter += 1
        gradient = -g(x_old, *args)             # Computes the
                                                # negative gradient
        direction = gradient / np.linalg.norm(gradient)   # Normalizes gradient
                                                          # to unit length

        step = line_search(f, g, x_old,
                           direction, args=args)  # Computes step length
                                                  # using line search

        if step[0] is None:                     # If the line search
            distance = 1.0                      # fails, make it 1.0.
        else:
            distance = step[0]

        x_new = x_old + distance * direction    # Computes
        descent_path[n_iter] = x_new            # the update

        err = np.linalg.norm(x_new - x_old)     # Computes the change from
                                                # the previous iteration
        if err <= 1e-3 or n_iter >= max_iter:
            converged = True                    # Converges if change is small or
                                                # maximum iterations are reached
        x_old = x_new                           # Gets ready for
                                                # the next iteration
    return x_new, descent_path
```

We can test drive this gradient descent procedure on the Branin function. To do this, in addition to the function itself, we'll also need its gradient. We can compute the gradient explicitly by dredging up the basics of calculus (if not the memories of it).

The gradient is a vector with two components: the gradient of f with respect to w_1 and w_2, respectively. With this gradient, we can compute the direction of steepest increase everywhere:

$$g(w_1, w_2) = \begin{bmatrix} \frac{\partial f(w_1, w_2)}{\partial w_1} \\ \frac{\partial f(w_1, w_2)}{\partial w_2} \end{bmatrix} = \begin{bmatrix} 2a\left(w_2 - bw_1^2 + cw_1 - r\right) \cdot (-2bw_1 + c) - s(1 - t)\sin(w_1) \\ 2a\left(w_2 - bw_1^2 + cw_1 - r\right) \end{bmatrix}$$

We can implement the Branin function and its gradient as shown here:

```
def branin(w, a, b, c, r, s, t):
    return a * (w[1] - b * w[0] ** 2 + c * w[0] - r) ** 2 + \
        s * (1 - t) * np.cos(w[0]) + s

def branin_gradient(w, a, b, c, r, s, t):
    return np.array([2 * a * (w[1] - b * w[0] ** 2 + c * w[0] - r) *
                    (-2 * b * w[0] + c) - s * (1 - t) * np.sin(w[0]),
                    2 * a * (w[1] - b * w[0] ** 2 + c * w[0] - r)])
```

In addition to the function and the gradient, listing 5.1 also requires an initial guess x_init. Here, we'll initialize gradient descent with w_ini=[-4,-5]' (transposed because these are column vectors, mathematically speaking). Now, we can call the gradient descent procedure:

```
a, b, c, r, s, t = 1, 5.1/(4 * np.pi**2), 5/np.pi, 6, 10, 1/(8 * np.pi)
w_init = np.array([-4, -5])
w_optimal, w_path = gradient_descent(branin, branin_gradient,
                                     w_init, args=(a, b, c, r, s, t))
```

Gradient descent returns an optimal solution w_optimal=[3.14, 2.27] and the optimization path w_path, which is the sequence of intermediate solutions that the procedure iterated through on its way to the optimal solution.

And voila! In figure 5.3, we see that gradient descent is able to reach one of the four local minimizers of the Branin function. There are several important things to note about gradient descent, as we'll discuss next.

PROPERTIES OF GRADIENT DESCENT

First, observe that the gradient steps become smaller and smaller as we approach one of the minimizers. This is because gradients vanish at minimizers. More importantly, gradient descent exhibits zigzagging behavior because the gradient doesn't point at the local minimizer itself; rather, it points in the direction of steepest ascent (or descent, if negative).

The gradient at a point essentially captures local information, that is, the nature of the function close to that point. Gradient descent chains several such gradient steps to get to a minimizer. When the gradient descent has to pass through steep valleys, it's

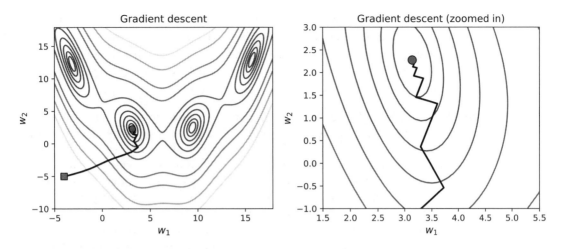

Figure 5.3 The figure on the left shows the full descent path of gradient descent, starting from [–4,–5]' (square) and converging to one of the local minima (circle). The figure on the right shows the zoomed-in version of the same descent path as gradient descent approaches the solution. Note that the gradient steps become smaller, and the descent algorithm tends to zigzag as it approaches the solution.

tendency to use local information causes it to bounce around the valley walls as it moves toward the minimum.

Second, gradient descent converged to one of the four local minimizers of the Branin function. You can get it to converge to a different minimizer by changing the initialization. Figure 5.4 illustrates various gradient descent paths for different initializations.

The sensitivity of gradient descent to initialization is illustrated in figure 5.4, where different random initializations cause gradient descent to converge to different local minimizers. This behavior may be familiar to those of you who have used k-means clustering: different initializations will often produce different clusterings, each of which is a different local solution.

An interesting challenge with gradient descent is in identifying the appropriate initialization as different initializations lead gradient descent to different local minimiz-

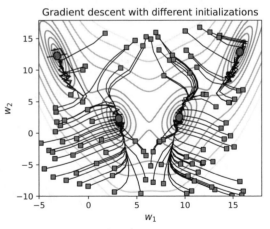

Figure 5.4 Different initializations will cause gradient descent to reach different local minima.

ers. From an optimization perspective, it's not always easy to identify the correct initialization beforehand.

However, from a machine-learning perspective, the different local solutions may demonstrate the same generalization behavior. That is, the locally optimal learned models all have similar predictive performance. This situation is commonly encountered with neural networks and deep learning, which is why training procedures for many deep models are initialized from pretrained solutions.

> **TIP** The sensitivity of gradient descent to initialization depends on the type of function being optimized. If the function is convex or cup-shaped everywhere, then any local minimizer that gradient descent identifies will always be a global minimizer too! This is the case with models learned by support vector machine (SVM) optimizers. However, a good initial guess is still important as it may cause the algorithm to converge faster. Many real-world problems are typically non-convex and have several local minima. Gradient descent will converge to one of them, depending on the initialization and shape of the function in the locality of the initial guess. The objective function of k-means clustering is non-convex, which is why different initializations produce different clusterings. See *Algorithms for Optimization* by Mykel Kochenderfer and Tim Wheeler (MIT Press, 2019) for a solid and hands-on introduction to optimization.

5.1.2 *Gradient descent over loss functions for training*

Now that we understand the basics of how gradient descent works on a simple example (the Branin function), let's build a classification task from scratch using a loss function of our own. Then, we'll use gradient descent to train a model. First, we create a 2D classification problem as follows:

```
from sklearn.datasets import make_blobs
X, y = make_blobs(n_samples=200, n_features=2,
                  centers=[[-1.5, -1.5], [1.5, 1.5]], random_state=42)
```

This synthetic classification data set is visualized in figure 5.5.

We specifically create a linearly separable data set (with some noise, of course) so that we can train a linear separator or classification function. This will keep our loss function formulation simple and make our gradients easy to calculate.

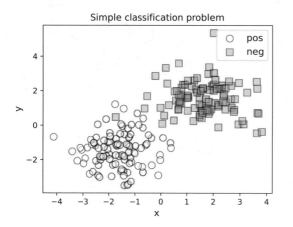

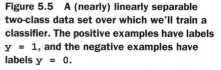

Figure 5.5 A (nearly) linearly separable two-class data set over which we'll train a classifier. The positive examples have labels y = 1, and the negative examples have labels y = 0.

The classifier we want to train, $h_w(x)$, takes 2D data points $x = [x_1, x_2]'$ and returns a prediction using a linear function:

$$h_w(x) = w_1 x_1 + w_2 x_2$$

The classifier is parameterized by $w = [w_1, w_2]'$, which we have to learn using the training examples. To learn, we'll need a loss function over the true label and predicted label. We'll use the familiar squared loss (or squared error) that measures the cost for an individual labeled training example (x,y):

$$f_{\text{loss}}(y, x) = \frac{1}{2} (y - h_w(x))^2 = \frac{1}{2}(y - w_1 x_1 - w_2 x_2)^2$$

The squared loss function computes the loss between the prediction of the current candidate model (h_w) on a single training example (x) and its true label (y). For the n training examples in the data set, the overall loss can be written as follows:

$$f_{\text{loss}}(y, x) = \frac{1}{2} \sum_{i=1}^{n} (y - h_w(x_i))^2 = \frac{1}{2} \sum_{i=1}^{n} \left(y - w_1 x_1^i - w_2 x_2^i \right)^2 = \frac{1}{2}(y - Xw)'(y - Xw)$$

The expression for the overall loss is just the sum of the individual losses of the n training examples in the data set.

The expression $\frac{1}{2}(y - Xw)'(y - Xw)$ is simply the *vectorized* version of the overall loss, which uses dot products instead of loops. In the vectorized version, the boldface y is an $n \times 1$ vector of true labels; x is an $n \times 2$ data matrix, where each row is a 2D training example; and w is a 2×1 model vector that we want to learn.

As before, we'll need the gradient of the loss function:

$$g(w_1, w_2) = \begin{bmatrix} \frac{\partial f_{\text{loss}}(w_1, w_2)}{\partial w_1} \\ \frac{\partial f_{\text{loss}}(w_1, w_2)}{\partial w_2} \end{bmatrix} = \begin{bmatrix} -\sum_{i-1}^{n} (y_i - w_1 x_1^i - w_2 x_2^i) x_1^i \\ -\sum_{i=1}^{n} (y_i - w_1 x_1^i - w_2 x_2^i) x_2^i \end{bmatrix} = -X'(y - Xw)$$

We implement the vectorized versions because they are more compact and more efficient as they avoid explicit loops for summation:

```
def squared_loss(w, X, y):
    return 0.5 * np.sum((y - np.dot(X, w))**2)

def squared_loss_gradient(w, X, y):
    return -np.dot(X.T, (y - np.dot(X, w)))
```

TIP If you're alarmed at the prospect of hand-computing gradients, despair not; alternatives are available that can numerically approximate the gradients and are used for training many machine-learning models, including deep learning and gradient boosting. These alternatives rely on finite difference approximations or autodifferentiation (which is based on the first principles of numerical calculus and linear algebra) to compute gradients efficiently. An easy-to-use tool is the function `scipy.optimize.approx_fprime` available in the `scipy` scientific package. A far more powerful tool is JAX (https://github.com/google/jax), which is free and open source. JAX is intended for computing gradients of complex functions representing deep neural networks with many layers. JAX can differentiate through loops, branches, and even recursion, and it has GPU support for large-scale gradient computations.

What does our loss function look like? We can visualize it as before, as shown in figure 5.6. This loss function is bowl-shaped and convex, and has one global minimum, which is our optimal classifier, *w*.

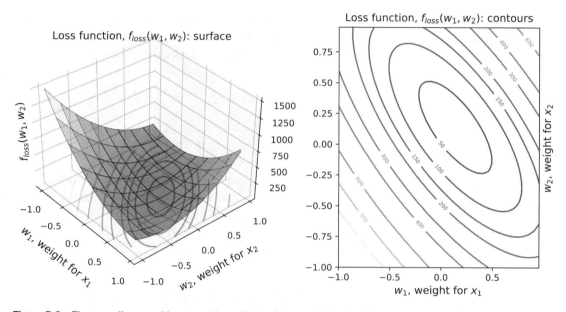

Figure 5.6   The overall squared loss over the entire training set, visualized

As before, we perform gradient descent, this time initializing at $w = [0.0, -0.99]'$ using the following code snippet, with the gradient descent path shown in figure 5.7:

```
w_init = np.array([0.0, -0.99])
w, path = gradient_descent(squared_loss, squared_loss_gradient,
                           w_init, args=(X, y))
print(w)
[0.17390066 0.11937649]
```

Gradient descent has learned a final learned model: $w^* = [0.174, 0.119]'$. The linear classifier learned by our gradient descent procedure is visualized in figure 5.7 (right). In addition to visually confirming that the gradient descent procedure learned a useful model, we can also compute training accuracy.

Recall that linear classifier $h_w(\boldsymbol{x}) = w_1 x_1 + w_2 x_2$ returns real-valued predictions, which we need to convert to 0 or 1. This is straightforward: we simply assign all positive predictions (examples above the line, geometrically) to the class $y_{pred} = 1$ and assign negative predictions (examples below the line, geometrically) to the class $y_{pred} = 0$:

```
ypred = (np.dot(X, w) >= 0).astype(int)
from sklearn.metrics import accuracy_score
accuracy_score(y, ypred)
0.995
```

Success! The training accuracy learned by our implementation of gradient descent is 99.5%.

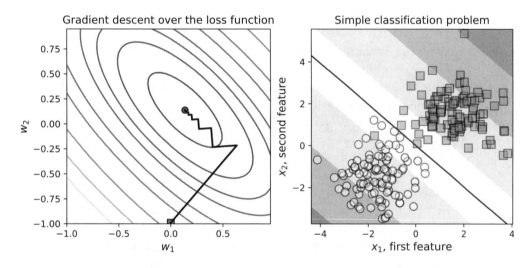

Figure 5.7 Left: Gradient descent over our squared loss function starting at `w_init` (square) and converging at the optimal solution (circle). Right: The learned model $w^* = [0.174, 0.119]'$ is a linear classifier that fits the training data quite well as it separates both the classes.

Now that we understand how gradient descent uses gradient information sequentially to minimize a loss function during training, let's see how we can extend it with boosting to train a sequential ensemble.

5.2 Gradient boosting: Gradient descent + boosting

In gradient boosting, we aim to train a sequence of weak learners that approximate the gradient at each iteration. Gradient boosting and its successor, Newton boosting, are currently considered state-of-the-art ensemble methods and are widely implemented and deployed for several tasks in diverse application areas.

We'll first look at the intuition of gradient boosting and contrast it with another familiar boosting method: AdaBoost. Armed with this intuition, as before, we'll implement our own version of gradient boosting to visualize what is really going on under the hood.

Then, we'll look at two gradient-boosting approaches available in scikit-learn: the `GradientBoostingClassifier`, and its more scalable counterpart, `Histogram-GradientBoostingClassifer`. This will set us up nicely for LightGBM, a powerful and flexible implementation of gradient boosting widely used for practical applications.

5.2.1 *Intuition: Learning with residuals*

The key component of sequential ensemble methods, such as AdaBoost and gradient boosting, is that they aim to train a new weak estimator at each iteration to fix the errors made by the weak estimator at the previous iteration. However, AdaBoost and gradient boosting train new weak estimators on poorly classified examples in rather different ways.

ADABOOST VS. GRADIENT BOOSTING

AdaBoost identifies high-priority training examples by weighting them such that misclassified examples have higher weights than correctly classified ones. In this way, AdaBoost can tell the base-learning algorithm which training examples it should focus on in the current iteration. In contrast, gradient boosting uses residuals or errors (between the true and predicted labels) to tell the base-learning algorithm which training examples it should focus on in the next iteration.

What exactly is a residual? For a training example, it's simply the error between the true label and the corresponding prediction. Intuitively, a correctly classified example must have a small residual, and a misclassified example must have a large residual. More concretely, if a classifier h makes a prediction $h(x)$ on a training example x, a naïve way of computing the residual would be to directly measure the difference between them:

$$\text{residual(true, predicted)} = \text{residual}(y, h(x)) = y - h(x)$$

Recall the squared loss function we were using previously: $f_{\text{loss}}(y, x) = \frac{1}{2}(y - h(x))^2$. The gradient of this loss f with respect to our model h is as follows:

$$\text{gradient(true, predicted)} = \frac{\partial f_{\text{loss}}}{\partial h}(y, h(x)) = -(y - h(x))$$

The negative gradient of the squared loss is exactly the same as our residual! This means that the gradient of the loss function is a measure of the misclassification and is the residual.

Training examples that are badly misclassified will have large gradients (residuals) as the gap between the true and predicted labels will be large. Training examples that are correctly classified will have small gradients.

This is evident in figure 5.8, where the magnitude and sign of the residuals indicate the training examples that require the most attention. Thus, analogous to Ada-Boost, we have a measure of how badly each training example is misclassified. How can we use this information to train a weak learner?

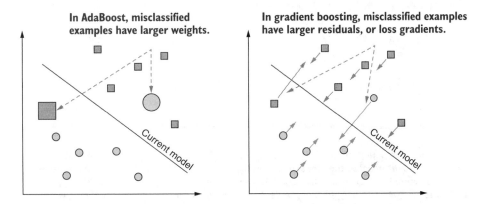

Figure 5.8 Comparing AdaBoost (left) to gradient boosting (right). Both approaches train weak estimators that improve classification performance on misclassified examples. AdaBoost uses weights, with misclassified examples being assigned higher weights. Gradient boosting uses residuals, with misclassified examples having higher residuals. The residuals are nothing but negative loss gradients.

USING WEAK LEARNERS TO APPROXIMATE GRADIENTS

Continuing our analogy with AdaBoost, recall that once it assigns weights to all the training examples, we have a weight-augmented data set (x_i, y_i, D_i) with i = 1, ..., n, of weighted examples. Thus, training a weak learner in AdaBoost is an instance of a weighted classification problem. With an appropriate base classification algorithm, AdaBoost trains a weak classifier.

In gradient boosting, we no longer have weights D_i. Instead, we have residuals (or negative loss gradients), r_i, and a residual-augmented data set (x_i, r_i). Instead of classification labels ($y_i = 0$ or 1) and example weights (D_i), each training example now has an associated residual, which can be viewed as a real-valued label.

Thus, training a weak learner in gradient boosting is an instance of a regression problem, which requires a base-learning algorithm such as decision-tree regression. When trained, weak estimators in gradient boosting can be viewed as approximate gradients.

Figure 5.9 illustrates how gradient descent differs from gradient boosting and how gradient boosting is conceptually similar to gradient descent. The key difference between the two is that gradient descent directly uses the negative gradient, while gradient boosting trains a weak regressor to approximate the negative gradient. We now have all the ingredients to formalize the algorithmic steps of gradient boosting.

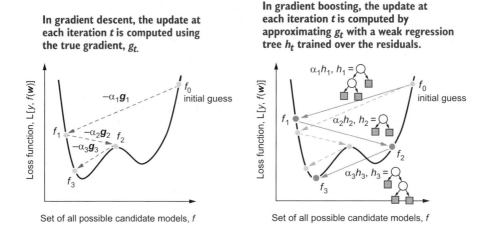

Figure 5.9   Comparing gradient descent (left) to gradient boosting (right). At iteration t, gradient descent updates the model using the negative gradient, $-g_t$. At iteration t, gradient boosting approximates the negative gradient by training a weak regressor, h_t, on the negative residuals $-r_t^i$. The step length α_t in gradient descent is equivalent to the hypothesis weight of each base estimator in a sequential ensemble.

> **NOTE**   Gradient boosting aims to fit a weak estimator to residuals, which are real-valued. Thus, gradient boosting will *always* need to use a regression algorithm as a base-learning algorithm and learn regressors as weak estimators. This will be the case even when the loss function corresponds to binary or multiclass classification, regression, or ranking.

GRADIENT BOOSTING IS GRADIENT DESCENT + BOOSTING

To summarize, gradient boosting combines gradient descent and boosting:

- Like AdaBoost, gradient boosting trains a weak learner to fix the mistakes made by the previous weak learner. AdaBoost uses example weights to focus learning on misclassified examples, while gradient boosting uses example residuals to do the same.
- Like gradient descent, gradient boosting updates the current model with gradient information. Gradient descent uses the negative gradient directly, while gradient boosting trains a weak regressor over the negative residuals to approximate the gradient.

Finally, both gradient descent and gradient boosting are additive algorithms; that is, they generate sequences of intermediate terms that are additively combined to produce the final model. This is apparent in figure 5.10.

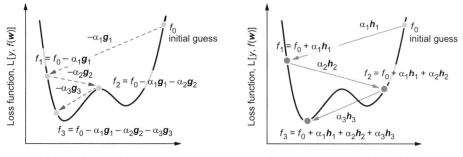

Figure 5.10   Both gradient descent (left) and gradient boosting (right) produce a sequence of updates. In gradient descent, each iteration additively updates the current model with the new negative gradient ($-g_t$). In gradient boosting, each iteration additively updates the current model with the new approximate weak gradient estimate (the regression tree, h_t).

At each iteration, AdaBoost, gradient descent, and gradient boosting all update the current model using an additive expression of the following form:

$$\text{new model} = \text{old model} + (\text{step length}) * (\text{update direction})$$

More formally, this appears as follows:

$$F_{t+1}(\boldsymbol{x}) = F_t(\boldsymbol{x}) + \alpha_t \cdot h_t(\boldsymbol{x})$$

We can unravel this expression for iterations $t, t - 1, t - 2, \ldots, 0$ to obtain the overall update sequence AdaBoost, gradient descent, and gradient boosting produce:

$$F_{t+1}(\boldsymbol{x}) = F_0(\boldsymbol{x}) + \alpha_1 \cdot h_1(\boldsymbol{x}) + \alpha_2 \cdot h_2(\boldsymbol{x}) + \cdots + \alpha_{t-1} \cdot h_{t-1}(\boldsymbol{x}) + \alpha_t \cdot h_t(\boldsymbol{x})$$

The key differences between the three algorithms are in how we compute the updates h_t and the hypothesis weights (also known as step lengths) α_t. We can summarize the update steps of all three algorithms in table 5.1.

Table 5.1   Comparing AdaBoost, gradient descent, and gradient boosting

Algorithm	Loss function	Base-learning algorithm	Update direction $h_t(x)$	Step length α_t
AdaBoost for classification	Exponential	Classification with weighted examples	Weak classifier	Computed in closed form
Gradient descent	User-specified	None	Gradient vector	Line search
Gradient boosting	User-specified	Regression with examples and residuals	Weak regressor	Line search

The reason gradient boosting = gradient descent + boosting is because it *generalizes* the boosting procedure from the exponential loss function used by AdaBoost to any user-specified loss function. For gradient boosting to flexibly adapt to a wide variety of loss functions, it adopts two general procedures: (1) approximate gradients using weak regressors, and (2) compute the hypothesis weights (or step lengths) using line search.

5.2.2   *Implementing gradient boosting*

As before, we'll put our intuition to practice by implementing our own version of gradient boosting. The basic algorithm can be outlined with the following pseudocode:

```
initialize: F = f_0, some constant value
for t = 1 to T:
1. compute the negative residuals for each example,  r_i^t = -∂L/∂F (x_i)
2. fit a weak decision tree regressor h_t(x) using the training set (x_i, r_i)_{i=1}^n
3. compute the step length (α_t) using line search
4. update the model: F_t = F + α_t · h_t(x)
```

This training procedure is almost the same as that of gradient descent except for a couple of differences: (1) instead of using the negative gradient, we use an approximate gradient trained on the negative residuals, and (2) instead of checking for convergence, the algorithm terminates after a finite, maximum number of iterations T. The following listing implements this pseudocode specifically for the squared loss. It uses a type of line search called *golden section search* to find the best step length.

Listing 5.2   Gradient boosting for the squared loss

```python
from scipy.optimize import minimize_scalar
from sklearn.tree import DecisionTreeRegressor

def fit_gradient_boosting(X, y, n_estimators=10):      Gets dimensions
    n_samples, n_features = X.shape                    of the data set
    n_estimators = 10
    estimators = []                                    Initializes an
                                                       empty ensemble
    F = np.full((n_samples, ), 0.0)
                                                       Predicts the ensemble
                                                       on the training set
    for t in range(n_estimators):
        residuals = y - F                              Computes residuals as negative
        h = DecisionTreeRegressor(max_depth=1)         gradients of the squared loss
        h.fit(X, residuals)
                                                       Gets predictions of the
                                                       weak learner, h_t
        hreg = h.predict(X)
        loss = lambda a: np.linalg.norm(               Sets up the line
                         y - (F + a * hreg))**2        search problem
        step = minimize_scalar(loss, method='golden')  Finds the best step
        a = step.x                                     length using the
                                                       golden section search
        F += a * hreg
        estimators.append((a, h))                      Updates the
                                                       ensemble
    return estimators
```

Fits weak regression tree (h_t) to the examples and residuals

Updates the ensemble predictions

Once the model is trained, we can make predictions (see the following listing) as with the AdaBoost ensemble. Note that, just like our AdaBoost implementation previously, this model returns predictions of –1/1 rather than 0/1.

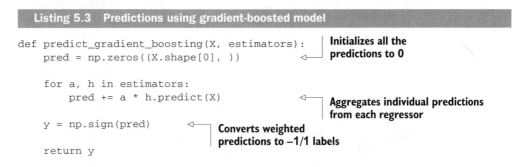

Listing 5.3   Predictions using gradient-boosted model

```
def predict_gradient_boosting(X, estimators):
    pred = np.zeros((X.shape[0], ))          ⟵  Initializes all the
                                                 predictions to 0

    for a, h in estimators:
        pred += a * h.predict(X)             ⟵  Aggregates individual predictions
                                                 from each regressor
    y = np.sign(pred)       ⟵  Converts weighted
                               predictions to –1/1 labels
    return y
```

We can test drive this implementation on a simple two-moons classification example. Note that we convert the training labels from 0/1 to –1/1 to ensure that we learn and predict correctly:

```
from sklearn.datasets import make_moons
X, y = make_moons(n_samples=200, noise=0.15, random_state=13)    ⟵  Converts training
y = 2 * y - 1                                                        labels to –1/1
from sklearn.model_selection import train_test_split    ⟵  Splits into train
Xtrn, Xtst, ytrn, ytst = train_test_split(X, y,            and test sets
                                    test_size=0.25, random_state=11)

estimators = fit_gradient_boosting(Xtrn, ytrn)
ypred = predict_gradient_boosting(Xtst, estimators)

from sklearn.metrics import accuracy_score    ⟵  Trains and gets
tst_err = 1 - accuracy_score(ytst, ypred)        the test error
tst_err
0.06000000000000005
```

The error rate of this model is 6%, which is pretty good.

VISUALIZING GRADIENT-BOOSTING ITERATIONS

Finally, to comprehensively nail down our understanding of gradient boosting, let's step through the first few iterations to see how gradient boosting uses residuals to boost classification. In our implementation, we initialize our predictions to be $F(x_i) = 0$. This means that in the first iteration, the residuals for examples in Class 1 will be $r_i = 1 - 0 = 1$, and the residuals for the examples in Class 0 will be $r_i = -1 - 0 = -1$. This is evident in figure 5.11.

In the first iteration, all the training examples have high residuals (either +1 or –1), and the base-learning algorithm (decision-tree regression) has to train a weak regressor taking all these residuals into account. The trained regression tree (h_1) is shown in figure 5.11 (right).

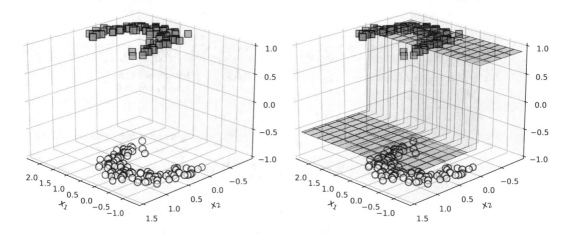

Figure 5.11   Iteration 1: residuals (left) and the weak regressor trained over the residuals (right)

The current ensemble consists of only one regression tree: $F = \alpha_1 h_1$. We can also visualize the classification predictions of h_1 and the ensemble F. The resulting classifications achieve an overall error rate of 16%, as shown in figure 5.12.

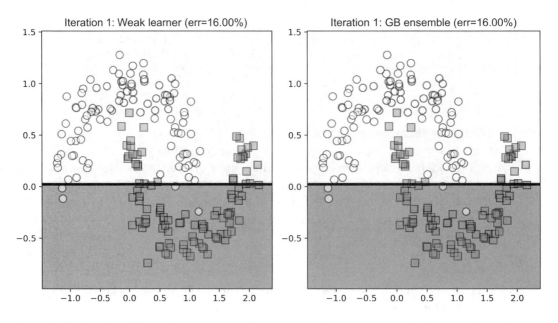

Figure 5.12   Iteration 1: Predictions of the weak learner (h_1) and the whole ensemble (F). Since this is the first iteration, the ensemble consists of only one weak regressor.

In iteration 2, we compute the residuals again. Now, the residuals begin to show more separation, which reflects how well they are classified by the current ensemble. The decision-tree regressor attempts to fit the residuals again (figure 5.13, right), though this time, it focuses on examples that have been misclassified previously.

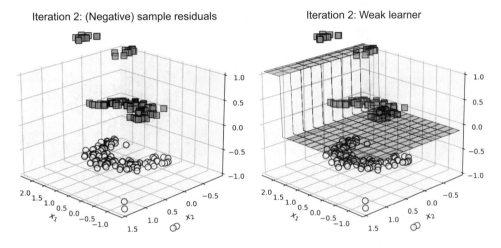

Figure 5.13   Iteration 2: residuals (left) and the weak regressor trained over the residuals (right)

The ensemble now consists of two regression trees: $F = \alpha_1 h_1 + \alpha_2 h_2$. We can now visualize the classification predictions of the newly trained regressor h_2 and the overall ensemble F (see figure 5.14).

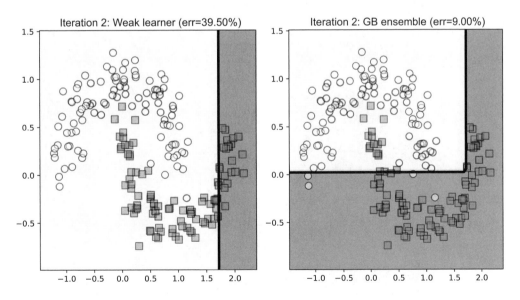

Figure 5.14   Iteration 2: predictions of the weak learner (h_2) and the overall ensemble (F)

The weak learner trained in iteration 2 has an overall error rate of 39.5%. Yet the first two weak learners have already boosted ensemble performance up to 91% accuracy, that is, 9% error. This process continues in iteration 3, as shown in figure 5.15.

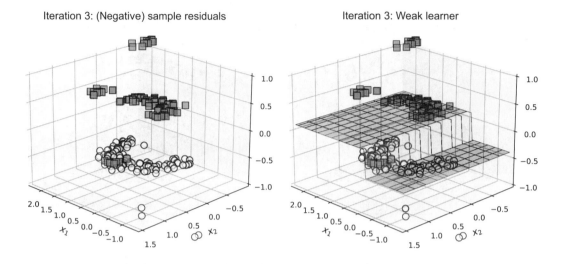

Figure 5.15   Iteration 3: residuals (left) and the weak regressor trained over the residuals (right)

In this manner, gradient boosting continues to sequentially train and add base regressors to the ensemble. Figure 5.16 shows the model trained after 10 iterations; the ensemble consists of 10 weak regressor estimators and has boosted overall training accuracy to 97.5%!

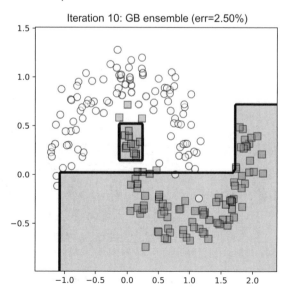

Figure 5.16   Final gradient boosting ensemble after 10 iterations

There are several publicly available and efficient implementations of gradient boosting that you can use for your machine-learning tasks. For the rest of this section, we'll focus on the most familiar: scikit-learn.

5.2.3   *Gradient boosting with scikit-learn*

We'll now look at how to use two scikit-learn classes: `GradientBoostingClassifier` and a new version called `HistogramGradientBoostingClassifier`. The latter trades exactness for speed to train models significantly faster than `GradientBoostingClassifier`, making it ideally suited for larger data sets.

scikit-learn's `GradientBoostingClassifier` essentially implements the same gradient-boosting algorithm that we have ourselves implemented in this section. Its usage is similar to other scikit-learn classifiers such as `AdaBoostClassifier`. There are two key differences from `AdaBoostClassifier`, however:

- Unlike `AdaBoostClassifier`, which supports several different types of base estimators, `GradientBoostingClassifier` only supports tree-based ensembles. Therefore, it will always use decision trees as base estimators, and there is no mechanism to specify other types of base-learning algorithms.
- `AdaBoostClassifier` optimizes the exponential loss (by design). `GradientBoostingClassifier` allows the user to select either the logistic or exponential loss functions. The logistic loss (also known as cross entropy) is a commonly used loss function for binary classification (and also has a multiclass variant).

NOTE   Training a `GradientBoostingClassifier` with the exponential loss very is similar to (but not exactly the same as) training an `AdaBoostClassifier`.

In addition to selecting the loss function, we can also set additional learning parameters. These parameters are often selected by cross validation (CV), much like any other machine-learning algorithm (see section 4.3 for parameter selection in `AdaBoostClassifier`):

- We can control the complexity of the base tree estimators directly with `max_depth` and `max_leaf_nodes`. Higher values mean that the base tree learning algorithm has greater flexibility in training more complex trees. The caveat here, of course, is that deeper trees, or trees with more leaf nodes, tend to overfit the training data.
- `n_estimators` caps the number of weak learners that will be trained sequentially by `GradientBoostingClassifier` and is essentially the number of algorithm iterations.
- Like AdaBoost, gradient boosting also trains weak learners (h_t in iteration t) sequentially and constructs an ensemble incrementally and additively: $F_t(x) = F_{t-1}(x) + \eta \cdot \alpha_t \cdot h_t(x)$. Here, α_t is the weight of weak learner h_t (or the step length), and η is the learning rate. The learning rate is a user-defined learning parameter that lies in the range $0 < \eta \leq 1$. Recall that a slower learning rate

means that it will often take more iterations to train an ensemble. It may be necessary to opt for slower learning rates to make successive weak learners more robust to outliers and noise. Learning rate is controlled by the `learning_rate` parameter.

Let's look at an example of gradient boosting in action on the breast cancer data set. We train and evaluate a `GradientBoostingClassifier` model using this data set:

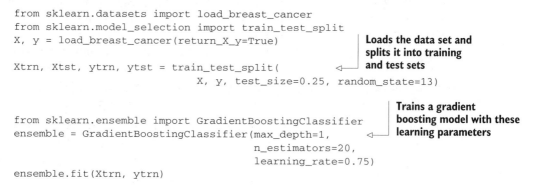

```
from sklearn.datasets import load_breast_cancer
from sklearn.model_selection import train_test_split
X, y = load_breast_cancer(return_X_y=True)          Loads the data set and
                                                     splits it into training
Xtrn, Xtst, ytrn, ytst = train_test_split(          and test sets
                    X, y, test_size=0.25, random_state=13)


                                                     Trains a gradient
                                                     boosting model with these
from sklearn.ensemble import GradientBoostingClassifier   learning parameters
ensemble = GradientBoostingClassifier(max_depth=1,
                            n_estimators=20,
                            learning_rate=0.75)
ensemble.fit(Xtrn, ytrn)
```

And how well did this model do? This gradient boosting classifier achieves 4.9% test error, which is pretty good:

```
ypred = ensemble.predict(Xtst)
err = 1 - accuracy_score(ytst, ypred)
print(err)
0.04895104895104896
```

A key limitation of `GradientBoostingClassifier`, however, is its speed; while effective, it does tend to be rather slow on large data sets. The efficiency bottleneck, as it turns out, is in tree learning. Recall that gradient boosting has to learn a regression tree at each iteration as a base estimator. For large data sets, the number of splits a tree learner has to consider becomes prohibitively large. This has led to the emergence of histogram-based gradient boosting, which aims to speed up base estimator tree learning, allowing gradient boosting to scale up to larger data sets.

5.2.4   *Histogram-based gradient boosting*

To understand the need for histogram-based tree learning, we have to revisit how a decision-tree algorithm learns a regression tree. In tree learning, we learn a tree in a top-down fashion, one decision node at a time. The standard way to do this is by presorting the feature values, enumerating all possible splits, and then evaluating all of them to find the best split. Let's say we have 1 million (10^6) training examples, each of dimension 100. Standard tree learning will enumerate and evaluate (on the order of) 100 million splits ($10^6 \times 100 = 10^8$) to identify a decision node! This is clearly untenable.

One alternative is to reorganize the feature values into a small number of bins. In this hypothetical example, suppose we binned each feature column into 100 bins.

Now, to find the best split, we have to only search over 10,000 splits ($100 \times 100 = 10^4$), which can speed up training rather dramatically!

Of course, this means that we're trading off exactness for speed. However, there is usually a large amount of redundancy or repeated information in many (big) data sets, which we compress by binning the data into smaller buckets. Figure 5.17 illustrates this tradeoff.

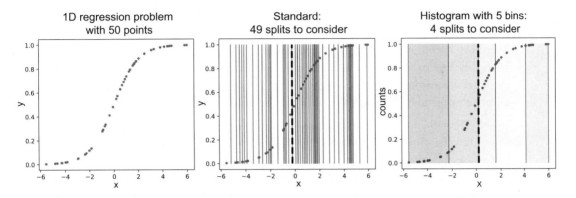

Figure 5.17   Left: A simple 1D regression problem with 50 data points. Center: Standard tree learning evaluates every possible split, which is illustrated by a line between each pair of data points. The best split is the one with the lowest split criterion (here, squared loss). Right: Histogram-based binning first puts the data into five buckets, and then evaluates the splits between each pair of data buckets. Again, the best split is the one with the lowest split criterion (also squared loss).

In figure 5.17, we contrast the behaviors of standard tree learning and histogram-based tree learning. In standard tree learning, each split considered is between two successive data points (figure 5.17, center); for 50 data points, we have to evaluate 49 splits.

In histogram-based splitting, we first bin the data (figure 5.17, right) into five bins. Now, each split considered is between two successive data buckets; for five bins, we only have to evaluate four splits! Now imagine how this would scale to millions of data points.

scikit-learn 0.21 introduced a version of gradient boosting called `Histogram-GradientBoostingClassifier` that implements histogram-based gradient boosting such that its training time is significantly improved. The following snippet shows how to train and evaluate `HistogramGradientBoostingClassifier` on the breast cancer data set:

```
from sklearn.ensemble import HistGradientBoostingClassifier

ensemble = HistGradientBoostingClassifier(max_depth=2,
                                          max_iter=20,
                                          learning_rate=0.75)
ensemble.fit(Xtrn, ytrn)
```

Initializes a histogram-based gradient-boosting classifier

Trains the ensemble

```
ypred = ensemble.predict(Xtst)
err = 1 - accuracy_score(ytst, ypred)
print(err)
0.04195804195804198
```

On the breast cancer data set, `HistGradientBoostingClassifier` achieved a test error of 4.2%. scikit-learn's histogram-based boosting implementation itself is inspired by another popular gradient-boosting package: LightGBM.

5.3   *LightGBM: A framework for gradient boosting*

Light Gradient Boosted Machines (LightGBM)[1] is an open source gradient boosting framework that was originally developed and released by Microsoft. At its core, LightGBM is essentially a histogram-based gradient-boosting approach. However, it also has several modeling and algorithmic features that enable it to handle large-scale data. In particular, LightGBM offers the following advantages:

- Algorithmic speedups such as gradient-based one-sided sampling and exclusive feature bundling that result in faster training and lower memory usage (these are described in more detail in section 5.3.1)
- Support for a large number of loss functions for classification, regression, and ranking, as well as application-specific custom loss functions (see section 5.3.2)
- Support for parallel and GPU learning, which enables LightGBM to handle large-scale data sets (parallel/GPU-based machine learning is out-of-scope for this book)

We'll also delve into how to apply LightGBM to some practical learning situations to avoid overfitting (section 5.4.1), and ultimately a case study on a real-world data set (section 5.5). It's impossible to detail all the features available in LightGBM in this limited space, of course. Instead, this section and the next introduce LightGBM and illustrate its usage and applications in practical settings. This should enable you to springboard further into advanced use cases of LightGBM for your applications through its documentation.

5.3.1   *What makes LightGBM "light"?*

Recall from our earlier discussion that the biggest computational bottleneck in scaling gradient boosting to large (with many training examples) or high-dimensional (with many features) data sets is tree learning, specifically, identifying optimal splits in the regression tree base estimators. As we saw in the previous section, histogram-based gradient boosting attempts to address this computational bottleneck. This works reasonably well for medium-sized data sets. However, histogram-bin construction can itself be slow if we have a very large number of data points, a large number of features, or both.

---

[1] LightGBM is available for Python, R, and many other platforms. See the LightGBM installation guide for detailed instructions on installation at http://mng.bz/v1K1.

In this section, we'll look at two key conceptual improvements LightGBM implements that often lead to significant speedups in training times in practice. The first, Gradient-based One-Side Sampling (GOSS), aims to reduce the number of *training examples*, while the second, Exclusive Feature Bundling (EFB), aims to reduce the number of *features*.

GRADIENT-BASED ONE-SIDE SAMPLING

A well-known approach to dealing with a very large number of training examples is to downsample the data set, that is, randomly sample a smaller subset of the data set. We've already seen examples of this in other ensemble approaches such as pasting (which is bagging without replacement; see chapter 2, section 2.4.1).

There are two problems with randomly downsampling the data set. First, not all examples are equally important; as in AdaBoost, some training examples are more important than others depending on the extent of their misclassification. Thus, it's imperative that downsampling not throw away high-importance training examples.

Second, sampling should also ensure that some fraction of correctly classified examples is also included. This is important in order to not overwhelm the base-learning algorithm with misclassified examples, which will inevitably lead to overfitting.

This is addressed by downsampling the data smartly using the Gradient-based One-Side Sampling (GOSS) procedure. Briefly, GOSS performs the following steps:

1 Use the gradient magnitude, similar to AdaBoost, which uses sample weights. Remember that the gradient indicates how much more the prediction can be improved: well-trained examples have small gradients, while under-trained (typically, misclassified or confusing) examples have large gradients.
2 Select the top $a\%$ of examples with the largest gradients; call this subset `top`.
3 Randomly sample $b\%$ of the remaining examples; call this subset `rand`.
4 Assign weights to examples in both sets: $w_{\text{top}} = 1$, $w_{\text{rand}} = \frac{100-a}{b}$.
5 Train a base regressor over this sampled data (examples, residuals, weights).

The weights computed in step 4 ensure that there is a good balance between undertrained and well-trained samples. Overall, such sampling also fosters ensemble diversity, which ultimately leads to better ensembles.

EXCLUSIVE FEATURE BUNDLING

Aside from a large number of training examples, big data also often provides the challenge of very high dimensionality, which can adversely affect histogram construction and slow down the overall training process. Similar to downsampling training examples, if we're able to downsample the features as well, it's possible to gain (sometimes very big) improvements in training speed. This is especially so when feature space is sparse, and features are mutually exclusive.

One common example of such a feature space is when we apply one-hot vectorization to categorical variables. For instance, consider a categorical variable that takes 10 unique values. When one-hot vectorized, this variable is expanded to 10 binary variables of which only one is nonzero, and all others are zero. This makes the 10 columns corresponding to this feature highly sparse.

Exclusive Feature Bundling (EFB) works in reverse, exploits this sparsity, and aims to compress mutually exclusive columns into one column to reduce the number of effective features. At a high level, EFB performs two steps:

1 Identify features that can be bundled together by measuring conflicts or the number of times both features are *nonzero simultaneously*. The intuition here is that if two features are often mutually exclusive, they are low conflict and can be bundled together.

2 Merge the identified low-conflict features into a feature bundle. The idea here is to preserve information carefully when merging nonzero values, which is typically done by adding offsets to feature values to prevent overlaps.

Intuitively, this is like having two features: `pass` and `fail`. Since one can't pass and fail an exam at the same time, we can merge them both into one feature (i.e., collapse two columns in the data set into one).

`pass` and `fail`, of course, are zero-conflict features and will never overlap. More often, two or more features might not be perfectly zero-conflict, but low conflict with some small number of overlaps. In such cases, EFB will still bundle these features together, which compresses several data columns into one column! By merging features in this manner, EFB effectively reduces the overall number of features, which often makes training much faster.

5.3.2 *Gradient boosting with LightGBM*

LightGBM is available for various platforms, including Windows, Linux, and macOS, and it can either be built from scratch or installed using tools such as `pip`. Its usage syntax is quite similar to that of scikit-learn.

Continuing with the breast cancer data set from section 5.2.3, we can train a gradient boosting model using LightGBM as follows:

```
from lightgbm import LGBMClassifier
gbm = LGBMClassifier(boosting_type='gbdt', n_estimators=20, max_depth=1)
gbm.fit(Xtrn, ytrn)
```

Here, we instantiate an instance of `LGBMClassifier` and set it to train an ensemble of 20 regression stumps (i.e., the base estimators will be regression trees of depth 1). The other important specification here is `boosting_type`. LightGBM can be trained in four modes:

- `boosting_type='rf'`—Trains traditional random forest ensembles (see chapter 2, section 2.3)
- `boosting_type='gbdt'`—Trains an ensemble using traditional gradient boosting (refer to section 5.2)
- `boosting_type='goss'`—Trains an ensemble using GOSS (refer to section 5.3.1)

- `boosting_type='dart'`—Trains an ensemble using Dropouts meet Multiple Additive Regression Trees (DART; see section 5.5)

The last three gradient-boosting modes essentially trade off between training speed and predictive performance, and we'll explore this in our case study. For now, check out how well the model we just trained using `boosting_type='gbdt'` turns out:

```
from sklearn.metrics import accuracy_score
ypred = gbm.predict(Xtst)
accuracy_score(ytst, ypred)
0.9473684210526315
```

Our first LightGBM classifier achieves 94.7% accuracy on the test set held out from the breast cancer data set. Now that we've familiarized ourselves with the basic functionality of LightGBM, let's look at how we can train models for real-world use cases with LightGBM.

5.4   *LightGBM in practice*

In this section, we describe how to train models in practice using LightGBM. As always, this means ensuring that LightGBM models generalize well and don't overfit. As with AdaBoost, we look to set the learning rate (section 5.4.1) or employ early stopping (section 5.4.2) as a means to control overfitting:

- *Learning rate*—By selecting an effective learning rate, we try to control the rate at which the model learns so that it doesn't rapidly fit, and then overfit the training data. We can think of this as a proactive modeling approach, where we try to identify a good training strategy so that it leads to a good model.
- *Early stopping*—By enforcing early stopping, we try to stop training as soon as we observe that the model is starting to overfit. We can think of this as a reactive modeling approach, where we contemplate terminating training as soon as we think we have a good model.

Finally, we also explore one of the most powerful functionalities of LightGBM: its support for custom loss functions. Recall that one of the major benefits of gradient boosting is that it's a general procedure, widely applicable to many loss functions.

While LightGBM provides support for many standard loss functions for classification, regression, and ranking, sometimes it may be necessary to train with application-specific loss functions. In section 5.4.3, we'll see precisely how we can do this with LightGBM.

5.4.1   *Learning rate*

When using gradient boosting, as with other machine-learning algorithms, it's possible to overfit on the training data. This means that, while we achieve very good training set performance, this doesn't result in a similar test set performance. That is, the model we've trained fails to generalize well. LightGBM, like scikit-learn, provides us with the means to control model complexity before overfitting.

LEARNING RATE VIA CROSS VALIDATION

LightGBM allows us to control the learning rate through the `learning_rate` training parameter (a positive number that has a default value of 0.1). This parameter also has a couple of aliases, `shrinkage_rate` and `eta`, which are other terms for the learning rate commonly used in machine-learning literature. Though all of these parameters have the same effect, care must be taken to set only one of them.

How can we figure out an effective learning rate for our problem? As with any other learning parameter, we can use CV. Recall that we also used CV to select the learning rate for AdaBoost in the previous chapter.

LightGBM plays nicely with scikit-learn, and we can combine the relevant functionalities from both packages to perform model learning. In listing 5.4, we combine scikit-learn's `StratifiedKFold` class to split the training data into 10 folds of training and validation sets. `StratifiedKFold` ensures that we preserve class distributions, that is, the fractions of different classes across the folds. Once the CV folds are set up, we can train and validate models on these 10 folds for different choices of learning rates: 0.1, 0.2, ..., 1.0.

Listing 5.4   Cross validation with LightGBM and scikit-learn

```
from sklearn.model_selection import StratifiedKFold
import numpy as np
                                              Initializes learning rates and
                                              number of cross validation folds
n_learning_rate_steps, n_folds = 10, 10    ◁
learning_rates = np.linspace(0.1, 1.0, num=n_learning_rate_steps)

                                         Splits data into training
                                         and validation folds
splitter = StratifiedKFold(         ◁
                n_splits=n_folds, shuffle=True, random_state=42)

trn_err = np.zeros((n_learning_rate_steps, n_folds))   Saves training and
val_err = np.zeros((n_learning_rate_steps, n_folds))   validation errors

                                              Trains a LightGBM classifier for each
                                              fold with different learning rates
for i, rate in enumerate(learning_rates):   ◁
    for j, (trn, val) in enumerate(splitter.split(X, y)):
        gbm = LGBMClassifier(boosting_type='gbdt', n_estimators=10,
                             max_depth=1, learning_rate=rate)
        gbm.fit(X[trn, :], y[trn])
        trn_err[i, j] = (1 - accuracy_score(y[trn],
                                            gbm.predict(X[trn, :]))) * 100
        val_err[i, j] = (1 - accuracy_score(y[val],
                                            gbm.predict(X[val, :]))) * 100

trn_err = np.mean(trn_err, axis=1)    Averages training and
val_err = np.mean(val_err, axis=1)    validation errors across folds
```

Saves training and
validation errors

We can visualize the training and validation errors for different learning rates in figure 5.18.

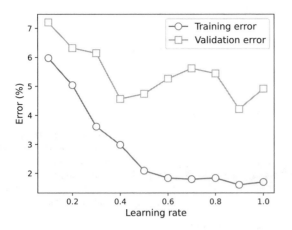

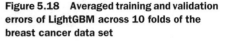

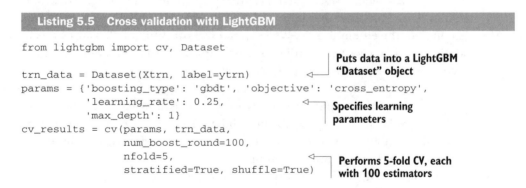

Figure 5.18 Averaged training and validation errors of LightGBM across 10 folds of the breast cancer data set

Unsurprisingly, as the learning rate increases, the training error continues to decrease, suggesting that the model first fits and then begins to overfit the training data. The validation error doesn't show the same trend. It decreases initially, and then increases; a learning rate of 0.4 produces the lowest validation error. This, then, is the best choice of learning rate.

CROSS VALIDATION WITH LIGHTGBM

LightGBM provides its own functionality to perform CV with given parameter choices through a function called `cv`, as shown in the following listing.

Listing 5.5 Cross validation with LightGBM

```
from lightgbm import cv, Dataset

trn_data = Dataset(Xtrn, label=ytrn)          ⟵  Puts data into a LightGBM
params = {'boosting_type': 'gbdt', 'objective': 'cross_entropy',   "Dataset" object
          'learning_rate': 0.25,              ⟵  Specifies learning
          'max_depth': 1}                         parameters
cv_results = cv(params, trn_data,
                num_boost_round=100,
                nfold=5,                       ⟵  Performs 5-fold CV, each
                stratified=True, shuffle=True)    with 100 estimators
```

In listing 5.5, we perform 5-fold CV over 100 boosting rounds (thus eventually training 100 base estimators). Setting `stratified=True` ensures that we preserve class distributions, that is, the fractions of different classes across the folds. Setting `shuffle=True` randomly shuffles the training data before splitting the data into folds.

We can visualize the training objective as training progresses. In listing 5.5, we train our classification model by optimizing cross entropy, set via `'objective': 'cross_entropy'`. As shown in figure 5.19, as we add more base estimators to our sequential ensemble, the average 5-fold cross-entropy objective decreases.

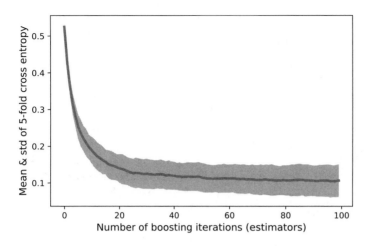

Figure 5.19 The average cross entropy across the folds decreases with increasing iterations, as we add more base estimators to the ensemble.

5.4.2 *Early stopping*

Another way of reining in overfitting behavior is through early stopping. As we've seen with AdaBoost, the idea of early stopping is pretty straightforward. As we train sequential ensembles, we train one base estimator at each iteration. This process continues until we reach the user-specified ensemble size (in LightGBM, there are several aliases to specify this: n_estimators, num_trees, num_rounds).

As the number of base estimators in the ensemble increases, the complexity of the ensemble also increases, which eventually leads to overfitting. To avoid this, we employ early stopping; that is, instead of training the model, we stop before we reach the limit of the ensemble size. We keep track of overfitting behavior by means of a validation set. Then, we train until we see no improvement in validation performance for a certain prespecified number of iterations.

For example, let's say that we've started training an ensemble of 500 base estimators and set early stopping iterations to 5. This is how early stopping works: when training, we keep a close eye on the validation error as we grow our ensemble, and when the validation error doesn't improve over a window of five iterations or early stopping rounds, we terminate training.

In LightGBM, we can incorporate early stopping if we specify a value for the parameter early_stopping_rounds. As long as the overall validation score (say, accuracy) improves over the last early_stopping_rounds, LightGBM will continue to train. However, if the score hasn't improved after early_stopping_rounds, LightGBM terminates.

As with AdaBoost, LightGBM also needs us to explicitly specify a validation set as well as a scoring metric for early stopping. In listing 5.6, we use the area under the receiver-operator curve (AUC) as the scoring metric to determine early stopping.

The AUC is an important evaluation metric for classification problems and can be interpreted as the probability that the model will rank a randomly chosen positive example higher than a randomly chosen negative example. Thus, high values of AUC are preferred as it means that the model is more discriminative.

> **Listing 5.6   Early stopping with LightGBM**

```
from sklearn.model_selection import train_test_split
Xtrn, Xval, ytrn, yval = train_test_split(              Splits data into train
                    X, y, test_size=0.2,           ◁─── and validation sets
                    shuffle=True, random_state=42)

                                                Performs early stopping if there's
                                                no change in the validation score
gbm = LGBMClassifier(boosting_type='gbdt', n_estimators=50,   after five rounds
                max_depth=1, early_stopping=5)         ◁───

                                          Uses AUC as the
gbm.fit(Xtrn, ytrn,                       validation scoring metric
        eval_set=[(Xval, yval)], eval_metric='auc')  ◁─── for early stopping
```

Let's look at the output produced by LightGBM. In listing 5.6, we set n_estimators=50, which means training will add one base estimator per iteration:

```
Training until validation scores don't improve for 5 rounds
[1]  valid_0's auc: 0.885522      valid_0's binary_logloss: 0.602321
[2]  valid_0's auc: 0.961022      valid_0's binary_logloss: 0.542925
...
[27] valid_0's auc: 0.996069      valid_0's binary_logloss: 0.156152
[28] valid_0's auc: 0.996069      valid_0's binary_logloss: 0.153942
[29] valid_0's auc: 0.996069      valid_0's binary_logloss: 0.15031
[30] valid_0's auc: 0.996069      valid_0's binary_logloss: 0.145113
[31] valid_0's auc: 0.995742      valid_0's binary_logloss: 0.143901
[32] valid_0's auc: 0.996069      valid_0's binary_logloss: 0.139801
Early stopping, best iteration is:
[27] valid_0's auc: 0.996069      valid_0's binary_logloss: 0.156152
```

First, observe that training terminates after 32 iterations, meaning that LightGBM did indeed terminate before going all the way to training a full set of 50 base estimators. Next, note that the best iteration was 27, which had a score (in this case, AUC) of 0.996069.

Over the next 5 (early_stopping_rounds) iterations, from 28 to 32, LightGBM observed that adding additional estimators didn't improve the validation score significantly. This triggers the early stopping criterion, causing LightGBM to terminate and return an ensemble with 32 base estimators.

> **NOTE**   In its output, LightGBM reports two metrics: AUC, which we specified as the evaluation metric, and binary logistic loss, which is its default evaluation metric. Since we specified early stopping with respect to AUC, the algorithm terminates even though the binary logistic loss keeps decreasing. Put another way, if we'd used binary logistic loss as our evaluation metric, early stopping would not have terminated this early and would've kept going. In practical situations, such metrics are often task dependent and should be chosen carefully with the downstream application in mind.

We also visualize the training and validation errors as well as the ensemble size for different choices of `early_stopping_rounds`.

Small values of `early_stopping_rounds` make LightGBM very "impatient" and aggressive in that it doesn't wait too long to see if there is any improvement before stopping learning early. This leads to underfitting; in figure 5.20, for instance, setting `early_stopping_rounds` to 1 leads to an ensemble of just five base estimators, hardly enough to even fit the training data properly!

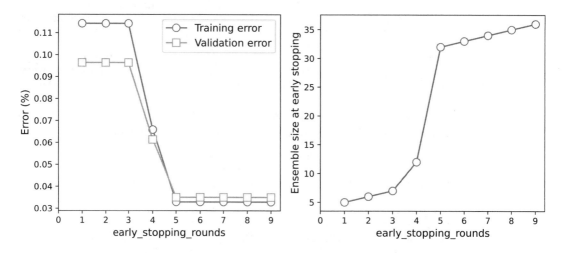

Figure 5.20   Left: Training and validation errors for different values of `early_stopping_rounds`. Right: Ensemble sizes for different values of `early_stopping_rounds`.

Large values of `early_stopping_rounds` make LightGBM too passive in that it waits for longer periods to see if there is any improvement. The choice of `early_stopping_rounds` ultimately depends on your problem: how big it is, what your performance metric is, and the complexity of the models you're willing to tolerate.

5.4.3   *Custom loss functions*

Recall that one of the most powerful features of gradient boosting is that it's applicable to a wide variety of loss functions. This means that it's also possible for us to design our own, problem-specific loss functions to handle specific properties of our data set and task. Perhaps our data set is imbalanced, meaning that different classes have different amounts of data. In such situations, rather than high accuracy, we might require high recall (fewer false negatives, e.g., in medical diagnoses) or high precision (fewer false positives, e.g., in spam detection). In many such scenarios, it's often necessary to design our own problem-specific loss functions.

> **NOTE**   For more details on evaluation metrics such as precision and recall, as well metrics for other machine-learning tasks such as regression and ranking, see *Evaluating Machine Learning Models* by Alice Zheng (O'Reilly, 2015).

With gradient boosting generally, and LightGBM specifically, once we have a loss function, we can rapidly train and evaluate models that are targeted toward our problem. In this section, we'll explore how to use LightGBM for a custom loss function called the *focal loss*.

THE FOCAL LOSS

The focal loss was introduced for dense object detection, or the problem of object detection in a large number of densely packed windows in an image. Ultimately, such object-detection tasks come down to a foreground versus background classification problem, which is highly imbalanced as there are often many more windows with background than foreground objects of interest.

The focal loss, in general, was designed for and is well suited for classification problems with such class imbalances. It's a modification of the classic cross-entropy loss that puts more focus on harder-to-classify examples, while ignoring the easier examples.

More formally, recall that the standard cross-entropy loss between a true label and a predicted label can be computed as

$$L_{ce}\left(y_{true}, y_{pred}\right) = -y_{true}\log\left(p_{pred}\right) - (1 - y_{true})\log\left(1 - p_{pred}\right)$$

where p_{pred} is the probability of predicting class 1, that is, $prob(y_{pred} = 1) = p_{pred}$. Note that, for a binary classification problem, since the only other label is 0, the probability of negative prediction will be $prob(y_{pred} = 0) = 1 - p_{pred}$.

The focal loss introduces a *modulating factor* to each term in the cross-entropy loss:

$$L_{fo}\left(y_{true}, y_{pred}\right) = -y_{true}\log\left(p_{pred}\right) \cdot \left(1 - p_{pred}\right)^{\gamma} - (1 - y_{true})\log\left(1 - p_{pred}\right) \cdot \left(p_{pred}\right)^{\gamma}$$

The modulating factor suppresses the contribution of well-classified examples, forcing a learning algorithm to focus on poorly classified examples. The extent of this focus is determined by a user-controllable parameter, $\gamma > 0$. To see how modulation works, let's compare the cross-entropy loss with the focal loss with $\gamma = 2$:

- *Well-classified example*—Let's say the true label is $y_{true} = 1$ with high predicted label probability $p_{pred} = 0.95$. The cross-entropy loss is $L_{ce} = -1 \cdot \log 0.95 - 0 \cdot \log 0.05 = 0.0513$, while the focal loss is $L_{fo} = -1 \cdot \log 0.95 \cdot 0.05^2 - 0 \cdot \log 0.05 \cdot 0.95^2 = 0.0001$. The modulating factor in the focal loss, thus, down-weights the loss if an example is classified with high confidence.
- *Poorly classified example*—Let's say the true label is $y_{true} = 1$ with low predicted label probability $p_{pred} = 0.05$. The cross-entropy loss is $L_{ce} = -1 \cdot \log 0.05 - 0 \cdot \log 0.95 = 2.9957$, while the focal loss is $L_{fo} = -1 \cdot \log 0.05 \cdot 0.95^2 - 0 \cdot \log 0.95 \cdot 0.05^2 = 2.7036$. The modulating factor affects the loss for this example far less because it's classified with low confidence.

This effect can be seen in figure 5.21, where the focal loss is plotted for different values of γ. For bigger values of γ, well-classified examples (with high probability of $y = 1$) have lower losses, while poorly classified examples have higher losses.

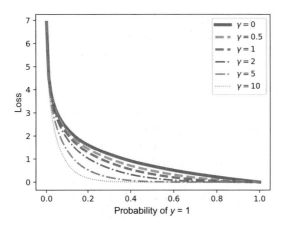

Figure 5.21 **The focal loss visualized for various values of** γ**. When** $\gamma = 0$**, the original cross-entropy loss is recovered. As** γ **increases, the part of the curve corresponding to well-classified examples becomes longer, reflecting the loss function's focus on poor classification.**

GRADIENT BOOSTING WITH THE FOCAL LOSS

To use the focal loss to train gradient boosted decision trees (GBDT), we have to provide LightGBM with two functions:

- The actual loss function itself, which will be used for function evaluations and scoring during learning
- The first derivative (gradient) and second derivative (Hessian) of the loss function, which will be used for learning the constituent base-estimator trees

LightGBM uses the Hessian information for learning at leaf nodes. For the moment, we can put this small detail aside, as we'll revisit it in the next chapter.

Listing 5.7 shows how we can define custom loss functions. The `focal_loss` function is the loss itself, implemented exactly as defined at the start of this subsection. The `focal_loss_metric` function turns `focal_loss` into a scoring metric for use with LightGBM.

The `focal_loss_objective` function returns the gradient and the Hessian of the loss function for LightGBM to use in tree learning. This function is rather unintuitively suffixed with "`objective`" to be consistent with LightGBM's usage, as will become apparent shortly.

Listing 5.7 Defining custom loss functions

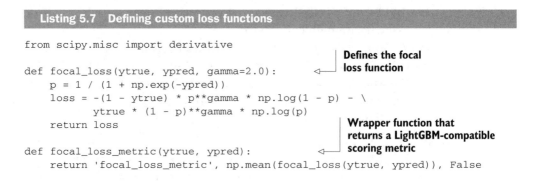

```
from scipy.misc import derivative

def focal_loss(ytrue, ypred, gamma=2.0):          ⟵┐ Defines the focal
    p = 1 / (1 + np.exp(-ypred))                        loss function
    loss = -(1 - ytrue) * p**gamma * np.log(1 - p) - \
           ytrue * (1 - p)**gamma * np.log(p)
    return loss                                   ┌─ Wrapper function that
                                                  │  returns a LightGBM-compatible
def focal_loss_metric(ytrue, ypred):          ⟵──┘  scoring metric
    return 'focal_loss_metric', np.mean(focal_loss(ytrue, ypred)), False
```

```
def focal_loss_objective(ytrue, ypred):
    func = lambda z: focal_loss(ytrue, z)
    grad = derivative(func, ypred, n=1, dx=1e-6)
    hess = derivative(func, ypred, n=2, dx=1e-6)
    return grad, hess
```

Autodifferentiation computes gradient and Hessian derivatives

Care must be taken to ensure that the loss function, metric, and objective are all vector-compatible; that is, they can take array-like objects `ytrue` and `ypred` as inputs. In listing 5.7, we've used `scipy`'s `derivative` functionality to approximate the first and second derivatives. It's also possible to analytically derive and implement the first and second derivatives for some loss functions. Once we've defined our custom loss function, it's straightforward to use it with LightGBM:

```
gbm_focal_loss = \
    LGBMClassifier(
        objective=focal_loss_objective,
        learning_rate=0.25, n_estimators=20,
        max_depth=1)
gbm_focal_loss.fit(Xtrn, ytrn,
                   eval_set=[(Xval, yval)],
                   eval_metric=focal_loss_metric)
```

Sets objective to ensure that LightGBM uses the gradients of the focal loss for learning

Sets metric to ensure that LightGBM uses the focal loss for evaluation

```
from scipy.special import expit
probs = expit(gbm_focal_loss.predict(Xval,
                            raw_score=True))

ypred = (probs > 0.5).astype(float)

accuracy_score(yval, ypred)
0.9649122807017544
```

Imports the sigmoid function from "scipy"

Gets raw scores and then computes the probability of class=1 using the sigmoid function

Converts to a 0/1 label, where the prediction is class=1 if probability > 0.5, and class=0 otherwise

GBDT with focal loss achieves a validation score of 96.5% on the breast cancer data set.

5.5   Case study: Document retrieval

Document retrieval is the task of retrieving documents from a database to match a user's query. For example, a paralegal at a law firm might need to search for information about previous cases from legal archives to establish precedent and research case law. Or perhaps a graduate student might need to search for articles from a journal's database during the course of a literature survey of work in a specific area. You may also have seen a feature called "related articles" on many websites that lists articles that may be related to the article you're currently reading. There are many such use cases for document retrieval in a wide range of domains, where a user searches for specific terms, and the system must return a list of documents relevant to the search.

This challenging problem has two key components: first, finding the documents that match the user's query, and second, ranking the documents according to some notion of relevance to the user. In this case study, the problem is set up as a three-class classification problem of identifying the relevance rank/class (least relevant, moderately relevant, or highly relevant) given a query-document pair. We'll explore the performance of different LightGBM classifiers for this task.

5.5.1   *The LETOR data set*

The data set we'll use for this case study is called LEarning TO Rank (LETOR) v4.0, which was itself created from a large corpus of web pages called GOV2. The GOV2 data set (http://mng.bz/41aD) is a collection of about 25 million web pages extracted from the .gov domain.

The LETOR 4.0 data collection (http://mng.bz/Q8DR) is derived from the GOV2 corpus and is made freely available by Microsoft Research. The collection contains several data sets, and we'll use the data set that was originally developed for the Million Query track of the 2008 Text Retrieval Conference (TREC), specifically, MQ2008.rar.

Each training example in the MQ2008 data set corresponds to a query-document *pair*. The data itself is in LIBSVM format, and several examples are shown in this section. Each row in the data set is a labeled training example in the format:

```
<relevance label> qid:<query id> 1:<feature 1 value> 2:<feature 2 value>
3:<feature 3 value> ... 46:<feature 46 value> # meta-information
```

Every example has 46 features extracted from a query-document pair, and a relevance label. The features include the following:

- Low-level content features extracted from the body, anchor, title, and URL. These include features commonly used in text mining such as term frequency, inverse document frequency, document length, and various combinations.
- High-level content features extracted from the body, anchor, and title. These features are extracted using two well-known retrieval systems: Okapi BM25 and language-model approaches for information retrieval (LMIR).
- Hyperlink features extracted from hyperlinks using several tools such as Google PageRank and variations.
- Hybrid features containing both content and hyperlink information.

The label for each query-document example is a relevance rank that takes three unique values: 0 (least relevant), 1 (moderately relevant), and 2 (highly relevant). In our case study, these are treated as class labels, making this an instance of a three-class classification problem. Following are some examples of the data:

```
0 qid:10032 1:0.130742 2:0.000000 3:0.333333 4:0.000000 5:0.134276 ...
45:0.750000 46:1.000000
#docid = GX140-98-13566007 inc = 1 prob = 0.0701303

1 qid:10032 1:0.593640 2:1.000000 3:0.000000 4:0.000000 5:0.600707 ...
45:0.500000 46:0.000000
#docid = GX256-43-0740276 inc = 0.0136292023050293 prob = 0.400738

2 qid:10032 1:0.056537 2:0.000000 3:0.666667 4:1.000000 5:0.067138 ...
45:0.000000 46:0.076923
#docid = GX029-35-5894638 inc = 0.0119881192468859 prob = 0.139842
```

Much more detail can be found in the documentation and references provided with the LETOR 4.0 data collection. A part of this data set that we'll use for the case study is available in the companion GitHub repository. We first load this data set and split into training and test sets:

```
from sklearn.datasets import load_svmlight_file
from sklearn.model_selection import train_test_split

query_data_file = './data/ch05/MQ2008/Querylevelnorm.txt'
X, y = load_svmlight_file(query_data_file)

Xtrn, Xtst, ytrn, ytst = train_test_split(X, y,
                                    test_size=0.2, random_state=42)

print(Xtrn.shape, Xtst.shape)
(12168, 46) (3043, 46)
```

We now have a training set with 12,000 examples and a test set with 3,000 examples.

5.5.2 Document retrieval with LightGBM

We'll learn four models using LightGBM. Each of these models represents a tradeoff between speed and accuracy:

- *Random forest*—Our now-familiar parallel homogeneous ensemble of randomized decision trees. This method will serve as a baseline approach.
- *Gradient boosted decision trees (GBDT)*—This is the standard approach to gradient boosting and represents a balance between models with good generalization performance and training speed.
- *Gradient-based One-Side Sampling (GOSS)*—This variant of gradient boosting downsamples the training data and is ideally suited for large data sets; due to downsampling, it may lose out on generalization, but is typically very fast to train.
- *Dropouts meet Multiple Additive Regression Trees (DART)*—This variant incorporates the notion of dropout from deep learning, where neural units are randomly and temporarily dropped during backpropagation iterations to mitigate overfitting. Similarly, DART randomly and temporarily drops base estimators from the overall ensemble during gradient-fitting iterations to mitigate overfitting. DART is often the slowest of all the gradient-boosting options available in LightGBM.

We'll train a model using each of these four approaches with the following learning hyperparameters. Specifically, observe that all the models are trained using the multiclass logistic loss, a generalization of the binary logistic loss function that is used in logistic regression. The number of `early_stopping_rounds` is set to 25:

```
fixed_params = {'early_stopping_rounds': 25,
                'eval_metric' : 'multi_logloss',
                'eval_set' : [(Xtst, ytst)],
                'eval_names': ['test set'],
                'verbose': 100}
```

Beyond these parameters that are common to all models, we'll also need to identify other model-wise hyperparameters such as learning rate (to control the rate of learning) or the number of leaf nodes (to control the complexity of the base estimator trees). These hyperparameters are selected using scikit-learn's randomized CV module: RandomizedSearchCV. Specifically, we perform 5-fold CV over a grid of various parameter choices; however, instead of exhaustively evaluating all possible learning-parameter combinations the way GridSearchCV does, RandomizedSearchCV samples a smaller number of model combinations for faster parameter selection:

```
num_random_iters = 20
num_cv_folds = 5
```

The following snippet is used to train random forests using LightGBM:

```
from scipy.stats import randint, uniform
from sklearn.model_selection import RandomizedSearchCV
import lightgbm as lgb

rf_params = {'bagging_fraction': [0.4, 0.5, 0.6, 0.7, 0.8],
             'bagging_freq': [5, 6, 7, 8],
             'num_leaves': randint(5, 50)}

ens = lgb.LGBMClassifier(boosting='rf', n_estimators=1000,
                         max_depth=-1,
                         random_state=42)
cv = RandomizedSearchCV(estimator=ens,
                        param_distributions=rf_params,
                        n_iter=num_random_iters,
                        cv=num_cv_folds,
                        refit=True,
                        random_state=42, verbose=True)
cv.fit(Xtrn, ytrn, **fixed_params)
```

Similarly, LightGBM is also trained with boosting='gbdt', boosting='goss', and boosting='dart' with code similar to the following:

```
gbdt_params = {'num_leaves': randint(5, 50),
               'learning_rate': [0.25, 0.5, 1, 2, 4, 8, 16],
               'min_child_samples': randint(100, 500),
               'min_child_weight': [1e-2, 1e-1, 1, 1e1, 1e2],
               'subsample': uniform(loc=0.2, scale=0.8),
               'colsample_bytree': uniform(loc=0.4, scale=0.6),
               'reg_alpha': [0, 1e-1, 1, 10, 100],
               'reg_lambda': [0, 1e-1, 1, 10, 100]}

ens = lgb.LGBMClassifier(boosting='gbdt', n_estimators=1000,
                         max_depth=-1,
                         random_state=42)
cv = RandomizedSearchCV(estimator=ens,
                        param_distributions=gbdt_params,
                        n_iter=num_random_iters,
                        cv=num_cv_folds,
                        refit=True,
                        random_state=42, verbose=True)

cv.fit(Xtrn, ytrn, **fixed_params)
```

The CV-based learning-parameter selection procedure explores several different values for the following parameters:

- `num_leaves`, which limits the number of leaf nodes and hence base-estimator complexity to control overfitting
- `min_child_samples` and `min_child_weight`, which limit each leaf node either by size or by the sum of Hessian values to control overfitting
- `subsample` and `colsample_bytree`, which specify the fractions of training examples and features to sample from the training data, respectively, to accelerate training
- `reg_alpha` and `reg_lambda`, which specify the amount of regularization of the leaf node values, to control overfitting as well
- `top_rate` and `other_rate`, the sampling rate for GOSS (specifically)
- `drop_rate`, the dropout rate for DART (specifically)

For each of these approaches, we're interested in looking at two performance measures: the test set accuracy and overall model development time, which includes parameter selection and training time. These are shown in figure 5.22. The key takeaways are as follows:

- GOSS and GBDT perform similarly, including overall modeling times. This difference will become much more pronounced for increasingly larger data sets, especially those with hundreds of thousands of training examples.
- DART achieves the best performance. However, this comes at the cost of significantly increased training time. Here, for instance, DART has a running time of close to 20 minutes, compared to 3 minutes for random forest and under 30 seconds for GBDT and GOSS.

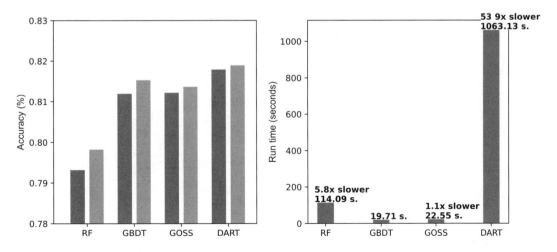

Figure 5.22 All algorithms trained using LightGBM. Left: Comparing test set accuracy of random forest, GBDT, GOSS, and DART; Right: Comparing the overall training times of random forest, GBDT, GOSS, and DART. GBDT is the fastest at 19.71 seconds and the other methods are slower as indicated, compared to GBDT.

- Note that LightGBM supports both multi-CPU as well as GPU processing, which may be able to significantly improve running times.

Summary

- Gradient descent is often used to minimize a loss function to train a machine-learning model.
- Residuals, or errors between the true labels and model predictions, can be used to characterize correctly classified and poorly classified training examples. This is analogous to how AdaBoost uses weights.
- Gradient boosting combines gradient descent and boosting to learn a sequential ensemble of weak learners.
- Weak learners in gradient boosting are regression trees that are trained over the residuals of the training examples and approximate the gradient.
- Gradient boosting can be applied to a wide variety of loss functions arising from classification, regression, or ranking tasks.
- Histogram-based tree learning trades off exactness for efficiency, allowing us to train gradient-boosting models very rapidly and scale up to larger data sets.
- Learning can be sped up even further by smartly sampling training examples (Gradient-based One-Side Sampling, GOSS) or smartly bundling features (Exclusive Feature Bundling, EFB).
- LightGBM is a powerful, publicly available framework for gradient boosting that incorporates both GOSS and EFB.
- As with AdaBoost, we can avoid overfitting in gradient boosting by choosing an effective learning rate or via early stopping. LightGBM provides support for both.
- In addition to a wide variety of loss functions for classification, regression, and ranking, LightGBM also provides support for incorporation of our own custom, problem-specific loss functions for training.

Sequential ensembles: Newton boosting

In the previous two chapters, we saw two approaches to constructing sequential ensembles: In chapter 4, we introduced a new ensemble method called adaptive boosting (AdaBoost), which uses weights to identify the most misclassified examples. In chapter 5, we introduced another ensemble method called gradient boosting, which uses gradients (residuals) to identify the most misclassified examples. The fundamental intuition behind both of these boosting methods is to target the most misclassified (essentially, the worst behaving) examples at every iteration to improve classification.

In this chapter, we introduce a third boosting approach—Newton boosting—which combines the advantages of both AdaBoost and gradient boosting and uses *weighted gradients* (or weighted residuals) to identify the most misclassified examples. As with gradient boosting, the framework of Newton boosting can be applied to any loss function, which means that any classification, regression, or ranking problem can be boosted using weak learners. In addition to this flexibility, packages such as XGBoost are now available that can scale Newton boosting to big data through parallelization. Unsurprisingly, Newton boosting is currently considered by many practitioners to be a state-of-the-art ensemble approach.

Because Newton boosting builds on Newton's descent, we kick off the chapter with examples of Newton's descent and how it can be used to train a machine-learning model (section 6.1). Section 6.2 aims to provide intuition for learning with weighted residuals, the key intuition behind Newton boosting. As always, we implement our own version of Newton boosting to understand how it combines gradient descent and boosting to train a sequential ensemble.

Section 6.3 introduces XGBoost, a free and open source gradient-boosting and Newton-boosting package, which is widely used for building and deploying real-world machine-learning applications. In section 6.4, we see how we can avoid overfitting with strategies such as early stopping and adapting the learning rate with XGBoost. Finally, in section 6.5, we'll reuse the real-world study of document retrieval from chapter 5 to compare the performance of XGBoost to LightGBM, its variants, and random forests.

The origins and motivation for devising Newton boosting are analogous to those of the gradient-boosting algorithm: the optimization of loss functions. Gradient descent, which gradient boosting is based on, is a first-order optimization method in that it uses first derivatives during optimization.

Newton's method, or Newton's descent, is a second-order optimization method, in that it uses both first and second-derivative information together to compute a Newton step. When combined with boosting, we obtain the ensemble method of Newton boosting. We begin this chapter by discussing how Newton's method inspires a powerful and widely used ensemble method.

6.1   *Newton's method for minimization*

Iterative optimization methods such as gradient descent and Newton's method perform an update within each iteration: next = current + (step × direction). In gradient descent (figure 6.1, left), first-derivative information only allows us to construct a local linear approximation at best. While this gives us a descent direction, different step lengths can give us vastly different estimates and may ultimately slow down convergence.

Incorporating second-derivative information, as Newton's descent does, allows us to construct a local quadratic approximation! This extra information leads to a better local approximation, resulting in better steps and faster convergence.

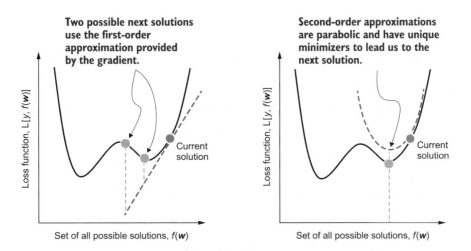

Figure 6.1 Comparing gradient descent (left) and Newton's method (right). Gradient descent only uses local first-order information near the current solution, which leads to a linear approximation of the function being optimized. Different step lengths will then lead to different next steps. Newton's method uses both local first- and second-order information near the current solution, leading to a quadratic (parabolic) approximation of the function being optimized. This provides a better estimate of the next step.

NOTE The approach described in this chapter, Newton's method for optimization, is derived from a more general root-finding method, also called Newton's method. We'll often use the term Newton's descent to refer to Newton's method for minimization.

More formally, gradient descent computes the next update as

$$w_{t+1} = w_t + \alpha_t \cdot \left(-f'(w_t)\right)$$

where α_t is the step length, and $(-f'(w_t))$ is the negative gradient, or the negative of the first derivative. Newton's method computes the next update as

$$w_{t+1} = w_t + \alpha_t \cdot \left(-\frac{f'(w_t)}{f''(w_t)}\right)$$

where $f''(w_t)$ is the second derivative, and the step length α_t is 1.

NOTE Unlike gradient descent, Newton's descent computes exact steps and doesn't require a step-length computation. However, we'll explicitly include the step length for two reasons: (1) to enable us to immediately compare and understand the differences between gradient descent and Newton's descent; and (2) more importantly, unlike Newton's descent, Newton boosting can only approximate the step and will require us to specify a step length similar to gradient descent and gradient boosting. As we'll see, this step length in Newton boosting is nothing more than the learning rate.

THE SECOND DERIVATIVE AND THE HESSIAN MATRIX

For univariate functions (i.e., functions in one variable), the second derivative is easy to compute: we simply differentiate the function twice. For instance, for the function $f(w) = x^5$, the first derivative is $f'(x) = \frac{\partial f}{\partial x} = 5x^4$, and the second derivative is $f''(x) = \frac{\partial f}{\partial x \partial y} = 20x^3$.

For multivariate functions, or functions in many variables, the calculation of the second derivative is a little more involved. This is because we now have to consider differentiating the multivariate function with respect to pairs of variables.

To see this, consider a function in three variables: $f(x,y,z)$. The gradient of this function is straightforward to compute: we differentiate the function with respect to each of the variables x, y, and z (where w.r.t. is "with respect to"):

$$\nabla f = \begin{bmatrix} \text{derivative of } f \text{ w.r.t. } x \\ \text{derivative of } f \text{ w.r.t. } y \\ \text{derivative of } f \text{ w.r.t. } z \end{bmatrix} = \begin{bmatrix} \frac{\partial f}{\partial x} \\ \frac{\partial f}{\partial y} \\ \frac{\partial f}{\partial z} \end{bmatrix}$$

To compute the second derivative, we have to further differentiate each entry of the gradient with respect to x, y, and z again. This produces a matrix known as the Hessian:

$$\nabla^2 f = \begin{bmatrix} \text{deriv. of } \frac{\partial f}{\partial x} \text{ w.r.t. } x & \text{deriv. of } \frac{\partial f}{\partial x} \text{ w.r.t. } y & \text{deriv. of } \frac{\partial f}{\partial x} \text{ w.r.t. } z \\ \text{deriv. of } \frac{\partial f}{\partial y} \text{ w.r.t. } x & \text{deriv. of } \frac{\partial f}{\partial y} \text{ w.r.t. } y & \text{deriv. of } \frac{\partial f}{\partial y} \text{ w.r.t. } z \\ \text{deriv. of } \frac{\partial f}{\partial z} \text{ w.r.t. } x & \text{deriv. of } \frac{\partial f}{\partial z} \text{ w.r.t. } y & \text{deriv. of } \frac{\partial f}{\partial z} \text{ w.r.t. } z \end{bmatrix}$$

$$= \begin{bmatrix} \frac{\partial}{\partial x}\left(\frac{\partial f}{\partial x}\right) & \frac{\partial}{\partial x}\left(\frac{\partial f}{\partial y}\right) & \frac{\partial}{\partial x}\left(\frac{\partial f}{\partial z}\right) \\ \frac{\partial}{\partial y}\left(\frac{\partial f}{\partial x}\right) & \frac{\partial}{\partial y}\left(\frac{\partial f}{\partial y}\right) & \frac{\partial}{\partial y}\left(\frac{\partial f}{\partial z}\right) \\ \frac{\partial}{\partial z}\left(\frac{\partial f}{\partial x}\right) & \frac{\partial}{\partial z}\left(\frac{\partial f}{\partial y}\right) & \frac{\partial}{\partial z}\left(\frac{\partial f}{\partial z}\right) \end{bmatrix}$$

The Hessian is a symmetric matrix because the order of differentiation doesn't change the result, meaning that

$$\frac{\partial}{\partial x}\left(\frac{\partial f}{\partial y}\right) = \frac{\partial}{\partial y}\left(\frac{\partial f}{\partial x}\right)$$

and so on, for all pairs of variables in f. In the multivariate case, the extension of Newton's method is given by

$$w_{t+1} = w_t + \alpha_t \cdot \left(-\nabla^2 f(w_t)^{-1} \nabla f(w_t)\right)$$

where $\nabla f(w_t)$ is the gradient vector of the multivariate function f, and $-\nabla^2(w_t)^{-1}$ is the inverse of the Hessian matrix. Inverting the second-derivative Hessian matrix is the multivariate equivalent of dividing by the term $f''(w_t)$.

For large problems with many variables, inverting the Hessian matrix can become quite computationally expensive, slowing down overall optimization. As we'll see in section 6.2, Newton boosting circumvents this problem by computing second derivatives for individual examples to avoid inverting the Hessian.

For now, let's continue to explore the differences between gradient descent and Newton's method. We return to the two examples we used in section 5.1: the simple illustrative Branin function and the squared-loss function. We'll use these examples to illustrate the differences between gradient descent and Newton's descent.

6.1.1 Newton's method with an illustrative example

Recall from chapter 5 that the Branin function comprises two variables (w_1 and w_2), defined as

$$f(w_1, w_2) = a \left(w_2 - bw_1^2 + cw_1 - r \right)^2 + s(1 - t)\cos(w_1) + s$$

where $\alpha = 1$, $b = \frac{5.1}{4\pi^2}$, $c = \frac{5}{\pi}$, $r = 6$, $s = 10$, and $t = \frac{1}{8\pi}$ are fixed constants. This function is shown in figure 6.2 and has four minimizers at the centers of the elliptical regions.

We'll take our gradient descent implementation from the previous section and modify it to implement Newton's method. There are two key differences: (1) we compute the descent direction using the gradient and the Hessian, that is, using both the first- and second-derivative information; and (2) we drop the computation of the step

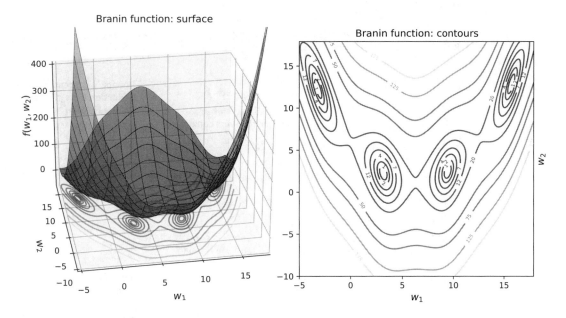

Figure 6.2 The surface plot (left) and contour plot (right) of the Branin function. We can visually verify that this function has four minima, which are the centers of the elliptical regions in the contour plot.

length, that is, we assume that the step length is 1. The modified pseudocode is shown here:

```
initialize: w_old = some initial guess, converged=False
while not converged:
1. compute the gradient vector g and Hessian matrix H at the current
   estimate, w_old
2. compute the descent direction d = -H⁻¹g
3. set step length α = 1
4. update the solution: c + distance * direction = w_old + α · d
5. if change between w_new and w_old is below some specified tolerance:
   converged=True, so break
6. w_new = w_old, get ready for the next iteration
```

The key steps in this pseudocode are steps 1 and 2, where the descent direction is computed using the inverse Hessian matrix (second derivatives) and the gradient (first derivatives). Note that, as with gradient descent, the Newton's descent direction is negated.

Step 3 is included to explicitly illustrate that, unlike gradient descent, Newton's method doesn't require the computation of a step length. Instead, the step length can be set ahead of time, much like a learning rate. Once the descent direction is identified, step 4 implements the Newton update: $w_{t+1} = w_t + \left(-\nabla^2 f(w_t)^{-1} \nabla f(w_t)\right)$.

After we compute each update, similar to gradient descent, we check for convergence; here, our convergence test is to see how close w_{t+1} and w_t are to each other. If they are close enough, we terminate; if not, we continue on to the next iteration. The following listing implements Newton's method.

Listing 6.1 Newton's descent

```python
import numpy as np
def newton_descent(f, g, h,                          ◁── Newton's descent requires
                   x_init, max_iter=100, args=()):       a function f, its gradient g,
    converged = False         ◁──┐ Initializes Newton's   and its Hessian h.
    n_iter = 0                    │ descent to not converged

    x_old, x_new = np.array(x_init), None
    descent_path = np.full((max_iter + 1, 2), fill_value=np.nan)
    descent_path[n_iter] = x_old

    while not converged:
        n_iter += 1

        gradient = g(x_old, *args)     │ Computes the gradient
        hessian = h(x_old, *args)      │ and the Hessian

        direction = -np.dot(np.linalg.inv(hessian),    │ Computes the
                            gradient)                   │ Newton direction

        distance = 1                              ◁──┐ Sets step length
        x_new = x_old + distance * direction          │ to 1, for simplicity
        descent_path[n_iter] = x_new
```

Computes the update ──▷

```
                   err = np.linalg.norm(x_new - x_old)
                   if err <= 1e-3 or n_iter >= max_iter:
                       converged = True

                   x_old = x_new

               return x_new, descent_path
```

Computes change from previous iteration

Converges if change is small or maximum iterations are reached

Gets ready for the next iteration

Note that the step length is set to 1, although for Newton boosting, as we'll see, the step length will become the learning rate.

Let's take our implementation of Newton's descent for a spin. We've already implemented the Branin function and its gradient in the previous section. This implementation is shown here again:

```
def branin(w, a, b, c, r, s, t):
    return a * (w[1] - b * w[0] ** 2 + c * w[0] - r) ** 2 + \
           s * (1 - t) * np.cos(w[0]) + s

def branin_gradient(w, a, b, c, r, s, t):
    return np.array([2 * a * (w[1] - b * w[0] ** 2 + c * w[0] - r) *
                     (-2 * b * w[0] + c) - s * (1 - t) * np.sin(w[0]),
                     2 * a * (w[1] - b * w[0] ** 2 + c * w[0] - r)])
```

We also need the Hessian (second derivative) matrix for Newton's descent. We can compute it by analytically differentiating the gradient (first derivative) vector:

$$H(w_1, w_2) = \begin{bmatrix} \frac{\partial}{\partial w_1}\left(\frac{\partial f}{\partial w_1}\right) & \frac{\partial}{\partial w_2}\left(\frac{\partial f}{\partial w_1}\right) \\ \frac{\partial}{\partial w_1}\left(\frac{\partial f}{\partial w_2}\right) & \frac{\partial}{\partial w_2}\left(\frac{\partial f}{\partial w_2}\right) \end{bmatrix}$$

$$= \begin{bmatrix} 2a(-2bw_1 + c)^2 - 4ab(w_2 - bw_1^2 + cw_1 - r) - s(1-t)\cos w_1 & 2a\left(-2bw_1 + c\right) \\ 2a(-2bw_1 + c) & 2a \end{bmatrix}$$

This can also be implemented as shown here:

```
def branin_hessian(w, a, b, c, r, s, t):
    return np.array([[2 * a * (- 2 * b * w[0] + c)** 2 -
                      4 * a * b * (w[1] - b * w[0] ** 2 + c * w[0] - r) -
                      s * (1 - t) * np.cos(w[0]),
                      2 * a * (- 2 * b * w[0] + c)],
                     [2 * a * (- 2 * b * w[0] + c),
                      2 * a]])
```

As with gradient descent, Newton's descent (refer to listing 6.1) also requires an initial guess x_init. Here, we'll initialize gradient descent with $w_{init} = [2,-5]'$. Now, we can call the Newton's descent procedure:

```
a, b, c, r, s, t = 1, 5.1/(4 * np.pi**2), 5/np.pi, 6, 10, 1/(8 * np.pi)
w_init = np.array([2, -5])
w_optimal, w_newton_path = newton_descent(branin, branin_gradient,
                                          branin_hessian,
                                          w_init, args=(a, b, c, r, s, t))
```

Newton's descent returns an optimal solution w_optimal (which is [3.142, 2.275]') and the solution path w_path. So how does Newton's descent compare to gradient descent? In figure 6.3, we plot the solution paths of both optimization algorithms together.

The result of this comparison is pretty striking: Newton's descent is able to exploit the additional local information about the curvature of the function provided by the Hessian matrix to take a more direct path to the solution. In contrast, gradient descent only has the first-order gradient information to work with and takes a round-about path to the same solution.

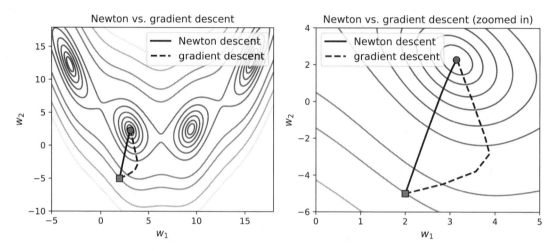

Figure 6.3 We compare the solution paths of Newton's descent and gradient descent starting from [2,–5] (square) and both converging to one of the local minima (circle). Newton's descent (solid line) progresses toward the local minimum in a more direct way compared to gradient descent (dotted line). This is because Newton's descent uses a more informative second-order local approximation with each update, while gradient descent only uses a first-order local approximation.

PROPERTIES OF NEWTON'S DESCENT

We note a couple of important things about Newton's descent and its similarities to gradient descent. First, unlike gradient descent, Newton's method computes the descent step exactly and doesn't require a step length. Keep in mind that our purpose is to extend Newton's descent to Newton boosting. From this perspective, the step length can be interpreted as a learning rate.

Choosing an effective learning rate (say, using cross validation like we did for Ada-Boost or gradient boosting) is very much akin to choosing a good step length. Instead of selecting a learning rate to accelerate convergence, in boosting algorithms, we select the learning rate to help us avoid overfitting and to generalize better to the test set and future data.

A second important point to keep in mind is that, like gradient descent, Newton's descent is also sensitive to our choice of initial point. Different initializations will lead Newton's descent to different local minimizers.

In addition to local minimizers, a bigger problem is that our choice of initial point can also lead Newton's descent to converge to *saddle points*. This is a problem faced by all descent algorithms and is illustrated in figure 6.4.

A saddle point mimics a local minimizer: at both locations, the gradient of the function becomes zero. However, saddle points aren't true local minimizers: the saddle-like shape means that it's curving upwards in one direction and curving downwards in another. This is in contrast to local minimizers, which are bowl-shaped. However, both local minimizers and saddle points have zero gradients. This means that descent algorithms can't distinguish between the two and sometimes converge to saddle points instead of minimizers.

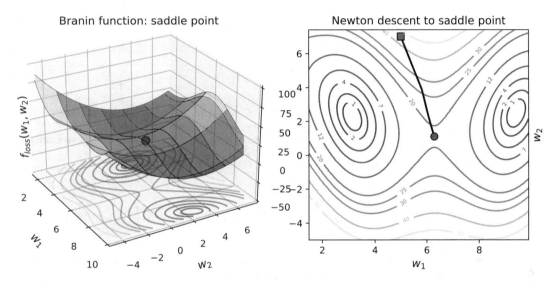

Figure 6.4   A saddle point of the Branin function lies between two minimizers and, like the minimizers, it has a zero gradient at its location. This causes all descent methods to converge to saddle points.

The existence of saddle points and local minimizers depends on the functions being optimized, of course. For our purposes, most common loss functions are convex and "well shaped," meaning that we can safely use Newton's descent and Newton boosting. Care should be taken, however, to ensure convexity when creating and using custom loss functions. Handling such non-convex loss functions is an active and ongoing research area.

6.1.2   Newton's descent over loss functions for training

So how does Newton's descent fare on a machine-learning task? To see this, we can revisit the simple 2D classification problem from chapter 5, section 5.1.2, on which we've previously trained a model using gradient descent. The task is a binary classification problem, with data generated as shown here:

```
from sklearn.datasets import make_blobs
X, y = make_blobs(n_samples=200, n_features=2,
                  centers=[[-1.5, -1.5], [1.5, 1.5]])
```

We visualize this synthetic data set in figure 6.5.

Recall that we want to train a linear classifier $h_w(x) = w_1 x_1 + w_2 x_2$. This classifier takes 2D data points $x = [x_1, x_2]'$ and returns a prediction. As in chapter 5, section 5.1.2, we'll use the squared loss function for this task.

The linear classifier is parameterized by weights $w = [w_1, w_2]'$. The weights, of course, have to be learned such that they minimize some loss over the data to achieve the best training fit.

The squared loss measures the error between true labels y_i and their corresponding predictions $h_w(x_i)$ as shown here:

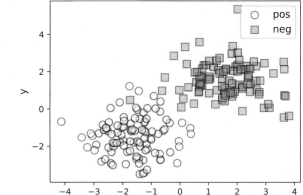

Figure 6.5   A (nearly) linearly separable two-class data set over which we'll train a classifier. The positive examples have labels y = 1, and the negative examples have labels y = 0.

$$f_{\text{loss}}(w) = \frac{1}{2} \sum_{i=1}^{n} (y_i - h_w(x_i))^2 = \frac{1}{2} \sum_{i=1}^{n} \left(y_i - w_1 x_1^i - w_2 x_2^i\right)^2 = \frac{1}{2} (y - Xw)' (y - Xw)$$

Here, X is an $n \times d$ data matrix of n training examples with d features each, and y is a $d \times 1$ vector of true labels. The expression on the far right is a compact way of representing the loss over the entire data set using vector and matrix notation.

For Newton's descent, we'll need the gradient and Hessian of this loss function. These can be obtained by differentiating the loss function analytically, just as with the Branin function. In vector-matrix notation, these can also be compactly written as

$$g(w) = -X'(y - Xw),$$

$$He(w) = X'X.$$

Note that the Hessian is a 2×2 matrix. The implementations of the loss function, its gradient, and Hessian are as follows:

```
def squared_loss(w, X, y):
    return 0.5 * np.sum((y - np.dot(X, w))**2)

def squared_loss_gradient(w, X, y):
    return -np.dot(X.T, (y - np.dot(X, w)))

def squared_loss_hessian(w, X, y):
    return np.dot(X.T, X)
```

Now that we have all the components of the loss function, we can use Newton's descent to compute an optimal solution, that is, "learn a model." We can compare the model learned by Newton's descent to the one learned by gradient descent (which we implemented in chapter 5). We initialize both gradient descent and Newton's descent with $w = [0,0,0.99]'$:

```
w_init = np.array([0.0, -0.99])
w_gradient, path_gradient = gradient_descent(squared_loss,
                                             squared_loss_gradient,
                                             w_init, args=(X, y))
w_newton, path_newton = newton_descent(squared_loss,
                                       squared_loss_gradient,
                                       squared_loss_hessian,
                                       w_init, args=(X, y))
print(w_gradient)
[0.13643511 0.13862275]

print(w_newton)
[0.13528094 0.13884772]
```

The squared loss function we're optimizing is convex and has only one minimizer. Both gradient descent and Newton's descent essentially learn the same model, though they terminate as soon as they reach the threshold 10^{-3}, roughly the third decimal place. We can easily verify that this learned model achieves a training accuracy of 99.5%:

```
ypred = (np.dot(X, w_newton) >= 0).astype(int)
from sklearn.metrics import accuracy_score
accuracy_score(y, ypred)
0.995
```

While both gradient descent and Newton's descent learn the same model, they arrive there in decidedly different ways, as figure 6.6 illustrates.

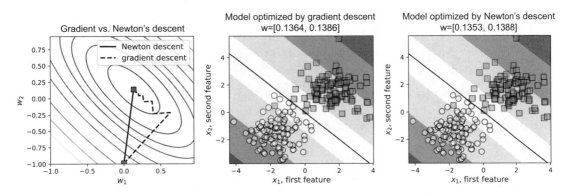

Figure 6.6 The solution paths of Newton's descent (solid line) versus gradient descent (dotted line) as well as the models produced by Newton's and gradient descent. Gradient descent takes 20 iterations to learn this model, while Newton's descent takes 12 iterations.

The key takeaway is that Newton's descent is a powerful optimization method in the family of descent methods. It converges to solutions much faster because it takes local second-order derivative information (essentially curvature) into account in constructing descent directions.

This additional information about the shape of the objective (or loss) function being optimized greatly aids convergence. This comes at a computational cost, however: with more variables, the second derivative, or the Hessian, which holds the second-order information, becomes increasingly difficult to manage, especially as it has to be inverted.

As we'll see in the next section, Newton boosting avoids computing or inverting the entire Hessian matrix by using an approximation with *pointwise second derivatives*, essentially second derivatives computed and inverted per training example, which keeps training efficient.

6.2   *Newton boosting: Newton's method + boosting*

We begin our deep dive into Newton boosting by gaining an intuitive understanding of how Newton boosting differs from gradient boosting. We'll compare the two methods side by side to see exactly what Newton boosting adds to each iteration.

6.2.1   *Intuition: Learning with weighted residuals*

As with other boosting methods, Newton boosting learns a new weak estimator every iteration such that it fixes the misclassifications or errors made by the previous iteration. AdaBoost identifies and characterizes misclassified examples that need attention by assigning *weights* to them: badly misclassified examples are assigned higher weights. A weak classifier trained on such weighted examples will focus on them more during learning.

Gradient boosting characterizes misclassified examples that need attention through *residuals*. A residual is simply another means to measure the extent of misclassification and is computed as the gradient of the loss function.

Newton boosting does both and uses *weighted residuals*! The residuals in Newton boosting are computed in exactly the same way as in gradient boosting: using the gradient of the loss function (the first derivative). The weights, on the other hand, are computed using the Hessian of the loss function (the second derivative).

NEWTON BOOSTING IS NEWTON'S DESCENT + BOOSTING

As we saw in chapter 5, each gradient-boosting iteration mimics gradient descent. At iteration t, gradient descent updates the model f_t using the gradient of the loss function ($\nabla L(f_t) = g_t$):

$$f_{t+1} = f_t - \alpha_t \cdot \nabla L(f_t) = f_t - \alpha_t \cdot g_t$$

Rather than compute the overall gradient directly, g_t, gradient boosting learns a weak estimator (h_t^{GB}) over the individual gradients, which are also residuals. That is, a weak estimator is trained over the data and corresponding residuals $(x_i, -g_t(x_i))_{i=1}^n$. The model is then updated as follows:

$$f_{t+1} = f_t + \alpha_t \cdot h_t^{GB}$$

Similarly, Newton boosting mimics Newton's descent. At iteration t, Newton's descent updates the model f_t using the gradient of the loss function ($\nabla L(f_t) = g_t$) (exactly as with the earlier gradient descent) and the Hessian of the loss function ($\nabla^2 L(f_t) = He_t$):

$$f_{t+1} = f_t - \alpha_t \cdot \nabla^2 L (f_t)^{-1} \cdot \nabla L (f_t) = f_t - \alpha_t \cdot He_t^{-1} g_t$$

Computing the Hessian can often be very computationally expensive. Newton boosting avoids the expense of computing the gradient or the Hessian by learning a weak estimator over the individual gradients and Hessians.

For each training example, in addition to the gradient residual, we have to incorporate the Hessian information as well, all the while ensuring that the overall weak estimator that we want to train approximates Newton's descent. How do we do this?

Observe that the Hessian matrix is inverted in the Newton update (He_t^{-1}). For a single training example, the second (functional) derivative will be a scalar (a single number instead of a matrix). This means that the term $He_t^{-1} g_t$ becomes $\frac{g_t(x_i)}{He_t(x_i)}$; these are simply the residuals $g_t(x_i)$ weighted by the Hessians $\frac{g_t(x_i)}{He_t(x_i)}$.

Thus, for Newton boosting, we train a weak estimator (h_t^{NB}) using Hessian-weighted gradient residuals, that is, $\left(x_i, -\frac{g_t(x_i)}{He_t(x_i)}\right)_{i=1}^n$, and, voilà, we can update our ensemble in exactly the same way as gradient boosting:

$$f_{t+1} = f_t + \alpha_t \cdot h_t^{NB}$$

In summary, Newton boosting uses Hessian-weighted residuals, while gradient boosting uses unweighted residuals.

WHAT DO THE HESSIANS ADD?

So, what kind of additional information do these Hessian-based weights add to boosting? Mathematically, Hessians, or second derivatives, correspond to the curvature or how "curvy" a function is. In Newton boosting, we weight gradients by second-derivative information for each training example x_i:

$$\frac{g_t(x_i)}{He_t(x_i)}$$

A large value of the second derivative $He_t(x_i)$ implies that the curvature of the function is large at x_i. At these curvy regions, the Hessian weight decreases the gradient, which, in turn, leads Newton boosting to take smaller, more conservative steps.

Conversely, if the second derivative $He_t(x_i)$ is small, then the curvature at x_i is small, meaning that the function is rather flat. In such situations, the Hessian weight allows Newton's descent to take large, bolder steps so it can traverse the flat area faster.

Thus, second derivatives combined with first-derivative residuals can capture the notion of "misclassification" very effectively. Let's see this in action over a commonly used loss function—the logistic loss—which measures the extent of the misclassification:

$$L(y, f(x)) = \log\left(1 + e^{-y \cdot f(x)}\right)$$

The logistic loss is compared to the squared loss function in figure 6.7 (left).

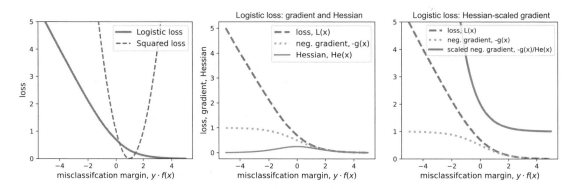

Figure 6.7   Left: Logistic loss versus squared loss function; Center: Negative gradient and Hessian of the logistic loss; Right: Hessian-scaled negative gradient of the logistic loss

In figure 6.7 (center), we look at the logistic loss function and its corresponding gradient (first derivative) and Hessian (second derivative). All of these are functions of the misclassification margin: the product of the true label (y) and the prediction ($f(x)$). If y and $f(x)$ have opposite signs, then we have $y \cdot f(x) < 0$. In this case, the true label doesn't match the predicted label, and we have a misclassification. Thus, the left part of the logistic loss curve (with negative margins) corresponds to misclassified examples and measures the extent of the misclassification. Similarly, the right part of the logistic loss (with positive margins) corresponds to correctly classified examples, whose loss is nearly 0, as we expect.

The second derivative achieves its highest values around 0, which corresponds to the elbow of the logistic loss function. This isn't surprising because we can see that the logistic loss function is curviest around the elbow and flat to the left and right of the elbow.

In figure 6.7 (right), we can see the effect of weighting the gradients. For well-classified examples ($y \cdot f(x) > 0$), the overall gradient as well as the weighted gradient are 0. This means that these examples won't participate in the boosting iteration.

On the other hand, for misclassified examples ($y \cdot f(x) < 0$), the overall weighed gradient $\frac{g(x_i)}{He(x_i)}$ increases steeply with misclassification. In general, it increases far more steeply than the unweighted gradient.

Now, we can answer the question of what the Hessians do: they incorporate local curvature information to ensure that badly misclassified training examples get higher weights. This is illustrated in figure 6.8.

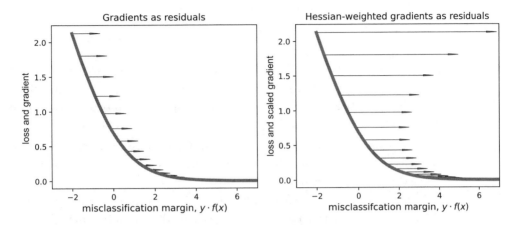

Figure 6.8 **Unweighted residuals (left) used by gradient boosting compared to Hessian-weighted residuals (right) used by Newton boosting. Positive values of misclassification margin ($y \cdot f(x) > 0$) indicate correct classification. For misclassifications, we have $y \cdot f(x) < 0$. For badly misclassified examples, the Hessian-weighted gradients capture that notion more effectively than unweighted gradients.**

The more badly misclassified a training example is, the further to the left it will be in figure 6.8. Hessian weighting of residuals ensures that training examples further to the left will get higher weights. This is in sharp contrast to gradient boosting, which is unable to differentiate training examples as effectively because it only uses unweighted residuals.

To summarize, Newton boosting aims to use both first-derivative (gradient) information and second-derivative (Hessian) information to ensure that misclassified training examples receive focus based on the extent of the misclassification.

6.2.2 *Intuition: Learning with regularized loss functions*

Before proceeding, let's introduce the notion of *regularized loss functions*. A regularized loss function contains an additional smoothing term along with the loss function, making it more convex, or bowl-like.

Regularizing a loss function introduces additional structure to the learning problem, which often stabilizes and accelerates the resulting learning algorithms. Regularization also allows us to control the complexity of the model being learned and improves the overall robustness and generalization capabilities of the model.

Essentially, a regularized loss function explicitly captures the fit versus complexity tradeoff inherent in most machine-learning models (see chapter 1, section 1.3).

A regularized loss function is of the following form:

$$\alpha \cdot \underbrace{\text{regularization}(f(x))}_{\textbf{measures model complexity}} + \overbrace{\text{loss}(f(x), \text{data})}^{\textbf{measures model fit}}$$

The regularization term measures the flatness (the opposite of "curviness") of the model: the more it's minimized, the less complex the learned model is.

The loss term measures the fit to the training data through a loss function: the more it's minimized, the better the fit to the training data. The regularization parameter α trades off between these two competing objectives (in section 1.3, this tradeoff was achieved by the parameter C, which is essentially the inverse of α):

- A large value of α means the model will focus more on regularization and simplicity and less on training error, which causes the model to have higher training error and underfit.
- A small value of α means the model will focus more on training errors and learn more complex models, which causes the model to have lower training errors and possibly overfit.

Thus, a regularized loss function allows us to trade off between fit and complexity during learning, ultimately leading to models that generalize well in practice.

As we saw in chapter 1, section 1.3, there are several ways to introduce regularization and control model complexity during learning. For example, limiting the maximum depth of trees or the number of nodes prevents trees from overfitting.

Another common approach is through L2 regularization, which amounts to introducing a penalty over the model directly. That is, if we have a model $f(x)$, L2 regularization introduces a penalty over model by $f(x)^2$:

$$\alpha \cdot \underbrace{f(x)^2}_{\textbf{penalizes model complexity}} + \overbrace{\text{loss}(f(x), \text{data})}^{\textbf{measures model fit}}$$

The loss functions of many common machine-learning approaches can be expressed in this form. In chapter 5, we implemented the gradient-boosting algorithm for the *unregularized* squared loss function as

$$0 \cdot \underbrace{f(x)^2}_{\textbf{L2 regularization}} + \overbrace{\frac{1}{2}(y - f(x))^2}^{\textbf{squared loss}}$$

between the true label y and the predicted label $f(x)$. In this setting, unregularized loss functions simply have the regularization parameter $\alpha = 0.1$.

We've already seen an example of a regularized loss function (chapter 1, section 1.3.2) with support vector machines (SVMs), which use the regularized hinge loss function:

$$L\left(y, f\left(x\right)\right) = \alpha \underbrace{f\left(x\right)^2}_{\text{L2 regularization}} + \underbrace{\max\left(0, 1 - y \cdot f\left(x\right)\right)}_{\text{hinge loss}}$$

In this chapter, we consider the *regularized logistic loss* function, which is commonly used in logistic regression as

$$L(y, f\left(x\right)) = \alpha \underbrace{f\left(x\right)^2}_{\text{L2 regularization}} + \underbrace{\log\left(1 + e^{-y \cdot f\left(x\right)}\right)}_{\text{logistic loss}}$$

which augments the standard logistic loss $\log\left(1 + e^{-y \cdot f\left(x\right)}\right)$, with a regularization term $\alpha \cdot f(x)^2$. Figure 6.9 illustrates the regularized logistic loss for $\alpha = 0.1$. Observe how the regularization term makes the overall loss function's profile curvier and more bowl-like.

Regularization parameter α trades off between fit and complexity: as α is increased, the regularization effect will increase, making the overall surface more convex and ignoring the contributions of the loss function. Because the loss function affects the fit, over-regularizing the model (by setting high values of alpha) will lead to underfitting.

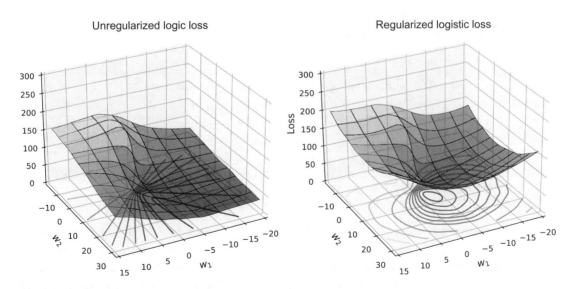

Figure 6.9 The standard logistic loss function (left) versus the regularized logistic loss function (right), which is curvier and has a better-defined minimum

The gradient and Hessian of the regularized logistic loss function can be computed as the first and second derivatives with respect to the model's prediction ($f(x)$):

$$g\left(y, f\left(x\right)\right) = \frac{-y}{1 + e^{-y \cdot f(x)}} + 2\alpha f\left(x\right)$$

$$He\left(y, f\left(x\right)\right) = \frac{e^{y \cdot f(x)}}{\left(1 + e^{y \cdot f(x)}\right)^2} + 2\alpha$$

The following listing implements functions to compute the regularized logistic loss, with the value of the parameter $\alpha = 0.1$.

Listing 6.2   Regularized logistic loss, gradient, and Hessian with $\lambda = 0.1$

```
def log_loss_func(y, F):
    return np.log(1 + np.exp(-y * F)) + 0.1 * F**2

def log_loss_grad(y, F):
    return -y / (1 + np.exp(y * F)) + 0.2 * F

def log_loss_hess(y, F):
    return np.exp(y * F) / (1 + np.exp(y * F))**2 + 0.2
```

These functions can now be used to compute the residuals and corresponding Hessian weights that we'll need for Newton boosting.

6.2.3   *Implementing Newton boosting*

In this section, we'll develop our own implementation of Newton boosting. The basic algorithm can be outlined with the following pseudocode:

```
initialize: F = f₀, some constant value
for t = 1 to T:
1. compute first and second derivatives for each example,
```

$$g_i^t = \frac{\partial L}{\partial F}\left(x_i\right), \; He_i^t = \frac{\partial^2 L}{\partial F^2}\left(x_i\right)$$

```
2. compute the weighted residuals for each example r_i^t = -g_i^t/He_i^t
3. fit a weak decision tree regressor hₜ(x) using the training set (x_i, r_i^t)_{i=1}^n
4. compute the step length (αₜ) using line search
5. update the model: F_{t+1} = F_t + αₜhₜ(x)
```

Unsurprisingly, this training procedure is the same as gradient boosting, with the only change being the computation of Hessian-weighted residuals in steps 1 and 2. Because the general algorithmic framework for gradient and Newton boosting is the same, we can combine and implement them together. The following listing extends listing 5.2

to incorporate Newton boosting, which it uses for training only with the following flag: use_Newton=True.

Listing 6.3   Newton boosting for the regularized logistic loss

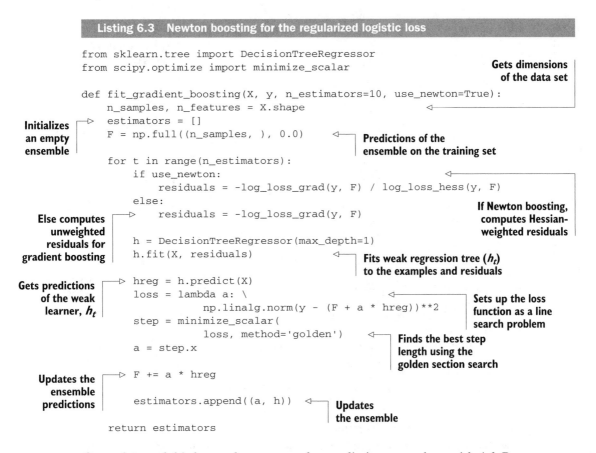

```
from sklearn.tree import DecisionTreeRegressor
from scipy.optimize import minimize_scalar          Gets dimensions
                                                     of the data set
def fit_gradient_boosting(X, y, n_estimators=10, use_newton=True):
    n_samples, n_features = X.shape     ◁
    estimators = []
    F = np.full((n_samples, ), 0.0)     ◁    Predictions of the
                                             ensemble on the training set
    for t in range(n_estimators):      ◁
        if use_newton:
            residuals = -log_loss_grad(y, F) / log_loss_hess(y, F)
        else:
            residuals = -log_loss_grad(y, F)    If Newton boosting,
                                                computes Hessian-
                                                weighted residuals
        h = DecisionTreeRegressor(max_depth=1)
        h.fit(X, residuals)     ◁    Fits weak regression tree (h_t)
                                     to the examples and residuals
        hreg = h.predict(X)
        loss = lambda a: \
                np.linalg.norm(y - (F + a * hreg))**2    Sets up the loss
        step = minimize_scalar(                          function as a line
                loss, method='golden')    ◁              search problem
        a = step.x                        Finds the best step
                                          length using the
                                          golden section search
        F += a * hreg

        estimators.append((a, h))    ◁    Updates
                                           the ensemble
    return estimators
```

Initializes an empty ensemble → `estimators = []` `F = np.full((n_samples, ), 0.0)`

Else computes unweighted residuals for gradient boosting → `residuals = -log_loss_grad(y, F)`

Gets predictions of the weak learner, h_t → `hreg = h.predict(X)`

Updates the ensemble predictions → `F += a * hreg`

Once the model is learned, we can make predictions exactly as with AdaBoost or gradient boosting because the ensemble learned is a sequential ensemble. The following listing is the same prediction function used by these previously introduced methods, repeated here for convenience.

Listing 6.4   Predictions of Newton boosting

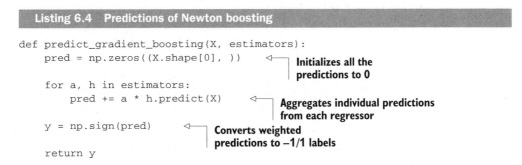

```
def predict_gradient_boosting(X, estimators):
    pred = np.zeros((X.shape[0], ))    ◁    Initializes all the
                                             predictions to 0
    for a, h in estimators:
        pred += a * h.predict(X)    ◁    Aggregates individual predictions
                                         from each regressor
    y = np.sign(pred)     ◁    Converts weighted
                               predictions to −1/1 labels
    return y
```

Let's compare the performance of our implementations of gradient boosting (from the previous chapter) and Newton boosting:

```
from sklearn.datasets import make_moons
X, y = make_moons(n_samples=200, noise=0.15, random_state=13)
y = 2 * y - 1
```
◁—⌐ **Converts training labels to –1/1**

```
from sklearn.model_selection import train_test_split
from sklearn.metrics import accuracy_score
```

```
Xtrn, Xtst, ytrn, ytst = \
    train_test_split(X, y, test_size=0.25, random_state=11)
```
◁—⌐ **Splits into train and test sets**

```
estimators_nb = fit_gradient_boosting(Xtrn, ytrn, n_estimators=25,
                                  use_newton=True)
ypred_nb = predict_gradient_boosting(Xtst, estimators_nb)
print('Newton boosting test error = {0}'.
            format(1 - accuracy_score(ypred_nb, ytst)))
```
◁—⌐ **Newton boosting**

```
estimators_gb = fit_gradient_boosting(Xtrn, ytrn, n_estimators=25,
                                  use_newton=False)
ypred_gb = predict_gradient_boosting(Xtst, estimators_gb)
print('Gradient boosting test error = {0}'.
            format(1 - accuracy_score(ypred_gb, ytst)))
```
◁—⌐ **Gradient boosting**

We see that Newton boosting produces a test error of around 8% compared to gradient boosting, which achieves 12%:

```
Newton boosting test error = 0.07999999999999996
Gradient boosting test error = 0.12
```

VISUALIZING GRADIENT-BOOSTING ITERATIONS

Now that we have our joint gradient-boosting and Newton-boosting implementation (listing 6.3), we can compare the behaviors of both of these algorithms. First, note that they both train and grow their ensembles in roughly the same way. The key difference between them is in the residuals they use for ensemble training: gradient boosting uses the negative gradients directly as residuals, whereas Newton boosting uses the negative Hessian-weighted gradients.

Let's step through the first few iterations to see what the effect of Hessian weighting is. In the first iteration, both gradient and Newton boosting are initialized with $F(x_i) = 0$.

Both gradient and Newton boosting use residuals as a means to measure the extent of misclassification so that the most misclassified training examples can get more attention in the current iteration. In figure 6.10, the very first iteration, the effect of Hessian weighting is immediately observable. Using second-derivative information to weight the residuals increases the separation between the two classes, making them easier to classify.

This behavior can also be seen in the second (figure 6.11) and third (figure 6.12) iterations, where Hessian weighting enables greater stratification of misclassifications, enabling the weak learning algorithm to construct more effective weak learners.

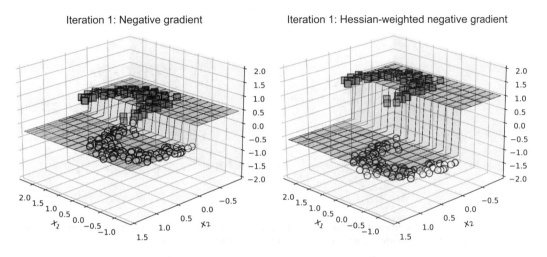

Figure 6.10   Iteration 1: Negative gradients (left) as residuals in gradient boosting versus Hessian-weighted negative gradients (right) as residuals in Newton boosting

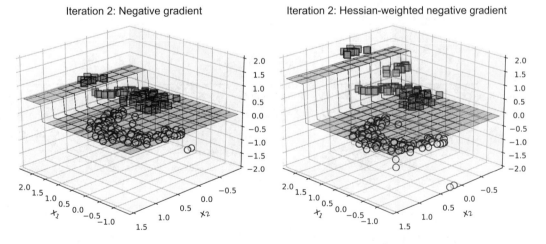

Figure 6.11   Iteration 2: Negative gradients (left) as residuals in gradient boosting versus Hessian-weighted negative gradients (right) as residuals in Newton boosting

In summary, Newton boosting aims to use both first-derivative (gradient) information and second-derivative (Hessian) information to ensure that misclassified training examples receive increased attention dependent on the extent of the misclassification.

Figure 6.12 illustrates how Newton boosting grows the ensemble and decreases the error steadily over successive iterations.

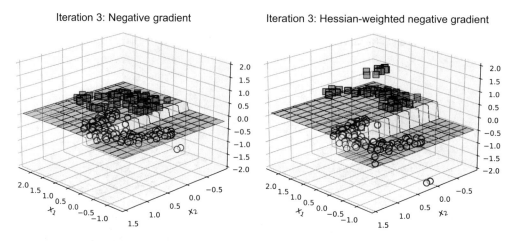

Figure 6.12   Iteration 3: Negative gradients (left) as residuals in gradient boosting versus Hessian-weighted negative gradients (right) as residuals in Newton boosting

We can observe the progression of the Newton-boosting classifier in figure 6.13 across many iterations, as more and more base estimators are added to the ensemble.

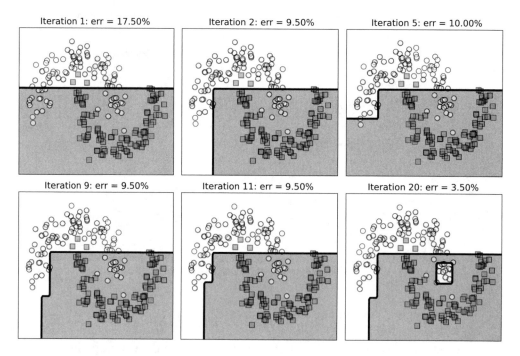

Figure 6.13   Newton boosting across 20 iterations

6.3　*XGBoost: A framework for Newton boosting*

XGBoost, or eXtreme Gradient Boosting, is an open source gradient-boosting framework (originated from a research project by Tianqi Chen). It gained widespread recognition and adoption, especially in the data science competition community, after its success in the Higgs Boson Machine Learning Challenge.

XGBoost has since evolved into a powerful boosting framework that provides parallelization and distributed processing capabilities that allow it to scale to very large data sets. Today, XGBoost is available in many languages, including Python, R, and C/C++, and it's deployed on several data science platforms such as Apache Spark and H2O.

XGBoost has several key features that make it applicable in a variety of domains as well as for large-scale data:

- Newton boosting on regularized loss functions to directly control the complexity of the regression tree functions (weak learners) that constitute the ensemble (section 6.3.1)
- Algorithmic speedups such as weighted quantile sketch, a variant of the histogram-based split-finding algorithm (that LightGBM uses) for faster training (section 6.3.1)
- Support for a large number of loss functions for classification, regression, and ranking, as well as application-specific custom loss functions, similar to LightGBM
- Block-based system design that stores data in memory in smaller units called blocks; this allows for parallel learning, better caching, and efficient multithreading (these details are out of scope for this book)

Because it's impossible to detail all the features available in XGBoost in this limited space, this section and the next introduce XGBoost, its usage, and applications in practical settings. This will enable you to springboard further into advanced use cases of XGBoost for your applications through its documentation.

6.3.1　*What makes XGBoost "extreme"?*

In a nutshell, XGBoost is extreme due to Newton boosting with regularized loss functions, efficient tree learning, and a parallelizable implementation. In particular, the success of XGBoost lies in the fact that its boosting implementation feature conceptual and algorithmic improvements designed *specifically* for tree-based learning. In this section, we'll focus on how XGBoost improves the robustness and generalizability of tree-based ensembles so efficiently.

REGULARIZED LOSS FUNCTIONS FOR LEARNING

In section 6.2.2, we saw several examples of L2-regularized loss functions of the following form:

$$\alpha \cdot \underbrace{f(x)^2}_{\text{measures model complexity}} + \overbrace{\text{loss}(f(x), \text{data})}^{\text{measures model fit}}$$

If we only consider tree-based learners for weak models in our ensemble, there are other ways to *directly control* the complexity of the trees during learning. XGBoost does this by introducing another regularization term to limit the number of leaf nodes:

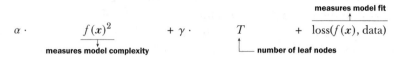

How does this control the complexity of a tree? By limiting the number of leaf nodes, this additional term will force tree learning to train shallower trees, which in turn makes the trees weaker and less complex.

XGBoost uses this regularized objective function in many ways. For instance, during tree learning, instead of using a scoring function such as the Gini criterion or entropy for split finding, XGBoost uses the regularized learning objective described previously. Thus, this criterion is used to determine the *structure* of the individual trees, which are the weak learners in the ensemble.

XGBoost also uses this objective to compute the leaf values themselves, which are essentially the regression values that gradient boosting aggregates. Thus, this criterion is used to determine the *parameters* of the individual trees as well.

An important caveat before we move on: the additional regularization term allows direct control over model complexity and downstream generalization. This comes at a price, however, in that we now have an extra parameter γ to worry about. Because γ is a user-defined parameter, we have to set this value, along with α and many others. These will often have to be selected by CV and can add to the overall model development time and effort.

WEIGHTED QUANTILE-BASED NEWTON BOOSTING

Even with a regularized learning objective, the biggest computational bottleneck is in scaling learning to large data sets, specifically, in identifying optimal splits for use during learning of the regression tree base estimators.

The standard approach to tree learning exhaustively enumerates all possible splits in the data. As we've seen in chapter 5, section 5.2.4, this isn't a good idea for large data sets. Efficient modifications, such as histogram-based splitting, bin the data instead so that we evaluate far fewer splits.

Implementations such as LightGBM incorporate further improvements, such as sampling and feature bundling, to speed up tree learning. XGBoost also aims to bring these notions into its implementation. However, there is one key consideration unique to XGBoost. Packages such as LightGBM implement gradient boosting, while XGBoost implements Newton boosting. This means that XGBoost's tree learning has to consider Hessian-weighted training examples, unlike LightGBM, where all the examples are weighted equally!

XGBoost's approximate split-finding algorithm, *weighted quantile sketch*, aims to find ideal split points using quantiles in the features. This is analogous to histogram-based splitting, which uses bins employed by gradient-boosting algorithms.

The details of weighted quantile sketch and its implementation are considerable and can't be covered here owing to limited space. However, here are our key takeaways:

- Conceptually, XGBoost also uses approximate split-finding algorithms; these algorithms consider additional information unique to Newton boosting (e.g., Hessian weights). Ultimately, they are similar to histogram-based algorithms and aim to bin the data. Unlike other histogram-based algorithms that bucket data into evenly sized bins, XGBoost bins data into feature-dependent buckets. At the end of the day, XGBoost trades off exactness for efficiency by adapting clever strategies for split finding.
- From an implementation standpoint, XGBoost presorts and organizes data into blocks both in memory and on disk. Once this is done, XGBoost further exploits this organization by caching access patterns, using block compression, and chunking the data into easily accessible shards. These steps significantly improve the efficiency of Newton boosting, allowing it to scale to very large data sets.

6.3.2 *Newton boosting with XGBoost*

We kick off our explorations of XGBoost with the breast cancer data set, which we've used several times in the past as a pedagogical data set:

```
from sklearn.datasets import load_breast_cancer
from sklearn.model_selection import train_test_split
X, y = load_breast_cancer(return_X_y=True)
Xtrn, Xtst, ytrn, ytst = train_test_split(X, y, test_size=0.2,
                                          shuffle=True, random_state=42)
```

NOTE XGBoost is available for Python, R, and many platforms. See the XGBoost installation guide for detailed instructions on installation at http://mng.bz/61eZ.

For Python users, especially those who are familiar with scikit-learn, XGBoost provides a familiar interface that is designed to look and feel like scikit-learn. Using this interface, it's very easy to set up and train an XGBoost model:

```
from xgboost import XGBClassifier
ens = XGBClassifier(n_estimators=20, max_depth=1,
                    objective='binary:logistic')
ens.fit(Xtrn, ytrn)
```

We set the loss function to be the logistic loss, set the number of iterations (with 1 estimator trained per iteration) to 20, and set the maximum tree depth to 1. This results in an ensemble of 20 decision stumps (trees of depth 1).

It's also similarly easy to predict labels on test data and evaluate model performance:

```
from sklearn.metrics import accuracy_score
ypred = ens.predict(Xtst)
accuracy_score(ytst, ypred)
0.9649122807017544
```

Alternatively, we can use XGBoost's native interface, which was originally designed to read data in the LIBSVM format, which is well-suited for storing sparse data with lots of zeros efficiently.

In the LIBSVM format (which was introduced in the case study in chapter 5, section 5.5.1), each line of the data file contains a single training example represented as follows:

```
<label> qid:<example id> 1:<feature 1 value> 2:<feature 2 value> …
k:<feature k value> ... # other information as comments
```

XGBoost uses a data object called `DMatrix` to group data and corresponding labels together. `DMatrix` objects can be created by reading data directly from files or from other array-like objects. Here, we create two `DMatrix` objects called `trn` and `tst` to represent the train and test data matrices:

```
import xgboost as xgb
trn = xgb.DMatrix(Xtrn, label=ytrn)
tst = xgb.DMatrix(Xtst, label=ytst)
```

We also set up the training parameters using a dictionary and train an XGBoost model using `trn` and the parameters:

```
params = {'max_depth': 1, 'objective':'binary:logistic'}
ens2 = xgb.train(params, trn, num_boost_round=20)
```

Care must be taken while using this model for prediction, however. Models trained with certain loss functions will return prediction probabilities rather than the predictions directly. The logistic loss function is one such case.

These prediction probabilities can be converted to binary classification labels 0/1 by thresholding at 0.5. That is, all test examples with prediction probability ≥ 0.5 are classified into Class 1 and the rest into Class 0:

```
ypred_proba = ens2.predict(tst)
ypred = (ypred_proba >= 0.5).astype(int)
accuracy_score(ytst, ypred)
0.9649122807017544
```

Finally, XGBoost supports three different types of boosting approaches, which can be set through the `booster` parameter:

- `booster='gbtree'` is the default setting and implements Newton boosting using trees as weak learners trained using tree-based regression.
- `booster='gblinear'` implements Newton boosting using linear functions as weak learners trained using linear regression.

- `booster='dart'` trains an ensemble using Dropouts meet Multiple Additive Regression Trees (DART), as previously described in chapter 5, section 5.4.

We can also train (parallel) random forest ensembles using XGBoost by carefully setting the training parameters to ensure training examples and feature subsampling. This is generally only useful when you want to use XGBoost's parallel and distributed training architecture to explicitly train parallel ensembles.

6.4   *XGBoost in practice*

In this section, we describe how to train models in practice using XGBoost. As with AdaBoost and gradient boosting, we look to set the learning rate (section 6.4.1) or employ early stopping (section 6.4.2) as a means to control overfitting, as follows:

- By selecting an effective learning rate, we try to control the rate at which the model learns so that it doesn't rapidly fit and then overfit the training data. We can think of this as a proactive modeling approach, where we try to identify a good training strategy so that it leads to a good model.
- By enforcing early stopping, we try to stop training as soon as we observe that the model is starting to overfit. We can think of this as a reactive modeling approach, where we contemplate terminating training as soon as we think we have a good model.

6.4.1   *Learning rate*

Recall from section 6.1 that the step length is analogous to the learning rate and is a measure of each weak learner's contribution to the entire ensemble. The learning rate allows greater control over how quickly the complexity of the ensemble grows. Therefore, it's essential that we identify the best learning rate for our data set in practice so that we can avoid overfitting and generalize well after training.

LEARNING RATE VIA CROSS VALIDATION

As we've seen in the preceding section, XGBoost provides an interface that plays nicely with scikit-learn. This subsection shows how we can combine the functionalities of both packages to effectively perform parameter selection using CV. While we use CV to set the learning rate here, CV can be used to select other learning parameters such as maximum tree depth, number of leaf nodes, and even loss-function-specific parameters.

We combine scikit-learn's `StratifiedKFold` class to split the training data into 10 folds of training and validation sets. `StratifiedKFold` ensures that we preserve class distributions, that is, the fractions of different classes across the folds.

First, we initialize the learning rates we're interested in exploring:

```
import numpy as np
learning_rates = np.concatenate([np.linspace(0.02, 0.1, num=5),
                                 np.linspace(0.2, 1.8, num=9)])
n_learning_rate_steps = len(learning_rates)
print(learning_rates)
[0.02 0.04 0.06 0.08 0.1  0.2  0.4  0.6  0.8  1.   1.2  1.4  1.6  1.8 ]
```

Next, we set up `StratifiedKFold` to split the training data into 10 folds:

```
from sklearn.model_selection import StratifiedKFold
n_folds = 10
splitter = StratifiedKFold(n_splits=n_folds, shuffle=True, random_state=42)
```

In the following listing, we perform CV by training and evaluating models on each of the 10 folds with XGBoost.

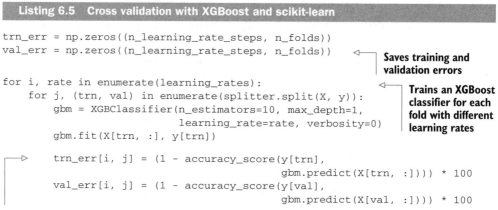

Listing 6.5   Cross validation with XGBoost and scikit-learn

```
trn_err = np.zeros((n_learning_rate_steps, n_folds))          ◁── Saves training and
val_err = np.zeros((n_learning_rate_steps, n_folds))              validation errors

for i, rate in enumerate(learning_rates):          ◁── Trains an XGBoost
    for j, (trn, val) in enumerate(splitter.split(X, y)):       classifier for each
        gbm = XGBClassifier(n_estimators=10, max_depth=1,       fold with different
                            learning_rate=rate, verbosity=0)    learning rates
        gbm.fit(X[trn, :], y[trn])

        trn_err[i, j] = (1 - accuracy_score(y[trn],     ◁── Saves training and
                                 gbm.predict(X[trn, :]))) * 100    validation errors
        val_err[i, j] = (1 - accuracy_score(y[val],
                                 gbm.predict(X[val, :]))) * 100

trn_err = np.mean(trn_err, axis=1)          Averages training and
val_err = np.mean(val_err, axis=1)          validation errors across folds
```

When applied to the breast cancer data set (see section 6.3.2), we obtain the averaged training and validation errors for this data set. We visualize these errors for different learning rates in figure 6.14.

As the learning rate decreases, XGBoost's performance degrades as the boosting process becomes increasingly more conservative and exhibits underfitting behavior. As the learning rate increases, XGBoost's performance, once again, degrades as the boosting process becomes increasingly more aggressive and exhibits overfitting behavior. The best value among our parameter choices appears to be `learning_rate=1.2`, which is generally in the region between 1.0 and 1.5.

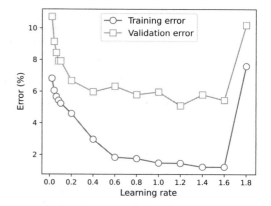

Figure 6.14   Averaged training and validation errors of XGBoost across 10 folds of the breast cancer data set

CROSS VALIDATION WITH XGBOOST

Beyond parameter selection, CV can also be useful to characterize model performance. In listing 6.6, we use XGBoost's built-in CV functionality to characterize how XGBoost's performance changes as we increase the number of estimators in the ensemble.

We use the `XGBoost.cv` function to perform 10-fold CV, as shown in the following listing. Observe that `xgb.cv` is called in nearly the same way as `xgb.fit` from the previous section.

Listing 6.6   Cross validation with XGBoost

```
import xgboost as xgb
trn = xgb.DMatrix(Xtrn, label=ytrn)
tst = xgb.DMatrix(Xtst, label=ytst)

params = {'learning_rate': 0.25, 'max_depth': 2,
          'objective': 'binary:logistic'}
cv_results = xgb.cv(params, trn, num_boost_round=60,
                    nfold=10, metrics={'error'}, seed=42)
```

In this listing, the model performance is characterized by error, which is passed to `XGBoost.cv` using the argument `metrics={'error'}`. The training and test cross-validation errors are shown in figure 6.15.

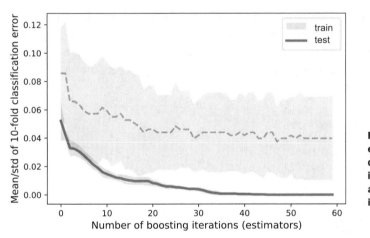

Figure 6.15   The average error across the folds decreases with increasing iterations, as we add more and more base estimators into the ensemble.

Another interesting observation from figure 6.15 is that training and validation performance stop improving meaningfully at around 35 iterations. This suggests that there's no significant performance improvement to be gained by prolonging training beyond this point. This brings us, rather neatly, to the notion of early stopping, which we've encountered before with both AdaBoost and gradient boosting.

6.4.2   *Early stopping*

As the number of base estimators in the ensemble increases, the complexity of the ensemble also increases, which eventually leads to overfitting. To avoid this, instead of training the model, we can stop before we reach the limit of ensemble size.

Early stopping with XGBoost works pretty similarly to LightGBM, where we specify a value for the parameter `early_stopping_rounds`. The performance of the ensemble is scored after each iteration on a validation set, which is split from the training set for the purpose of identifying a good early stopping point.

As long as the overall score (say, accuracy) improves over the last `early_stopping_rounds`, XGBoost will continue to train. However, when the score doesn't improve after `early_stopping_rounds`, XGBoost terminates training.

The following listing illustrates early stopping using XGBoost. Note that `train_test_split` is used to create an independent validation set that is used by XGBoost to identify an early stopping point.

Listing 6.7   Early stopping with XGBoost

```
from sklearn.model_selection import train_test_split
Xtrn, Xval, ytrn, yval = train_test_split(X, y, test_size=0.2,
                                           shuffle=True, random_state=42)
ens = XGBClassifier(n_estimators=50, max_depth=2,
                    objective='binary:logistic')
ens.fit(Xtrn, ytrn, early_stopping_rounds=5,
        eval_set=[(Xval, yval)], eval_metric='auc')
```

The three key parameters for early stopping in the preceding listing are the number of early stopping rounds and the evaluation set: `early_ stopping_rounds=5` and `eval_set=[(Xval, yval)]`, and the evaluation metric `eval_metric='auc'`. With these parameters, training terminates after 13 rounds even though `n_estimators` was initialized to 50 in `XGBClassifier`:

```
[0]validation_0-auc:0.95480
[1]validation_0-auc:0.96725
[2]validation_0-auc:0.96757
[3]validation_0-auc:0.99017
[4]validation_0-auc:0.99099
[5]validation_0-auc:0.99181
[6]validation_0-auc:0.99410
[7]validation_0-auc:0.99640
[8]validation_0-auc:0.99476
[9]validation_0-auc:0.99148
[10]validation_0-auc:0.99050
[11]validation_0-auc:0.99050
[12]validation_0-auc:0.98985
```

Thus, early stopping can greatly improve training times, while ensuring that model performance doesn't degrade excessively.

6.5   *Case study redux: Document retrieval*

To conclude this chapter, we revisit the case study from chapter 5 that addressed the task of document retrieval, which identifies and retrieves documents from a database to match a user's query. In chapter 5, we compared several gradient-boosting approaches available in LightGBM.

In this chapter, we'll train Newton boosting models using XGBoost on the document retrieval task and compare the performance of XGBoost and LightGBM. In addition to this comparison, this case study also illustrates how to set up randomized CV for effective parameter selection in XGBoost over large data sets.

6.5.1 *The LETOR data set*

We use the LEarning TO Rank (LETOR) v4.0 data set, which is made freely available by Microsoft Research. Each training example corresponds to a query-document pair, with features describing the query, the document, and the matches between them. Each training label is a relevance rank: least relevant, moderately relevant, or highly relevant.

This problem is set up as a three-class classification problem of identifying the relevance class (least, moderately, or highly relevant) given a training example: a query-document pair. For purposes of convenience and consistency, we'll use the functionalities provided by XGBoost's scikit-learn wrapper along with modules from scikit-learn itself. First, let's load the LETOR data set:

```
from sklearn.datasets import load_svmlight_file
from sklearn.model_selection import train_test_split
import numpy as np

query_data_file = './data/ch05/MQ2008/Querylevelnorm.txt'
X, y = load_svmlight_file(query_data_file)
```

Next, let's split this into train and test sets:

```
Xtrn, Xtst, ytrn, ytst = train_test_split(X, y,
                                           test_size=0.2, random_state=42)
```

6.5.2 *Document retrieval with XGBoost*

As we have a three-class (multiclass) classification problem, we train a tree-based XGBoost classifier using the softmax loss function. Softmax loss is a generalization of the logistic loss function to multiclass classification and is commonly used in many multiclass learning algorithms, including multinomial logistic regression and deep neural networks.

We set the loss function for training with `objective='multi:softmax'`, and the evaluation function for testing with `eval_metric='merror'`. The evaluation function is a multiclass error, that is, a generalization of a 0–1 misclassification error from the binary to multiclass case. We don't use `merror` as the training objective because it's not differentiable and isn't amenable to computing gradients and Hessians:

```
xgb = XGBClassifier(booster='gbtree', objective='multi:softmax',
                    eval_metric='merror', use_label_encoder=False,
                    n_jobs=-1)
```

We also set `n_jobs=-1` to enable XGBoost to use all available CPU cores to accelerate training with parallelization.

As with LightGBM, XGBoost also requires that we set several training hyperparameters, such as learning rate (to control the rate of learning) or the number of leaf nodes (to control the complexity of the base-estimator trees). These hyperparameters are selected using scikit-learn's randomized CV module: `RandomizedSearchCV`. Specifically, we perform 5-fold CV over a grid of various parameter choices; however, instead of exhaustively evaluating all possible learning parameter combinations the way GridSearchCV does, RandomizedSearchCV samples a smaller number of model combinations for faster parameter selection:

```
num_random_iters = 20
num_cv_folds = 5
```

We can explore several different values of some key parameters as described here:

- learning_rate—Controls overall contribution of each tree to the ensemble
- max_depth—Limits tree depth to accelerate training and decrease complexity
- min_child_weight—Limits each leaf node by the sum of the Hessian values to control overfitting
- colsample_bytree—Specifies the fraction of features to sample from the training data, respectively, to accelerate training (similar to feature subsampling performed by random forests or random subspaces)
- reg_alpha and reg_lambda—Specifies the amount of regularization of the leaf node values to control overfitting as well

The following code specifies the ranges of values for the parameters we're interested in searching over to identify an effective training parameter combination:

```
from scipy.stats import randint, uniform
xgb_params = {'max_depth': randint(2, 10),
              'learning_rate': 2**np.linspace(-6, 2, num=5),
              'min_child_weight': [1e-2, 1e-1, 1, 1e1, 1e2],
              'colsample_bytree': uniform(loc=0.4, scale=0.6),
              'reg_alpha': [0, 1e-1, 1, 10, 100],
              'reg_lambda': [0, 1e-1, 1, 10, 100]}
```

As mentioned earlier, the grid over these parameters produces too many combinations to evaluate efficiently. Thus, we adopt randomized search with CV and randomly sample a much smaller number of parameter combinations:

```
cv = RandomizedSearchCV(estimator=xgb,
                        param_distributions=xgb_params,
                        n_iter=num_random_iters,
                        cv=num_cv_folds,
                        refit=True,
                        random_state=42, verbose=1)
cv.fit(Xtrn, ytrn, eval_metric='merror', verbose=False)
```

Observe that we've set refit=True in RandomizedSearchCV, which enables the training of one final model using the optimal parameter combination identified by RandomizedSearchCV.

After training, we compare the performance of XGBoost with four models trained by LightGBM in chapter 5, section 5.5:

- *Random forest*—Parallel homogeneous ensemble of randomized decision trees.

- *Gradient boosted decision trees (GBDT)*—This is the standard approach to gradient boosting that represents a balance between models with good generalization performance and training speed.
- *Gradient-based with One-Side Sampling (GOSS)*—This variant of gradient boosting downsamples the training data and is ideally suited for large data sets. Due to downsampling, it may lose out on generalization, but it's typically very fast to train.
- *Dropouts meet Multiple Additive Regression Trees (DART)*—This variant incorporates the notion of dropout from deep learning, where neural units are randomly and temporarily dropped during backpropagation iterations to mitigate overfitting. DART is often the slowest of all the gradient-boosting options available in LightGBM.

XGBoost uses regularized loss functions and Newton boosting. In contrast, the random forest ensemble doesn't use any gradient information, while GBDT, GOSS, and DART use gradient boosting.

As before, we compare the performance of all algorithms using test set accuracy (figure 6.16, left) and overall model development time (figure 6.16, right), which includes CV-based parameter selection as well as training time.

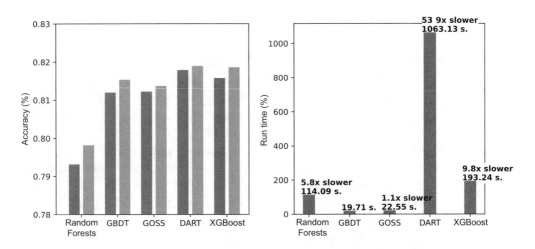

Figure 6.16 Left: Comparing test set accuracy of random forest, GBDT, GOSS, and DART; Right: Comparing the overall training times of random forest, GBDT, GOSS, and DART (all trained using LightGBM)

Following are the key takeaways from this experiment (see figure 6.16):

- On training performance, XGBoost performs comparably to DART, GOSS, and GBDT and outperforms random forest. On test set performance, XGBoost is second only to DART.

- On training time, the overall model development time of XGBoost is significantly shorter than DART. This suggests that there is an application-dependent tradeoff to be made here between the need for the additional performance improvement and the accompanying computational overhead incurred.
- Finally, these results are dependent on various choices made during modeling, such as learning parameter ranges and randomization. Further performance gains are possible with careful feature engineering, loss function selection, and using distributed processing for efficiency.

Summary

- Newton's descent is another optimization algorithm, similar to gradient descent.
- Newton's descent uses second-order (Hessian) information to accelerate optimization as compared to gradient descent, which only uses first-order (gradient) information.
- Newton boosting combines Newton's descent and boosting to train a sequential ensemble of weak learners.
- Newton boosting uses weighted residuals to characterize correctly classified and poorly classified training examples. This is analogous to both how AdaBoost uses weights and how gradient boosting uses residuals.
- Weak learners in Newton boosting are regression trees that are trained over the weighted residuals of the training examples and approximate the Newton step.
- Like gradient boosting, Newton boosting can be applied to a wide variety of loss functions arising from classification, regression, or ranking tasks.
- Optimizing a regularized loss function helps control the complexity of the weak learners in the learned ensemble, prevent overfitting, and improve generalization.
- XGBoost is a powerful, publicly available framework for tree-based Newton boosting that incorporates Newton boosting, efficient split finding, and distributed learning.
- XGBoost optimizes a regularized learning objective consisting of the loss function (to fit the data) and two regularization functions: L2 regularization and number of leaf nodes.
- As with AdaBoost and gradient boosting, we can avoid overfitting in Newton boosting by choosing an effective learning rate or via early stopping. XGBoost supports both.
- XGBoost implements an approximate split-finding algorithm called weighted quantile sketch, which is similar to histogram-based split finding but adapted and optimized for efficient Newton boosting.
- In addition to a wide variety of loss functions for classification, regression, and ranking, XGBoost also provides support for incorporation of our own custom, problem-specific loss functions for training.

Part 3

Ensembles in the wild:
Adapting ensemble methods to your data

The world of data is a wild and dangerous place for a data scientist. We must contend with different types of data, such as counts, categories, and strings, strewn with missing values and noise. We are asked to build predictive models for different types of tasks: binary classification, multiclass classification, regression, and ranking.

We have to build our machine-learning pipelines and preprocess our data with care to avoid data leakage. They have to be accurate, fast, robust, and meme-worthy (ok, that last one is probably optional). After all this, we end up with models that may well do the job they were trained for but are ultimately black boxes that no one understands.

In this final part of the book, you'll learn how to tackle these challenges, armed with the arsenal of ensemble methods from the previous part of the book, as well as a few new ensemble methods. This is your last stop from ensembler-in-training to seasoned ensembler-explorer of the wild world of data.

Chapter 7 covers ensemble learning for regression tasks, where you'll learn how to adapt different ensemble methods to handle continuous and count-valued labels.

Chapter 8 covers ensemble learning with nonnumeric features, where you'll learn how to encode categorical and string-valued features before or during ensembling. You'll also learn about two pervasive issues that arise during such preprocessing (and sometimes in other ways)—data leakage and prediction shift—and how they often mess with our ability to accurately evaluate model performance. In addition, chapter 8 introduces another variant of gradient boosting called ordered boosting and another powerful gradient boosting package called CatBoost, which is similar to LightGBM and XGBoost.

Chapter 9 covers the exciting new area of explainable AI, which seeks to create models that humans can understand and trust. While this chapter is presented from the perspective of ensemble methods, many explainability methods (e.g., surrogate models, LIME, and SHAP) covered in this chapter can be applied to any machine-learning model. Chapter 9 also introduces explainable boosting machines, a type of ensemble method that is explicitly designed to be directly explainable.

This part of the book covers advanced topics in ensemble methods and builds on some key concepts from part 2, especially gradient boosting. Don't hesitate to jump back to part 2 as a refresher or reference, as needed.

Learning with continuous and count labels

This chapter covers

- Regression in machine learning
- Loss and likelihood functions for regression
- When to use different loss and likelihood functions
- Adapting parallel and sequential ensembles for regression problems
- Using ensembles for regression in practical settings

Many real-world modeling, prediction, and forecasting problems are best framed and solved as regression problems. Regression has a rich history predating the advent of machine learning and has long been a part of the standard statistician's toolkit.

Regression techniques have been developed and widely applied in many areas. Here are just a few examples:

- *Weather forecasting*—To predict the precipitation tomorrow using data from today, including temperature, humidity, cloud cover, wind, and more

- *Insurance analytics*—To predict the number of automobile insurance claims over a period of time, given various vehicle and driver attributes
- *Financial forecasting*—To predict stock prices using historical stock data and trends
- *Demand forecasting*—To predict the residential energy load for the next three months using historical, demographic, and weather data

Whereas chapters 2–6 introduced ensembling techniques for classification problems, in this chapter, we'll see how to adapt ensembling techniques to regression problems.

Consider the task of detecting fraudulent credit card transactions. This is a *classification problem* because we're aiming to distinguish between two types of transactions: fraudulent (e.g., with class label 1) and not fraudulent (e.g., with class label 0). The labels (or targets) we want to predict in classification are *categorical* (0, 1, . . .) and represent different categories.

On the other hand, consider the task of predicting a cardholder's monthly credit card balance. This is an instance of a *regression* task. Unlike classification, the labels (or targets) we want to predict are *continuous* values (e.g., $650.35).

Consider yet another task of predicting the number of times a cardholder uses their card every week. This is also an instance of a regression task, though with a subtle difference. The labels, or targets, we want to predict are *counts*. We typically distinguish between *continuous regression* and *count regression* because it doesn't always make sense to model counts as continuous values (e.g., what does it even mean to predict that a cardholder will use their card 7.62 times?).

In this chapter, we'll learn about these types of problems and others that can be modeled with regression, as well as how we can train regression ensembles. Section 7.1 introduces regression formally, shows some commonly used regression models, and explains how regression can be used to model continuous and count-valued labels (and even categorical labels) under a single framework called the generalized linear model (GLM). Sections 7.2 and 7.3 show how we can adapt ensemble methods to regression problems. Section 7.3 introduces loss and likelihood functions for continuous and count-valued targets, along with guidelines on when and how to use them. We conclude with a case study in section 7.4, this time from the realm of demand forecasting.

7.1   *A brief review of regression*

This section reviews the terminology and background material for regression. We begin with the more familiar and traditional framing of regression as learning with continuous labels. We'll then discuss Poisson regression, an important technique for learning with count labels, and logistic regression, another important technique for learning with categorical labels.

In particular, we'll see that linear, Poisson, and logistic regression are all individual variations within the GLM framework. We'll also briefly review two important nonlinear regression methods—decision-tree regression and artificial neural networks (ANNs)—as they are both often used as base estimators or meta-estimators in ensemble methods.

7.1.1   *Linear regression for continuous labels*

The most fundamental regression method is *linear regression*, where the model to be trained is a linear, weighted combination of the input features:

$$f(x) = w_0 + w_1 x_1 + \cdots + w_d x_d = w_0 + w' x$$

The linear regression model $f(x)$ takes an example x as input and is parameterized by feature weights, w, and the intercept (also known as the bias) w_0. This model is trained by identifying the weights that minimize the *mean squared error* (MSE) between the true labels (y_i) and predicted labels ($f(x_i)$) over all n training examples where

$$\text{squared loss} = \frac{1}{2n} \sum_{i=1}^{n} (y_i - f(x_i))^2 = \frac{1}{2n} \sum_{i=1}^{n} \left(y_i - w' x_i - w_0 \right)^2$$

The MSE is nothing but the (mean) squared loss. Since we minimize the loss function to learn the model, linear regression is also known by another name that may be familiar to you: *ordinary least squares* (OLS) regression.

Recall from chapter 6, section 6.2 (and also from chapter 1), that most machine-learning problems can be cast as combinations of regularization and loss functions, where the regularization function controls model complexity, and the loss function controls model fit:

$$\text{learning objective} = \alpha \cdot \underbrace{\text{regularization}(f)}_{\text{measures model complexity}} + \overbrace{\text{loss}(f, \text{data})}^{\text{measures model fit}}$$

α, of course, is the regularization parameter that trades off between fit and complexity. It must be determined and set by the user, typically through practices such as cross validation (CV).

Optimizing (specifically, minimizing) this learning objective essentially amounts to training a model. From this perspective, ordinary least squares regression can be framed as an *unregularized learning problem* where only the squared-loss function is optimized:

$$\text{OLS learning objective} = \alpha \cdot \underbrace{0}_{\text{measures model complexity}} + \overbrace{\text{squared loss}}^{\text{measures model fit}}$$

Is it possible to use different regularization functions to come up with other linear regression methods? Absolutely, and this is precisely what the statistics community has been up to for the better part of the past century.

COMMON LINEAR REGRESSION METHODS

Let's see some common linear regression methods in practice through scikit-learn's `linear_model` subpackage, which implements several linear regression models. We'll use a synthetic data set, where the true underlying function is given by $f(x) = -2.5x + 3.2$. This is a univariate function, or a function of one variable (for our purposes, one feature). In practice, we'll often not know the true underlying function, of course. The following code snippet generates a small, noisy data set of 100 training examples:

```
import numpy as np
n = 100

rng = np.random.default_rng(seed=42)
X = rng.uniform(low=-4.0, high=4.0, size=(n, 1))    ← Creates a seeded random
                                                       number generator in NumPy
f = lambda x: -2.5 * x + 3.2
y = f(X)                                             Generates noisy labels according
y += rng.normal(scale=0.15 * np.max(y), size=(n, 1))   to this (linear) function
```

We can visualize this data set in figure 7.1.

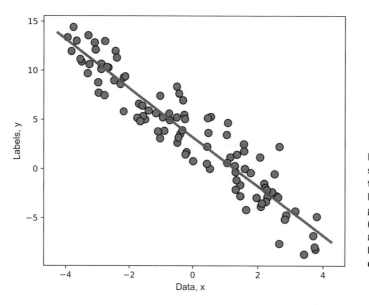

Figure 7.1   Data for a synthetic regression problem to which we fit several linear regression models, generated by the univariate (1D), noisy function $f(x) = -2.5x + 3.2$ shown by the line overlaid on the data points.

Different regularization methods serve diverse modeling needs and can handle different types of data problems. The most common data problem that linear regression models must contend with is that of *multicollinearity*.

Multicollinearity in data arises when one feature depends on others, that is, when the features are *correlated with each other*. For example, in medical data, patient weight and blood pressure are often highly correlated. In practical terms, this means that both features convey nearly the *same information,* and it should be possible to train a less complex model by selecting and using only one of them.

To understand the effect of different regularization methods, we'll explicitly create a data set with multicollinearity using our recently generated univariate data. Specifically, we'll create a data set with two features, where one feature is dependent on the other:

```
X = np.concatenate([X, 3*X + 0.25*np.random.uniform(size=(n, 1))], axis=1)
```

This produces a data set of two features, where the second feature is three times the first (with some added random noise to keep it more realistic). We now have a 2D data set, where the second feature is highly correlated with the first. As before, we'll split the data set into training (75%) and test (25%) sets:

```
from sklearn.model_selection import train_test_split
Xtrn, Xtst, ytrn, ytst = train_test_split(X, y, test_size=0.25,
                                           random_state=42)
```

We now train four commonly used linear regression models:

- OLS regression, with no regularization
- Ridge regression, which uses L2 regularization
- Least Absolute Shrinkage and Selection Operator (LASSO), which uses L1 regularization
- Elastic net, which uses a combination of L1 and L2 regularization

The following listing initializes and trains all 4 models.

Listing 7.1 Linear regression models

```
from sklearn.linear_model import LinearRegression, Ridge, Lasso, ElasticNet
from sklearn.metrics import mean_squared_error, mean_absolute_error

models = ['OLS Regression', 'Ridge Regression', 'LASSO', 'Elastic Net']
regressors = [LinearRegression(),
              Ridge(alpha=0.5),               Initializes four common
              Lasso(alpha=0.5),               linear regression models
              ElasticNet(alpha=0.5, l1_ratio=0.5)]

for (model, regressor) in zip(models, regressors):
    regressor.fit(Xtrn, ytrn)               Gets predictions
    ypred = regressor.predict(Xtst)         on the test set
    mse = mean_squared_error(ytst, ypred)   Computes the test error
    mad = mean_absolute_error(ytst, ypred)  using MSE and MAD

    print('{0}\'s test set performance: MSE = {1:4.3f}, MAD={2:4.3f}'.
          format(model, mse, mad))
    print('{0} model: {1} * x + {2}\n'.
          format(model, regressor.coef_, regressor.intercept_))     Prints the
                                                                    regression
                                                                    weights
```

Trains the regression model

The unregularized OLS model will serve as our baseline for comparing the others:

```
OLS Regression's test set performance: MSE = 2.786, MAD=1.300
OLS Regression model: [[-1.46397043 -0.32220113]] * x + [3.3541317]
```

We'll use two metrics to evaluate the performance of each model: mean squared error (MSE) and mean absolute deviation (MAD). This model has an MSE of 2.786 and a MAD of 1.3. The next linear regression model, ridge regression, uses L2 regularization, which is just the sum of squares of the weights, that is,

$$\text{ridge regression learning objective} = \alpha \cdot \underbrace{\frac{1}{2}\left(w_1^2 + \cdots w_d^2\right)}_{\textbf{measures model complexity}} + \overbrace{\text{squared loss}}^{\textbf{measures model fit}}$$

So, what does L2 regularization do? Learning involves minimizing the learning objective; when the regularization term, or sum of squares, is minimized, it pushes individual weights to zero. This is known as *shrinkage* of the model weights, which reduces model complexity.

The squared loss term in the objective is critical because, without it, we would train a degenerate model with all zero weights. Thus, a ridge regression model trades off complexity for fit, the balance of which is controlled by appropriately setting the parameter $\alpha > 0$. Listing 7.1 produces the following ridge regression model (with $\alpha > 0.5$):

```
Ridge Regression's test set performance: MSE = 2.760, MAD=1.301
Ridge Regression model: [[-0.34200341 -0.69592603]] * x + [3.39572877]
```

The effect of regularization and the resultant shrinkage is immediately evident when we compare the weights learned by L2-regularized ridge regression, [–0.34, –0.7], to those learned by unregularized OLS regression, [–1.46, –0.322].

As mentioned earlier, another popular linear regression method is Least Absolute Shrinkage and Selection Operator (LASSO), which is rather similar to ridge regression except that it uses L1 regularization to control model complexity. That is, the learning objective with L1 regression becomes

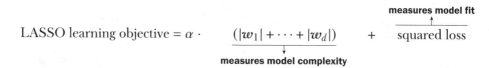

$$\text{LASSO learning objective} = \alpha \cdot \underbrace{(|w_1| + \cdots + |w_d|)}_{\textbf{measures model complexity}} + \overbrace{\text{squared loss}}^{\textbf{measures model fit}}$$

L1 regularization is the sum of absolute values of the weights, rather than the sum of squares in L2 regularization. The effect, overall, is similar to L2 regularization, except that L1 regularization shrinks the weights for less-predictive features. In contrast, L2 regularization shrinks the weights for all the features uniformly.

Put another way, L1 regularization pushes the weights of less-informative features down to zero, which makes it well suited for feature selection. L2 regularization pushes the weights of all features down together, which makes it well suited for handling correlated and covariant features.

Listing 7.1 produces the following LASSO model (with $\alpha > 0.5$):

```
LASSO's test set performance: MSE = 2.832, MAD=1.304
LASSO model: [-0.          -0.79809073] * x + [3.41650036]
```

Contrast the LASSO model's weights, [0, –0.798], to those learned by ridge regression, [–0.34, –0.7]: LASSO has actually learned a zero weight for the first feature!

We can see that L1 regularization induces *model sparsity*. That is, LASSO performs implicit feature selection during learning to identify a small set of features needed to build a less-complex model, while maintaining or even improving performance.

Put another way, this LASSO model only depends on one feature, while the OLS model requires two. This makes the LASSO model less complex than the OLS model. While this may not mean much for this toy data set, this has significant scalability implications when deployed for a data set that has thousands of features.

Recall that our synthetic data set was carefully constructed to have two highly correlated features. LASSO has identified this, determined that it doesn't require both, and hence learned a zero weight for one, effectively zeroing out its contribution to the final model.

The final linear regression model we'll look at is called elastic net, a celebrated, widely used, and well-studied model. Elastic net regression uses a combination of both L1 and L2 regularization:

$$\text{elastic net objective} = \underbrace{\alpha \cdot \rho \left(|\boldsymbol{w}_1| + \cdots + |\boldsymbol{w}_d| \right) + \alpha \cdot \frac{1-\rho}{2} \left(w_1^2 + \cdots + w_d^2 \right)}_{\textbf{measures model complexity}} + \underbrace{\text{squared loss}}_{\textbf{measures model fit}}$$

The proportions of L1 and L2 regularizers in the overall regularization are controlled by the L1 ratio, $0 \leq \rho \leq 1$, while the parameter $\alpha > 0$ still controls the tradeoff between the overall regularization and the loss function.

The L1 ratio allows us to tune the contribution of L1 and L2 objectives. For example, if $\rho = 0$, the elastic net objective becomes a ridge regression objective. Alternately, if $\rho = 1$, the elastic net objective becomes a LASSO objective. For all other values between 0 and 1, the elastic net objective is some combination of ridge regression and LASSO.

Listing 7.1 produces the following elastic net model, with $\alpha = 0.5$, $\rho = 0.5$, and elastic net's test set performance as MSE = 2.824, MAD = 1.304:

```
Elastic Net model: [-0.          -0.79928498] * x + [3.41567834]
```

As we see from the results, the elastic net model still has the sparsity-inducing characteristics of LASSO (observe that the first learned weight is zero), while incorporating the robustness of ridge regression to correlations in the data (compare the test set performances of ridge regression and elastic net).

Table 7.1 summarizes several common linear regression models, all of which can be cast into the squared loss + regularization framework discussed previously.

Table 7.1 Four popular linear regression methods that all use the squared-loss function but use different regularization approaches to contribute to model robustness and sparsity

Model	Loss function	Regularization	Comment
OLS regression	Squared loss $(y - f(\boldsymbol{x}))^2$	None	Classical linear regression; becomes unstable with highly correlated features
Ridge regression	Squared loss $(y - f(\boldsymbol{x}))^2$	L2 penalty $1/2(w_1^2 + \cdots + w_d^2)$	Shrinks the weights to control model complexity, and encourages robustness to highly correlated features
LASSO	Squared loss $(y - f(\boldsymbol{x}))^2$	L1 penalty $|w_1| + \cdots + |w_d|$	Shrinks the weights even more, encourages sparse models, performs implicit feature selection
Elastic net	Squared loss $(y - f(\boldsymbol{x}))^2$	ρL1 + $(1 - \rho)$L2 $0 \leq \rho \leq 1$	Weighted combination of both regularizers to balance between sparsity and robustness

During model training, these regularized loss functions are often optimized through gradient descent, Newton's descent, or their variants, as discussed in chapter 5, section 5.1, and chapter 6, section 6.1.

All the linear regression methods in table 7.1 use the squared loss. Other regression methods can be derived using different loss functions. We'll see examples in section 7.3, and again in the case study in section 7.4.

7.1.2 *Poisson regression for count labels*

The previous section introduced regression as a machine-learning approach suited for modeling problems with continuous-valued targets (labels). There are often situations, however, where we have to develop models in which the labels are counts.

In health informatics, for instance, we may want to build a model to predict the number (essentially, the count) of doctor visits given specific patient data. In insurance pricing, a common problem is that of modeling claim frequency to predict the count of how many insurance claims we can expect for different types of insurance policies. Urban planning is another example in which we may want to model different count variables for census regions, such as household size, number of crimes, number of births and deaths, and many more. In all of these problems, we're still interested in building a regression model of the form $y = f(\boldsymbol{x})$; however, the target label y is no longer a continuous value, but a count.

ASSUMPTIONS OF CONTINUOUS-VALUED REGRESSION MODELS

One approach is to simply treat counts as continuous values, but this doesn't always work. For one, continuous-valued predictions of count variables can't always be interpreted meaningfully. If we were predicting the number of doctor visits per patient, for example, a prediction of 2.41 visits isn't really helpful because it's not clear whether it's two visits or three. What's worse, a continuous-valued predictor may even predict negative values that may be completely meaningless. What does –4.7 visits to a doctor even mean? This discussion shows that continuous and count-valued targets mean completely different things and should be treated differently.

First, let's look at how linear regression fits continuous-valued targets. Figure 7.2 (left) shows a (noisy) univariate data set, where the continuous-valued label (y) depends on a single feature (x).

A linear regression model assumes that for an input x, the prediction errors or residuals $y = f(x)$ are distributed according to the normal distribution. In figure 7.2 (left), we overlay several such normal distributions on the data, labels, and linear regression model (the dotted line).

To put it simply, linear regression tries to fit a linear model so that the residuals have a normal distribution. The normal distribution, also called the Gaussian distribution, is a *probability distribution*, or a mathematical description of the spread and shape of the possible values a (random) variable can take. As we can see in figure 7.2 (right), the normal distribution is a continuous-valued distribution and a reasonable choice for continuous-valued labels.

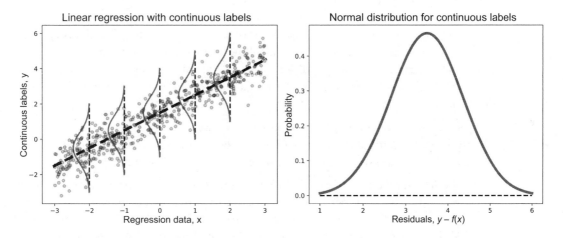

Figure 7.2   Linear regression (left) fits continuous-valued targets by assuming that the *spread* of the targets can be modeled by the continuous-valued normal distribution (right). More precisely, linear regression assumes that the predictions $f(x)$ for an example x are distributed according to the normal distribution.

But what of count data? In figure 7.3, we visualize the difference between our data set from figure 7.2 with continuous-valued targets (left) and a second data set with count-valued targets (right).

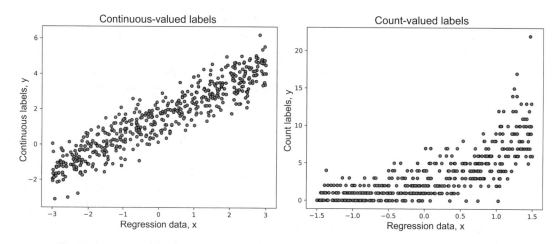

Figure 7.3   Visualizing the differences between continuous-valued targets (left) and count-valued targets (right) shows us that linear regression won't work well because the distribution (spread and shape) of the count labels is quite different from that of continuous labels.

We begin to see some rather stark differences between continuous-valued and count-valued labels. Intuitively, a regression model designed for continuous targets would struggle to build a viable model with count-valued targets.

This is because regression models for continuous targets assume that the residuals have a certain shape: the normal distribution. As we'll see, count-valued targets are *not* normally distributed, but, in fact, often follow a Poisson distribution. Because count-valued labels are fundamentally different from continuous-valued labels, a regression approach designed for continuous-valued labels won't generally work well on count-valued labels.

NEW ASSUMPTIONS FOR COUNT-VALUED REGRESSION MODELS

Can we keep the general framework of linear regression, then, but extend it to be able to handle count-valued data? We can indeed, with some modeling changes:

- We'll have to change how we link the label (prediction target) to the input features. Linear regression relates labels to features through a linear function: $y = \beta_0 + \beta'x$. For count labels, we'll introduce a link function $g(y)$ into model $g(y) = \beta_0 + \beta'x$; in particular, we'll use the log-link function—$log(y) = \beta_0 + \beta'x$— or equivalently, by inverting the log as $y = e^{\beta_0 + \beta'x}$. Link functions are often chosen based on two key factors: (1) the underlying probability distribution that we think is best suited for the data and how it behaves, and (2) task- and application-dependent considerations.

- We'll have to change our assumptions on how we think the predictions $f(x)$ are distributed. Linear regression assumes the normal distribution for continuous-valued labels. For count-valued labels, we'll need the Poisson distribution, which is one of several distributions that can be used to model counts.

- The Poisson distribution is a discrete probability distribution, so it's well suited to handle discrete count-valued labels and expresses the probability of how many events can occur in a fixed interval of time. In this case, the log-link function is a natural fit for the Poisson distribution and other distributions that have an exponential form.

Figure 7.4 illustrates the need for a log-link function as well as the Poisson distribution for developing regression models for count-valued data:

- Observe the mean (average) trend of the count labels (y) in relation to the regression data (x) in figure 7.4 (left), illustrated by the dashed line. Intuitively, this is a gentle exponential trend and shows how the features (x) can be linked to the labels (y).
- Observe how the Poisson distributions overlaid on the visualization model the nature of counts (discrete) as well as their spread far better than the normal distribution.

A regression model with these changes allows us to model count-valued targets and is appropriately called *Poisson regression*.

To recap, Poisson regression still uses a linear model to capture the effect of the various input features from the examples. However, it introduces a log-link function and the Poisson distribution assumption to effectively model count-labeled data.

The Poisson regression approach just described is an extension of ordinary linear regression, meaning that it has no regularization. Unsurprisingly, however, we can add different regularization terms to induce robustness or sparsity, as we saw in section 7.1.

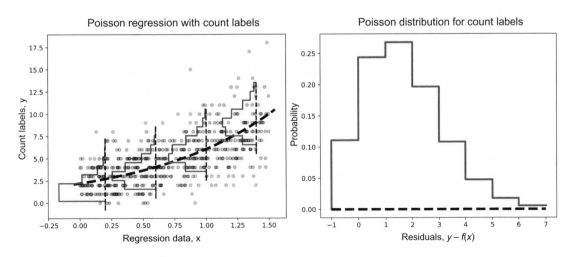

Figure 7.4 Poisson regression (left) fits count-valued targets by assuming that the *spread* of the targets can be modeled by the discrete-valued Poisson distribution (right). More precisely, Poisson regression assumes that the predictions $f(x)$ for an example x are distributed according to the Poisson distribution.

scikit-learn's implementation of Poisson regression is part of the `sklearn.linear_model` subpackage. It implements Poisson regression with L2 regularization, where the effect of regularization can be controlled through the argument `alpha`.

Thus, the hyperparameter `alpha` is the regularization parameter, analogous to the regularization parameter in ridge regression. Setting `alpha=0` causes the model to learn an unregularized Poisson regressor, which, as with unregularized linear regression, can't handle feature correlations as effectively.

In the following example, we call Poisson regression with `alpha=0.01`, which trains a regression model for count labels and is *also* robust to feature correlations in the data:

```
from sklearn.linear_model import PoissonRegressor
poiss_reg = PoissonRegressor(alpha=0.01)
poiss_reg.fit(Xtrn, ytrn)
ypred = poiss_reg.predict(Xtst)
mse = mean_squared_error(ytst, ypred)
mad = mean_absolute_error(ytst, ypred)
print('Poisson regression test set performance: MSE={0:4.3f}, MAD={1:4.3f}'.
    format(mse, mad))
```

This snippet, executed on the data in figure 7.4 (see the companion Python code to generate this data), results in the following output:

```
Poisson regression test set performance: MSE = 3.963, MAD=1.594
```

We can train a ridge regression model on this synthetic data set with count-valued features. Remember that ridge regression uses the MSE as the loss function, which is unsuited for count variables, as shown here:

```
Ridge regression test set performance: MSE = 4.219, MAD=1.610
```

7.1.3   *Logistic regression for classification labels*

In the previous section, we saw that it's possible to extend linear regression to count-valued labels with an appropriate choice of link function and target distribution. What other label types can we handle? Can this idea (of adding link functions and introducing other types of distributions) be extended to categorical labels? Categorical (or class) labels are used to describe classes in binary classification problems (0 or 1) or multiclass classification problems (0, 1, 2).

The question, then, is can we apply a regression framework to a classification problem? Amazingly, yes! For simplicity, let's focus on binary classification, where labels can take only two values, 0 or 1:

- We'll have to change how we *link* the target label to the input features. For class/categorical labels, we use the logit link function $g(y) = \ln\left(\frac{y}{1-y}\right)$. Thus, the model we'll learn will be $\ln\left(\frac{y}{1-y}\right) = \beta_0 + \boldsymbol{\beta}' \boldsymbol{x}$. This may seem like a rather arbitrary choice at first, but a slightly deeper look demystifies this choice.

  First, by inverting the logit function, we have the equivalent link $y = \frac{1}{1+e^{-\left(\beta_0 + \boldsymbol{\beta}' \boldsymbol{x}\right)}}$ between the labels y and the data x. That is, y is modeled with the sigmoid function, also known as the *logistic function*! Thus, using the logit link function in a regression model turns it into logistic regression, a well-known classification algorithm!

Second, we can think of $\frac{y}{1-y}$ as a ratio of $y : (1 - y)$, which we interpret as the odds of y being Class 0 to being Class 1. These odds are exactly the same as the odds offered in gambling and betting. The logit link function is simply the logarithm of the odds, or *log-odds*. This link function, essentially, is providing a measure of likelihood of the class being 0 or 1.

- Linear regression assumed the normal distribution for continuous-valued labels, and Poisson regression assumed the Poisson distribution for count-valued labels. Logistic regression assumes the Bernoulli distribution for binary class labels.

  The Bernoulli, like the Poisson distribution, is another discrete probability distribution. However, rather than describing counts of events, the Bernoulli distribution models the outcomes of yes/no questions. This is ideally suited for the binary classification case, where we ask the question, "Does this example belong to Class 0 or Class 1?"

Putting all of this together, we visualize logistic regression analogously to linear regression or Poisson regression in figure 7.5.

Figure 7.5 (left) shows a binary classification data set, where the data has only one feature and the targets belong to one of two categories. In this case, the binary labels follow the Bernoulli distribution, and the sigmoid link function (dotted line) allows us to relate the data (x) to the labels (y) nicely. Figure 7.5 (right) shows us a closer look at the Bernoulli distribution.

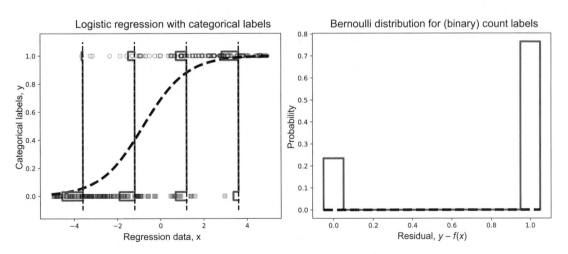

Figure 7.5 Logistic regression (left) fits 0/1-valued targets by assuming that the *spread* of the targets can be modeled by the discrete-valued Bernoulli distribution (right). Observe how the prediction probabilities (the heights of the bars) of Class 0 and Class 1 change with the data.

Logistic regression, of course, is one of many different classification algorithms, though one with a close connection to regression. This segue into classification problems is only intended to highlight the various types of problems the general regression framework can handle.

7.1.4 *Generalized linear models*

The generalized linear model (GLM) framework includes different combinations of link functions and probability distributions (and many other models) to create problem-specific regression variants. Linear regression, Poisson regression, logistic regression, and many other models are all different GLM variants. A (regularized) GLM regression model has four components:

- Probability distribution (formally, from the exponential family of distributions)
- Linear model $\eta = \beta_0 + \beta'x$
- Link function $g(y) = \eta$
- Regularization function $R(\beta)$

Why do we care about GLMs? First, they're obviously a cool modeling approach that allows us to handle several different types of regression problems in one unified framework. Second, and more importantly, GLMs are often used as weak learners in sequential models, especially in many gradient-boosting packages such as XGBoost. Third, and most important, GLMs allow us to think about problems in a principled manner; in practice, this means that during data set analysis, as we begin to get a good sense of the labels and their distribution, we can see which GLM variant best suits the problem at hand.

Table 7.2 shows different GLM variants, link function–distribution combinations, and types of labels they're best suited for. Some of these approaches, such as Tweedie regression, may be new to you, and we'll get into them more in sections 7.3 and 7.4.

Table 7.2   GLMs for different types of labels

Model	Link function	Distribution	Type of label
Linear regression	Identity $g(y) = y$	Normal	Real-valued
Gamma regression	Negative inverse $g(y) = -\frac{1}{y}$	Gamma	Positive real-valued
Poisson regression	Log $g(y) = log(y)$	Poisson	Counts/occurrences; integer-valued
Logistic regression	Logit $g(y) = \frac{y}{1-y}$	Bernoulli	0–1; binary class labels; yes/no outcomes
Multiclass logistic regression	Multiclass logit $g(y) = \frac{y}{K-y}$	Binomial	0–K; multiclass labels; multichoice outcomes
Tweedie regression	Log $g(y) = ln(y)$	Tweedie	Labels with many zeros, right-skewed targets

The last method, Tweedie regression, is a particularly important GLM variant that is widely used for regression modeling in agriculture, insurance, weather, and many other areas.

7.1.5 *Nonlinear regression*

Unlike linear regression, where the model to be learned is cast as a weighted sum of the features, $f(w) = w_0 + w_1 x_1 + \cdots + w_d x_d$, the model to be learned in nonlinear regression can be made up of any combination of features and functions of features. For example, a polynomial regression model of three features can be constructed from weighted combinations of all possible feature interactions:

$$f(x_1, x_2, x_3) = w_0 + w_1 x_1 + w_2 x_2 + w_3 x_3 + w_4 x_1 x_2 + w_5 x_2 x_3 + w_6 x_3 x_1 + w_7 x_1 x_2 x_3$$

From a modeling perspective, nonlinear regression poses two challenges:

- *Which feature combinations should we use?* In the preceding example, with three features, we have $2^3 = 8$ feature combinations, each with its own weight. In general, with d features, we would have 2^d feature combinations to consider and as many weights to learn. Doing this exhaustively can be extremely computationally expensive, and even more so since the example doesn't include any higher-order terms (e.g., $x_2^2 x_3$), which are often also included to build nonlinear models!
- *Which nonlinear functions should we use?* All sorts of functions and combinations beyond polynomials are admissible: trigonometric, exponential, logarithmic, and many others, as well as many more combinations. Searching through this space of functions exhaustively is simply computationally infeasible.

While many different nonlinear regression techniques have been proposed, studied, and used, two approaches are especially relevant in the modern context: decision trees and neural networks. We'll discuss them both briefly, though we'll focus more on decision trees as they are the building blocks of most ensemble methods.

Tree-based methods use decision trees to define the space of nonlinear functions to explore. During learning, decision trees are grown using the same loss functions as described previously, such as the squared loss. Each time a new decision node is added, it introduces a new feature interaction/combination into the tree.

Thus, decision trees induce feature combinations greedily and recursively during learning via the loss function as a scoring metric. As the tree grows, its nonlinearity (or complexity) also increases. The learning objective of decision trees, then, can be written as follows:

$$\text{decision tree learning objective} = \alpha \cdot \underbrace{\text{tree depth}}_{\text{measures model complexity}} + \overbrace{\text{squared loss}}^{\text{measures model fit}}$$

On the other hand, ANNs use layers of neurons to successively induce increasingly complex feature combinations at each layer. The nonlinearity of a neural network increases with network depth, which directly influences the number of network weights that must be learned:

$$\text{neural network learning objective} = \alpha \cdot \underbrace{\text{number of nodes}}_{\text{measures model complexity}} + \overbrace{\text{squared loss}}^{\text{measures model fit}}$$

The scikit-learn package provides many nonlinear regression approaches. Let's take a quick look at how we can train decision tree and neural network regressors for a simple problem.

As before, let's generate a simple, univariate data set to visualize these two regression approaches. The data is generated with $f(x) = e^{-0.5x}\sin(1.25\pi x - 1.414)$, which is the true underlying nonlinear relationship between the data x and the continuous labels y:

```
n = 150
X = rng.uniform(low=-1.0, high=5.0, size=(n, 1))
g = lambda x: np.exp(-0.5*x) * np.sin(1.25 * np.pi * x - 1.414)
y = g(X)  # Generate labels according to this nonlinear function
y += rng.normal(scale=0.08 * np.max(y), size=(n, 1))
y = y.reshape(-1, )
```

Split into train and test sets:

```
Xtrn, Xtst, ytrn, ytst = train_test_split(X, y, test_size=0.25,
                                           random_state=42)
```

Now, train a decision-tree regressor of maximum depth 5:

```
from sklearn.tree import DecisionTreeRegressor
dt = DecisionTreeRegressor(max_depth=5)
dt.fit(Xtrn, ytrn)

ypred_dt = dt.predict(Xtst)
mse = mean_squared_error(ytst, ypred_dt)
mad = mean_absolute_error(ytst, ypred_dt)
print('Decision Tree''s test set performance: MSE = {0:4.3f}, MAD={1:4.3f}'.
      format(mse, mad))
```

The learned decision tree function is shown in figure 7.6 (right). A decision tree with a univariate (single-variable) split function learns axis-parallel fits, which is reflected in the decision-tree model in the figure: the model is made up of segments that are parallel to the x- or y-axes.

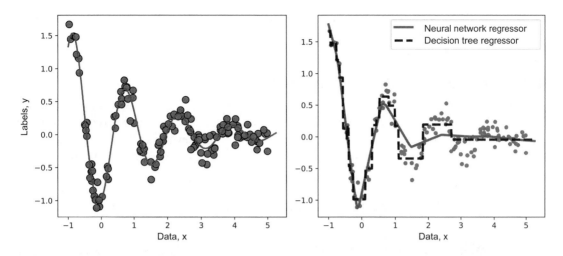

Figure 7.6   Left: The true function relating labels to data (solid curve) and the generated data samples. Right: Two nonlinear regression models fit to this synthetic data set, decision tree and neural network regressors.

In similar fashion, we can train an ANN for regression, also known as a multilayer perceptron (MLP) regressor:

```
from sklearn.neural_network import MLPRegressor
ann = MLPRegressor(hidden_layer_sizes=(50, 50, 50),
                   alpha=0.001, max_iter=1000)
ann.fit(Xtrn, ytrn.reshape(-1, ))
ypred_ann = ann.predict(Xtst)
mse = mean_squared_error(ytst, ypred_ann)
mad = mean_absolute_error(ytst, ypred_ann)

print('Neural Network''s test set performance: MSE = {0:4.3f}, MAD={1:4.3f}'.
      format(mse, mad))
```

This neural network is made up of three hidden layers, each containing 50 neurons, which are specified during network initialization through `hidden_layer _sizes=(50, 50, 50)`.

`MLPRegressor` uses the piecewise-linear rectifier function ($relu(x) = max(x,0)$) as the activation for each neuron. The regression function learned by the neural network is in figure 7.6 (right). Since the neural network activation functions were piecewise linear, the final learned neural network model is nonlinear, though made up of several linear components (hence, piecewise). Comparing the performance of both networks, we see that they are quite similar:

```
Decision Trees test set performance: MSE = 0.027, MAD=0.131
Neural Networks test set performance: MSE = 0.043, MAD=0.164
```

Finally, ensemble methods for regression are typically trained nonlinear regression models (except with specific choices of base estimators), much like the ones discussed in this subsection.

7.2   *Parallel ensembles for regression*

In this section, we revisit parallel ensembles, both homogeneous (chapter 2) and heterogeneous (chapter 3), and see how they can be applied to regression problems. Before we dive into how, let's refresh ourselves on how parallel ensembles work. Figure 7.7 illustrates a generic parallel ensemble, where base estimators are regressors.

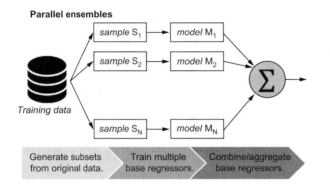

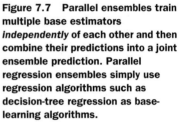

Figure 7.7   Parallel ensembles train multiple base estimators *independently* **of each other and then combine their predictions into a joint ensemble prediction. Parallel regression ensembles simply use regression algorithms such as decision-tree regression as base-learning algorithms.**

Parallel ensemble methods train each component estimator independently of the others, which means that they can be trained in parallel. Parallel ensembles typically use strong learners, or high-complexity, high-fit learners as base learners. This is in contrast to sequential ensembles, which typically use weak learners, or low-complexity, low-fit learners as base learners.

As with all ensemble methods, ensemble diversity among the component base estimators is the key. Parallel ensembles achieve this in two ways:

- *Homogeneous ensembles*—The base-learning algorithm is fixed, but the training data is randomly subsampled to induce ensemble diversity. In section 7.2.1, we look at two such approaches: random forest and Extra Trees.
- *Heterogeneous ensembles*—The base-learning algorithm is changed for diversity, while the training data is fixed. In sections 7.2.2 and 7.2.3, we look at two such approaches: fusing base estimator predictions with a combining function (or aggregator) and stacking base estimator predictions by learning a second-level estimator (or meta-estimator).

We focus on a problem with continuous-valued labels called AutoMPG, which is a popular regression data set that is often used as a benchmark to evaluate regression methods. The regression task is to predict the fuel efficiency of various car models or miles per gallon (MPG). The features consist of various engine-related attributes such as number of cylinders, displacement, horsepower, weight, and acceleration. The data set is available from the UCI Machine Learning Repository (http://mng.bz/Y6Yo), as well as with the source code for this book.

Listing 7.2 shows how to load the data and split it into training and test sets. The listing also includes a preprocessing step, where the data is centered and rescaled so that each feature has a mean of 0 and standard deviation of 1. This step, called normalization or standardization, ensures that all the features are in the same range of values and improves the performance of downstream learning algorithms.

Listing 7.2   Loading and preprocessing the AutoMPG data set

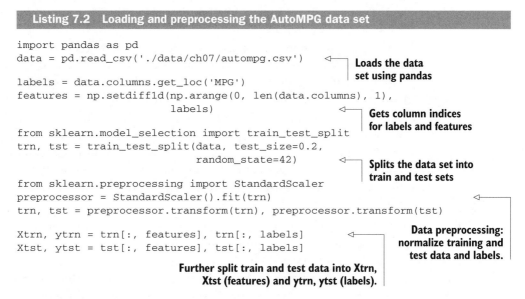

```
import pandas as pd
data = pd.read_csv('./data/ch07/autompg.csv')          ◁─── Loads the data
                                                            set using pandas
labels = data.columns.get_loc('MPG')
features = np.setdiff1d(np.arange(0, len(data.columns), 1),
                        labels)
                                                  ◁─── Gets column indices
                                                       for labels and features
from sklearn.model_selection import train_test_split
trn, tst = train_test_split(data, test_size=0.2,
                            random_state=42)
                                                  ◁─── Splits the data set into
                                                       train and test sets
from sklearn.preprocessing import StandardScaler
preprocessor = StandardScaler().fit(trn)                                    ◁───
trn, tst = preprocessor.transform(trn), preprocessor.transform(tst)

Xtrn, ytrn = trn[:, features], trn[:, labels]          ◁───      Data preprocessing:
Xtst, ytst = tst[:, features], tst[:, labels]                    normalize training and
                                                                 test data and labels.
              Further split train and test data into Xtrn,
              Xtst (features) and ytrn, ytst (labels).
```

We'll be using this data set as a running example for this and the next section.

7.2.1   Random forests and Extra Trees

Homogeneous parallel ensembles are some of the oldest ensemble methods and are generally variants of *bagging*. Chapter 2 introduced homogeneous ensemble methods in the context of classification. To recap, each base estimator in a parallel ensemble method such as bagging can be trained *independently* using the following steps:

1   Generate a bootstrap sample (by sampling with replacement, which means an example can be sampled multiple times) from the original data set.
2   Fit a base estimator to the bootstrap sample; since each bootstrap sample will be different, the base estimators will be diverse.

We can follow the same for regression ensembles. The only difference is in how the individual base estimator predictions are aggregated. For classification, we use majority voting; for regression, we use the mean (essentially, the average prediction), though others (e.g., the median) can also be used.

NOTE   Each base estimator in bagging is a fully trained strong estimator; therefore, if the bagging ensemble contains 10 base regressors, it will take 10 times as long to train. Of course, this training procedure can be parallelized over multiple CPU cores; however, the overall computational resources needed for full-blown bagging is often prohibitive.

As bagging can be rather computationally expensive to train, two important tree-based and randomized variants are used:

- *Random forest*—This is essentially bagging with *randomized decision trees* as base estimators. In other words, random forests perform bootstrap sampling to generate a training subset (exactly like bagging), and then use randomized decision trees as base estimators.

  Randomized decision trees are trained using a modified decision-tree learning algorithm, which introduces randomness when growing trees. Specifically, instead of considering all the features to identify the best split, a *random* subset of features is evaluated to identify the best feature to split on.

- *Extra Trees (extremely randomized trees)*—These randomized trees take the idea of randomized decision trees to the extreme by selecting not just the splitting variable from a random subset of features but also the splitting threshold. This extreme randomization is so effective, in fact, that we can construct an ensemble of extremely randomized trees directly from the original data set without bootstrap sampling!

Randomization has two important and beneficial consequences. One, as we expect, is that it improves training efficiency and reduces the computational requirements. The other is that it improves ensemble diversity! Random forests and Extra Trees can be adapted to regression by modifying the underlying learning algorithm to train regression trees to make continuous-valued predictions rather than classification trees.

Regression trees use different splitting criteria during training compared to classification trees. In principle, any loss function for regression can be used as the splitting criterion. However, two commonly implemented splitting criteria are mean squared error (MSE) and mean absolute error (MAE). We'll look at other loss functions for regression in section 7.3.

Listing 7.3 shows how we can use scikit-learn's `RandomForestRegressor` and `ExtraTreesRegressor` to train regression ensembles for the AutoMPG data set. Two versions of each method are trained: one using MSE and one using MAE as the training criteria.

Listing 7.3 Random forest and Extra Trees for regression

```
from sklearn.ensemble import RandomForestRegressor, ExtraTreesRegressor
from sklearn.metrics import mean_squared_error, mean_absolute_error

ensembles = {
    'Random Forest MSE': RandomForestRegressor(criterion='squared_error'),
    'Random Forest MAE': RandomForestRegressor(criterion='absolute_error'),
    'ExtraTrees MSE': ExtraTreesRegressor(criterion='squared_error'),
    'ExtraTrees MAE': ExtraTreesRegressor(criterion='absolute_error')}
```

Initializes
ensembles

```
results = pd.DataFrame()
ypred_trn = {}
ypred_tst = {}
```
Creates data structures to store model predictions and evaluation results

```
for method, ensemble in ensembles.items():
    ensemble.fit(Xtrn, ytrn)
```
Trains the ensemble

```
    ypred_trn[method] = ensemble.predict(Xtrn)
    ypred_tst[method] = ensemble.predict(Xtst)
```
Gets ensemble predictions on both train and test sets

```
    res = {'Method-Loss': method,
           'Train MSE': mean_squared_error(ytrn, ypred_trn[method]),
           'Train MAE': mean_absolute_error(ytrn, ypred_trn[method]),
           'Test MSE': mean_squared_error(ytst, ypred_tst[method]),
           'Test MAE': mean_absolute_error(ytst, ypred_tst[method])}
```
Evaluates train and test set performance with MAE and MSE

Saves results
```
    results = pd.concat([results,
                        pd.DataFrame.from_dict([res])], ignore_index=True)
```

All models are also evaluated using MSE and MAE as the evaluation criteria. These evaluation metrics are added to the `results` variable:

```
  Package-Method-Loss   Train MSE   Train MAE   Test MSE   Test MAE
0   Random Forest MSE      0.0176      0.0919     0.0872     0.2061
1   Random Forest MAE      0.0182      0.0964     0.0998     0.2293
2       ExtraTrees MSE     0.0000      0.0000     0.0806     0.2030
3       ExtraTrees MAE     0.0000      0.0000     0.0702     0.1914
```

In the preceding example, we used the default parameter settings for both `Random-ForestRegressor` and `ExtraTreesRegressor`. For instance, each trained ensemble is of size 100 as `n_estimators=100`, by default.

As with any other machine-learning algorithm, we have to identify the best model hyperparameters (e.g., `n_estimators`) through a grid search or randomized search. There are several examples of this in the case study in section 7.4.

7.2.2 Combining regression models

Another classic ensembling approach, especially when we have different types of models, is to simply combine their predictions. This is essentially one of the simplest heterogeneous parallel ensembling approaches.

Why combine regression models? It's quite common, during the data exploration phase, to experiment with different machine-learning algorithms. This means that we often have several different models available to us for ensembling. For example, in section 7.2.1, we trained four different regression models. Because we have the predictions of four different models, we can happily combine them into one ensemble prediction—but what combination functions should we use?

- *For continuous-valued targets*—Use combining functions/aggregators such as weighted mean, median, min, or max. In particular, the median is especially effective when combining heterogenous predictions where the models are in greater disagreement.

For example, if we have five models in the ensemble predicting [0.29, 0.3, 0.32, 0.35, 0.85], then most of the models agree, though there is one outlier with 0.85. The mean of these predictions is 0.42, while the median is 0.32. Thus, the median tends to discard the influence of the outliers (and behaves similarly to majority voting), while the mean tends to include them. This is because the median is simply (and literally) the middle value, while the mean is the averaged value.

- *For count-valued targets*—Use combining functions/aggregators such as mode and median. We can think of the mode, in particular, as the generalization of majority voting to counts. The mode is simply the most common answer.

  For example, if we have five models in the ensemble predicting [12, 15, 15, 15, 16], the mode is 15. If there are conflicts, with equal counts we can use random selection to break ties.

Listing 7.4 illustrates the use of four simple aggregators for continuous-valued data. In this listing, we use the four regressors trained in listing 7.3 as the (heterogeneous) base estimators whose values we'll combine: `RandomForestRegressor` and `ExtraTrees-Regressor`, each trained with MSE and MAE as the loss function/split criteria.

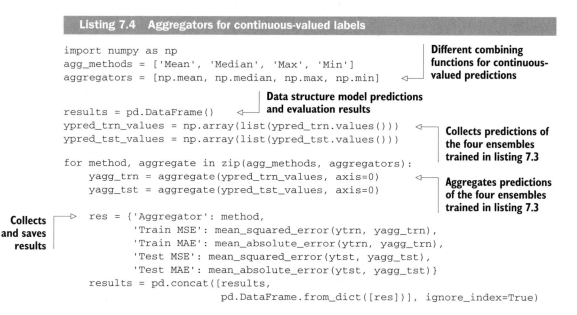

Listing 7.4   Aggregators for continuous-valued labels

```
import numpy as np
agg_methods = ['Mean', 'Median', 'Max', 'Min']          Different combining
aggregators = [np.mean, np.median, np.max, np.min]       functions for continuous-
                                                          valued predictions

                          Data structure model predictions
results = pd.DataFrame()    and evaluation results
ypred_trn_values = np.array(list(ypred_trn.values()))    Collects predictions of
ypred_tst_values = np.array(list(ypred_tst.values()))    the four ensembles
                                                          trained in listing 7.3
for method, aggregate in zip(agg_methods, aggregators):
    yagg_trn = aggregate(ypred_trn_values, axis=0)       Aggregates predictions
    yagg_tst = aggregate(ypred_tst_values, axis=0)       of the four ensembles
                                                          trained in listing 7.3
    res = {'Aggregator': method,
           'Train MSE': mean_squared_error(ytrn, yagg_trn),
           'Train MAE': mean_absolute_error(ytrn, yagg_trn),
           'Test MSE': mean_squared_error(ytst, yagg_tst),
           'Test MAE': mean_absolute_error(ytst, yagg_tst)}
    results = pd.concat([results,
                         pd.DataFrame.from_dict([res])], ignore_index=True)
```

Collects and saves results

Again, all models are also evaluated using MSE and MAE as the evaluation criteria. These evaluation metrics are added to the `results` variable:

```
  Aggregator  Train MSE  Train MAE  Test MSE  Test MAE
0       Mean     0.0044     0.0466    0.0805    0.2044
1     Median     0.0035     0.0392    0.0809    0.2024
2        Max     0.0091     0.0557    0.0993    0.2247
3        Min     0.0128     0.0541    0.0737    0.1981
```

7.2.3 Stacking regression models

Another way to combine the predictions of different (heterogeneous) regressors is through stacking or meta-learning. Instead of making up a function ourselves (e.g., the mean or median), we train a second-level model to learn how to combine the predictions of the base estimators. This second-level regressor is known as the meta-learner or the meta-estimator.

The meta-estimator is often a nonlinear model that can effectively combine the predictions of the base estimators in a nonlinear manner. The price we pay for this added complexity is that stacking can often overfit, especially in the presence of noisy data.

To guard against overfitting, stacking is often combined with k-fold CV such that each base estimator isn't trained on the exact same data set. This often leads to more diversity and robustness, while decreasing the chances of overfitting.

In chapter 3, listing 3.1, we implemented a stacking model for classification from scratch. An alternate implementation uses scikit-learn's `StackingClassifier` and `StackingRegressor`. This is illustrated for regression problems in listing 7.5.

Here, we train four nonlinear regressors: kernel ridge regression (a nonlinear extension of ridge regression), support vector regression, k-nearest neighbor regression, and Extra Trees. We use an ANN as a meta-learner, which allows us to combine predictions of various heterogeneous regression models in a learnable and highly nonlinear fashion.

Listing 7.5　Stacking regression models

```
from sklearn.ensemble import StackingRegressor
from sklearn.neural_network import MLPRegressor
from sklearn.kernel_ridge import KernelRidge
from sklearn.svm import SVR
from sklearn.tree import DecisionTreeRegressor
from sklearn.neighbors import KNeighborsRegressor
from sklearn.gaussian_process import GaussianProcessRegressor

estimators = \                      Initializes first-level
    [('Kernel Ridge', KernelRidge(kernel='rbf', gamma=0.1)),
     ('Support Vector Machine', SVR(kernel='rbf', gamma=0.1)),
     ('K-Nearest Neighbors', KNeighborsRegressor(n_neighbors=3)),
     ('ExtraTrees', ExtraTreesRegressor(criterion='absolute_error'))]

meta_learner = MLPRegressor(hidden_layer_sizes=(50, 50, 50),
                            max_iter=1000)

stack = StackingRegressor(estimators, final_estimator=meta_learner, cv=3)
stack.fit(Xtrn, ytrn)

ypred_trn = stack.predict(Xtrn)
ypred_tst = stack.predict(Xtst)
```

Initializes first-level (base) regressors

Initializes second-level (meta) regressor

Trains a stacking regressor with 3-fold CV

Computes train and test errors

```
print('Train MSE = {0:5.4f}, Train MAE = {1:5.4f}\n' \
      'Test MSE = {2:5.4f}, Test MAE = {3:5.4f}'.format(
      mean_squared_error(ytrn, ypred_trn),
      mean_absolute_error(ytrn, ypred_trn),
      mean_squared_error(ytst, ypred_tst),
      mean_absolute_error(ytst, ypred_tst)))
```

The stacking regression produces the following output:

```
Train MSE = 0.0427, Train MAE = 0.1478
Test MSE = 0.0861, Test MAE = 0.2187
```

It should be noted here that default parameters were used with the individual base regressors. The performance of this stacking ensemble can further be improved with effective hyperparameter tuning of the base estimator models, which improves the performance of each ensemble component and hence the ensemble overall.

7.3   *Sequential ensembles for regression*

In this section, we revisit sequential ensembles, specifically gradient boosting (with LightGBM; refer to chapter 5) and Newton boosting (with XGBoost; refer to chapter 6), and see how they can be adapted to regression problems.

Both of these approaches are very general in that they can be trained on a wide variety of loss functions. This means they can easily be adapted to different types of problem settings, allowing for problem-specific modeling of continuous-valued and count-valued labels. Before we dive into how, let's refresh ourselves on how sequential ensembles work. Figure 7.8 illustrates a generic sequential ensemble where base estimators are regressors. Unlike parallel ensembles, sequential ensembles grow the ensemble one estimator at a time, where successive estimators aim to improve on the predictions of the previous ones.

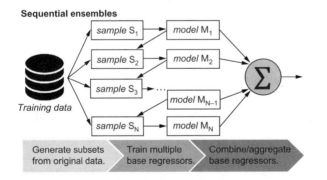

Figure 7.8   **Unlike parallel ensembles that train base estimators *independently* of each other, sequential ensembles, such as boosting, train successive base estimators stagewise to identify and minimize the errors made by the previous base estimator.**

Each successive base estimator uses the *residual* as a means of identifying which training examples need attention in the current iteration. In regression problems, the residual tells the base estimator how much the model is underestimating or overestimating the prediction (see figure 7.9).

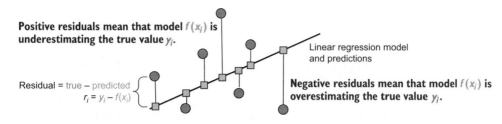

Figure 7.9 **A linear regression model and its predictions (squares) fit to a data set (circles). The residuals are a measure of the *error* between the true label (y_i) and predicted label $f(x_i)$. The size of the residual of each training example indicates the extent of the error in fitting, while the sign of the residual indicates whether the model is underestimating or overestimating.**

More concretely, regression residuals convey two important pieces of information to the base learners. For each training example, the magnitude of the residual can be interpreted in a straightforward manner: bigger residuals mean more errors.

The sign of the residual also conveys important information. A positive residual suggests that the current model's prediction is *underestimating* the true value; that is, the model has to increase its prediction. A negative residual suggests that the current model's prediction is *overestimating* the true value; that is, the model has to decrease its prediction.

The loss function and, more importantly, its derivatives allow us to measure the residual between the current model's prediction and the true label. By changing the loss function, we're essentially changing how we prioritize different examples.

Both gradient boosting and Newton boosting use shallow regression trees as weak base learners. Weak learners (contrast with bagging and its variants, which use strong learners) are essentially low-complexity, low-fit models. By training a sequence of weak learners to fix the mistakes of the previously learned weak learners, both methods boost the performance of the ensemble in stages:

- *Gradient boosting*—Uses the negative gradient of the loss function as the residual to identify training examples to focus on.
- *Newton boosting*—Uses Hessian-weighted gradients of the loss function as the residual to identify training examples to focus on. The Hessians (second derivatives) of the loss functions incorporate local "curvature" information to increase the weight on training examples with higher loss values.

Loss functions, then, are a key ingredient in developing effective sequential ensembles.

7.3.1 Loss and likelihood functions for regression

In this section, we'll take a look at some common (and uncommon) loss functions for different types of labels: continuous-valued, continuous-valued but positive, and count-valued. Each of these loss functions penalizes errors differently and will result in learning models with different properties, much like how different regularization functions produced models with different properties (in section 7.1).

Many loss functions are ultimately derived from how we assume the residuals are distributed. We've already seen this in section 7.1, where we assume that the residuals of continuous-valued targets can be modeled using the Gaussian distribution, count-valued targets can be modeled using the Poisson distribution, and so on.

Here, we formalize that notion. Note that some loss functions don't have a closed-form expression. In such cases, it's useful to visualize the *negative log of the underlying distribution*. This term, called the *negative log-likelihood*, is sometimes optimized instead of the loss function and ultimately has the same effect in the final model.

We consider three types of labels and their corresponding loss functions. These are visualized in figure 7.10.

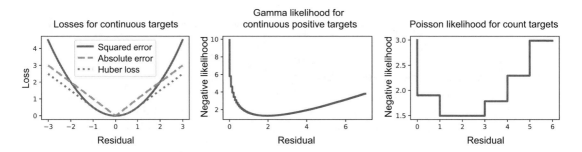

Figure 7.10   Loss and log-likelihood functions for three different types of targets: continuous-valued (left), positive continuous-valued (center), and count-valued (right)

CONTINUOUS-VALUED LABELS

There are several well-known loss functions for continuous-valued targets. Two of the most common are as follows:

- Squared error (SE), $\frac{1}{2} \cdot (y - f(x))^2$—Directly corresponds to assuming a Gaussian distribution over the residuals
- Absolute error (AE), $|y - f(x)|$—Corresponds to assuming the Laplacian distribution over the residuals

The SE penalizes errors far more heavily than the AE, as is evident from the loss values at the extremes in figure 7.10. This makes the SE highly sensitive to outliers. The SE is also a doubly differentiable loss function, which means that we can compute both the first and second derivatives. Thus, we can use it for both gradient boosting (which uses residuals) and Newton boosting (which uses Hessian-boosted residuals). The AE isn't doubly differentiable, meaning it can't be used in Newton boosting.

The *Huber loss* is a hybrid of the SE and the AE and switches its behavior between the two at some user-specified threshold τ:

$$L(y, f(x)) = \begin{cases} \frac{1}{2}(y - f(x))^2, & \text{for } |y - f(x)| \leq \tau, \\ \tau \cdot |y - f(x)| - \frac{\tau^2}{2}, & \text{otherwise} \end{cases}$$

For residuals smaller than τ, the Huber loss behaves like the SE, and beyond the threshold, it behaves like the scaled AE (refer to figure 7.10). This makes the Huber loss ideal in situations where we desire to limit the influence of outliers.

Note that the Huber loss can't be directly used with Newton boosting as it contains the AE as one of its components. For this reason, Newton-boosting implementations use a smooth approximation called the *pseudo-Huber loss*:

$$L(y, f(x)) = \tau^2 \left(\sqrt{1 + \frac{1}{\tau^2}(y - f(x))^2} - 1 \right)$$

The pseudo-Huber loss behaves like the Huber loss, though it's an approximate version that outputs $\frac{1}{2} \cdot (y - f(x))^2$ for residuals $(y - f(x))$ close to zero.

CONTINUOUS-VALUED POSITIVE LABELS

In some domains, such as insurance claims analytics, the target labels that we want to predict only take positive values. For example, the claim amount is continuous-valued but can only be positive.

In such situations, where the Gaussian distribution isn't appropriate, we can use the *gamma distribution*. The gamma distribution is a highly flexible distribution that can fit many target distribution shapes. This makes it ideally suited for modeling problems where the target distributions have long tails—that is, outliers that can't be ignored.

The gamma distribution doesn't correspond to a closed-form loss function. Shown earlier in figure 7.10 (center), we plot the negative log-likelihood instead, which functions as a surrogate loss function.

First, observe that the loss function is only defined for positive real values (x-axis). Next, observe how the log-likelihood function only gently penalizes errors to the further right. This allows the underlying models to fit to right-skewed data.

COUNT-VALUED LABELS

Beyond continuous-valued labels, some regression problems require us to fit count-valued targets. We've already seen examples of this in section 7.1, where we learned that counts, which are discrete-valued, can be modeled using the Poisson distribution.

Like the gamma distribution, the Poisson distribution also doesn't correspond to a closed-form loss function. Figure 7.10 (right) illustrates the negative log-likelihood of the Poisson distribution, which can be used to build regression models (called Poisson regression).

HYBRID LABELS

In some problems, the underlying labels can't be modeled by a single distribution. For example, in weather analytics, if we want to model rainfall, we can expect that (1) on most days, we'll have no rain at all; (2) on some days, we'll have varying degrees of rainfall; and (3) on some rare occasions, we'll have very heavy rainfall.

Figure 7.11 shows the distribution of rainfall data, where we have a big "point mass" or spike at 0 (corresponding to most days that receive no rainfall). In addition, this distribution is also right skewed as there are a small number of days with very high rainfall.

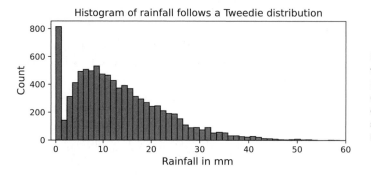

Figure 7.11 Modeling some types of labels effectively requires combinations of distributions, called compound distributions. One such compound distribution is the Tweedie distribution.

To model this problem, we need a loss function corresponding to a hybrid distribution, specifically a Poisson-gamma distribution: the Poisson distribution to model the big point mass at 0, and the gamma distribution to model the right-skewed, positive, continuous data. For such labels, we can use a powerful family of probability distributions called the Tweedie distributions, which are parameterized by the Tweedie power parameter p. Different values of p give rise to different distributions:

- $p = 0$: Gaussian (normal) distribution
- $p = 1$: Poisson distribution
- $1 < p < 2$: Poisson-gamma distributions for different p
- $p = 2$: Gamma distribution
- $p = 3$: Inverse Gaussian distribution

Other choices of p produce many other distributions. For our purposes, we're mostly interested in using $1 < p < 2$, to create hybrid Poisson-gamma loss functions.

Both LightGBM and XGBoost come with support for the Tweedie distribution, which has led to their widespread adoption in domains such as weather analytics, insurance analytics, and health informatics. We'll see how to use this in our case study in section 7.4.

7.3.2 Gradient boosting with LightGBM and XGBoost

Now, armed with the knowledge of various loss functions, let's see how we can apply gradient-boosting regressors to the AutoMPG data set.

GRADIENT BOOSTING WITH LIGHTGBM

First, let's apply standard gradient boosting, that is, LightGBM's `LGBMRegressor` with the Huber loss function. There are several LightGBM hyperparameters that we also have to select. These parameters control various components of LightGBM:

- *Loss function parameters*—`alpha` is the Huber loss parameter, the threshold where it switches from behaving like the MSE to behaving like the MAE loss.
- *Learning control parameters*—`learning_rate` is used to control the rate at which the model learns so that it doesn't rapidly fit and then overfit the training data; and `subsample` is used to randomly sample a smaller fraction of the data during training to induce additional ensemble diversity and improve training efficiency.

- *Regularization parameters*—`lambda_l1` and `lambda_l2` are the weights on the L1 and L2 regularizations functions, respectively; these correspond to *a* and *b* in the elastic net objective (refer to table 7.1).
- *Tree learning parameters*—`max_depth` limits the maximum depth of each weak tree in the ensemble.

There are other hyperparameters in each category that also allow for finer-grained control over training. We select hyperparameters using a combination of randomized search (since an exhaustive grid search would be too slow) and CV. Listing 7.6 shows an example of this with LightGBM.

In addition to hyperparameter selection, the listing also implements early stopping, where training is terminated if no performance improvement is observed on an evaluation set.

Listing 7.6 LightGBM with Huber loss

```
from lightgbm import LGBMRegressor
from sklearn.model_selection import RandomizedSearchCV          Ranges of
                                                                hyperparameters that
parameters = {'alpha': [0.3, 0.9, 1.8],          ◁─────────     we want to search over
              'max_depth': np.arange(2, 5, step=1),
              'learning_rate': 2**np.arange(-8., 2., step=2),
              'subsample': [0.6, 0.7, 0.8],
              'lambda_l1': [0.01, 0.1, 1],
              'lambda_l2': [0.01, 0.1, 1e-1, 1]}               Initializes a
                                                              LightGBM
lgb = LGBMRegressor(objective='huber', n_estimators=100)  ◁──  regressor
param_tuner = RandomizedSearchCV(lgb, parameters,
                                 n_iter=20, cv=5,    ◁───  Since GridSearchCV will be slow,
 Fits the regressor               refit=True, verbose=1)    searches more than 20 random
 with early stopping                                        parameter combinations
                                                            with 5-fold CV
  └─▷ param_tuner.fit(Xtrn, ytrn,
                  eval_set=[(Xtst, ytst)], eval_metric='mse', verbose=False)

ypred_trn = param_tuner.best_estimator_.predict(Xtrn)  ◁───  Computes train
ypred_tst = param_tuner.best_estimator_.predict(Xtst)       and test errors
print('Train MSE = {0:5.4f}, Train MAE = {1:5.4f}\n' \
      'Test MSE = {2:5.4f}, Test MAE = {3:5.4f}'.format(
      mean_squared_error(ytrn, ypred_trn),
      mean_absolute_error(ytrn, ypred_trn),
      mean_squared_error(ytst, ypred_tst),
      mean_absolute_error(ytst, ypred_tst)))
```

This produces the following output:

```
Fitting 5 folds for each of 20 candidates, totalling 100 fits
Train MSE = 0.0476, Train MAE = 0.1497
Test MSE = 0.0951, Test MAE = 0.2250
```

The LightGBM (gradient boosting) model trained with the Huber loss achieves test MSE of 0.0951, highlighted in bold in the preceding code snippet.

NEWTON BOOSTING WITH XGBOOST

We can repeat this training and evaluation with XGBoost's `XGBRegressor`. Since Newton boosting requires second derivatives, which can't be computed for the Huber loss, XGBoost doesn't provide this loss directly. Instead, XGBoost provides a pseudo-Huber loss, the differentiable approximation of the Huber loss introduced in section 7.3.1. Again, as with LightGBM, we have to set several different hyperparameters. Many of XGBoost's parameters correspond exactly to LightGBM's parameters, though they have different names:

- *Learning control parameters*—`learning_rate` is used to control the rate at which the model learns so that it doesn't rapidly fit and then overfit the training data; and `colsample_bytree` is used to randomly sample a smaller fraction of the features (similar to random forests) during training to induce additional ensemble diversity and improve training efficiency.

- *Regularization parameters*—`reg_alpha` and `reg_lambda` are the weights on the L1 and L2 regularizations functions, respectively; these correspond to *a* and *b* in the elastic net objective (refer to table 7.1).

- *Tree learning parameters*—`max_depth` limits the maximum depth of each weak tree in the ensemble.

The following listing shows how we can train an `XGBRegressor`, including a randomized hyperparameter search.

Listing 7.7 Using XGBoost with pseudo-Huber loss

```
from xgboost import XGBRegressor
parameters = {'max_depth': np.arange(2, 5, step=1),          ◁── Ranges of
              'learning_rate': 2**np.arange(-8., 2., step=2),     hyperparameters
              'colsample_bytree': [0.6, 0.7, 0.8],                that we want to
              'reg_alpha': [0.01, 0.1, 1],                        search over
              'reg_lambda': [0.01, 0.1, 1e-1, 1]}

xgb = XGBRegressor(objective='reg:pseudohubererror')    ◁── Initializes an
                                                            XGBoost regressor

param_tuner = RandomizedSearchCV(xgb, parameters,
                                 n_iter=20, cv=5,       ◁── Since GridSearchCV will
                                 refit=True, verbose=1)     be slow, searches more
Fits the regressor                                          than 20 random
with early stopping                                         parameter combinations
   └─▷ param_tuner.fit(Xtrn, ytrn, eval_set=[(Xtst, ytst)],   with 5-fold CV
                       eval_metric='rmse', verbose=False)

ypred_trn = param_tuner.best_estimator_.predict(Xtrn)   ◁── Computes train
ypred_tst = param_tuner.best_estimator_.predict(Xtst)       and test errors
print('Train MSE = {0:5.4f}, Train MAE = {1:5.4f}\n' \
      'Test MSE = {2:5.4f}, Test MAE = {3:5.4f}'.format(
      mean_squared_error(ytrn, ypred_trn),
      mean_absolute_error(ytrn, ypred_trn),
      mean_squared_error(ytst, ypred_tst),
      mean_absolute_error(ytst, ypred_tst)))
```

This produces the following output:

```
Fitting 5 folds for each of 20 candidates, totalling 100 fits
Train MSE = 0.0451, Train MAE = 0.1572
Test MSE = 0.0947, Test MAE = 0.2244
```

The XGBoost model trained with the pseudo-Huber loss achieves a test MSE of 0.0947 (highlighted in bold in the output of listing 7.7). This is similar to the performance of the LightGBM model, which achieved a test MSE of 0.0951 (see output produced by listing 7.6).

This illustrates that the pseudo-Huber loss is a reasonable substitute for the Huber loss when the situation calls for it. We'll shortly see how we can use LightGBM and XGBoost with other loss functions discussed in this section on the task of bike demand prediction in the chapter case study.

7.4   Case study: Demand forecasting

Demand forecasting is an important problem that arises in many business contexts when the goal is to predict the demand for a certain product or commodity. Accurately predicting demand is critical for downstream supply chain management and optimization: to ensure that there is enough supply to meet needs and not too much that there is waste.

Demand forecasting is often cast as a regression problem of using historical data and trends to build a model to predict future demand. The target labels can be continuous or count-valued.

For example, in energy demand forecasting, the label to predict (energy demand in gigawatt hours) is continuous valued. Alternately, in product demand forecasting, the label to predict (number of items to be shipped) is count-valued.

In this section, we study the problem of bike rental forecasting. As we see in this section, the nature of the problem (and, especially, the targets/labels) is quite similar to those arising in the areas of weather prediction and analytics, insurance and risk analytics, health informatics, energy demand forecasting, business intelligence, and many others.

We analyze the data set and then build progressively more complex models, beginning with single linear models, then moving on to ensemble nonlinear models. At each stage, we'll perform hyperparameter tuning to select the best hyperparameter combinations.

7.4.1   The UCI Bike Sharing data set

The Bike Sharing data set[1] was the first of several similar publicly available data sets that tracks the usage of bicycle-sharing services in major metropolitan areas. These

---

[1] "Event labeling combining ensemble detectors and background knowledge," by H. Fanaee-T and J. Gama. *Progress in Artificial Intelligence* 2, 113–127 (2014).

data sets are made publicly available through the UCI Machine Learning Repository (http://mng.bz/GRrM).

This data set, first made available in 2013, tracks hourly and daily bicycle rentals of casual riders and registered member riders of Capital Bike Sharing in Washington, DC. In addition, the data set also contains several features describing the weather as well as the time of day and day of the year.

The overall goal of the problem in this case study is to predict the bike rental demand of casual riders depending on the time of day, the season, and the weather. The demand is measured in total number of users—a count!

Why only model casual riders? The number of registered users appears to be fairly consistent across the year, since these are users who presumably use bike sharing as a regular transportation option rather than a recreational activity. This is akin to commuters who have a monthly/annual bus pass for their daily commutes as opposed to tourists who only buy bus tickets as needed.

Keeping this in mind, we construct a derived data set for our case study that can be used to build a model to forecast the rental bike demand of casual users. The (modified) data set for this case study is available with the book's code and can be loaded thus:

```
import pandas as pd
data = pd.read_csv('./data/ch07/bikesharing.csv')
```

We can look at the statistics of the data set with the following:

```
data.describe()
```

This will compute various statistics of all the features in the data set, as shown in figure 7.12, which is helpful in getting a sense of the various features and how their values are distributed at a high level.

	season	mnth	hr	holiday	weekday	workingday	weathersit	temp	atemp	hum	windspeed	casual
count	17,379.000	17,379.000	17,379.000	17,379.000	17,379.000	17,379.000	17,379.000	17,379.000	17,379.000	17,379.000	17,379.000	17,379.000
mean	2.502	6.538	11.547	0.029	3.004	0.683	1.425	0.497	0.476	0.627	0.190	35.676
std	1.107	3.439	6.914	0.167	2.006	0.465	0.639	0.193	0.172	0.193	0.122	49.305
min	1.000	1.000	0.000	0.000	0.000	0.000	1.000	0.020	0.000	0.000	0.000	0.000
25%	2.000	4.000	6.000	0.000	1.000	0.000	1.000	0.340	0.333	0.480	0.104	4.000
50%	3.000	7.000	12.000	0.000	3.000	1.000	1.000	0.500	0.485	0.630	0.194	17.000
75%	3.000	10.000	18.000	0.000	5.000	1.000	2.000	0.660	0.621	0.780	0.254	48.000
max	4.000	12.000	23.000	1.000	6.000	1.000	4.000	1.000	1.000	1.000	0.851	367.000

Figure 7.12   Statistics of the Bike Sharing data set. The "casual" column is the prediction target (label).

The data set contains several continuous weather features: temp (normalized temperature), atemp (normalized "feels like" temperature), hum (humidity), and windspeed.

The categorical feature `weathersit` describes the type of weather seen at that time with four categories:

- 1: Clear, Few Clouds, Partly Cloudy
- 2: Mist + Cloudy, Mist + Broken Clouds, Mist + Few Clouds, Mist
- 3: Light Snow, Light Rain + Thunderstorm + Scattered Clouds, Rain + Scattered Clouds
- 4: Heavy Rain + Ice Pellets + Thunderstorm + Mist, Snow + Fog

The data set also contains discrete features: `season` (1: winter, 2: spring, 3: summer, 4: fall), `mnth` (1 to 12 for January through December), and `hr` (hour from 0 to 23) to describe the time. In addition, the binary features `holiday`, `weekday`, and `working-day` encode whether the day in question is a holiday, weekday, or workday.

PREPROCESSING THE FEATURES

Let's preprocess this data set by normalizing the features, that is, ensuring each feature is zero mean, unit standard deviation. Normalization isn't always the best approach to deal with discrete features. For now, though, let's use this simple preprocessing and keep our focus on ensembles for regression. In chapter 8, we delve more into preprocessing strategies for these types of features.

Listing 7.8 shows our preprocessing steps: it splits the data into training (80% of the data) and test sets (remaining 20% of the data) and applies normalization to the features. As always, we'll hold out the test set from the training process so that we can evaluate the performance of each of our trained models on the test set.

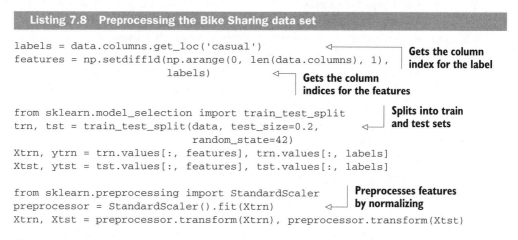

Listing 7.8 Preprocessing the Bike Sharing data set

```
labels = data.columns.get_loc('casual')          ◁——  Gets the column
features = np.setdiff1d(np.arange(0, len(data.columns), 1),    index for the label
                        labels)        ◁——  Gets the column
                                             indices for the features

from sklearn.model_selection import train_test_split      Splits into train
trn, tst = train_test_split(data, test_size=0.2,    ◁——┘   and test sets
                            random_state=42)
Xtrn, ytrn = trn.values[:, features], trn.values[:, labels]
Xtst, ytst = tst.values[:, features], tst.values[:, labels]

from sklearn.preprocessing import StandardScaler      Preprocesses features
preprocessor = StandardScaler().fit(Xtrn)    ◁——  by normalizing
Xtrn, Xtst = preprocessor.transform(Xtrn), preprocessor.transform(Xtst)
```

COUNT-VALUED TARGETS

The target label we want to predict is `casual`, that is, the number of casual users, which is count-valued, ranging from 0 to 367. We plot the histogram of these targets in figure 7.13 (left). This data set has a large point mass at 0, indicating that, on many days, there are no casual users. Further, we can see that this distribution has a *long tail*, which makes it *right skewed*.

We can further analyze these labels by applying a log transformation, that is, transform each count label y to $log(1 + y)$, where we add 1 to avoid taking the logarithm of zero count data. This is shown in figure 7.13 (right).

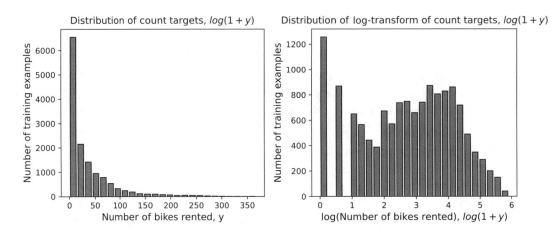

Figure 7.13   Histogram of count-valued targets, the number of casual users (left); histogram of the count targets after log transformation (right)

This gives us two great insights regarding how we might want to model the problem:

- *Use Tweedie distribution*—The distribution of the log-transformed count target looks very similar to the histogram of rainfall shown earlier in figure 7.11, which suggests that a Tweedie distribution might be appropriate for modeling this problem. Recall that a Tweedie distribution with parameter $1 < p < 2$ can model a compound Poisson-gamma distribution: the Poisson distribution to model the big point mass at 0, and the gamma distribution to model the right-skewed, positive continuous data.
- *Use GLM*—The log transformation itself suggests a connection between the target and the features. If we were to model this regression task as a GLM, we would have to use the log-link function. We would like to extend this notion to ensemble methods (which are usually nonlinear).

As we'll see shortly, LightGBM and XGBoost provide support for modeling both the log link (and other link functions) and distributions such as Poisson, gamma, and Tweedie. This allows them to emulate the intuition of GLMs to capture the nuances of the data set, while going beyond the restriction of GLMs to learning only linear models.

7.4.2   *GLMs and stacking*

Let's first train individual general linear regression models that capture the intuitions gleaned previously. In addition, we'll also stack these individual models to combine their predictions. We'll train three individual regressors:

- *Tweedie regression with the log-link function*—Uses the Tweedie distribution to model the positive, right-skewed targets. We use scikit-learn's `Tweedie Regressor`, which requires that we choose two parameters: `alpha`, parameter for the L2 regularization term, and `power`, which should be between 1 and 2.

- *Poisson regression with the log-link function*—Uses the Poisson distribution to model count variables. We use scikit-learn's `PoissonRegressor`, which requires that we choose only one parameter: `alpha`, parameter for the L2 regularization term. It should be noted that setting `power=1` in `TweedieRegressor` is equivalent to using `PoissonRegressor`.

- *Ridge regression*—Uses the normal distribution to model continuous variables. This, in general, isn't well suited for this data and is included as a baseline, as it's one of the most common methods we'll encounter in the wild.

The following listing demonstrates how we can train these regressors with the hyperparameter search through the exhaustive grid search and combined with CV.

Listing 7.9 Training GLMs for bike rental prediction

```
from sklearn.model_selection import GridSearchCV
from sklearn.metrics import (
    mean_squared_error, mean_absolute_error, r2_score)
from sklearn.linear_model import Ridge, PoissonRegressor, TweedieRegressor

parameters = {                          Ranges of hyperparameters for ridge,
                                        Poisson, and Tweedie regressors
    'GLM: Linear': {'alpha': 10 ** np.arange(-4., 1.)},
    'GLM: Poisson': {'alpha': 10 ** np.arange(-4., 1.)},
    'GLM: Tweedie': {
        'alpha': 10 ** np.arange(-4., 1.),        Tweedie regression has an
        'power': np.linspace(1.1, 1.9, num=5)}}   additional parameter: power.

glms = {'GLM: Linear': Ridge(),                    Initializes GLMs
        'GLM: Poisson': PoissonRegressor(max_iter=1000),
        'GLM: Tweedie': TweedieRegressor(max_iter=1000)}

best_glms = {}                   Saves individual
results = pd.DataFrame()         GLMs after CV

for glm_type, glm in glms.items():      Performs grid search for
    param_tuner = GridSearchCV(         each GLM with 5-fold CV
                    glm, parameters[glm_type],
                    cv=5, refit=True, verbose=2)

    param_tuner.fit(Xtrn, ytrn)

    best_glms[glm_type] = param_tuner.best_estimator_      Gets the final refit GLM
    ypred_trn = best_glms[glm_type].predict(Xtrn)          and computes train
    ypred_tst = best_glms[glm_type].predict(Xtst)          and test predictions
```

```
res = {'Method': glm_type,
       'Train MSE': mean_squared_error(ytrn, ypred_trn),
       'Train MAE': mean_absolute_error(ytrn, ypred_trn),
       'Train R2': r2_score(ytrn, ypred_trn),
       'Test MSE': mean_squared_error(ytst, ypred_tst),
       'Test MAE': mean_absolute_error(ytst, ypred_tst),
       'Test R2': r2_score(ytst, ypred_tst)}
results = pd.concat([results,
                     pd.DataFrame.from_dict([res])], ignore_index=True)
```

> **Computes and saves three metrics for each GLM: MAE, MSE, and R^2 score**

If we use `print(results)`, we'll see what the three models have learned. We evaluate the train and test set performance using these metrics: MSE, MAE, and R^2 score. Recall that the R^2 score (or the coefficient of determination) is the proportion of the target variance that is explainable from the data.

R^2 scores range from negative infinity to 1, with higher scores indicating better performance. MSE and MAE range from 0 to infinity, with lower errors indicating better performance:

	Method	Train MSE	Train MAE	Train R2	Test MSE	Test MAE	Test R2
GLM:	Linear	1,368.677	24.964	0.444	1,270.174	23.985	0.447
GLM:	Poisson	1,354.006	21.726	0.450	1,228.898	20.641	0.465
GLM:	Tweedie	1,383.374	21.755	0.438	1,254.304	20.661	0.454

The test set performance immediately confirms one of our intuitions: classical regression approaches, which assume a normal distribution over the data, fare the worst. Poisson or Tweedie distributions, however, show promise.

We've now have trained our first three machine-learning models: let's ensemble them by stacking them. The following listing shows how to do this using ANN regression. While the GLMs we trained are linear, this stacked model will be nonlinear!

Listing 7.10   Stacking GLMs for bike rental prediction

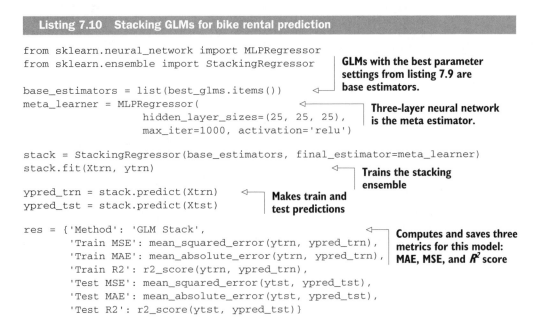

```
from sklearn.neural_network import MLPRegressor
from sklearn.ensemble import StackingRegressor

base_estimators = list(best_glms.items())
meta_learner = MLPRegressor(
                hidden_layer_sizes=(25, 25, 25),
                max_iter=1000, activation='relu')

stack = StackingRegressor(base_estimators, final_estimator=meta_learner)
stack.fit(Xtrn, ytrn)

ypred_trn = stack.predict(Xtrn)
ypred_tst = stack.predict(Xtst)

res = {'Method': 'GLM Stack',
       'Train MSE': mean_squared_error(ytrn, ypred_trn),
       'Train MAE': mean_absolute_error(ytrn, ypred_trn),
       'Train R2': r2_score(ytrn, ypred_trn),
       'Test MSE': mean_squared_error(ytst, ypred_tst),
       'Test MAE': mean_absolute_error(ytst, ypred_tst),
       'Test R2': r2_score(ytst, ypred_tst)}
```

> **GLMs with the best parameter settings from listing 7.9 are base estimators.**
>
> **Three-layer neural network is the meta estimator.**
>
> **Trains the stacking ensemble**
>
> **Makes train and test predictions**
>
> **Computes and saves three metrics for this model: MAE, MSE, and R^2 score**

```
results = pd.concat([results,
                     pd.DataFrame.from_dict([res])], ignore_index=True)
```

Now, we can compare the results of stacking with the individual models

```
    Method   Train MSE   Train MAE   Train R2   Test MSE   Test MAE   Test R2
GLM Stack      975.428      19.011      0.604    927.214     18.199     0.596
```

The stacked GLM ensemble already improves test set performance noticeably, indicating that nonlinear models are the way to go.

7.4.3 *Random forest and Extra Trees*

Now, let's train some more parallel ensembles for the bike rental prediction task using scikit-learn's `RandomForestRegressor` and `ExtraTreesRegressor`. Both modules support MSE, MAE, and Poisson as the loss function. However, unlike GLMs, random forest and Extra Trees don't use a log-link function. We'll train two different ensembles: one for each MSE and Poisson loss functions, and with similar hyperparameter sweeps for each.

For both methods, we're looking to identify the best choice of two hyperparameters: ensemble size (`n_estimators`) and the maximum depth of each base estimator (`max_depth`). We can set the loss functions through the criterion argument for each method as `'squared_error'` or `'poisson'`.

The following listing demonstrates how we can train these regressors with hyperparameter search through exhaustive grid search and combined with CV—similar to what we did for GLMs.

> **Listing 7.11 Random forest and Extra Trees for bike rental prediction**

```
from sklearn.ensemble import RandomForestRegressor
from sklearn.ensemble import ExtraTreesRegressor
                                                      Ranges of hyperparameters for both
parameters = {                                        random forest and Extra Trees
    'n_estimators': np.arange(200, 600, step=100),
    'max_depth': np.arange(4, 7, step=1)}
                                                      Both ensembles use MSE
ensembles = {                                         as the training criterion.
    'RF: Squared Error': RandomForestRegressor(criterion='squared_error'),
    'RF: Poisson': RandomForestRegressor(criterion='poisson'),
    'XT: Squared Error': ExtraTreesRegressor(criterion='squared_error'),
    'XT: Poisson': ExtraTreesRegressor(criterion='poisson')}

for ens_type, ensemble in ensembles.items():          Hyperparameter tuning with
    param_tuner = GridSearchCV(ensemble, parameters,  grid search and 5-fold CV
                               cv=5, refit=True, verbose=2)
    param_tuner.fit(Xtrn, ytrn)

    ypred_trn = \
        param_tuner.best_estimator_.predict(Xtrn)     Gets train and test
    ypred_tst = param_tuner.best_estimator_.predict(Xtst)  predictions for
                                                      each ensemble
```

```
res = {'Method': ens_type,
       'Train MSE': mean_squared_error(ytrn, ypred_trn),
       'Train MAE': mean_absolute_error(ytrn, ypred_trn),
       'Train R2': r2_score(ytrn, ypred_trn),
       'Test MSE': mean_squared_error(ytst, ypred_tst),
       'Test MAE': mean_absolute_error(ytst, ypred_tst),
       'Test R2': r2_score(ytst, ypred_tst)}
results = pd.concat([results,
                     pd.DataFrame.from_dict([res])], ignore_index=True)
```

> Computes and saves three metrics for each ensemble: MAE, MSE, and R^2 score

Compare the results of these parallel ensemble models with stacking and individual GLMs. In particular, observe the sharp improvement in performance compared to single models, which demonstrates the power of ensemble methods, even when trained on suboptimal loss functions:

```
             Method  Train MSE  Train MAE  Train R2  Test MSE  Test MAE  Test R2
RF: Squared Error    497.514     12.530      0.798    487.923   12.264    0.788
      RF: Poisson    566.552     13.081      0.770    549.014   12.684    0.761
XT: Squared Error    567.141     13.911      0.770    559.725   13.700    0.756
      XT: Poisson    576.096     13.946      0.766    566.706   13.754    0.753
```

Can we get similar or better performance with gradient and Newton-boosting methods? Let's find out.

7.4.4   *XGBoost and LightGBM*

Finally, let's train sequential ensembles using both XGBoost and LightGBM on this data set. Both packages have support for a wide variety of loss functions:

- Some of the loss and likelihood functions that XGBoost supports include the MSE, pseudo-Huber, Poisson, and Tweedie losses with the log-link function. Note again that XGBoost implements Newton boosting, which requires computing second derivatives; this means that XGBoost can't implement the MAE or Huber losses directly. Instead, XGBoost provides support for the pseudo-Huber loss.

- Like XGBoost, LightGBM supports the MSE, Poisson, and Tweedie losses with the log-link function. However, since it implements gradient boosting, which only requires first derivatives, it directly supports the MAE and the Huber loss.

For both models, we'll need to tune for several hyperparameters that control various aspects of ensembling (e.g., learning rate and early stopping), regularization (e.g., weights on the L1 and L2 regularizations), and tree learning (e.g., maximum tree depth).

Many of the previous models we trained only required tuning of a small number of hyperparameters, which allowed us to identify them through a grid search procedure. Grid search is time consuming, and the computational expense becomes prohibitive, so it should be avoided in instances such as this. Instead of an exhaustive grid search, randomized search can be an efficient alternative.

In a randomized hyperparameter search, we sample a smaller number of random hyperparameter combinations from the full list. If necessary, we can perform more fine-tuning once we've identified a good combination to attempt to refine and improve our results further.

The following listing shows the steps for randomized parameter search and ensemble training for XGBoost with different loss functions.

Listing 7.12 XGBoost for bike rental prediction

```
from xgboost import XGBRegressor
from sklearn.model_selection import RandomizedSearchCV          ⟵  Ranges of
                                                                    hyperparameters for all
parameters = {'max_depth': np.arange(2, 7, step=1),         ⟵──  XGBoost loss functions
              'learning_rate': 2**np.arange(-8., 2., step=2),
              'colsample_bytree': [0.4, 0.5, 0.6, 0.7, 0.8],
              'reg_alpha': [0, 0.01, 0.1, 1, 10],
              'reg_lambda': [0, 0.01, 0.1, 1e-1, 1, 10]}
print(parameters)
                                                    Initializes XGBoost models, each
ensembles = {                                   ⟵   with a different loss function
    'XGB: Squared Error': XGBRegressor(objective='reg:squarederror',
                                       eval_metric='poisson-nloglik'),
    'XGB: Pseudo Huber': XGBRegressor(objective='reg:pseudohubererror',
                                      eval_metric='poisson-nloglik'),
    'XGB: Poisson': XGBRegressor(objective='count:poisson',
                                 eval_metric='poisson-nloglik'),
    'XGB: Tweedie': XGBRegressor(objective='reg:tweedie',
                                 eval_metric='poisson-nloglik')}

for ens_type, ensemble in ensembles.items():    For the Tweedie loss, we have an
    if ens_type == 'XGB: Tweedie':          ⟵   additional hyperparameter: power.
        parameters['tweedie_variance_power'] = np.linspace(1.1, 1.9, num=9)

    param_tuner = RandomizedSearchCV(                       ⟵
                     ensemble, parameters, n_iter=50,           Hyperparameter tuning
                     cv=5, refit=True, verbose=2)               using randomized
    param_tuner.fit(Xtrn, ytrn,                    ⟵            search with 5-fold CV
                    eval_set=[(Xtst, ytst)], verbose=False)
                                                            Selects the best model
                                                            using negative Poisson
    ypred_trn = \                                  ⟵        log-likelihood
        param_tuner.best_estimator_.predict(Xtrn)
    ypred_tst = param_tuner.best_estimator_.predict(Xtst)   Gets train and test
                                                            predictions for
                                                            each ensemble
    res = {'Method': ens_type,
           'Train MSE': mean_squared_error(ytrn, ypred_trn),
           'Train MAE': mean_absolute_error(ytrn, ypred_trn),
           'Train R2': r2_score(ytrn, ypred_trn),
           'Test MSE': mean_squared_error(ytst, ypred_tst),
           'Test MAE': mean_absolute_error(ytst, ypred_tst),
           'Test R2': r2_score(ytst, ypred_tst)}

    results = pd.concat([results, pd.DataFrame([res])], ignore_index=True)
```

Computes and saves three metrics for each XGBoost ensemble: MAE, MSE, and R^2 score

NOTE Listing 7.12 uses early stopping to terminate training early if there is no noticeable performance improvement on an evaluation set. When we last employed early stopping on the AutoMPG data set (refer to listing 7.6), we used the MSE as the evaluation metric to track performance improvement. Here, we use the negative Poisson log-likelihood (`eval_metric='poisson-nloglik'`). Recall from our discussion in section 7.3.1 that negative log-likelihood is often used as a surrogate for loss functions without a closed form. In this case, because we're modeling count targets (which follow a Poisson distribution), it may be more appropriate to measure model performance with negative Poisson log-likelihood. It would've also been appropriate to compare test set performances of different models with this metric alongside MSE, MAE, and R^2, as we've been doing. However, this metric isn't always available or exposed in most packages.

The performance of XGBoost with different loss functions is shown here:

Method	Train MSE	Train MAE	Train R2	Test MSE	Test MAE	Test R2
XGB: Squared Err	134.926	7.227	0.945	254.099	9.475	0.889
XGB: Pseudo Huber	335.578	9.999	0.864	360.987	11.274	0.843
XGB: Poisson	181.602	7.958	0.926	250.034	8.958	0.891
XGB: Tweedie	139.167	6.958	0.944	231.110	8.648	0.899

These results are dramatically improved, with XGBoost trained with Poisson and Tweedie losses performing the best.

We can repeat a similar experiment with LightGBM. The implementation for this (which can be found in the companion code) is quite similar to how we trained LightGBM models for the AutoMPG data set in listing 7.6 and XGBoost models for the Bike Sharing data set in listing 7.11. The performance of LightGBM with MSE, MAE, Huber, Poisson, and Tweedie losses are shown here:

Method	Train MSE	Train MAE	Train R2	Test MSE	Test MAE	Test R2
LGBM: Squared Err	184.264	8.293	0.925	260.745	9.535	0.887
LGBM: Absolute Er	302.753	9.071	0.877	321.206	9.756	0.860
LGBM: Huber	744.769	12.485	0.698	702.736	12.204	0.694
LGBM: Quantile	852.409	18.726	0.654	815.393	18.671	0.645
LGBM: Poisson	223.913	8.776	0.909	264.663	9.215	0.885
LGBM: Tweedie	182.309	8.035	0.926	245.714	8.939	0.893

LightGBM's performance is similar to that of XGBoost, with Poisson and Tweedie losses, again, performing the best, and XGBoost edging LightGBM out slightly.

Figure 7.14 summarizes the test set performance (with R^2 score) of all the models we've trained for the bike rental demand prediction tasks. We note the following:

- Individual GLMs perform far worse than any ensemble method. This is unsurprising since ensemble methods combine the power of many individual models into a final prediction. Furthermore, many of the ensemble regressors are nonlinear and fit the data better, while all GLMs are linear and limited.
- The appropriate choice of loss functions is critical to training a good model. In this case, LightGBM and XGBoost models trained with Tweedie fit and

generalize best. This is because the Tweedie loss captures the distribution of the bike demand, which is a count-valued target.

- Packages such as LightGBM and XGBoost provide loss functions such as the Tweedie, while scikit-learn's ensemble method implementations (random forest, Extra Trees) only support MSE and MAE losses (at the time of this writing). It's possible to push the performance of these methods up further by adopting losses such as the Tweedie, but this would require custom loss implementations.

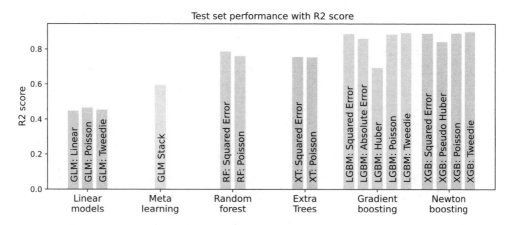

Figure 7.14 The test set performance (with the R^2 score metric) of the various ensemble methods for regression as we progressed through our analysis and modeling. Gradient-boosting (LightGBM) and Newton-boosting (XGBoost) ensembles are the current state of the art. Among these methods, performance can further be improved through a judicious choice of loss function and systematic parameter selection.

Summary

- Regression can be used to model continuous-valued, count-valued, and even discrete-valued targets.
- Classical linear models such as ordinary least squares (OLS), ridge regression, Least Absolute Shrinkage and Selection (LASSO), and elastic net all use the squared loss function, but they use different regularization functions.
- Poisson regression uses a linear model with a log-link function and the Poisson distribution assumption on the targets to effectively model count-labeled data.
- Gamma regression uses a linear model with a log-link function and the gamma distribution assumption on the targets to effectively model continuous, but positively valued and right-skewed data.
- Tweedie regression uses a linear model with a log-link function and the Tweedie distribution assumption to model compound distributions on data arising in many practical applications, such as insurance, weather, and health analytics.
- Classic mean squared regression, Poisson regression, gamma regression, Tweedie regression, and even logistic regression are all different variants of generalized linear models (GLMs).

- Random forests and Extra Trees use randomized regression tree learning to induce ensemble diversity.
- Common statistical measures such as mean and median can be used to combine the predictions of continuous targets and mode and median to combine predictions of count targets.
- Artificial neural network (ANN) regressors are good choices for meta-estimators when learning stacking ensembles.
- Loss functions such as mean squared error (MSE), mean average deviation (MAD), and Huber loss are well suited for continuous-valued labels.
- The gamma likelihood function is well suited for continuous-valued but positive labels (i.e., they don't take negative values).
- The Poisson likelihood function is well suited for count-valued labels.
- Some problems contain a mix of these labels and can be modeled with a Tweedie likelihood function.
- LightGBM and XGBoost provide support for modeling both the log link (and other link functions) and distributions such as Poisson, gamma, and Tweedie.
- Hyperparameter selection, either through exhaustive grid search (slow, but thorough) or randomized search (fast, but approximate), is essential for good ensemble development in practice.

Learning with categorical features

8

This chapter covers

- Introducing categorical features in machine learning
- Preprocessing categorical features using supervised and unsupervised encoding
- Understanding ordered boosting
- Using CatBoost for categorical variables
- Handling high-cardinality categorical features

Data sets for supervised machine learning consist of features that describe objects and labels that describe the targets we're interested in modeling. At a high level, features, also known as attributes or variables, are usually classified into two types: continuous and categorical.

A *categorical* feature is one that takes a discrete value from a set of finite, nonnumeric values, called categories. Categorical features are ubiquitous and appear in nearly every data set and in every domain. For example:

235

- *Demographic features*—These features, such as `gender` or `race`, are common attributes in many modeling problems in medicine, insurance, finance, advertising, recommendation systems, and many more. For instance, the US Census Bureau's `race` attribute is a categorical feature that admits five choices or categories: (1) American Indian or Alaska Native, (2) Asian, (3) Black or African American, (4) Native Hawaiian or Other Pacific Islander, (5) White.
- *Geographical features*—These features, such as `US State` or `ZIP code`, are also categorical features. The feature `US State` is a categorical variable with 50 categories. The feature `ZIP code` is also a categorical variable, with 41,692 unique categories (!) in the United States, from 00501, belonging to the Internal Revenue Service in Holtsville, NY, to 99950 in Ketchikan, AK.

Categorical features are usually represented as strings or in specific formats (e.g., ZIP codes, which have to be exactly five digits long and can start with zeros).

Since most machine-learning algorithms require numeric inputs, categorical features must be *encoded* or converted to numeric form before training. The nature of this encoding must be carefully chosen to capture the true underlying nature of the categorical features.

The ensemble setting has two approaches for handling categorical features:

- *Approach 1*—Preprocess categorical features using one of several standard or general-purpose encoding techniques available in libraries such as scikit-learn, and then train ensemble models with packages such as LightGBM or XGBoost with the preprocessed features.
- *Approach 2*—Use an ensemble method, such as CatBoost, that is designed to handle categorical features to train ensembles directly and carefully.

Section 8.1 covers approach 1. It introduces commonly used preprocessing methods for categorical features and how we can use them in practice (using the `category_encoders` package) with any machine-learning algorithm, including ensemble methods. Section 8.1 also discusses two common problems: training-to-test-set leakage and training-to-test-set distribution shift, or prediction shift, which affect our ability to accurately evaluate the generalization ability of our models to future, unseen data.

Section 8.2 covers approach 2 and introduces a new ensemble approach called ordered boosting, which is an extension of boosting approaches we've already seen but is specially modified to address leakage and shift for categorical features. This section also introduces the CatBoost package and shows how we can use it to train ensemble methods on data sets with categorical features. We explore both approaches in a real-world case study in section 8.3, where we compare random forest, LightGBM, XGBoost, and CatBoost on an income-prediction task.

Finally, many general-purpose approaches don't scale well to high-cardinality categorical features (where the number of categories is very high, such as ZIP code) or in the presence of noise, or so-called "dirty" categorical variables. Section 8.4 shows how we can effectively handle such high-cardinality categories with the `dirty_cat` package.

8.1   Encoding categorical features

This section reviews the different types of categorical features and introduces two classes of standard approaches to handling them: unsupervised encoding (specifically, ordinal and one-hot encoding) and supervised encoding (specifically, with target statistics).

Encoding techniques, like machine-learning methods, are either *unsupervised* or *supervised*. Unsupervised encoding methods use only the features to encode categories, while supervised encoding methods use both features and targets.

We'll also see how supervised encoding techniques can lead to degraded performance in practice owing to a phenomenon called *target leakage*. This will help us understand the motivations behind the development of the ordinal boosting approach, which we'll explore in section 8.3.

8.1.1   Types of categorical features

A categorical feature contains information about a category or group that a training example belongs to. The values, or categories, that make up such variables are often represented using strings or other nonnumeric tags.

Broadly, categorical features are of two types: *ordinal*, where an ordering exists between the categories, and *nominal*, where no ordering exists between the categories. Let's look closely at nominal and ordinal categorical features in the context of a hypothetical fashion task, where the goal is to train a machine-learning algorithm to predict the cost of a T-shirt. Each T-shirt is described by two attributes: color and size (figure 8.1).

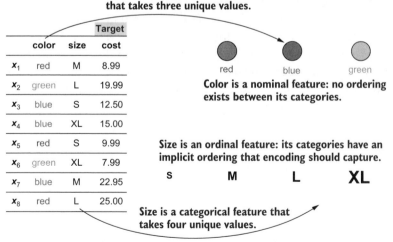

Figure 8.1   T-shirts in this example data set are described using two categorical features: color **and** size**. Categorical features can be either (1) nominal, where there is no ordering between the various categories, or (2) ordinal, where there is an ordering between the categories. The third feature in this data set,** cost**, is a continuous, numeric variable.**

The feature `color` takes three discrete values: `red`, `blue`, and `green`. No ordering exists between these categories, which makes `color` a nominal feature. Since it doesn't matter how we order `color`'s values, the ordering red-blue-green is equivalent to other ordering permutations such as blue-red-green or green-red-blue.

The feature `size` takes four discrete values: `S`, `M`, `L`, and `XL`. Unlike, `color`, however, there is an implicit ordering between the sizes: S < M < L < XL. This makes size an ordinal feature. While we can order sizes any way we want, ordering them in increasing order of size, S-M-L-XL, or in decreasing order of size, XL-L-M-S, is most sensible. Understanding the domain and the nature of each categorical feature is an important component of deciding how to encode them.

8.1.2 *Ordinal and one-hot encoding*

Categorical variables such as color and size have to be encoded, that is, converted to some sort of numeric representation prior to training a machine-learning model. Encoding is a type of feature engineering and must be done with care because an inappropriate choice of encoding can affect model performance and interpretability.

In this section, we'll look at two commonly used unsupervised methods of encoding categorical variables: *ordinal encoding* and *one-hot encoding*. They are unsupervised because they don't use the targets (labels) for encoding.

ORDINAL ENCODING

Ordinal encoding simply assigns each category a number. For example, the nominal feature `color` can be encoded by assigning `{'red': 0, 'blue': 1, 'green': 2}`. Since the categories don't have any implicit ordering, we could have also encoded by assigning other permutations such as `{'red': 2, 'blue': 0, 'green': 1}`.

On the other hand, since `size` is already an ordinal variable, it makes sense to assign numeric values to preserve this ordering. For `size`, either encoding with `{'S': 0, 'M': 1, 'L': 2, 'XL': 3}` (increasing) or `{'S': 3, 'M': 2, 'L': 1, 'XL': 0}` (decreasing) preserves the inherent relationship between the `size` categories.

scikit-learn's `OrdinalEncoder` can be used to create ordinal encodings. Let's encode the two categorical features (`color` and `size`) in the data set from figure 8.1 (denoted by X):

```
import numpy as np
X = np.array([['red', 'M'],
              ['green', 'L'],
              ['red', 'S'],
              ['blue', 'XL'],
              ['blue', 'S'],
              ['green', 'XL'],
              ['blue', 'M'],
              ['red', 'L']])
```

We'll specify our encoding for `color` assuming it can take four values: `red`, `yellow`, `green`, `blue` (even though we only see red, green, and blue in our data). We'll also specify the ordering for `size` as XL, L, M, S:

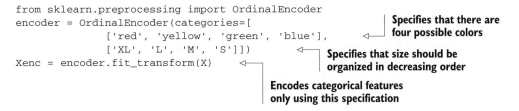

```
from sklearn.preprocessing import OrdinalEncoder
encoder = OrdinalEncoder(categories=[
                 ['red', 'yellow', 'green', 'blue'],
                 ['XL', 'L', 'M', 'S']])
Xenc = encoder.fit_transform(X)
```

Specifies that there are four possible colors

Specifies that size should be organized in decreasing order

Encodes categorical features only using this specification

Now, we can look at the encodings for these features:

```
encoder.categories_
[array(['red', 'yello', 'green', 'blue'], dtype='<U5'),
 array(['XL', 'L', 'M', 'S'], dtype='<U5')]
```

This encoding assigns numeric values to `color` as {`'red'`: 0, `'yellow'`: 1, `'blue'`: 2, `'green'`: 3} and to `size` as {`'XL'`: 0, `'L'`: 1, `'M'`: 2, `'S'`: 3}. This encoding transforms these categorical features to numeric values:

```
Xenc
array([[0., 2.],
       [2., 1.],
       [0., 3.],
       [3., 0.],
       [3., 3.],
       [2., 0.],
       [3., 2.],
       [0., 1.]])
```

Compare the encoded color (the first column of `Xenc`) with the raw data (the first column of `X`). All the `red` entries are encoded as 0, `green` as 2, and `blue` as 3. As there are no `yellow` entries, we have no encodings of value 1 in this column.

Note that ordinal encoding imposes an inherent ordering between variables. While this is ideal for ordinal categorical features, it may not always make sense for nominal categorical features.

ONE-HOT ENCODING

One-hot encoding is a way to encode a categorical feature without imposing any ordering among its values and is more suited for nominal features. Why use one-hot encoding? If we use ordinal encoding for nominal features, it would introduce an ordering that doesn't exist between the categories in the real world, thus misleading the learning algorithm into thinking there was one. Unlike ordinal encoding, which encodes each category using a single number, one-hot encoding encodes each category using a vector of 0s and 1s. The size of the vector depends on the number of categories.

For example, if we assume that `color` is a three-valued category (red, blue, green), it will be encoded as a length-3 vector. One such one-hot encoding can be {`'red'`: [1, 0, 0], `'blue'`: [0, 1, 0], `'green'`: [0, 0, 1]}. Observe the position of the 1s: `red` corresponds to the first encoding entry, `blue` corresponds to the second, and `green` to the third.

If we assume that `color` is a four-valued category (`red`, `yellow`, `blue`, `green`), one-hot encoding will produce length-4 vectors for each category. For the rest of this chapter, we'll assume that `color` is a three-valued category.

Because `size` takes four unique values, one-hot encoding produces length-4 vectors for each `size` category as well. One such one-hot encoding can be `{'S': [1, 0, 0, 0], 'M': [0, 1, 0, 0], 'L': [0, 0, 1, 0], 'XL': [0, 0, 0, 1]}`.

scikit-learn's `OneHotEncoder` can be used to create one-hot encodings. As before, let's encode the two categorical features (`color` and `size`) in the data set from figure 8.1:

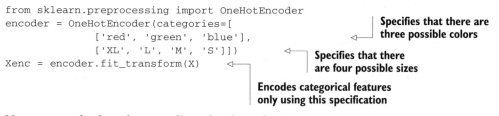

```
from sklearn.preprocessing import OneHotEncoder
encoder = OneHotEncoder(categories=[
            ['red', 'green', 'blue'],
            ['XL', 'L', 'M', 'S']])
Xenc = encoder.fit_transform(X)
```

Specifies that there are three possible colors

Specifies that there are four possible sizes

Encodes categorical features only using this specification

Now, we can look at the encodings for these features:

```
encoder.categories_
[array(['red', 'green', 'blue'], dtype='<U5'),
 array(['S', 'M', 'L', 'XL'], dtype='<U5')]
```

This encoding will introduce three one-hot features (first three columns in `Xenc`) to replace the `color` feature (first column in `X`) and four one-hot features (last four columns in `Xenc`) to replace the `size` feature (last column in `X`):

```
Xenc.toarray()
array([[1., 0., 0., 0., 1., 0., 0.],
       [0., 1., 0., 0., 0., 1., 0.],
       [1., 0., 0., 1., 0., 0., 0.],
       [0., 0., 1., 0., 0., 0., 1.],
       [0., 0., 1., 1., 0., 0., 0.],
       [0., 1., 0., 0., 0., 0., 1.],
       [0., 0., 1., 0., 1., 0., 0.],
       [1., 0., 0., 0., 0., 1., 0.]])
```

Each individual category has its own column now (three for each `color` category and four for each `size` category), and any ordering between them has been lost.

NOTE Since one-hot encoding removes any inherent ordering between categories, it's an ideal choice to encode nominal features. This choice, however, comes with a cost: we often tend to blow up the size of our data set as we have to replace one category column with a large number of binary feature columns, one for each category.

Our original fashion data set was 8 examples × 2 features. With ordinal encoding, it remained 8 × 2, though a forced ordering was imposed on the nominal feature, that is, `color`. With one-hot encoding, the size became 8 × 7, and the inherent ordering in the ordinal feature, `size`, was removed.

8.1.3 Encoding with target statistics

We now shift our focus to *encoding with target statistics,* or *target encoding,* which is an example of a supervised encoding technique. In contrast to unsupervised encoding methods, supervised encoding methods use labels to encode categorical features.

The idea behind encoding with target statistics is fairly straightforward: for each category, we compute a statistic such as the mean over the targets (i.e., labels) and replace the category with this newly computed numerical statistic. Encoding with label information often helps overcome the drawbacks of unsupervised encoding methods.

Unlike one-hot encoding, target encoding doesn't create any additional columns, meaning the dimensionality of the overall data set remains the same after encoding. Unlike ordinal encoding, target encoding doesn't introduce spurious relationships between the categories.

GREEDY TARGET ENCODING

In the original fashion data set from the previous section, recall that each training example is a T-shirt with two attributes—`color` and `size`—and the target to predict is `cost`. Let's say that we want to encode the `color` feature with target statistics. This feature has three categories—`red`, `blue`, and `green`—that need to be encoded.

Figure 8.2 illustrates how encoding with target statistics works for the category `red`.

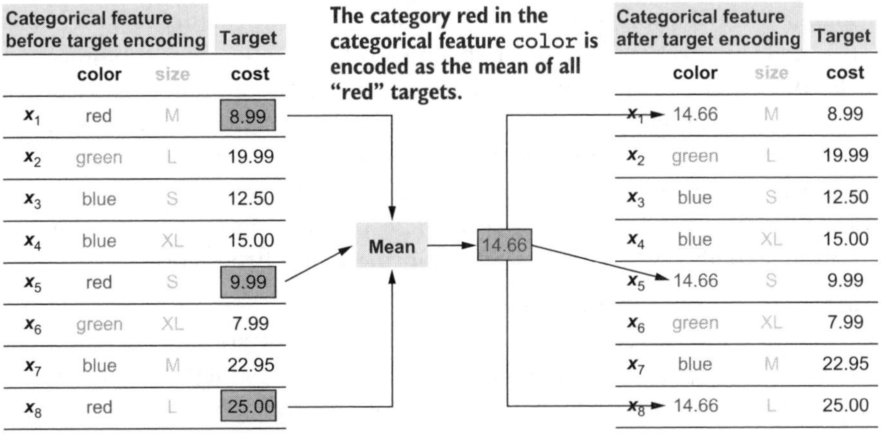

Figure 8.2 The category `red` of the feature `color` is replaced by its target statistic, the average (mean) of all the target values (`cost`) corresponding to the examples whose color is `red`. This is called greedy target encoding as all the training labels have been used for encoding.

There are three T-shirts, x_1, x_3, and x_8, whose color is `red`. Their corresponding target values (`cost`) are 8.99, 9.99, and 25.00. The target statistic is computed as the mean of these values: (8.99 + 9.99 + 25.00) / 3 = 14.66. Thus, each instance of `red` is replaced by its corresponding target statistic: 14.66. The other two categories, `blue` and `green`, can similarly be encoded with their corresponding target statistics, 16.82 and 13.99.

More formally, the target statistic for the kth category of the jth feature can be computed using the following formula:

$$s_k = \frac{\sum_{i=1}^{n} I\left(x_i^j = k\right) \cdot y_i + ap}{\sum_{i=1}^{n} I\left(x_i^j = k\right) + a}$$

Here, the notation $I\left(x_i^j = k\right)$ denotes an indicator function, which returns 1 if the condition within the parentheses is true and 0 if false. For example, in our fashion data set, $I\left(x_1^{color} = red\right) = 1$ because the first example corresponds to a medium red T-shirt, whereas $I\left(x_4^{color} = red\right) = 0$ because the fourth example corresponds to an XL blue T-shirt.

This formula for computing target statistics actually computes a *smoothed average* rather than just the average. Smoothing is performed by adding a parameter $a > 0$ to the denominator. This is to ensure that categories with a small number of values (and hence small denominators) don't end up with target statistics that are scaled differently to other categories. The constant p in the numerator is typically the average target value of the entire data set, and it serves as a *prior*, or as a means of regularizing the target statistic.

Generally, a prior is any additional knowledge we have that we can pass on to a learning algorithm to improve its training. For example, in Bayesian learning, a prior probability distribution is often specified to express our belief in how the data set is distributed. In this case, the prior specifies how the encoding should be applied on classes that occur very infrequently: simply replace with a value close to p.

This target encoding approach is called *greedy target encoding*, as it uses all the available training data to compute the encodings. As we'll see, a greedy encoding approach leaks information from the training to the test set. This "leakage" is problematic because a model identified as high performing during training and testing will often actually perform poorly in deployment and production.

INFORMATION LEAKAGE AND DISTRIBUTION SHIFT

Many preprocessing approaches are affected by one or both of two common practical problems: *training-to-test-set information leakage* and *training-to-test-set distribution shift*. Both problems affect our ability to evaluate our trained model and accurately estimate how it will behave on future, unseen data, that is, how it will generalize.

A key step in machine-learning model development is the creation of a hold-out test set, which is used to evaluate trained models. The test set must be completely held out from every stage of modeling (including preprocessing, training, and validation) and used purely for evaluating model performance to simulate model performance on unseen data. To do this effectively, we have to ensure that no part of the training data makes its way into test data. When this happens during modeling, it's called *information leakage from the training-to-test set*.

Data leakage occurs when information about features leaks into the test set, while target leakage occurs when information about targets (labels) leaks into the test set.

Greedy target encoding leads to target leakage, as illustrated in figure 8.3. In this example, a data set of 12 data points is partitioned into training and test sets. The training set is used to perform greedy target encoding of the category red of the feature color. More specifically, the target encoding from the training set is used to transform *both* the training *and* the test set. This leads to information leakage about the targets from the training set to the test set, making this an instance of target leakage.

	color	size	cost
x_1	red	M	8.99
x_2	green	L	19.99
x_3	blue	S	12.50
x_4	blue	XL	15.00
x_5	red	S	9.99
x_6	green	XL	7.99
x_7	blue	M	22.95
x_8	red	L	25.00
x_9	red	XL	12.95
x_{10}	blue	L	14.99
x_{11}	green	S	16.00
x_{12}	red	S	7.99

Training targets (labels) are used greedily for target encoding.

Mean → 14.66

Target (label) information from training set leaks to test set.

	color	size	cost
x_1	14.66	M	8.99
x_2	green	L	19.99
x_3	blue	S	12.50
x_4	blue	XL	15.00
x_5	14.66	S	9.99
x_6	green	XL	7.99
x_7	blue	M	22.95
x_8	14.66	L	25.00
x_9	14.66	XL	12.95
x_{10}	blue	L	14.99
x_{11}	green	S	16.00
x_{12}	14.66	S	7.99

Figure 8.3 Target leakage from the training to test set illustrated. All the targets (labels) in the training set are greedily used to create an encoding for red, which is used to encode this category in both the training and test sets, leading to target leakage.

Another consideration to keep in mind for the train-test split is ensuring that the training and hold-out test sets have similar distributions; that is, they have similar statistical properties. This is often achieved by randomly sampling the held-out test set from the overall set.

However, preprocessing techniques such as greedy target encoding can introduce disparities between the training and test sets, leading to a *prediction shift* between the training and test sets, as illustrated in figure 8.4. As before, the category red for the feature color is encoded using greedy target statistics. This encoding is computed as the mean of the targets corresponding to examples with color = red in the training data and is 14.66.

However, if we compute the mean of the targets corresponding to color = red in the test data only, the mean is 10.47. This discrepancy between the training and test sets is a by-product of greedy target encoding, which causes the test set distributions to become shifted from the training set distribution. Put another way, the statistical properties of the test set are now no longer similar to that of the training set, which has an inevitable and cascading influence on our model evaluation.

Both target leakage and prediction shift introduce a statistical bias into the performance metrics we use to evaluate the generalization performance of our trained models. Often, they overestimate generalization performance and make the trained model look better than it actually is, which causes a problem when this model is deployed and fails to perform according to expectations.

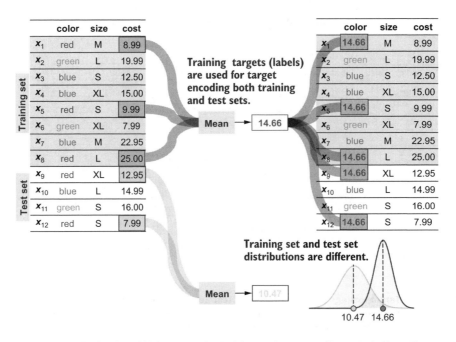

Figure 8.4 Distribution shift between the training and test sets illustrated. Since the target encoding for the test set is computed using the training set, it can lead to a shift in the distribution and statistical properties of the test set (yellow) compared to the training set (red).

HOLD-OUT AND LEAVE-ONE-OUT TARGET ENCODING

The best (and simplest) way to eliminate both target leakage and prediction shift is to hold out a part of the training data for encoding. Thus, in addition to the training and hold-out test sets, we also need to create a hold-out encoding set!

This approach, called *hold-out target encoding*, is illustrated in figure 8.5. Here, our data set from figure 8.3 and figure 8.4 is split into three sets—a training set, a hold-out encoding set, and a hold-out test set—each with four data points.

The hold-out encoding set is used to compute the target encoding for both the training and test sets. This ensures the independence of training and test sets and eliminates target leakage. Further, because the same target statistic is used for both training and test sets, it also avoids prediction shift.

A key drawback of hold-out target encoding is its data inefficiency. To avoid leakage, once the hold-out encoding set is used to compute the encoding, it needs to be discarded, which means that a good chunk of the total data available for modeling can potentially be wasted.

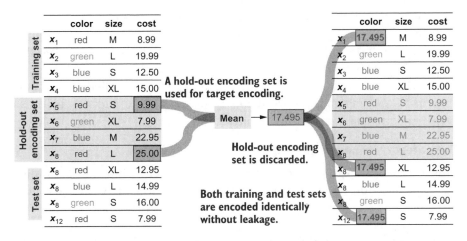

Figure 8.5 Hold-out encoding partitions the available data into three sets: training and test, as usual, and a third hold-out test set to be used exclusively for encoding with target statistics. This avoids both target leakage and distribution shift.

One (imperfect) alternative to avoid data inefficiency is to use *leave-one-out* (LOO) target encoding, which is illustrated in figure 8.6. LOO encoding works similarly to LOO cross validation (LOO CV), except that the left-out example is being encoded rather than being validated.

In figure 8.6, we see that to perform LOO target encoding for the red example x_5, we compute the target statistic using the other two red training examples x_1 and x_8, while leaving out x_5. This procedure is repeated for the other two red training examples, x_1 and x_8, in turn. Unfortunately, LOO encoding cannot include examples in the test set as we want to avoid leakage. Thus, we can apply greedy target encoding as before for the test set.

		color	size	cost			color	size	cost
Training set	x_1	red	M	8.99		x_1	red	M	8.99
	x_2	green	L	19.99		x_2	green	L	19.99
	x_3	blue	S	12.50		x_3	blue	S	12.50
	x_4	blue	XL	15.00		x_4	blue	XL	15.00
	x_5	red	S	9.99		x_5	16.995	S	9.99
	x_6	green	XL	7.99		x_6	green	XL	7.99
	x_7	blue	M	22.95		x_7	blue	M	22.95
	x_8	red	L	25.00		x_8	red	L	25.00
Test set	x_9	red	XL	12.95		x_9	14.66	XL	12.95
	x_{10}	blue	L	14.99		x_{10}	blue	L	14.99
	x_{11}	green	S	16.00		x_{11}	green	S	16.00
	x_{12}	red	S	7.99		x_{12}	14.66	S	7.99

Leave-one-out encodings used for the training set

Mean → 16.995

The example being encoded (here, x_5) is "left out" of the target statistic computation.

Greedy target encoding used for the test set

Figure 8.6 LOO target encoding is applied to the training data to avoid creating a wasteful hold-out encoding set. Instead of holding out a subset of the data, only the example being encoded is held out. Test data is encoded using greedy target encoding as before.

As we can see, the LOO target encoding procedure aims to emulate hold-out target encoding, while being significantly more data efficient. However, it should be noted that this overall procedure doesn't fully eliminate target leakage and prediction shift problems.

As we'll see in section 8.2, another encoding strategy called *ordered target statistics* aims to further mitigate the problems of target leakage and prediction shift while ensuring both data and computational efficiency.

8.1.4   *The category_encoders package*

This section provides examples of how to put together end-to-end encoding and training pipelines for data sets with categorical features. The subpackage `sklearn .preprocessing` provides some common encoders such as `OneHotEncoder` and `OrdinalEncoder`.

However, we'll use the `category_encoders` (http://mng.bz/41aQ) package, which provides many more encoding strategies, including for greedy and LOO target encoding. `category_encoders` is scikit-learn compatible, which means that it can be used with other ensemble method implementations that provide `sklearn`-compatible interfaces (e.g., LightGBM and XGBoost) discussed in this book.

We'll use the Australian Credit Approval data set from the UCI Machine Learning Repository (http://mng.bz/Q8D4). A clean version of this data set is available along with the source code for this book, and we'll use this version to demonstrate category encoding in practice. The data set contains six continuous features, four binary features, and four categorical features, and the task is to determine whether to approve or deny a credit card application, that is, binary classification.

First, let's load the data set and look at the feature names and the first few rows:

```
import pandas as pd
df = pd.read_csv('./data/ch08/australian-credit.csv')
df.head()
```

This code snippet prints the first few rows of the data set in tabular form, shown in figure 8.7.

The feature names are of the form `f1-bin`, `f2-cont`, or `f5-cat`, indicating the column index and whether the feature is binary, continuous, or categorical. To

	f1-bin	f2-cont	f3-cont	f4-cat	f5-cat	f6-cat	f7-cont	f8-bin	f9-bin	f10-cont	f11-bin	f12-cat	f13-cont	f14-cont	target
0	1	22.08	11.46	2	4	4	1.585	0	0	0	1	2	100	1213	0
1	0	22.67	7.00	2	8	4	0.165	0	0	0	0	2	160	1	0
2	0	29.58	1.75	1	4	4	1.250	0	0	0	1	2	280	1	0
3	0	21.67	11.50	1	5	3	0.000	1	1	11	1	2	0	1	1
4	1	20.17	8.17	2	6	4	1.960	1	1	14	0	2	60	159	1

Figure 8.7   The Australian Credit Approval data set from the UCI Machine Learning repository. Attribute names have been changed to protect confidentiality of the individuals represented in the data set.

protect applicant confidentiality, the category strings and names have been replaced with integer values; that is, the categorical features have already been processed with ordinal encoding!

Let's separate the columns into features and labels, and then further split into the training and test sets as usual:

```
X, y = df.drop('target', axis=1), df['target']
from sklearn.model_selection import train_test_split
Xtrn, Xtst, ytrn, ytst = train_test_split(X, y, test_size=0.2,
                                           random_state=13)
```

Furthermore, let's explicitly identify the categorical and continuous features we're interested in for preprocessing:

```
cat_features = ['f4-cat', 'f5-cat', 'f6-cat', 'f12-cat']
cont_features = ['f2-cont', 'f3-cont', 'f7-cont', 'f10-cont',
                 'f13-cont', 'f14-cont']
```

We'll preprocess the continuous and categorical features in different ways. The continuous features will be standardized; that is, each column of continuous features is rescaled to have zero mean and unit standard deviation. This rescaling ensures that different columns don't have drastically different scales, which can mess up downstream learning algorithms.

The categorical features will be preprocessed using one-hot encoding. For this, we'll use the `OneHotEncoder` from the `category_encoders` package. We'll create two separate preprocessing pipelines, one for continuous features and one for categorical features:

```
import category_encoders as ce
from sklearn.preprocessing import StandardScaler
from sklearn.pipeline import Pipeline

preprocess_continuous = Pipeline(steps=[('scaler', StandardScaler())])
preprocess_categorical = Pipeline(steps=[('encoder',
                             ce.OneHotEncoder(cols=cat_features))])
```

Note that `ce.OneHotEncoder` requires us to explicitly specify the columns corresponding to the categorical features, without which it will apply encoding to *all* the columns.

Now that we have two separate pipelines, we need to put these together to ensure that the correct preprocessing is applied to the correct feature type. We can do this with scikit-learn's `ColumnTransformer`, which allows us to apply different steps to different columns:

```
from sklearn.compose import ColumnTransformer
ct = ColumnTransformer(                           Preprocesses continuous
        transformers=[('continuous',              features here
                    preprocess_continuous, cont_features),    Preprocesses
                  ('categorical',                             categorical
                     preprocess_categorical, cat_features)],  features here
Keeps the remaining
    features as is      remainder='passthrough')
```

Now, we can fit a preprocessor on the training set and apply the transformation to both the training and test sets:

```
Xtrn_one_hot = ct.fit_transform(Xtrn, ytrn)
Xtst_one_hot = ct.transform(Xtst)
```

Observe how the test set isn't used to fit the preprocessor pipeline. This is a subtle but important practical step to ensure that the test set is held out and that there is no inadvertent data or target leakage due to preprocessing. Now, let's see what one-hot encoding has done to our feature set size:

```
print('Num features after ONE HOT encoding = {0}'.format(
                                    Xtrn_one_hot.shape[1]))
Num features after ONE HOT encoding = 38
```

Since one-hot encoding introduces one new column for each category of a categorical feature, the overall number of columns has increased from 14 to 38! Now let's train and evaluate a RandomForestClassifier on this preprocessed data set:

```
from sklearn.ensemble import RandomForestClassifier
model = RandomForestClassifier(n_estimators=200,
                             max_depth=6, criterion='entropy')
model.fit(Xtrn_one_hot, ytrn)

from sklearn.metrics import accuracy_score
ypred = model.predict(Xtst_one_hot)
print('Model Accuracy using ONE HOT encoding = {0:5.3f}%'.
      format(100 * accuracy_score(ypred, ytst)))

Model Accuracy using ONE HOT encoding = 89.855%
```

Our one-hot encoding strategy learned a model whose hold-out test accuracy is 89.9%. In addition to OneHotEncoder and OrdinalEncoder, the category_encoders package also provides many other encoders. Two of encoders of interest to us are the greedy TargetEncoder and the LeaveOneOutEncoder, which can be used in exactly the same way as OneHotEncoder. Specifically, we simply replace OneHotEncoder with TargetEncoder in the following:

```
preprocess_categorical = \
    Pipeline(steps=[('encoder', ce.TargetEncoder(cols=cat_features,
                                        smoothing=10.0))])
```

TargetEncoder takes one additional parameter, smoothing, a positive value that combines the effect of smoothing and the effect of applying the prior (see section 8.1.2). Higher values force higher smoothing and can counter overfitting. After preprocessing and training, we have the following:

```
Num features after GREEDY TARGET encoding = 14
Model Accuracy using GREEDY TARGET encoding = 91.304%
```

Unlike one-hot encoding, greedy target encoding doesn't add any new columns, which means that the overall dimensions of the data set remain unchanged. We can use `LeaveOneOutEncoder` in a similar way:

```
preprocess_categorical = Pipeline(steps=[('encoder',
                            ce.LeaveOneOutEncoder(cols=cat_features,
                                              sigma=0.4))])
```

The `sigma` parameter is a noise parameter that aims to decrease overfitting. The user manual recommends using values between 0.05 to 0.6. After preprocessing and training, we again have the following:

```
Num features after LEAVE-ONE-OUT TARGET encoding = 14
Model Accuracy using LEAVE-ONE-OUT TARGET encoding = 90.580%
```

As with `TargetEncoder`, the number of features remains unchanged due to preprocessing.

8.2   CatBoost: A framework for ordered boosting

CatBoost is another open source gradient-boosting framework developed by Yandex. CatBoost introduces three major modifications to the classical Newton-boosting approach:

- It's specialized to categorical features, unlike other boosting approaches that are more general.
- It uses ordered boosting as its underlying ensemble learning approach, which allows it to address target leakage and prediction shift implicitly during training.
- It uses oblivious decision trees as base estimators, which often leads to faster training times.

NOTE   CatBoost is available for Python on many platforms. See the CatBoost installation guide for detailed instructions on installation at http://mng.bz/ X5xE. At the time of this writing, CatBoost is only supported by the 64-bit version of Python.

8.2.1   Ordered target statistics and ordered boosting

CatBoost handles categorical features in two ways: (1) by encoding categorical features as described previously with target statistics, and (2) by cleverly creating categorical combinations of features (and encoding them with target statistics as well). While these modifications enable CatBoost to seamlessly handle categorical features, they do introduce some downsides that must be addressed.

As we've seen before, encoding with target statistics introduces target leakage and, more importantly, a prediction shift in the test set. The most ideal way to handle this is by creating a hold-out encoding set.

Holding out training examples for just encoding and nothing else is rather wasteful of data, meaning that this approach is rarely used in practice. The alternative, LOO encoding, is more data efficient, but doesn't completely mitigate prediction shift.

In addition to problems with encoding features, gradient boosting and Newton boosting both reuse data between iterations, leading to a gradient distribution shift, which ultimately causes a further prediction shift. In other words, even if we didn't have categorical features, we would still have a prediction shift problem, which would bias our estimates of model generalization!

CatBoost addresses this central problem of prediction shift by using permutation for ordering training examples to (1) compute target statistics for encoding categorical variables (called ordered target statistics), and (2) train its weak estimators (called ordered boosting).

ORDERED TARGET STATISTICS

At its heart, the ordering principle is simple and elegant and consists of two steps:

1   Reorder the training examples according to a random permutation.
2   To compute target statistics for the ith training example, use the previous $i - 1$ training examples according to this random permutation.

This is illustrated in figure 8.8 for eight training examples. First, the examples are permuted into a random ordering: 4, 7, 1, 8, 2, 6, 5, 3. Now, to compute target statistics for each training example, we assume that these examples arrive sequentially.

For example, to compute the target statistics for example 2, we can only use examples in the sequence that we've "previously seen": 4, 7, 1, and 8. Then, to compute the target statistics for example 6, we can only use examples in the sequence that we've previously seen, now: 4, 7, 1, 8, *and* 2, and so on.

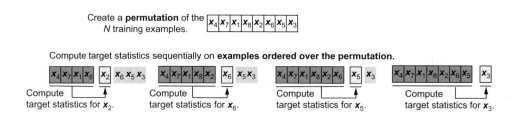

Figure 8.8   Ordered target statistics first permutes the examples into a random sequence, using only the previous examples in the ordered sequence to compute the target statistics.

Thus, to compute the encoding for the ith training example, ordered target statistics never uses its own target value; this behavior is similar to LOO target encoding. The key difference between the two is that ordered target statistics uses the notion of a "history" of examples it has already seen.

One downside to this approach is that training examples that occur early in a randomized sequence are encoded with far fewer examples. To compensate for this in practice and increase robustness, CatBoost maintains several sequences (i.e., histories), which are, in turn, randomly chosen. This means that CatBoost recomputes target statistics for categorical variables at each iteration.

ORDERED BOOSTING

CatBoost is fundamentally a Newton-boosting algorithm (see chapter 6); that is, it uses both the first and second derivative of the loss function to train its constituent weak estimators.

As mentioned previously, there are two sources of prediction shift: variable encoding and gradient computations themselves. To avoid prediction shift due to gradients, CatBoost extends the idea of ordering to training its weak learners. Another way to think about this is as Newton boosting + ordering = CatBoost.

Figure 8.9 illustrates ordered boosting, analogous to ordered target statistics. For example, to compute the residuals and gradients for example 2, ordered boosting uses a model only trained on the examples in the sequence that it has previously seen: 4, 7, 1, and 8. As with ordered target statistics, CatBoost uses multiple permutations to increase robustness. These residuals are now used to train its weak estimators.

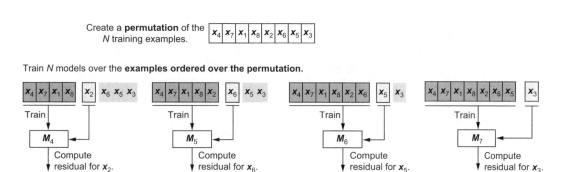

Figure 8.9 Ordered boosting also permutes the examples into a random sequence and uses only the previous examples in the ordered sequence to compute the gradients (residuals). Shown here is how the residuals are computed at iteration 4 (using estimator M4 for example x_2), at iteration 5 (using estimator M5 for example x_6), and so on.

8.2.2 Oblivious decision trees

Another key difference between Newton-boosting implementations such as XGBoost and CatBoost are the base estimators. XGBoost uses standard decision trees as weak estimators, while CatBoost uses *oblivious decision trees*.

Oblivious decision trees use the same splitting criterion in all the nodes across an entire level (depth) of the tree. This is illustrated in figure 8.10, which compares a standard decision tree with four leaf nodes with an oblivious decision tree with four leaf nodes.

In this example, observe that the second level of the oblivious tree (right) uses the same decision criterion, `size < 15`, at each node in the second level. While this is a simple example, note already that we only need to learn two split criteria for the oblivious tree, as opposed to the standard decision tree. This makes oblivious trees easier and more efficient to train, which has the effect of speeding up overall training. In

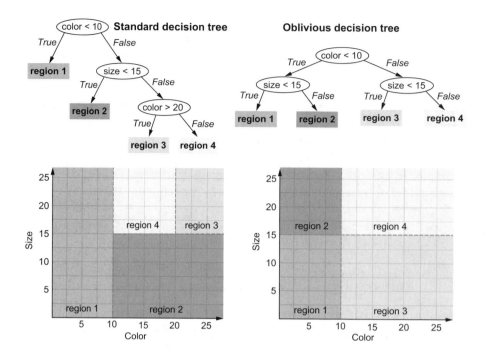

Figure 8.10 Comparing standard and oblivious decision trees, each with four leaf nodes. Observe that the decision nodes at depth 2 of the oblivious decision tree are both the same (`size < 15`). This is a key feature of oblivious decision trees: only one split criterion is learned for each depth.

addition, oblivious trees are balanced and symmetric, making them less complex and less prone to overfitting.

8.2.3   *CatBoost in practice*

This section shows how to create a training pipeline with CatBoost. We'll also look at an example of how to set the learning rate and employ early stopping as a means to control overfitting, as follows:

- By selecting an effective learning rate, we try to control the rate at which the model learns so that it doesn't rapidly fit and then overfit the training data. We can think of this as a proactive modeling approach, where we try to identify a good training strategy so that it leads to a good model.
- By enforcing early stopping, we try to stop training as soon as we observe that the model is starting to overfit. We can think of this as a reactive modeling approach, where we contemplate terminating training as soon as we think we have a good model.

We'll use the Australian Credit Approval data set that we used in section 8.1.4. The following listing provides a simple illustration of how to use CatBoost.

Listing 8.1   Using CatBoost

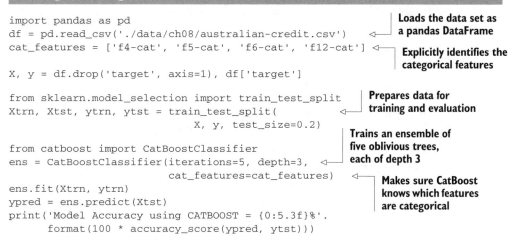

```
import pandas as pd
df = pd.read_csv('./data/ch08/australian-credit.csv')
cat_features = ['f4-cat', 'f5-cat', 'f6-cat', 'f12-cat']

X, y = df.drop('target', axis=1), df['target']

from sklearn.model_selection import train_test_split
Xtrn, Xtst, ytrn, ytst = train_test_split(
                         X, y, test_size=0.2)

from catboost import CatBoostClassifier
ens = CatBoostClassifier(iterations=5, depth=3,
                    cat_features=cat_features)
ens.fit(Xtrn, ytrn)
ypred = ens.predict(Xtst)
print('Model Accuracy using CATBOOST = {0:5.3f}%'.
      format(100 * accuracy_score(ypred, ytst)))
```

Loads the data set as a pandas DataFrame

Explicitly identifies the categorical features

Prepares data for training and evaluation

Trains an ensemble of five oblivious trees, each of depth 3

Makes sure CatBoost knows which features are categorical

This listing trains and evaluates a CatBoost model as follows:

```
Model Accuracy using CATBOOST = 83.333%
```

CROSS VALIDATION WITH CATBOOST

CatBoost provides support for many loss functions for regression and classification tasks, and many features to control various aspects of training. This includes hyperparameters to control overfitting by controlling the complexity of the ensemble (`iterations`, with one tree trained per iteration) and the complexity of the base estimators (`depth` of the oblivious decision trees).

In addition to these, another key hyperparameter is the `learning_rate`. Recall that the learning rate allows greater control over how quickly the complexity of the ensemble grows. Therefore, identifying an optimal learning rate for our data set in practice can help avoid overfitting and generalize well after training.

As with previous ensemble approaches, we'll use 5-fold CV to search over several different hyperparameter combinations to identify the best model. The following listing illustrates how to perform CV with CatBoost.

Listing 8.2   Cross validation with CatBoost

```
params = {'depth': [1, 3],
          'iterations': [5, 10, 15],
          'learning_rate': [0.01, 0.1]}

ens = CatBoostClassifier(cat_features=cat_features)
grid_search = ens.grid_search(params, Xtrn, ytrn,
                    cv=5, refit=True)

print('Best parameters: ', grid_search['params'])
ypred = ens.predict(Xtst)
print('Model Accuracy using CATBOOST = {0:5.3f}%'.
      format(100 * accuracy_score(ypred, ytst)))
```

Creates a grid of possible parameter combinations

Explicitly identifies the categorical features

Uses CatBoost's built-in grid search functionality

Performs 5-fold CV and then refits a model using the best parameters identified after grid search

This listing evaluates the (2 x 3 x 2 = 12) hyperparameter combinations specified in parameters using 5-fold CV to identify the best parameter combination and refits (i.e., retrains) a final model with it:

```
Best parameters:  {'depth': 3, 'iterations': 15, 'learning_rate': 0.1}
Model Accuracy using CATBOOST = 82.609%
```

EARLY STOPPING WITH CATBOOST

As with other ensemble methods, with each successive iteration, CatBoost adds a new base estimator to the ensemble. This causes the complexity of the overall ensemble to steadily increase during training until the model begins to overfit the training data. As with other ensemble methods, it's possible to employ early stopping with CatBoost, where we monitor the performance of CatBoost with the help of an evaluation set to stop training as soon as there is no significant improvement in performance.

In listing 8.3, we initialize CatBoost to train 100 trees. With early stopping of CatBoost, it's possible to terminate training early, thus ensuring a good model as well as training efficiency, similar to LightGBM and XGBoost.

Listing 8.3 Early stopping with CatBoost

```
ens = CatBoostClassifier(iterations=100, depth=3,       ◁─┐  Initializes a
                         cat_features=cat_features,        │  CatBoostClassifier with
                         loss_function='Logloss')          │  ensemble size 100

from catboost import Pool
eval_set = Pool(Xtst, ytst, cat_features=cat_features)  ◁─┐  Creates an evaluation
                                                           │  set by pooling "Xtst"
ens.fit(Xtrn, ytrn, eval_set=eval_set,                     │  and "ytst"
        early_stopping_rounds=5,                     ◁─── Stops training if no improvement
        verbose=False, plot=True)                    ◁─── detected after five rounds

ypred = ens.predict(Xtst)                            Sets plotting to "true" for
print('Model Accuracy using CATBOOST = {0:5.3f}%'.   CatBoost to plot training
      format(100 * accuracy_score(ypred, ytst)))     and evaluation curves
```

This code generates training and curves as shown in figure 8.11, where the effect of overfitting is observable. Around the 80th iteration, the training curve (dashed) is continuing to decrease, while the evaluation curve has begun to flatten.

This means that the training error is continuing to decrease without an equivalent decrease in our validation set, indicating overfitting. CatBoost observes this behavior for five more iterations (as `early_stopping_rounds=5`) and then terminates training.

The final model reports a test set performance of 82.61%, achieved after 88 rounds, with early stopping avoiding training all the way to 100 iterations as originally specified:

```
Model Accuracy using CATBOOST = 82.609%
```

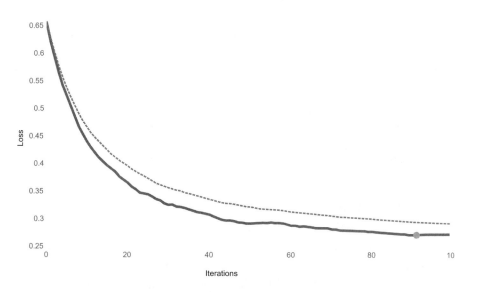

Figure 8.11   Training (dashed) and evaluation (solid) curves generated by CatBoost. The dot at the 88th iteration indicates the early stopping point.

8.3   *Case study: Income prediction*

In this section, we study the problem of *income prediction* from demographic data. Demographic data typically contains many different types of features, including categorical and continuous features. We'll explore two approaches to training ensemble methods:

- *Approach 1 (sections 8.3.2 and 8.3.3)*—Preprocess categorical features using the `category_encoders` package and then train ensembles using scikit-learn's random forest, LightGBM, and XGBoost with preprocessed features.
- *Approach 2 (section 8.3.4)*—Use CatBoost to directly handle categorical features during training through ordered target statistics and ordered boosting.

8.3.1   *Adult Data Set*

This case study uses the Adult Data Set from the UCI Machine Learning Repository. The task is to predict whether an individual will earn more or less than $50,000 per year based on several demographic indicators such as education, marital status, race, and gender.

This data set contains a nice mix of categorical and continuous features, which makes it an ideal choice for this case study. The data set is available along with the source code. Let's load the data set and visualize it (see figure 8.12):

```
import pandas as pd
df = pd.read_csv('./data/ch08/adult.csv')
df.head()
```

	age	workclass	fnlwgt	education	education-num	marital-status	occupation	relationship	race	sex	capital-gain	capital-loss	hours-per-week	native-country	salary
0	50	Self-emp-not-inc	83311	Bachelors	13	Married-civ-spouse	Exec-managerial	Husband	White	Male	0	0	13	United-States	<=50K
1	38	Private	215646	HS-grad	9	Divorced	Handlers-cleaners	Not-in-family	White	Male	0	0	40	United-States	<=50K
2	53	Private	234721	11th	7	Married-civ-spouse	Handlers-cleaners	Husband	Black	Male	0	0	40	United-States	<=50K
3	28	Private	338409	Bachelors	13	Married-civ-spouse	Prof-specialty	Wife	Black	Female	0	0	40	Cuba	<=50K
4	37	Private	284582	Masters	14	Married-civ-spouse	Exec-managerial	Wife	White	Female	0	0	40	United-States	<=50K

Figure 8.12   The Adult Data Set contains categorical and continuous features.

This data set contains several categorical features:

- workclass—Describes the classification of the type of employment and contains eight categories: Private, Self-emp-not-inc, Self-emp-inc, Federal-gov, Local-gov, State-gov, Without-pay, Never-worked.
- education—Describes the highest education level attained and contains 16 categories: Bachelors, Some-college, 11th, HS-grad, Prof-school, Assoc-acdm, Assoc-voc, 9th, 7th–8th, 12th, Masters, 1st–4th, 10th, Doctorate, 5th–6th, Preschool.
- marital-status—Describes the marital situation and has seven categories: Married-civ-spouse, Divorced, Never-married, Separated, Widowed, Married-spouse-absent, Married-AF-spouse.
- occupation—Describes the classification of the occupation area and contains 14 categories: Tech-support, Craft-repair, Other-service, Sales, Exec-managerial, Prof-specialty, Handlers-cleaners, Machine-op-inspct, Adm-clerical, Farming-fishing, Transport-moving, Priv-house-serv, Protective-serv, Armed-Forces.
- relationship—Describes relationship status and has six categories: Wife, Own-child, Husband, Not-in-family, Other-relative, Unmarried.
- sex—Describes gender and has two categories: male, female.
- native-country—This high(ish)-cardinality categorical variable describes the native country and contains 30 unique countries.

In addition, the data set also contains several continuous features, such as age, number of years of education, number of hours worked per week, capital gains and losses, and so on.

Fairness, bias, and the Adult Data Set

This data set was originally created from the 1994 Current Population Survey conducted by the US Census Bureau and has since been used in hundreds of research papers, machine-learning tutorials, and class projects, both as a benchmark data set and as a pedagogical tool.

In recent years, it has also become an important data set for research in the area of Fairness in AI, also known as algorithmic fairness, which explores approaches to ensure that machine-learning algorithms don't reinforce real-world biases and do strive for fair outcomes.

For example, let's say we were training an ensemble model to screen and then accept or reject job resumes for software engineering positions based on historical data. Historical hiring data would indicate that men are more likely to be hired for these positions than women. If we use such biased data for training, machine-learning models (including ensemble methods) will pick up this bias during learning and make biased hiring decisions when deployed, resulting in real world discriminatory outcomes!

The Adult Data Set is also similarly biased, and subtly so as both the prediction target ("Will an individual earn more or less than $50,000 per year?") and data features are disproportionately discriminative toward women and minorities. This means that models trained using this data set will also be discriminative and should not be used in practice for data-driven decision making. See the article by Ding et al.[a] for more details on this fascinating and extremely important area of machine learning.

Finally, it should be noted that this data set is used here solely as a teaching tool to illustrate different approaches to handling data sets with categorical variables.

[a] *Retiring Adult: New Datasets for Fair Machine Learning*, by Frances Ding, Moritz Hardt, John Miller, and Ludwig Schmidt. Proceedings of the 32nd International Conference on Neural Information Processing Systems (2021) (http://mng.bz/ydWe).

In the following listing, we explore some of the categorical features using the seaborn package, which provides some neat functions for quickly exploring and visualizing data sets.

Listing 8.4 Categorical features in the Adult Data Set

```python
import matplotlib.pyplot as plt
import seaborn as sns

fig, ax = plt.subplots(nrows=3, ncols=1, figsize=((12, 6)))
fig.suptitle('Category counts of select features in the adult data set')

sns.countplot(x='workclass', hue='salary', data=df, ax=ax[0])
ax[0].set(yscale='log')

sns.countplot(x='marital-status', hue='salary', data=df, ax=ax[1])
ax[1].set(yscale='log')

sns.countplot(x='race', hue='salary', data=df, ax=ax[2])
ax[2].set(yscale='log')
fig.tight_layout()
```

This listing produces figure 8.13.

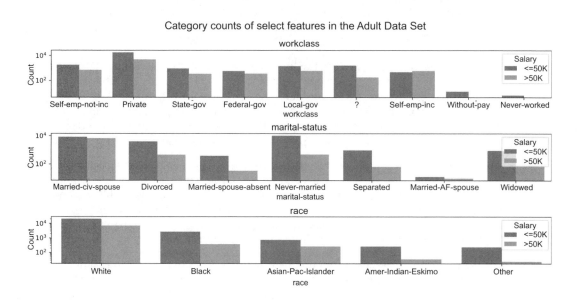

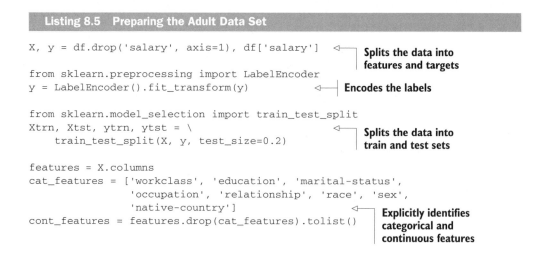

Figure 8.13 Visualizing the category counts of three categorical features in the Adult Data Set: workclass, marital-status, and race. Note that all the y-axes are in logarithmic (base 10) scale.

8.3.2 Creating preprocessing and modeling pipelines

Listing 8.5 describes how to prepare the data. In particular, we use `sklearn.preprocessing.LabelEncoder` to convert the target labels from string (<=50k, >50k) to numeric (0/1). `LabelEncoder` is identical to `OrdinalEncoder`, except that it's specifically designed to work with 1D data (targets).

Listing 8.5 Preparing the Adult Data Set

```
X, y = df.drop('salary', axis=1), df['salary']      ⊲─┐ Splits the data into
                                                       │ features and targets
from sklearn.preprocessing import LabelEncoder
y = LabelEncoder().fit_transform(y)                 ⊲─┤ Encodes the labels


from sklearn.model_selection import train_test_split
Xtrn, Xtst, ytrn, ytst = \                          ⊲─┐
    train_test_split(X, y, test_size=0.2)              │ Splits the data into
                                                       │ train and test sets

features = X.columns
cat_features = ['workclass', 'education', 'marital-status',
                'occupation', 'relationship', 'race', 'sex',
                'native-country']                   ⊲─┐ Explicitly identifies
cont_features = features.drop(cat_features).tolist()  │ categorical and
                                                       │ continuous features
```

Recall that the task is to predict if the income is greater than $50,000 (with labels y=1) or less than $50,000 (with labels y=0). One thing to note about this data set is that it's imbalanced; that is, it contains different proportions of the two classes:

```
import numpy as np
n_pos, n_neg = np.sum(y > 0)/len(y), np.sum(y <= 0)/len(y)
print(n_pos, n_neg)
0.24081695331695332 0.7591830466830467
```

Here, we see that the positive-negative distribution is 24.1% to 75.9% (unbalanced), rather than 50% to 50% (balanced). This means that evaluation metrics such as accuracy can unintentionally skew our view of model performance as they assume a balanced data set.

Next, we define a preprocessing function that can be reused with different types of category encoders. This function has two preprocessing pipelines, one to be applied to continuous features only, and the other for categorical features. The continuous features are preprocessed using StandardScaler, which normalizes each feature column to have zero mean and unit standard deviation.

In addition, both pipelines have a SimpleImputer to impute missing values. Missing continuous values are imputed with their corresponding median feature value, while missing categorical features are imputed as a new category called 'missing' prior to encoding.

For example, the feature workclass has missing values (indicated by '?'), which are treated as a separate category for modeling purposes. The following listing implements separate preprocessing pipelines for continuous and categorical features and returns a ColumnTransformer, which can be applied directly to any subset of training data from this domain.

Listing 8.6 Preprocessing pipelines

```
from sklearn.preprocessing import StandardScaler
from sklearn.impute import SimpleImputer
from sklearn.pipeline import Pipeline
from sklearn.compose import ColumnTransformer

import category_encoders as ce

def create_preprocessor(encoder):          Preprocessing pipeline
    preprocess_continuous = \            for continuous features
        Pipeline(steps=[
            ('impute_missing', SimpleImputer(strategy='median')),
            ('normalize', StandardScaler())])

    preprocess_categorical = \           Preprocessing pipeline
        Pipeline(steps=[               for categorical features
            ('impute_missing', SimpleImputer(strategy='constant',
                                             fill_value='missing')),
            ('encode', encoder())])
```

```
transformations = \
    ColumnTransformer(transformers=[
        ('continuous', preprocess_continuous, cont_features),
        ('categorical', preprocess_categorical, cat_features)])

return transformations
```

"ColumnTransformer" object used to combine the pipelines

This listing will create and return a scikit-learn `ColumnTransformer` object, which can apply a similar preprocessing strategy to training and test sets, ensuring consistency and minimizing data leakage.

Finally, we define a function to train and evaluate different types of ensembles, combining them with various types of category encoding. This will enable us to create different ensemble models by combining ensemble learning packages with various types of category encoders.

The function in listing 8.7 allows us to pass an `ensemble` as well as a grid of ensemble `parameters` for ensemble parameter selection. It uses k-fold CV combined with randomized search to identify the best ensemble parameters before training a final model with these best parameters.

Once trained, the function evaluates final model performance on the test set using three metrics: accuracy, balanced accuracy, and F1 score. Balanced accuracy and F1 score are especially useful metrics when the data set is imbalanced, as they take label imbalance into account by weighting model performance on each class based on how often they appear in the labels.

Listing 8.7   Training and evaluating combinations of encoders and ensembles

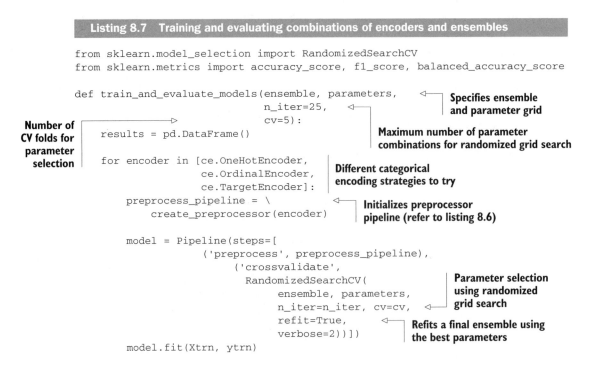

```
from sklearn.model_selection import RandomizedSearchCV
from sklearn.metrics import accuracy_score, f1_score, balanced_accuracy_score

def train_and_evaluate_models(ensemble, parameters,
                              n_iter=25,
                              cv=5):
    results = pd.DataFrame()

    for encoder in [ce.OneHotEncoder,
                    ce.OrdinalEncoder,
                    ce.TargetEncoder]:
        preprocess_pipeline = \
            create_preprocessor(encoder)

        model = Pipeline(steps=[
                    ('preprocess', preprocess_pipeline),
                        ('crossvalidate',
                            RandomizedSearchCV(
                                ensemble, parameters,
                                n_iter=n_iter, cv=cv,
                                refit=True,
                                verbose=2))])
        model.fit(Xtrn, ytrn)
```

Specifies ensemble and parameter grid

Maximum number of parameter combinations for randomized grid search

Number of CV folds for parameter selection

Different categorical encoding strategies to try

Initializes preprocessor pipeline (refer to listing 8.6)

Parameter selection using randomized grid search

Refits a final ensemble using the best parameters

```
ypred_trn = model.predict(Xtrn)
ypred_tst = model.predict(Xtst)

res = {'Encoder': encoder.__name__,
       'Ensemble': ensemble.__class__.__name__,
       'Train Acc': accuracy_score(ytrn, ypred_trn),
       'Train B Acc': balanced_accuracy_score(ytrn,
                                               ypred_trn),
       'Train F1': f1_score(ytrn, ypred_trn),
       'Test Acc': accuracy_score(ytst, ypred_tst),
       'Test B Acc': balanced_accuracy_score(ytst,
                                              ypred_tst),
       'Test F1': f1_score(ytst, ypred_tst)}
results = pd.concat([results,
                     pd.DataFrame.from_dict([res])], ignore_index=True)

    return results
```

> **Evaluates final ensemble performance and saves the results**

8.3.3 Category encoding and ensembling

In this section, we'll train various combinations of encoders and ensemble methods. In particular, we consider the following:

- *Encoders*—One-hot, ordinal, and greedy target encoding (from the `category_encoders` package)
- *Ensembles*—scikit-learn's random forest, gradient boosting with LightGBM, and Newton boosting with XGBoost

For each combination of encoder and ensemble, we follow the same steps implemented in listings 8.6 and 8.7: preprocess the features, perform ensemble parameter selection to get the best ensemble parameters, refit a final ensemble model with the best parameter combination, and evaluate the final model.

RANDOM FOREST

The following listing trains and evaluates the best combination of categorical encoding (one-hot, ordinal, and greedy target) and random forest.

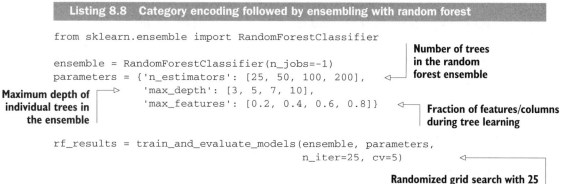

Listing 8.8   Category encoding followed by ensembling with random forest

```
from sklearn.ensemble import RandomForestClassifier

ensemble = RandomForestClassifier(n_jobs=-1)
parameters = {'n_estimators': [25, 50, 100, 200],
              'max_depth': [3, 5, 7, 10],
              'max_features': [0.2, 0.4, 0.6, 0.8]}

rf_results = train_and_evaluate_models(ensemble, parameters,
                                       n_iter=25, cv=5)
```

> **Number of trees in the random forest ensemble**

> **Maximum depth of individual trees in the ensemble**

> **Fraction of features/columns during tree learning**

> **Randomized grid search with 25 parameter combinations and 5-fold CV**

This listing returns the following results (edited to fit the page):

Encoder	Test Acc	Test B Acc	Test F1	Train Acc	Train B Acc	Train F1
OneHot	0.862	0.766	0.669	0.875	0.783	0.7
Ordinal	0.861	0.756	0.657	0.874	0.773	0.688
Target	0.864	0.774	0.679	0.881	0.797	0.72

Observe the difference between plain accuracy (Acc) and balanced accuracy (B Acc) or F1 score (F1) for both the training and test sets. Since balanced accuracy explicitly accounts for class imbalance, it provides a better estimate of model performance than accuracy. This illustrates the importance of using the right metric to evaluate our models.

While all encoding methods appear equally effective using plain accuracy as the evaluation metric, encoding with target statistics seems to be most effective in classifying between the positive and negative examples.

LightGBM

Next, we repeat this training and evaluation procedure with LightGBM, where we train an ensemble with 200 trees, as shown in following listing. Several other ensemble hyperparameters will be selected using 5-fold CV: maximum tree depth, learning rate, bagging fraction, and regularization parameters.

Listing 8.9   Category encoding followed by ensembling with LightGBM

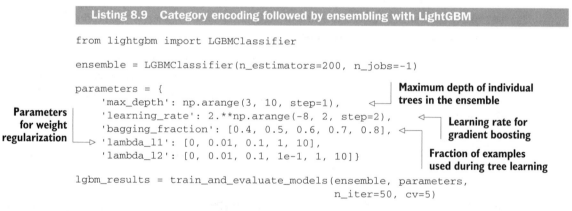

```
from lightgbm import LGBMClassifier

ensemble = LGBMClassifier(n_estimators=200, n_jobs=-1)

parameters = {
    'max_depth': np.arange(3, 10, step=1),               ← Maximum depth of individual trees in the ensemble
    'learning_rate': 2.**np.arange(-8, 2, step=2),       ← Learning rate for gradient boosting
    'bagging_fraction': [0.4, 0.5, 0.6, 0.7, 0.8],       ← Fraction of examples used during tree learning
    'lambda_l1': [0, 0.01, 0.1, 1, 10],
    'lambda_l2': [0, 0.01, 0.1, 1e-1, 1, 10]}

lgbm_results = train_and_evaluate_models(ensemble, parameters,
                                         n_iter=50, cv=5)
```

Parameters for weight regularization

This listing returns the following results (edited to fit the page):

Encoder	Test Acc	Test B Acc	Test F1	Train Acc	Train B Acc	Train F1
OneHot	0.874	0.802	0.716	0.891	0.824	0.754
Ordinal	0.874	0.802	0.717	0.892	0.825	0.757
Target	0.873	0.796	0.71	0.886	0.815	0.741

With LightGBM, all three encoding methods lead to ensembles with roughly similar generalization performance as evidenced by the test set balanced accuracy and F1 scores. The overall performance is also better than random forest.

XGBoost

Finally, we repeat this training and evaluation procedure with XGBoost as well, where we again train an ensemble of 200 trees, as shown in the following listing.

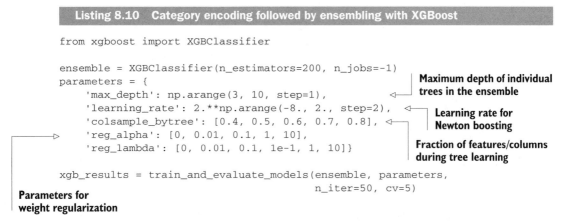

Listing 8.10 Category encoding followed by ensembling with XGBoost

```
from xgboost import XGBClassifier

ensemble = XGBClassifier(n_estimators=200, n_jobs=-1)
parameters = {
    'max_depth': np.arange(3, 10, step=1),
    'learning_rate': 2.**np.arange(-8., 2., step=2),
    'colsample_bytree': [0.4, 0.5, 0.6, 0.7, 0.8],
    'reg_alpha': [0, 0.01, 0.1, 1, 10],
    'reg_lambda': [0, 0.01, 0.1, 1e-1, 1, 10]}

xgb_results = train_and_evaluate_models(ensemble, parameters,
                                        n_iter=50, cv=5)
```

Maximum depth of individual trees in the ensemble

Learning rate for Newton boosting

Fraction of features/columns during tree learning

Parameters for weight regularization

This listing returns the following results (edited to fit the page):

Encoder	Test Acc	Test B Acc	Test F1	Train Acc	Train B Acc	Train F1
OneHot	0.875	0.799	0.715	0.896	0.829	0.764
Ordinal	0.873	0.799	0.712	0.891	0.823	0.753
Target	0.875	0.802	0.717	0.898	0.834	0.771

As with LightGBM, all three encoding methods lead to XGBoost ensembles with roughly similar generalization performance. The overall performance of XGBoost is similar to that of LightGBM, but better than random forest.

8.3.4 Ordered encoding and boosting with CatBoost

Finally, we explore the performance of CatBoost on this data set. Unlike the previous approaches, we won't use the `category_encoders` package. This is because CatBoost uses ordered target statistics along with ordered boosting. Therefore, as long as we clearly identify the categorical features that need encoding with ordered target statistics, CatBoost will take care of the rest without any additional preprocessing! The following listing performs ordered boosting with CV-based randomized parameter search.

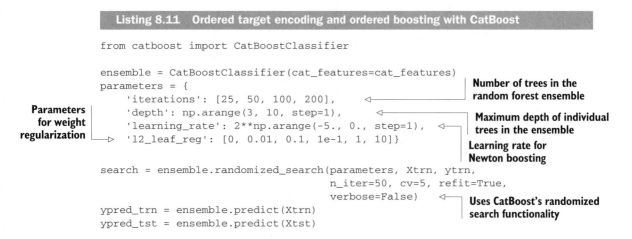

Listing 8.11 Ordered target encoding and ordered boosting with CatBoost

```
from catboost import CatBoostClassifier

ensemble = CatBoostClassifier(cat_features=cat_features)
parameters = {
    'iterations': [25, 50, 100, 200],
    'depth': np.arange(3, 10, step=1),
    'learning_rate': 2**np.arange(-5., 0., step=1),
    'l2_leaf_reg': [0, 0.01, 0.1, 1e-1, 1, 10]}

search = ensemble.randomized_search(parameters, Xtrn, ytrn,
                                    n_iter=50, cv=5, refit=True,
                                    verbose=False)
ypred_trn = ensemble.predict(Xtrn)
ypred_tst = ensemble.predict(Xtst)
```

Number of trees in the random forest ensemble

Maximum depth of individual trees in the ensemble

Learning rate for Newton boosting

Parameters for weight regularization

Uses CatBoost's randomized search functionality

```
res = {'Encoder': '',
        'Ensemble': ensemble.__class__.__name__,
        'Train Acc': accuracy_score(ytrn, ypred_trn),
        'Train B Acc': balanced_accuracy_score(ytrn, ypred_trn),
        'Train F1': f1_score(ytrn, ypred_trn),
        'Test Acc': accuracy_score(ytst, ypred_tst),
        'Test B Acc': balanced_accuracy_score(ytst, ypred_tst),
        'Test F1': f1_score(ytst, ypred_tst)}

cat_results = pd.DataFrame()
cat_results = pd.concat([cat_results,
                         pd.DataFrame.from_dict([res])], ignore_index=True)
```

CatBoost provides its own `randomized_search` feature, which can be initialized and invoked similarly to scikit-learn's `RandomizedGridCV`, which we used in the previous section:

Ensemble	Test Acc	Test B Acc	Test F1	Train Acc	Train B Acc	Train F1
CatBoost	0.87	0.796	0.708	0.888	0.82	0.747

CatBoost's performance on this data set is comparable to that of LightGBM and XGBoost, and better than random forests.

Now, let's put the results of all the approaches side by side; in figure 8.14, we look at how each approach performed with respect to balanced accuracy evaluated on the test set.

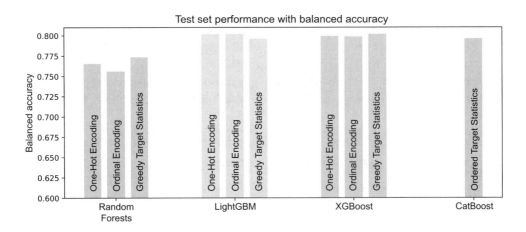

Figure 8.14 The test set performance (with the balanced accuracy metric) of various encoding and ensemble method combinations

In analyzing these results, always keep in mind that there is no free lunch, and no one method is best performing all the time. However, CatBoost does enjoy two key benefits:

- CatBoost allows for a consolidated approach to encoding and handling categorical features, unlike other ensemble approaches that necessarily use a two-step encode + ensemble approach.
- By design, CatBoost mitigates data and target leakage as well as distribution shift problems, which often need more care with other ensembling approaches.

8.4 Encoding high-cardinality string features

We wrap up this chapter by exploring encoding techniques for *high-cardinality categorical features*. The cardinality of a categorical feature is simply the number of unique categories in the feature. The number of categories is an important consideration in categorical encoding.

Real-world data sets often contain categorical string features, where feature values are strings. For example, consider a categorical feature of job titles at an organization. This feature can contain dozens to hundreds of job titles from "Intern" to "President and CEO," each with their own unique roles and responsibilities.

Such features contain a large number of categories and are inherently high-cardinality features. This disqualifies encoding approaches such as one-hot encoding (because it increases feature dimension significantly) or ordinal encoding (because a natural ordering might not always exist).

What's more, in real-world data sets, such high-cardinality features are also "dirty," in that there are several variations of the same category:

- Natural variations can arise because data is compiled from different sources. For example, two departments in the same organization may have different titles for the exact same role: "Lead Data Scientist" and "Senior Data Scientist."
- Many such data sets are manually entered into databases, which introduces noise due to typos and other errors. For example, "Data Scientsit" [sic] versus "Data Scientist."

Because two (or more!) such variants don't match exactly, they are treated as their own unique categories, even though common sense suggests that they should be cleaned and/or merged. This causes additional problems with high-cardinality string features by adding new categories to an already large set of categories.

To address this problem, we'll need to determine categories (and how to encode them) by *string similarity* rather than by exact matching. The intuition behind this approach is to encode similar categories together in a way that a human might in order to ensure that the downstream learning algorithm treats them similarly (as it should).

For example, similarity-based encoding would encode "Data Scientsit" [sic] and "Data Scientist" with similar features so that they appear nearly identical to a learning algorithm. Similarity-based encoding methods use the notion of *string similarity* to identify similar categories.

Such string similarity metrics, or measures, are widely used in natural language and text applications, for example, in autocorrect applications, database retrieval, or in language translation.

String similarity metrics

A *similarity metric* is a function that takes two objects and returns a numeric similarity measure between them. Higher values mean that the two objects are more similar to each other. A string similarity metric operates on strings.

Measuring the similarity between strings is challenging as strings can be of different lengths and can have similar substrings in different locations. To identify if two strings are similar potentially requires matching characters and subsequences of all possible lengths and locations. This combinatorial complexity means that computing string similarity can be computationally expensive.

Several efficient approaches to computing string similarity between strings of different lengths exist. Two common types are *character-based* string similarity and *token-based* string similarity, depending on the granularity of the string components being compared.

Character-based approaches measure string similarity by the number of operations at the character level (insertion, deletion, or substitution) needed to transform one string to another. These approaches are well suited for short strings.

Longer strings are often decomposed into tokens, typically substrings or words, called n-grams. Token-based approaches measure string similarity at the token level.

Irrespective of which string similarity metric you use, the similarity score can be used to encode both high-cardinality features (by grouping similar string categories together) and dirty features (by "cleaning" typos).

THE DIRTY_CAT PACKAGE

The `dirty_cat` package (https://dirty-cat.github.io/stable/index.html) provides category similarity metrics off the shelf and can be used seamlessly in modeling pipelines. The package provides three specialized encoders to handle so-called "dirty categories," which are essentially noisy and/or high-cardinality string categories:

- `SimilarityEncoder`—A version of one-hot encoding constructed using string similarities
- `GapEncoder`—Encodes categories by considering frequently co-occurring substring combinations
- `MinHashEncoder`—Encodes categories by applying hashing techniques to substrings

We use another salary data set to see how we can use the `dirty_cat` package in practice. This data set is a modified version of a publicly available Employee Salaries data set from Data.gov, with the goal being to predict an individual's salary given their job title and department.

First, we load the data set (available along with the source code) and visualize the first few rows:

```
import pandas as pd
df = pd.read_csv('./data/ch08/employee_salaries.csv')
df.head()
```

Figure 8.15 shows the first few rows of this data set.

gender	department_name	assignment_category	employee_position_title	underfilled_job_title	year_first_hired	salary
F	Department of Environmental Protection	Fulltime-Regular	Program Specialist II	NaN	2013	75362.93
F	Department of Recreation	Fulltime-Regular	Recreation Supervisor	NaN	1997	79522.62
F	Department of Transportation	Fulltime-Regular	Bus Operator	NaN	2014	42053.83
M	Fire and Rescue Services	Fulltime-Regular	Fire/Rescue Captain	NaN	1995	114587.02
F	Department of Public Libraries	Fulltime-Regular	Library Assistant I	NaN	1996	55139.67

Figure 8.15   The Employee Salaries data set mostly contains string categories.

The "salary" column is the target variable, making this a regression problem. We split this data frame into features and labels:

```
X, y = df.drop('salary', axis=1), df['salary']
print(X.shape)
(9211, 6)
```

We can get a sense of which are high-cardinality features by counting the number of unique categories or values per column:

```
for col in X.columns:
    print('{0}: {1} categories'.format(col, df[col].nunique()))

gender: 2 categories
department_name: 37 categories
assignment_category: 2 categories
employee_position_title: 385 categories
underfilled_job_title: 83 categories
year_first_hired: 51 categories
```

We see that the feature `employee_position_title` has 385 unique string categories, making this a high-cardinality feature. Directly encoding this using one-hot encoding, say, would introduce 385 new columns into our data set, thus increasing the number of columns greatly!

Instead, let's see how we can use the `dirty_cat` package to train an XGBoost ensemble on this data set. First, let's identify the different types of features in our data set explicitly:

```
lo_card = ['gender', 'department_name', 'assignment_category']
hi_card = ['employee_position_title']
continuous = ['year_first_hired']
```

Next, let's initialize the different `dirty_cat` encoders we want to use:

```
from dirty_cat import SimilarityEncoder, MinHashEncoder, GapEncoder
encoders = [SimilarityEncoder(),
            MinHashEncoder(n_components=100),
            GapEncoder(n_components=100)]
```

Encoding dimension →

← **Specifies the string similarity measure to use**

The most important encoding parameter for all encoding methods is the is `n_compo-`
`nents`, which is also known as the *encoding dimension.*

`SimilarityEncoder` measures n-gram similarity between two strings. An n-gram
is simply a sequence of *n* successive words. For example, the string "I love ensemble
methods." contains three 2-grams: "I love," "love ensemble," and "ensemble methods."
n-gram similarity between two strings first computes all possible n-grams in each string
and then computes similarity over the n-grams. By default, `SimilarityEncoder` constructs all 2-, 3-, and 4-grams, and then encodes all similar strings using one-hot encoding. This means that it will determine its own encoding dimension.

To understand the encoding dimension, consider that we're one-hot encoding the
feature `employee_position_title`, which contains 385 unique categories, which
can be grouped into 225 "similar" categories with a similarity metric. One-hot encoding will convert each categorical value to a 225-dimensional vector, making the encoding dimension 225.

`MinHashEncoder` and `GapEncoder`, on the other hand, can take in a user-specified encoding dimension and create an encoding of the specified size. In this case, the
encoding dimension is specified to be 100 for both, which is much smaller than one-
hot encoding would be forced to use.

Practically, the encoding dimension (`n_components`) is a modeling choice, and
the best value should be determined through k-fold CV, depending on the tradeoff
between model training time versus model performance.

We put all this together into the following listing, which trains three different
XGBoost models, one for each type of `dirty_cat` encoding.

> **Listing 8.12   Encoding and ensembling with high-cardinality features**

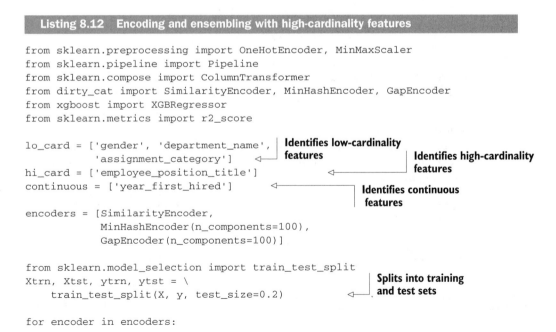

```
from sklearn.preprocessing import OneHotEncoder, MinMaxScaler
from sklearn.pipeline import Pipeline
from sklearn.compose import ColumnTransformer
from dirty_cat import SimilarityEncoder, MinHashEncoder, GapEncoder
from xgboost import XGBRegressor
from sklearn.metrics import r2_score

lo_card = ['gender', 'department_name',        Identifies low-cardinality
           'assignment_category']              features
hi_card = ['employee_position_title']                Identifies high-cardinality
continuous = ['year_first_hired']                    features
                                               Identifies continuous
                                               features
encoders = [SimilarityEncoder,
            MinHashEncoder(n_components=100),
            GapEncoder(n_components=100)]

from sklearn.model_selection import train_test_split
Xtrn, Xtst, ytrn, ytst = \                      Splits into training
    train_test_split(X, y, test_size=0.2)       and test sets

for encoder in encoders:
```

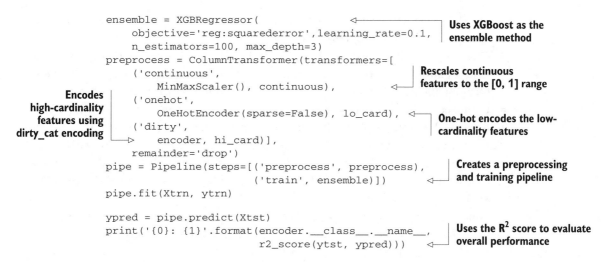

```
ensemble = XGBRegressor(                                    Uses XGBoost as the
    objective='reg:squarederror',learning_rate=0.1,         ensemble method
    n_estimators=100, max_depth=3)
preprocess = ColumnTransformer(transformers=[
    ('continuous',                                          Rescales continuous
        MinMaxScaler(), continuous),                        features to the [0, 1] range
    ('onehot',
        OneHotEncoder(sparse=False), lo_card),
    ('dirty',                                               One-hot encodes the low-
        encoder, hi_card)],                                 cardinality features
    remainder='drop')
pipe = Pipeline(steps=[('preprocess', preprocess),          Creates a preprocessing
                       ('train', ensemble)])                and training pipeline
pipe.fit(Xtrn, ytrn)

ypred = pipe.predict(Xtst)
print('{0}: {1}'.format(encoder.__class__.__name__,         Uses the R² score to evaluate
                        r2_score(ytst, ypred)))             overall performance
```

Encodes high-cardinality features using dirty_cat encoding

In this example, we identify three different types of features, each of which we preprocess differently:

- Low-cardinality features, such as gender (2 categories) and department_name (37 categories), are one-hot encoded.
- High-cardinality features, such as employee_position_title, are encoded using dirty_cat encoders.
- Continuous features, such as year_first_hired, are rescaled using MinMaxScaler to be in the range 0 to 1.

After encoding, we train an XGBoost regressor with 100 trees each of maximum depth 3 using the fairly standard mean squared error (MSE) loss function. The trained models are evaluated using the regression metric R^2 score (see chapter 1, section 1.3.1, for details), which ranges from $-\infty$ to 1, with values closer to 1 indicating better-performing regressors:

```
SimilarityEncoder: 0.8995625658800894
MinHashEncoder: 0.8996750692009536
GapEncoder: 0.8895356402510632
```

As with the other supervised methods, it's often necessary to use CV to determine which encoding parameters produce the best results for the data set at hand.

Summary

- A categorical feature is a type of data attribute that takes discrete values called classes or categories. For this reason, categorical features are also called discrete features.
- A nominal feature is a categorical variable whose values have no relationship between them (e.g., cat, dog, pig, cow).
- An ordinal feature is a categorical variable whose values are ordered, either increasing or decreasing (e.g., freshman, sophomore, junior, senior).

- One-hot vectorization/encoding and ordinal encoding are commonly used unsupervised encoding methods.

- One-hot encoding introduces binary (0–1) columns for each category into the data set and can be inefficient when a feature has a large number of categories. Ordinal encoding introduces integer values sequentially for each category.

- Using target statistics is a supervised encoding approach for categorical features; rather than a predetermined or learned encoding step, categorical features are replaced with a statistic that describes the category (e.g., mean).

- Greedy target statistics use all the training data for encoding, leading to train-to-test target leakage and distribution shift problems, which affect how we evaluate model generalization performance.

- Hold-out target statistics use a special hold-out encoding set in addition to a hold-out test set. This eliminates leakage and shift but is wasteful of data.

- Leave-one-out (LOO) target statistics and ordered target statistics are data-efficient ways to mitigate leakage and shift.

- Gradient-boosting techniques use training data for both residual computation and model training, which causes a prediction shift and overfitting.

- Ordered boosting is a modification of Newton boosting that uses a permutation-based approach to ensembling to further reduce prediction shift. Ordered boosting tackles prediction shift by training a sequence of models on different permutations and subsets of the data.

- CatBoost is a publicly available boosting library that implements ordered target statistics and ordered boosting.

- While CatBoost is well suited for categorical features, it can also be applied to regular features.

- CatBoost uses oblivious decision trees as weak learners. Oblivious decision trees use the same splitting criterion in all the nodes across an entire level/depth of the tree. Oblivious trees are balanced, less prone to overfitting, and allow speeding up execution significantly at testing time.

- High-cardinality features contain many unique categories; one-hot encoding high-cardinality features can introduce a large number of new data columns, most of them sparse (with many zeros), which leads to inefficient learning.

- `dirty_cat` is a package that produces more compact encodings for discrete-valued features and uses string and substring similarity and hashing to create effective encodings.

Explaining your ensembles 9

This chapter covers

- Understanding glass-box versus black-box and global versus local interpretability
- Using global black-box methods to understand pretrained ensemble behavior
- Using local black-box methods to explain pretrained ensemble predictions
- Training and using explainable global and local glass-box ensembles from scratch

When training and deploying models, we're usually concerned about *what* the model prediction is. Equally important, however, is *why* the model made the prediction that it did. Understanding a model's predictions is a critical component of building robust machine-learning pipelines. This is especially true when machine-learning models are used in high-stakes applications such as in health care or finance.

For example, in a medical diagnosis task such as diabetes diagnosis, understanding why the model made a specific diagnosis can provide users (in this case,

271

doctors) with additional insights that can guide them toward better prescriptions, preventative care, or palliative care. This increased transparency, in turn, increases trust in the machine-learning system, allowing the users for whom the models have been developed to use them with confidence.

Understanding the reasons behind a model's predictions is also extremely useful in model debugging, identifying failure cases, and finding ways to improve model performance. Furthermore, model debugging can also help pinpoint biases and problems with the data itself.

Machine-learning models can be characterized as black-box models and glass-box models. Black-box models are typically challenging to understand owing to their complexity (e.g., deep neural networks). The predictions of such models require specialized tools to be *explainable*. Many of the ensembles covered in this book, such as random forests and gradient boosting, are black-box machine-learning models.

Glass-box models are more intuitive and easier to understand (e.g., decision trees). The structure of such models makes them inherently *interpretable*. In this chapter, we explore the concepts of explainability and interpretability from the perspective of ensemble methods.

Interpretability methods are also characterized as global or local. Global methods attempt to broadly explain a model's features and relevance to decision making across different types of examples. Local methods attempt to specifically explain a model's decision-making process with respect to individual examples and predictions.

Section 9.1 introduces the basics of black-box and glass-box machine-learning models. This section also reintroduces two well-known machine-learning models from the perspective of interpretability: decision trees and generalized linear models (GLMs).

Section 9.2 introduces this chapter's case study: data-driven marketing. This application is used in the rest of the section to illustrate techniques for interpretability and explainability.

Section 9.3 introduces three techniques for global black-box explainability: permutation feature importance, partial dependence plots, and global surrogate models. Section 9.4 introduces two methods for local black-box explainability: LIME and SHAP. The black-box methods introduced in sections 9.3 and 9.4 are model-agnostic; that is, they can be used for any machine-learning black box. In these sections, we specifically focus on how they can be used for ensemble methods. Section 9.5 introduces a glass-box method called explainable boosting machines, a new ensemble method that is designed to be directly interpretable and provides both global and local interpretability.

9.1   *What is interpretability?*

We first introduce the basics of interpretability and explainability for machine-learning models generally, before moving to how these concepts apply to ensemble methods specifically. The notions of interpretability and explainability of a machine-learning model are related to its structure (e.g., a tree, a network, or a linear model) and its parameters (e.g., split and leaf values in trees, layer weights in neural networks, feature weights in linear models). Our goal is to understand a model's behavior in terms of its input features, output predictions, and the model internals (i.e., structure and parameters).

9.1.1   Black-box vs. glass-box models

Black-box machine-learning models are difficult to describe in terms of their model internals. This can be because we don't have access to the internal model structure and parameters (e.g., if it was trained by someone else). Even in cases where we do have access to the model internals, the model itself may be sufficiently complex that it's not easy to analyze and establish an intuitive understanding of the relationship between its inputs and outputs (see figure 9.1).

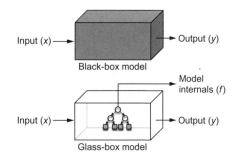

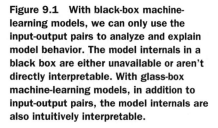

Figure 9.1   With black-box machine-learning models, we can only use the input-output pairs to analyze and explain model behavior. The model internals in a black box are either unavailable or aren't directly interpretable. With glass-box machine-learning models, in addition to input-output pairs, the model internals are also intuitively interpretable.

Neural networks and deep learning models are often cited as examples of black-box models, owing to the considerable complexity arising from their multilayered structure and large number of network parameters.

These models essentially function as black boxes: given an input example, they provide a prediction, but their inner workings are opaque to us. This makes interpreting model behavior pretty hard.

Many of the ensemble methods we've seen so far—random forests, AdaBoost, gradient boosting, and Newton boosting—are all effectively black-box models to us. This is because, even though the individual base estimators themselves may be intuitive and interpretable, the process of ensembling introduces complex interactions between the features, which, in turn, makes it hard to interpret the ensemble and its predictions. Black-box models typically require *black-box explainers*, which are explanation models that aim to explain model behavior using only a model's inputs and outputs, but not its internals.

Glass-box machine-learning models, on the other hand, are easier to understand. This is often because their model structures are immediately intuitive or comprehensible to humans.

For example, consider a simple task of diabetes diagnosis from only two features: age and blood-glucose test result (glc). Let's say that we've learned two machine-learning models that have identical predictive performance: a fourth-degree polynomial classifier and a decision-tree classifier.

The data set for this example is shown in figure 9.2, where patients who don't have diabetes (class=-1) are denoted by squares and patients who have diabetes (class=+1) are denoted by circles. The two classification models are also shown.

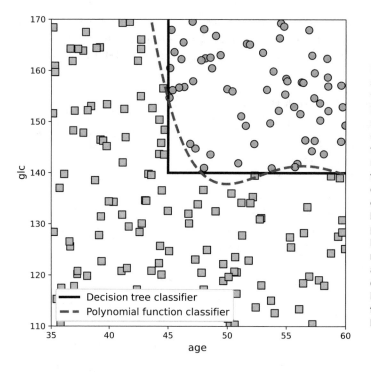

Figure 9.2   The problem space of diabetic patients who have to be classified as having diabetes (circles) or not having diabetes (squares) is based on two features: age and glc. Two machine-learning models—a fourth-degree polynomial classifier and a decision-tree classifier—are trained to have roughly similar predictive performance. However, the nature of their model internals (structure and parameters) means that decision trees are more intuitive for explanations and for understanding model behavior (see section 9.1.2).

The first model is a fourth-degree polynomial classifier. This classifier has an additive structure made up of weighted feature powers, and the weights are the model parameters:

$$f(\text{age,glc}) = \text{sign}\Big(0.0021\,\text{age}^4 - 0.497\,\text{age}^3 + 41.734\,\text{age}^2 - 1550.251\,\text{age}$$
$$+\, 21645.647 - \text{glc}\Big)$$

This function returns either +1 (diabetes = TRUE) or -1 (diabetes = FALSE). Even with the full model available to us, given a new patient and resulting diagnostic prediction (say, diabetes = TRUE), it's not immediately clear why the model made the decision it did. Was it because of the patient's age? Their blood-glucose test result? Both of these factors? This information is buried within complex mathematical calculations that aren't easy for us to infer by simply looking at the model, its structure, and parameters.

Now, let's consider a second model, a decision tree with a single decision node of the form

$$f(\text{age,glc}) = \begin{cases} \text{if age} > 45 \text{ and glc} > 140, & +1, \\ \text{otherwise}, & -1. \end{cases}$$

This function also returns either +1 (diabetes = TRUE) or -1 (diabetes = FALSE). However, the structure of this decision tree is easily interpretable as

```
if age > 45 AND glc > 140 then diabetes = TRUE else diabetes = FALSE.
```

This model's interpretation is pretty straightforward: any patient who is over the age of 45 and has a blood glucose test result over 140 will be diagnosed as having diabetes.

In summary, even though the full model internals of the polynomial classifier are available to us, the model might as well be a black box since the model internals aren't intuitive or interpretable. On the other hand, the inherent nature of how the decision tree represents the knowledge it has learned allows for easier interpretation, making it a glass-box model.

In the rest of this section, we'll explore two familiar machine-learning models that are also glass-box models: decision trees (and decision rules) and generalized linear models (GLMs). This will set us up to better understand the notions of interpretability and explainability for ensembles as both GLMs and decision trees are commonly used as base estimators in many ensemble methods.

9.1.2 Decision trees (and decision rules)

Decision trees are arguably the most interpretable of machine-learning models as they implement decision-making as a sequential process of asking and answering questions. The tree structure of a decision tree and its feature-based splitting functions are easy to interpret, as we'll see. This makes decision trees glass-box models.

Let's begin by training a decision tree on the well-known Iris data set, which is available in scikit-learn. The task is a three-way classification of irises into three species, *Iris setosa*, *Iris versicolour*, and *Iris virginica*, based on four features: sepal height, sepal width, petal height, and petal width. This exceedingly simple data set only has 150 training examples and will serve as a good teaching example for the notion of visualization.

INTERPRETING DECISION TREES IN PRACTICE

The following listing loads the data set, trains a decision-tree classifier, and visualizes it. Once visualized, we can interpret the learned decision-tree model.

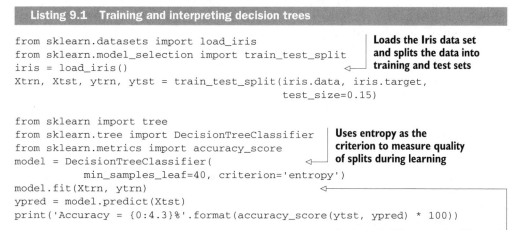

Listing 9.1 Training and interpreting decision trees

```
from sklearn.datasets import load_iris
from sklearn.model_selection import train_test_split
iris = load_iris()
Xtrn, Xtst, ytrn, ytst = train_test_split(iris.data, iris.target,
                                          test_size=0.15)


from sklearn import tree
from sklearn.tree import DecisionTreeClassifier
from sklearn.metrics import accuracy_score
model = DecisionTreeClassifier(
          min_samples_leaf=40, criterion='entropy')
model.fit(Xtrn, ytrn)
ypred = model.predict(Xtst)
print('Accuracy = {0:4.3}%'.format(accuracy_score(ytst, ypred) * 100))
```

Loads the Iris data set and splits the data into training and test sets

Uses entropy as the criterion to measure quality of splits during learning

Trains a decision-tree classifier and evaluates its test set performance

```
import graphviz, re, pydotplus
dot = tree.export_graphviz(model, feature_names=iris.feature_names,
                           class_names=['Iris-Setosa',
                                        'Iris-Versicolour',
                                        'Iris-Virginica'],
                           filled=True, impurity=False)
graphviz.Source(dot, format="png")
```

**Exports the tree internals
to dot format and then
renders using graphviz**

The resulting decision tree achieves 91.3% accuracy on the Iris data set. Note that, as Iris is a very simple data set, many different high-accuracy decision trees can be trained, one of which is shown here. We visualize it using the open source graph visualization software graph-viz package (see figure 9.3), which is used to render lists, trees, graphs, and networks.

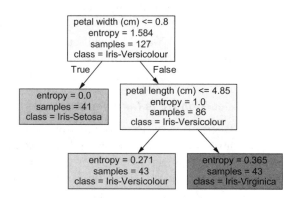

The first thing we notice is that only two of the four features, petal width and length, are enough to achieve over 90% accuracy. Thus, this decision tree has learned a *sparse model* by using only a subset of the features. But we can glean far more than that from this.

A nice property of decision trees is that each path from root node to leaf node represents it. At every split, since an example can either go left

Figure 9.3   Decision tree learned on the Iris data set for classification of irises into three species: *Iris setosa*, *Iris versicolour*, and *Iris virginica*. The standard convention for splits is followed here: if the split function evaluates to true, we proceed to the right branch; if it evaluates to false, the left branch.

or right only, the example can only end up at one of the three leaf nodes. This means that each leaf node (and by extension, each path from root to leaf, i.e., each rule) partitions the overall population into a subpopulation. Let's actually see this in action.

Since there are three leaf nodes, there are three decision rules, which we can write in Python syntax to understand them easily:

```
if petal_width <= 0.8:
    class = 'Iris-Setosa'
elif (petal_width > 0.8) and (petal_length <= 4.85):
    class = 'Iris-Versicolour'
elif (petal_width > 0.8) and (petal_length > 4.85):
    class = 'Iris-Virginica'
else:
    Can never reach here as all possibilities are covered above
```

In general, every decision tree can be expressed as a set of decision rules, which are more easily comprehensible to humans owing to their if-then structure.

NOTE   The interpretability of decision trees can be subjective and depends on the depth of the tree and the number of leaf nodes. Trees of small-to-medium depth (say, up to depth 3 or 4) and approximately 8–15 nodes are generally more intuitive and easier to understand. As the tree depth and number of leaf nodes increase, the number and length of decision rules we'll have to contend with and interpret also increase. This makes deep and complex decision trees more like black boxes and also rather difficult to interpret.

Remember that every example that passes through a decision tree must end up at one and only one of the leaf nodes. Thus, the set of paths from the root to the leaves will fully cover all the examples. What's more, the tree/rules will partition the space of all irises into three nonoverlapping subpopulations, each corresponding to one of the three species. This is very helpful for visualization and interpretation, as shown in figure 9.4.

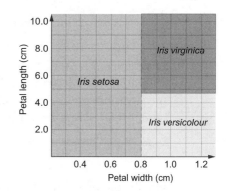

FEATURE IMPORTANCES

We know from the tree that two features are used: petal length and petal width. But how much did each feature contribute to the model? This is the notion of feature importance in which we ascribe a score to each feature depending on how much it influ-

Figure 9.4 Decision trees partition the feature space into nonoverlapping subspaces, where each subspace denotes a subpopulation of the examples.

ences overall decision making in a model. In a decision tree, feature importances can be computed very easily!

Let's compute the feature importances for each feature in the tree shown earlier in figure 9.3, keeping in mind a couple of important details. First, the training set consisted of 127 training examples (`samples = 127` in the root node). Next, this tree was trained using entropy as the split-quality criterion (refer to listing 9.1).

Thus, to measure feature importance, we simply compute how much each feature decreases entropy overall after the split. To avoid skewing our perception of splits with a very small or very large proportion of examples, we'll also weight the entropy decrease.

More precisely, for each split node, we compute how much its (weighted) entropy decreases with respect to its child nodes after the split:

$$\text{Importance}(node) = n_{node}H(node) - \left(n_{left}H(left) + n_{right}H(right)\right)$$

For the node [`petal_width <= 0.8`]:

$$\text{Importance(petal\_width)} = 127 \cdot 1.584 - (41 \cdot 0.0 + 86 \cdot 1.0) = 115.244$$

For the node [`petal_length <= 4.85`]:

$$\text{Importance(petal\_length)} = 86 \cdot 1.0 - (43 \cdot 0.271 + 43 \cdot 0.365) = 58.599$$

Since the other two features aren't used in the model, their feature importances will be zero. The final step is to normalize the feature importances so that they sum to 1:

$$\text{Importance(petal\_width)} = \frac{115.244}{115.244 + 58.599} = 0.663$$

$$\text{Importance(petal\_length)} = \frac{58.599}{115.244 + 58.599} = 0.337$$

In practice, we don't have to compute feature importances ourselves as most implementations of decision-tree learning do so. For example, the feature importances of the decision tree we just trained from listing 9.1 can be obtained directly from the model (compare with our preceding computation):

```
model.feature_importances_
array([0.        , 0.        , 0.33708016, 0.66291984])
```

Finally, the preceding example showed the interpretability of decision trees for classification problems. Decision-tree regressors can also be interpreted in the same way; the only difference is that the leaf nodes will be regression values instead of class labels.

9.1.3 *Generalized linear models*

We now revisit GLMs, which were originally introduced in chapter 7, section 7.1.4. Recall that GLMs extend linear models through a (nonlinear) link function, $g(y)$. For example, linear regression uses the identity link to relate the regression values y to the data x:

$$y = \beta_0 + \beta_1 x_1 + \cdots + \beta_d x_d$$

Here, the data point $x = [x_1, \cdots, x_d]'$ is described by d features, and the linear model is parameterized by the linear coefficients $\beta_1, \cdots, \beta_d$ and the intercept (sometimes called the bias) β_0. Another example of a GLM is logistic regression, which uses the logit link to relate class probabilities p to the data x:

$$\log \frac{p(y = 1)}{1 - p(y = 1)} = \beta_0 + \beta_1 x_1 + \cdots + \beta_d x_d$$

GLMs are interpretable due to their linear and additive structure. The linear parameters themselves give us an intuitive sense of each feature's contribution to the overall prediction. The additive structure ensures that the overall prediction depends on the individual contributions from each feature.

For example, consider that we've trained a logistic regression model for the diabetes diagnosis task discussed earlier, to classify if a patient has diabetes, using two features: `age` and blood-glucose test result (`glc`). Let's say the learned model is (with $p(y = 1)$ as p):

$$\log \frac{p}{1-p} = -0.1 + 0.5 \cdot \text{age} - 0.29 \cdot \text{glc}$$

Recall that if p is the probability of a positive diagnosis, then $\frac{p}{1-p}$ are the *odds* that the patient has the diagnosis. Thus, logistic regression represents the log-odds of a positive diabetes diagnosis as a weighted combination of the features `age` and `glc`.

FEATURE WEIGHTS

How can we interpret the feature weights? If `age` is increased by 1, $\log \frac{p}{1-p}$ will increase by 0.5 (because the model is linear and additive). Thus, for a patient who is a year older, their log-odds of a positive diabetes diagnosis are $\log \frac{p}{1-p} = 0.5$. Consequently, their odds of a positive diabetes diagnosis are $\frac{p}{1-p} = e^{0.5} = 1.65$, or 65% more.

In a similar vein, if `glc` is increased by 1, $\log \frac{p}{1-p}$ will decrease by 0.29 (note the minus in the weight, indicating a decrease). Thus, for a patient whose glc increases by 1, their odds of a positive diabetes diagnosis are $\frac{p}{1-p} = e^{-0.29} = 0.75$, or 25% less.

Let's take this intuition and see how we can interpret a more realistic logistic regression model. We begin by training a logistic regression model on the Breast Cancer data set that was first introduced in chapter 2's case study. The task is binary classification for breast cancer diagnosis. Each example in the data set is characterized by 30 features extracted from an image of the breast mass. These features represent properties such as the radius, perimeter, area, concavity, and so on of the breast mass.

INTERPRETING GLMs IN PRACTICE

The next listing loads the data set, trains a logistic regression classifier, and visualizes the increase or decrease in the odds of a positive breast cancer diagnosis of each feature.

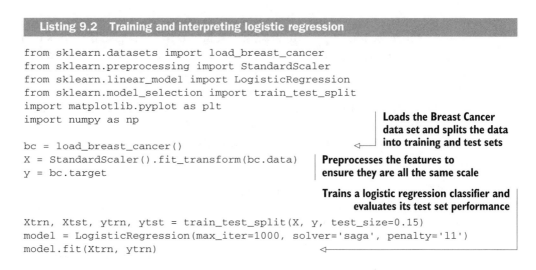

Listing 9.2 Training and interpreting logistic regression

```
from sklearn.datasets import load_breast_cancer
from sklearn.preprocessing import StandardScaler
from sklearn.linear_model import LogisticRegression
from sklearn.model_selection import train_test_split
import matplotlib.pyplot as plt
import numpy as np
                                                        Loads the Breast Cancer
                                                        data set and splits the data
bc = load_breast_cancer()                               into training and test sets
X = StandardScaler().fit_transform(bc.data)    Preprocesses the features to
y = bc.target                                  ensure they are all the same scale

                                               Trains a logistic regression classifier and
                                               evaluates its test set performance
Xtrn, Xtst, ytrn, ytst = train_test_split(X, y, test_size=0.15)
model = LogisticRegression(max_iter=1000, solver='saga', penalty='l1')
model.fit(Xtrn, ytrn)
```

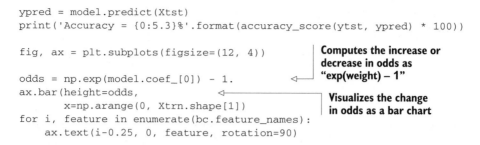

The odds of each feature i are calculated from the weights as $odds_i = e^{w_i}$. The change in odds is calculated as $change_i = odds_i - 1 = e^{w_i} - 1$, and visualized in figure 9.5.

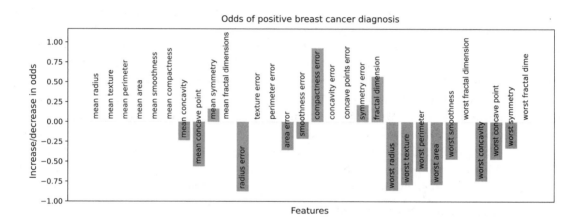

Figure 9.5 Interpreting a logistic regression, that is, a linear model for classification, for breast cancer diagnosis. Positive feature weights lead to increased odds of breast cancer, negative feature weights lead to decreased odds of breast cancer, and zero feature weights don't affect the odds of breast cancer.

If the feature weight $w_i > 0$, then $odds_i > 1$, and it will increase the odds of a positive diagnosis ($change_i > 0$). If a feature weight $w_i < 0$, then $odds_i < 1$, and it will decrease the odds of a positive diagnosis ($change_i < 0$). If a feature weight $w_i = 0$, then $odds_i = 1$ and that feature doesn't affect the diagnosis ($change_i = 0$).

This last part is an important component of learning *sparse linear models*, where we train a model as a mixture of zero and nonzero feature weights. A zero feature weight means that that feature doesn't contribute to the model and can be effectively dropped. This, in turn, allows for a sparser feature set and leaner, more interpretable models!

NOTE   The interpretability of linear models is dependent on the relative scaling between the features. For example, age might range from 18 to 65, while salary might range from \$30,000 to \$90,000. This disparity in features affects the underlying weight learning, and the feature with the higher weight range (in this case, salary) will dominate the models. When we interpret such models, we might incorrectly ascribe greater significance to such features. To train a robust model that considers all the features equally during learning, care must be taken to properly preprocess the data to ensure all features are in the same numerical range.

Linear regression models can also be interpreted similarly. In this case, rather than compute the odds, we can compute the contribution of each feature to the regression value directly, since the regression value $y = \beta_0 + \beta_1 x_1 + \cdots + \beta_d x_d$.

9.2   *Case study: Data-driven marketing*

In the rest of this chapter, we'll explore how we can train both black-box and glass-box ensembles in the context of a machine-learning task from the domain of data-driven marketing. Data-driven marketing aims to use customer and socioeconomic information to identify customers who will be most receptive to certain types of marketing strategies. This allows businesses to target specific customers with advertisements, offers, and sales in an optimal and personalized way.

9.2.1   *Bank Marketing data set*

We'll consider the Bank Marketing data set[1] from the UCI Machine Learning Repository (http://mng.bz/VpXP), where the data comes from a phone-based direct marketing campaign of a Portuguese bank. The task is to predict if a customer will subscribe to a fixed-term deposit.

This data set is also available with the source code. For each customer in the data set, there are four types of features: demographic attributes, details of the last phone contact, overall campaign information pertaining to this customer, and general socioeconomic indicators. The details are illustrated in table 9.1.

Table 9.1   Features and target of the Bank Marketing data set, grouped by the feature, type, and source

Feature	Type	Feature description
Client demographic attributes and financial indicators		
age	Continuous	Age of the customer
job	Categorical	Type of job (12 categories, e.g., blue-collar, retired, self-employed, student, services, etc., and unknown)
marital	Categorical	Marital status (divorced, married, single, unknown)
education	Categorical	Highest education (8 categories, e.g., high school, university degree, professional course, and unknown)
default	Categorical	Does customer have credit in default? (yes, no, unknown)
housing	Categorical	Does customer have a housing loan? (yes, no, unknown)
loan	Categorical	Does customer have a personal loan? (yes, no, unknown)

---

[1] S. Moro, P. Cortez and P. Rita, "A Data-Driven Approach to Predict the Success of Bank Telemarketing," *Decision Support Systems*, 62:22–31, June 2014.

Table 9.1   Features and target of the Bank Marketing data set, grouped by the feature, type, and source

Feature	Type	Feature description
Date and time conditions of last marketing contact		
contact	Binary	Contact communication type (cell phone, telephone)
month	Categorical	Last contact month (12 categories: January–December)
day-of-week	Categorical	Last contact weekday (5 categories: Monday–Friday)
Marketing campaign details from current and previous campaigns		
campaign	Continuous	Total number of contacts during this campaign
pdays	Continuous	Number of days since the last contact in previous campaign
previous	Continuous	Number of contacts performed before this campaign
poutcome	Categorical	Outcome of previous marketing campaign (3 categories: failure, nonexistent, success)
General social and economic indicators		
emp.var.rate	Continuous	Employment variation rate: quarterly indicator
cons.price.idx	Continuous	Consumer price index: monthly indicator
cons.conf.idx	Continuous	Consumer confidence index: monthly indicator
euribor3m	Continuous	Euribor three-month rate: daily indicator
nr.employed	Continuous	Number of employees: quarterly indicator
Prediction target		
subscribed?	Binary	Has the customer subscribed to a term deposit?

It's important to note that this data set is extremely imbalanced: only 10% of the customers in the data set subscribed to a term deposit as a result of this marketing campaign.

Listing 9.3 loads the data set, splits the data into training and test sets, and preprocesses them. The continuous features are scaled to between 0 and 1 using scikit-learn's `MinMaxEncoder`, and the categorical features are encoded with `OrdinalEncoder`.

Listing 9.3   Loading and preprocessing the Bank Marketing data set

```
import pandas as pd
data_file = './data/ch09/bank-additional-full.csv'          Loads the
df = pd.read_csv(data_file, sep=';')                        data set
df = df.drop('duration', axis=1)
                                                            Drops the "duration"
from sklearn.model_selection import train_test_split        column (see NOTE for a
y = df['y']                                                 more detailed explanation)
X = df.drop('y', axis=1)
                                            Splits the data frame into
                                            features and labels
```

```
Xtrn, Xtst, ytrn, ytst = \
    train_test_split(X, y, stratify=y, test_size=0.25)
```

◁─── **Splits into train and test sets with stratified sampling to preserve class balances**

```
from sklearn.preprocessing import LabelEncoder
preprocess_labels = LabelEncoder()
ytrn = preprocess_labels.fit_transform(ytrn).astype(float)
ytst = preprocess_labels.transform(ytst)
```

◁─── **Preprocesses labels using "LabelEncoder"**

```
from sklearn.preprocessing import MinMaxScaler, OrdinalEncoder
from sklearn.pipeline import Pipeline
from sklearn.compose import ColumnTransformer

cat_features = ['default', 'housing', 'loan', 'contact', 'poutcome',
                'job', 'marital', 'education', 'month', 'day_of_week']
cntnous_features = ['age', 'campaign', 'pdays', 'previous', 'emp.var.rate',
                    'cons.price.idx', 'cons.conf.idx', 'nr.employed',
                    'euribor3m']
```

Preprocesses continuous features with "MinMaxEncoder" and categorical features with "OrdinalEncoder"

```
preprocess_categorical = Pipeline(steps=[('encoder', OrdinalEncoder())])
preprocess_numerical = Pipeline(steps=[('scaler', MinMaxScaler())])
data_transformer = \                      ◁───
    ColumnTransformer(transformers=[
        ('categorical', preprocess_categorical, cat_features),
        ('numerical', preprocess_numerical, cntnous_features)])
all_features = cat_features + cntnous_features

Xtrn = pd.DataFrame(data_transformer.fit_transform(Xtrn),
                    columns=all_features)
Xtst = pd.DataFrame(data_transformer.transform(Xtst), columns=all_features)
```

To prevent data and target leakage (see chapter 8), we ensure that scaling and encoding functions are only fit to the training set before applying to the test set.

NOTE The original data set contains a feature called *duration*, which refers to the duration of the last phone call. Longer calls are highly correlated with the outcome of the call because longer calls indicate more engaged customers who are likelier to subscribe. However, unlike other features, which are known before making the call, we can't possibly know a call's duration ahead of time. In this way, the duration feature essentially behaves like a target variable since both `duration` and `subscribed` will immediately be known after a call. To build a realistic predictive model that can be deployed in practice with all features available *before* calling, we drop this feature from our modeling.

9.2.2 Training ensembles

We'll now train two ensembles (from two different packages) on this data set: `xgboost.XGBoostClassifier` and `sklearn.RandomForestClassifier`. Both these models will be complex ensembles of 200 decision trees (weighted ensembles, in the case of XGBoost) and are effectively black boxes. Once trained, we'll explore how to make these black boxes explainable in section 9.3.

Listing 9.4 shows how we can train an XGBoost ensemble over this data set. We use a randomized grid search combined with 5-fold cross validation (CV) and early stopping (see chapter 6 for additional details) to select among various hyperparameters such as learning rate and regularization parameters.

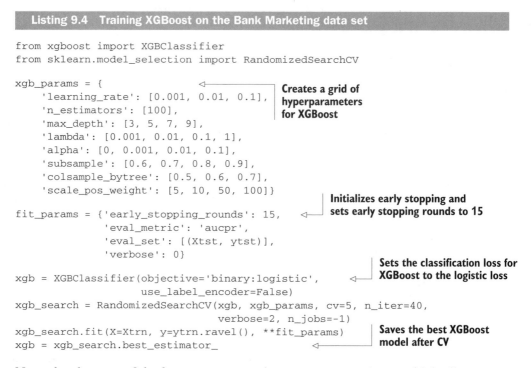

Listing 9.4   Training XGBoost on the Bank Marketing data set

```
from xgboost import XGBClassifier
from sklearn.model_selection import RandomizedSearchCV

xgb_params = {                              ◁       Creates a grid of
    'learning_rate': [0.001, 0.01, 0.1],           hyperparameters
    'n_estimators': [100],                          for XGBoost
    'max_depth': [3, 5, 7, 9],
    'lambda': [0.001, 0.01, 0.1, 1],
    'alpha': [0, 0.001, 0.01, 0.1],
    'subsample': [0.6, 0.7, 0.8, 0.9],
    'colsample_bytree': [0.5, 0.6, 0.7],
    'scale_pos_weight': [5, 10, 50, 100]}
                                                   Initializes early stopping and
fit_params = {'early_stopping_rounds': 15,   ◁     sets early stopping rounds to 15
              'eval_metric': 'aucpr',
              'eval_set': [(Xtst, ytst)],
              'verbose': 0}
                                                   Sets the classification loss for
xgb = XGBClassifier(objective='binary:logistic',  ◁  XGBoost to the logistic loss
                    use_label_encoder=False)
xgb_search = RandomizedSearchCV(xgb, xgb_params, cv=5, n_iter=40,
                                verbose=2, n_jobs=-1)
xgb_search.fit(X=Xtrn, y=ytrn.ravel(), **fit_params)   Saves the best XGBoost
xgb = xgb_search.best_estimator_            ◁          model after CV
```

Note also that one of the hyperparameters is `scale_pos_weight`, which allows us to weight positive and negative training examples differently. This is necessary since the Bank Marketing data set is imbalanced (10%:90% positive-to-negative example ratio). By weighting the positive examples more, we can ensure that their contribution isn't drowned out by the larger proportion of negative examples. Here, we use cross validation to identify a weight for positive examples from among 5, 10, 50 and 100.

This listing trains an `XGBoostClassifier` that achieves around 87.24% test set accuracy and 74.67% balanced accuracy. We can use a similar procedure to train a random forest over this data set. The main difference is that we set the class weights for positive examples to `10`.

Listing 9.5   Training a random forest on the Bank Marketing data set

```
from sklearn.ensemble import RandomForestClassifier
from sklearn.model_selection import RandomizedSearchCV

rf_params = {                           ◁       Creates a grid of
    'max_depth': [3, 5, 7],                     hyperparameters for
    'max_samples': [0.5, 0.6, 0.7, 0.8],        "RandomForestClassifier"
```

```
        'max_features': [0.5, 0.6, 0.7, 0.8]}

rf = RandomForestClassifier(
        class_weight={0: 1, 1: 10},
        n_estimators=200)
rf_search = RandomizedSearchCV(rf, rf_params, cv=5, n_iter=30,
                               verbose=2, n_jobs=-1)
rf_search.fit(X=Xtrn, y=ytrn)
rf = rf_search.best_estimator_
```

Sets the weights for negative-to-positive examples to be 1:10

Saves the best random forest after CV

This listing trains a `RandomForestClassifier` that achieves around 84% test set accuracy.

9.2.3   *Feature importances in tree ensembles*

Most of the ensembles in this book (including `XGBoostClassifier` and `Random-ForestClassifier` trained in the previous subsection) are tree ensembles as they use decision trees as their base estimators. One way to compute feature importances for an ensemble is to simply average the feature importances from the individual base decision trees!

In fact, the implementations of random forest (in scikit-learn) and XGBoost do this already, and we can obtain the ensemble feature importances using the following:

```
xgb_search.best_estimator_.feature_importances_
rf_search.best_estimator_.feature_importances_
```

We visualize and compare the feature importances of both these ensembles in figure 9.6 to interpret and understand their decision making.

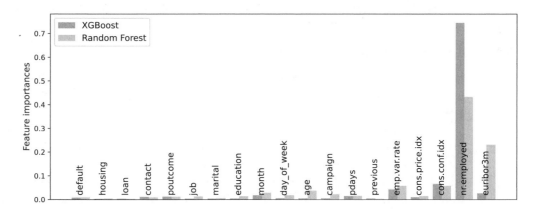

Figure 9.6   Feature importances of the ensembles learned by XGBoost (left bars) and random forest (right bars) classifiers

Both ensembles ascribe significant importance to the socioeconomic indicator variables, in particular, `nr.employed` and `emp.var.rate` (which indicate unemployment rates), `euribor3m` (interbanking interest rates, which indicate macroeconomic stability), and `cons.conf.idx` (which indicates consumer optimism regarding their expected financial situation).

The XGBoost model, however, is strongly reliant on just one of the variables over the others: `nr.employed`. The overall takeaway from interpreting this is that people are more likely to subscribe to a fixed-term deposit account when the overall economic picture is without uncertainty or fluctuations, and is optimistic.

Feature importances allow us to understand what a model is doing overall and over different types of examples. That is, feature importances are a type of global explainability method.

9.3   *Black-box methods for global explainability*

Methods for machine-learning model explainability can be categorized into two types:

- Global methods attempt to generally explain a model's decision-making process, and what factors are broadly relevant.
- Local methods attempt to specifically explain a model's decision-making process with respect to individual examples and predictions.

Global explainability speaks to a model's sensible behavior over a large number of examples when deployed or used in practice, whereas local explainability speaks to a model's individual predictions on single examples that allow the user to make decisions on what to do next.

In this section, we look at some global explainability methods for black-box models. These approaches only consider a model's inputs and outputs and don't use the model internals (hence, black box) to explain model behavior. For this reason, they can be used for global explainability of any machine-learning method and are also called *model-agnostic methods*.

9.3.1   *Permutation feature importance*

Feature importance in a machine-learning model refers to a score that indicates how good a feature is in a model, that is, how effective the feature is in a model's decision-making process.

We've already seen how we can compute feature importances for decision trees and, by aggregation, for tree-based ensembles that use decision trees as base estimators. For tree-based methods, the feature importance calculation uses model internals such as the tree structure and split parameters. But what if these model internals aren't available? Is there a black-box equivalent method for obtaining feature importances in such situations?

There is indeed: *permutation feature importance*. Recall that decision-tree feature importance scores each feature by how much it decreases the split criterion (e.g., Gini impurity or entropy for classification, squared error for regression). In contrast, permutation feature importance scores each feature by how much it increases the test error after we permute (shuffle) that feature's values.

The intuition here is straightforward: if a feature is more important, then "messing with it" affects its ability to contribute to predictions and will increase the test error. If a feature is less important, then messing with it won't have much of an effect on the model's predictions and won't affect the test error.

We "mess" with a feature by randomly permuting its values. This effectively snaps any relationship between that feature and its prediction. The procedure of permutation feature importance is illustrated in figure 9.7.

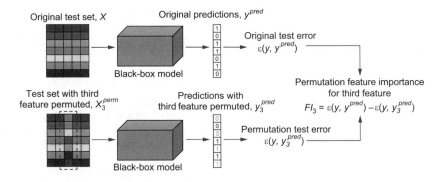

Figure 9.7   The procedure for computing permutation feature importance illustrated for the third feature. This procedure is repeated for all features. Permutation feature importance uses only inputs and outputs to estimate feature importance and doesn't use model internals (making this a model-agnostic approach).

The permutation feature importance is elegant and simple in how it scores features without access to model internals. Here are some important technical details to keep in mind, though:

- Permutation feature importance is a before-and-after score. It tries to estimate how the model's predictive performance changes from before to after we shuffle (permute) features. To get a robust and unbiased estimate of the before-and-after model performance, it's essential that we use a hold-out test set!

- There are many ways to evaluate a model's predictive performance depending on the task (classification or regression), the data set, and our own modeling goals. For this task, for instance, consider the following performance metrics:

  - *Balanced accuracy*—Since this is a classification task, accuracy is a natural choice for a model evaluation metric. However, this data set is imbalanced with a 1:10 ratio of positive-to-negative examples. To account for this, we can use balanced accuracy, which ensures this skew is considered by weighting predictions by class size.

  - *Recall*—The purpose of this model is to identify high-value customers who will subscribe to fixed-term deposits. From this perspective, we want to minimize false negatives, or customers that our model thinks won't subscribe, but who actually will! This type of wrong prediction costs us customers, and recall is a good metric to minimize such false negatives.

- This procedure randomly shuffles feature values. As with any randomized approach, it's a good idea to repeat the process several times and average the result (analogous to how we use *k* folds in cross validation).

PERMUTATION FEATURE IMPORTANCE IN PRACTICE

The following listing computes permutation feature importances for the XGB-Classifier trained in the previous section using `balanced_accuracy`.

Listing 9.6   Computing permutation feature importance

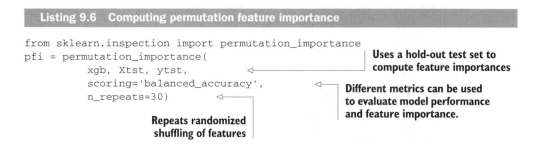

```
from sklearn.inspection import permutation_importance
pfi = permutation_importance(
        xgb, Xtst, ytst,                      ← Uses a hold-out test set to
                                                compute feature importances
        scoring='balanced_accuracy',          ← Different metrics can be used
        n_repeats=30)                     ←     to evaluate model performance
                                                and feature importance.
```
Repeats randomized shuffling of features

Figure 9.8 compares feature importance of the XGBoost model with the permutation importance computed using balanced accuracy and recall, and then visualizes the top-10 features identified by each approach.

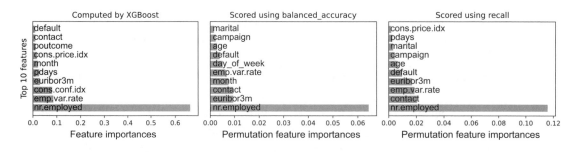

Figure 9.8   Feature importances computed by XGBoost versus black-box permutation feature importances computed for the XGBoost model using two different metrics: balanced accuracy and recall

Interestingly, while all three approaches identify the importance of `nr.employed` (the number of employees), `euribor3m` (the interbank borrowing rate) emerges as a key indicator when scoring features using balanced accuracy or recall. A little deeper reflection might shine a light as to why. In a healthier economy, better interbank borrowing rates allow for better interest rates, which, in turn, favorably influence customers to subscribe to a fixed deposit account.

Aside from the socioeconomic indicators, other features such as `contact` (cell phone vs. telephone contact) and `campaign` (total number of contacts during this campaign) also emerge as important indicators of whether a customer will subscribe to a fixed-term deposit.

Some demographic features such as `marital`, `age`, and `education` also begin to emerge as important when scored using recall, where we aim to decrease the false negatives and identify as many high-value customers as possible. Again, it's not hard to see that effectively identifying high-value customers is reliant on their personal demographic indicators.

> **NOTE**   Care must be taken with correlated features because they contain similar information. When two features, for example, are correlated, and one of them is permuted, the model can still use the other unpermuted feature without any decrease in performance (because they both contain similar, information). Since the scores before and after permutation are similar the permutation feature importance scores for both the correlated features will be small. From this, we may incorrectly conclude that both features are unimportant, when, in fact, they may both be important. This situation is even worse when we have three, four, or a cluster of correlated features. One way to handle this situation is to preprocess the data by clustering features into groups and using a representative feature from each feature group.

9.3.2   *Partial dependence plots*

Partial dependence plots (PDPs) are another useful black-box approach that helps us identify the nature of the relationship between a feature and the target. Unlike permutation feature importance, which uses randomization to elicit the importance of a feature, the partial dependence relationship is identified using *marginalization*, or summing out.

Let's say that we're interested in computing the partial dependence between the target y and the kth feature, X_k. Let the data set with the remaining features be X_{rest}. We have a black-box model $y = f([X_k, X_{rest}])$.

To obtain the partial dependence function $\hat{f}(X_k)$ from this black box, we simply have to sum over all possible values of all the other features X_{rest}; that is, we marginalize the other features. Mathematically, summing over all possible values of the other features is equivalent to integrating over them:

$$\hat{f}(X_k) = \int_{X_{rest}} f([X_k, X_{rest}]) \, dX_{rest}$$

However, since computing this integral isn't really feasible, we'll need to approximate it. We can do so very easily using a set of n examples:

$$\hat{f}(X_k = a) = \frac{1}{n} \sum_{i=1}^{n} f\left([a, X_{rest}^i]\right)$$

This equation gives us a straightforward way of computing the partial dependence function for a feature X_k.

For different values of a, we simply replace the entire column with a. Thus, for each a, we create a new data set $X^{[a]}$, where the kth feature takes the value a for every example. The predictions of this modified data set using our black-box model will be $y^{[a]} = f(X^{[a]})$. The prediction vector $y^{[a]}$ is a length-n vector, containing the predictions of each test example in the modified data set. We can now average over these predictions to give us one pair of points:

$$\left(X_k = a, \hat{f}\,(X_k = a) = \frac{1}{n} \sum_{i=1}^{n} y_i^{[a]} \right)$$

We repeat this procedure for different values of α to generate the full PDP. This is illustrated in figure 9.9 for two values, $a = 0,1$ and $a = 0.4$.

PDPs are intuitive to create and use, though they can be somewhat time consuming as new modified versions of the data set have to be created and evaluated for each point in the dependence plot. Here are some important technical details to keep in mind:

- Partial dependence tries to relate a model's output to input features, that is, model behavior in terms of what it has learned. For this reason, it's best to create and visualize a PDP with the training set.

- Remember that the overall partial dependence function is created by averaging across n examples; that is, each training example can be used to create an example-specific partial dependence function. This partial dependence between a specific example and its output is called the *individual conditional expectation* (ICE).

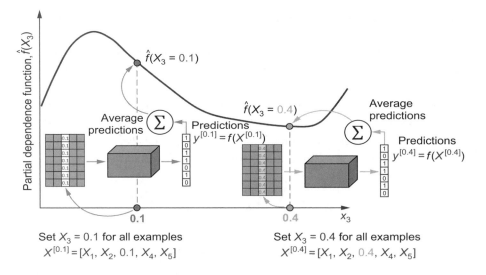

Figure 9.9   Two points in the PDP for the third feature computed at $X_3 = 0.1$ and $X_3 = 0.4$. Observe that we set the third column (feature) to 0.1 and 0.3, respectively, to get two data sets. Each of these data sets produce two sets of predictions, which are averaged to produce two points on the PDP.

PARTIAL DEPENDENCE PLOTS IN PRACTICE

The next listing illustrates how to construct PDPs for the `XGBoostClassifier` trained earlier in section 9.2 on the Bank Marketing data set.

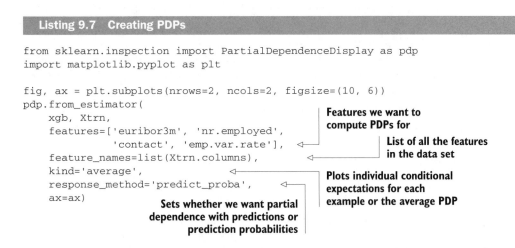

```
from sklearn.inspection import PartialDependenceDisplay as pdp
import matplotlib.pyplot as plt

fig, ax = plt.subplots(nrows=2, ncols=2, figsize=(10, 6))
pdp.from_estimator(
    xgb, Xtrn,                              Features we want to
    features=['euribor3m', 'nr.employed',  compute PDPs for
            'contact', 'emp.var.rate'],  ◁
    feature_names=list(Xtrn.columns),      ◁    List of all the features
    kind='average',                                 in the data set
    response_method='predict_proba',       ◁    Plots individual conditional
    ax=ax)                                          expectations for each
                   Sets whether we want partial     example or the average PDP
              dependence with predictions or
                  prediction probabilities
```

Figure 9.10 shows the partial dependence function of four high-scoring variables: `euribor3m`, `nr.employed`, `contact`, and `emp.var.rate` from the Bank Marketing data set.

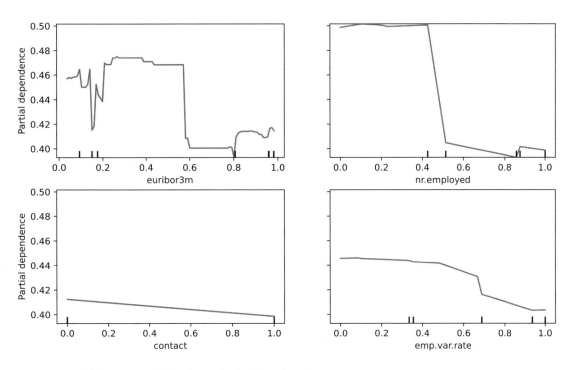

Figure 9.10   PDPs of four variables in the Bank Marketing data set

The PDPs give us further insight into how different variables behave and how they influence predictions. Note that, in listing 9.7, we set `response_method` to `'predict_proba'`. Thus, the plots in figure 9.10 show how each variable (partially) influences the prediction probability of a customer subscribing to a fixed-deposit account. Higher prediction probabilities indicate that those attributes are more helpful in identifying high-value customers.

For example, low values of `euribor3m` (e.g., in the range 0–0.5) generally correspond to higher subscription likelihoods. As discussed previously, this makes sense as lower bank borrowing rates typically mean lower customer interest rates, which would be attractive to a potential customer.

A similar conclusion—that lower unemployment rates are also likely to influence potential customers into opening fixed-deposit accounts—can also be drawn from the variables `emp.var.rate` and `nr.employed`.

> **NOTE** As with permutation feature importance, a key assumption in the procedure for PDPs is that the feature we're interested in, X_k, isn't correlated with the remaining features, X_{rest}. This independence assumption is what allows us to marginalize the remaining features by summing over them. If the features X_{rest} are correlated, then marginalizing over them destroys some component of X_k as well, and we no longer have an accurate view of how much X_k contributes to the predictions.

One important limitation of PDPs is that it's only possible to create plots of partial dependence functions of one variable (curves), two variables (contours), or three variables (surface plots). Beyond three variables, it becomes impossible to visualize multivariable partial dependence without breaking features down into smaller groups of two or three.

9.3.3   *Global surrogate models*

Black-box explanations such as feature importance and partial dependence attempt to identify the effect of an individual feature or group of features on predictions. In this section, we explore a more holistic approach that aims to approximate the behavior of the black-box model in an interpretable way.

The idea of a surrogate model is extremely simple: we train a second model that mimics the behavior of the black-box model. However, the surrogate model itself is a glass box and inherently explainable.

Once trained, we can use the surrogate glass-box model to explain the predictions of the black-box model, as illustrated in figure 9.11:

- A surrogate data set (X^s_{trn}, y^s_{trn}) is used to train the surrogate model. The original data that was used to train the black-box model can also be used to train the surrogate model, if it's available. If not, an alternate data sample from the original problem space is used. The key is to ensure that the surrogate data set has the same distribution as the original data set that was used to train the black-box model.

- The surrogate model is trained on the predictions of the original black-box model. This is because the idea is to fit a surrogate model to *mimic* the behavior of the black-box model so that we can explain the black box using the surrogate. Once trained, if the surrogate predictions (y_{pred}^s) match the black-box predictions (y_{pred}^b), then the surrogate model can be used to explain the predictions.
- Any glass-box model can be used as a surrogate model. This includes decision trees and GLMs, which can then be interpreted as shown earlier in section 9.11.

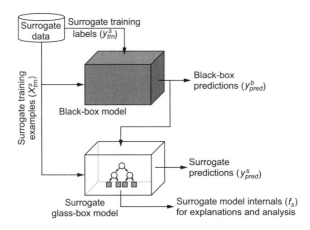

Figure 9.11   The procedure to train a global surrogate model from the predictions of a black-box model. Both models are trained on the same surrogate training examples. However, the surrogate model is trained on the predictions of the black-box model, so that it can learn to mimic its predictions. If the black box and surrogate make the same prediction, then the surrogate can be used to explain the black-box model's prediction.

THE FIDELITY-INTERPRETABILITY TRADEOFF

Let's train a surrogate decision tree to explain the behavior of the XGBoost model that was originally trained on the Bank Marketing data set. The original training set is also used as the surrogate training set.

Keep in mind that we want to trade off between two criteria while training the model: the surrogate's fidelity to the black-box model and the surrogate's explainability. The surrogate's fidelity measures how well it can mimic the black-box model's predictive behavior. More precisely, we measure how similar the surrogate model's predictions (y_{pred}^s) are to the black-box model's predictions (y_{pred}^b).

For binary classification problems, we can do this using metrics such as accuracy or R^2 score (see chapter 1). For regression problems, we can do this with metrics such as mean squared error (MSE), or R^2 again. Higher R^2 scores indicate better fidelity between the black-box model and its surrogate.

The surrogate's explainability depends on its complexity. Let's say that we want to train a decision-tree surrogate. Recall from our discussion in section 9.1 that we need to limit the number of leaf nodes in the surrogate model for it to be human-interpretable as too many leaf nodes might lead to model complexity and overwhelm the interpreter.

TRAINING GLOBAL SURROGATE MODELS IN PRACTICE

To train a useful surrogate model, we'll need to find the sweet spot in the fidelity-interpretability tradeoff. This sweet spot will be a surrogate model that approximates the black-box's predictions pretty well but is also not so complex that it defies any interpretation (possibly by inspection).

Figure 9.12 shows the fidelity-explainability tradeoff for a decision-tree surrogate trained for the XGBoost model. The surrogate is trained on the same Bank Marketing training set that was used to train the XGBoost model in section 9.1.

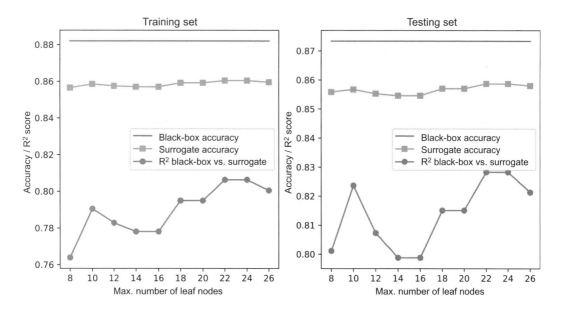

Figure 9.12 **The fidelity-explainability tradeoff for the Bank Marketing data set. The black-box model is an XGBoost ensemble, while the surrogate is a decision tree trained on the black-box predictions.**

We increase the surrogate's complexity (characterized by the number of leaf nodes), while keeping an eye on the fidelity (R^2 score) between the black-box and surrogate predictions. A decision-tree surrogate with 14 leaf nodes seems to achieve the ideal tradeoff between fidelity and complexity for explainability. Listing 9.8 trains a surrogate decision-tree model with these specifications.

Listing 9.8   Training a surrogate model

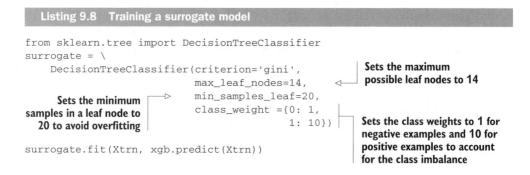

```
from sklearn.tree import DecisionTreeClassifier
surrogate = \
    DecisionTreeClassifier(criterion='gini',
                           max_leaf_nodes=14,
                           min_samples_leaf=20,
                           class_weight ={0: 1,
                                          1: 10})

surrogate.fit(Xtrn, xgb.predict(Xtrn))
```

Sets the maximum possible leaf nodes to 14

Sets the minimum samples in a leaf node to 20 to avoid overfitting

Sets the class weights to 1 for negative examples and 10 for positive examples to account for the class imbalance

Figure 9.13 shows the decision-tree surrogate for the XGBoost model.

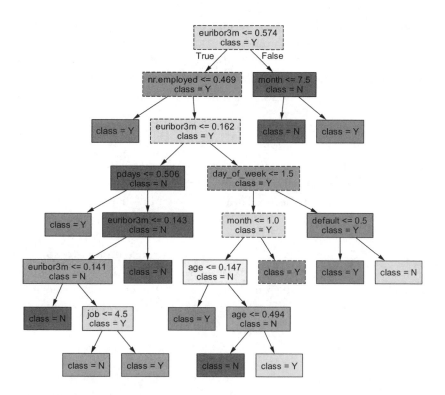

Figure 9.13 Surrogate model trained from the predictions of the XGBoost model, which was originally trained on the Bank Marketing data set. This tree has 14 leaf nodes. Inspecting and analyzing this tree can yield many insights, such as the highlighted path from root to leaf (nodes with dashed borders).

Several variables appear in the highlighted path from root node to leaf node. These variables describe a high-value subpopulation and provide insights into potentially successful strategies.

For example, the socioeconomic variables, such as `nr.employed` and `euribor3m`, identify favorable societal circumstances during which to launch a successful campaign. In addition, `[day_of_week <= 1.5]` suggests that calling these high-value customers on Monday (`day_of_week = 0`) or Tuesday (`day_of_week = 1`) is a good strategy.

We can also look at other paths and nodes to get further insights. The node `age <= 0.147` is obtained on the preprocessed data, where 0.147 corresponds to 40 before rescaling. This suggests that customers who are under 40 years of age are high value.

Yet another useful node is `[default <= 0.5]`, which suggests that customers who have no previous defaults are high value. You may be able to identify other viable strategies for identifying high-value customers and strategies as well.

9.4   *Black-box methods for local explainability*

The previous section introduced methods for global explainability, which aim to explain a model's global behavioral trends across different types of input examples and subpopulations. In this section, we'll explore methods for *local explainability*, which aim to explain a model's individual predictions. The explanations allow users (e.g., doctors using a diagnostic system) to trust the predictions and take actions based on them. This is tied to the user's ability to understand why a model made a particular decision.

9.4.1   *Local surrogate models with LIME*

The first method we'll look at is called *Locally Interpretable Model-Agnostic Explanations* (LIME). As the name rather transparently suggests, LIME is (1) a model-agnostic method, which means it can be used with any machine-learning model black box; and (2) a local interpretability method that is used to explain a model's individual predictions.

LIME is, in fact, a *local surrogate method.* It uses a linear model to approximate a black-box model in the locality of the example whose predictions we're interested in explaining. This intuition is shown in figure 9.14, in the complex surface of a black-box model and an interpretable linear surrogate model that approximates black-box behavior around a single example of interest.

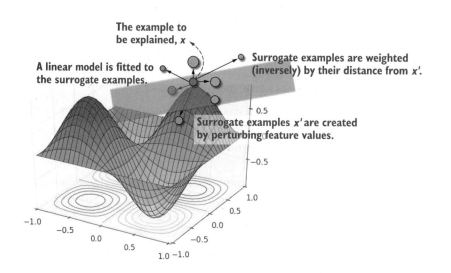

Figure 9.14   LIME creates a surrogate training set of examples in the locality of the example whose prediction needs to be explained. These examples are further weighted by their distance. This is indicated by the sizes of the surrogate examples, with closer examples getting higher weights (and shown larger). A weighted loss function is used to fit a linear surrogate model, which provides local explanations.

THE FIDELITY-INTERPRETABILITY TRADEOFF AGAIN

Given a training example whose predictions we want to explain, LIME trains a local surrogate to be the model with the best tradeoff between fidelity and interpretability. In the previous section, we trained a decision-tree surrogate to optimize the fidelity-interpretability tradeoff.

Let's write this down more formally. First, we denote the black-box model by $f_b(\boldsymbol{x})$ and the surrogate model by $f_s(\boldsymbol{x'})$. We measure fidelity between the predictions of the black box (f_b) and the surrogate (f_s) using the R^2 score. We measure interpretability of the surrogate model by using the number of leaf nodes in the tree: fewer leaf nodes generally lead to better interpretability.

Let's say that we want to explain the predictions of the black box on example $\boldsymbol{x}$. For decision-tree surrogate training, we try to find a decision tree that optimizes the following:

$$\text{surrogate training criteria for trees} = \underbrace{R^2\Big(f_b(\boldsymbol{x}), f_s(\boldsymbol{x'})\Big)}_{\text{fidelity}} + \overset{\text{interpretability}}{n_{leaf}(f_s)}$$

In a similar vein, LIME trains a linear surrogate by optimizing the following:

$$\text{surrogate training criteria for LIME} = \underbrace{L\Big(f_b(\boldsymbol{x}), f_s(\boldsymbol{x'}), \pi_x\Big)}_{\text{fidelity}} + \overset{\text{interpretability}}{n_{non-zeros}(f_s)}$$

Here, the examples $\boldsymbol{x'}$, called surrogate training examples, will be used to train the surrogate model. The loss function that is used to measure fidelity is a simple weighted MSE that measures the disparity in the predictions of the black box and the surrogate:

$$L\Big(f_b(\boldsymbol{x}), f_s(\boldsymbol{x'}), \pi_x\Big) = \sum_{x'} \underbrace{\pi_x(\boldsymbol{x'})}_{\text{local weight}} \cdot \Big(f_b(\boldsymbol{x}) - f_s(\boldsymbol{x'})\Big)^2$$

The surrogate is a linear model of the form $f_s(\boldsymbol{x'}) = \beta_0 + \beta_1 x_1' + \cdots + \beta_d x_d'$, and $\boldsymbol{x'}$ is a surrogate example. As we've seen in section 9.1, the interpretability of linear models depends on the number of features. Fewer features make analyzing their corresponding parameters β_k easier. Thus, LIME seeks to train sparser linear models with more zero parameters to promote interpretability (remember from chapter 7 that L1 regularization can help with this).

But what makes LIME local? How can we train a local surrogate model? How do we obtain surrogate examples $\boldsymbol{x'}$? And what are these local weights (π_x) in the preceding equation? The answers are in how LIME creates and uses surrogate examples.

SAMPLING SURROGATE EXAMPLES FOR LOCAL EXPLAINABILITY

We now have a well-defined fidelity-interpretability criterion to train our surrogate model. If we used the entire training set, we would obtain a global surrogate model.

To train a local surrogate model, we need data points that are close to or similar to our example of interest. LIME creates a local surrogate training set by sampling and smoothing.

Let's say that we're interested in explaining the prediction of the black box on an example with five features: $x = [x_1, x_2, x_3, x_4, x_5]$. LIME samples data in a neighborhood of x as follows:

- *Perturb*—Randomly generate perturbations for each feature. For continuous features, perturbations are randomly sampled from the normal distribution, $\epsilon \sim N(0,1)$. For categorical features, these are randomly sampled from the multivariate distribution over K category values, $\epsilon \sim Cat(K)$. This generates one surrogate example $x' = [x_1 + \epsilon_1, \ x_2 + \epsilon_2, \ x_3 + \epsilon_3, \ x_4 + \epsilon_4, \ x_5 + \epsilon_5]$. This example can now also be labeled using the black box, $y = f_b(x')$. This continues until we obtain a surrogate set Z in the locality of x.

- *Smooth*—Each surrogate training example is also assigned a weight using the exponential smoothing kernel: $\pi_x(x') = \exp(-\gamma \cdot D(x,x')^2)$. Here, $D(x,x')$ is the distance between our example that needs to be explained x and a perturbed sample x'. Surrogate training examples that are further from x get smaller weights, and those that are closer to x get higher weights. Thus, this function encourages the surrogate model to prioritize surrogate examples that are more local when training a linear approximation. The smoothing parameter $\gamma > 0$ controls the width of the kernel. Increasing γ allows LIME to consider larger neighborhoods, making the model less local.

Now that we have a surrogate training set in the locality of the example x, we can train a linear model. The goal is to train it to induce sparsity (as many zero parameters as possible). LIME supports training of sparse linear models with L1 regularization, such as Least Absolute Shrinkage and Selection (LASSO) or elastic net. These models are covered in chapter 7 for linear regression and can be easily extended to logistic regression for classification as well.

> **NOTE**   Keen observers may have noticed that the exponential kernel, with D as the Euclidean distance, is the same as a radial basis function (RBF) kernel that is used in support vector machines and other kernel methods. From that perspective, the exponential smoothing kernel is essentially a similarity function. Points that are closer are considered more similar and will have higher weights.

LIME IN PRACTICE

LIME is available as a package through Python's two most popular package managers: pip and conda. The package's GitHub page (https://github.com/marcotcr/lime) also contains additional documentation and a number of examples illustrating how to use LIME for classification, regression, and applications in text and image analytics.

In listing 9.9, we use LIME to explain the predictions of a test set example from the Bank Marketing data set. Test example 3104 is a customer who did subscribe, which the XGBoost model identified with 64% confidence, a true positive example.

Listing 9.9   Using LIME to explain XGBoost predictions

Identifies the categorical features and their indices explicitly (for visualization)

```
cat_features = ['default', 'housing', 'loan', 'contact', 'poutcome',
                'job', 'marital', 'education', 'month', 'day_of_week']
cat_idx = np.array(
            [cat_features.index(f) for f in cat_features])

from lime import lime_tabular
explainer = lime_tabular.LimeTabularExplainer(
    Xtrn.values,
    feature_names=list(Xtrn.columns),
    class_names=['Sub?=NO', 'Sub?=YES'],
    categorical_names=cat_features,
    categorical_features=cat_idx,
    kernel_width=75.0,
    discretize_continuous=False)

exp = explainer.explain_instance(
        Xtst.iloc[3104], xgb.predict_proba)
fig = exp.as_pyplot_figure()
```

Passes the training set, which is sometimes used for sampling, especially continuous features

Identifies the feature names and class names explicitly (for visualization)

Sets the kernel width for this data set (identified here by trial and error)

Explains the predictions of test example 3104

Visualizes the explanation as a bar chart

Figure 9.15 visualizes the local weights identified by LIME to explain this example.

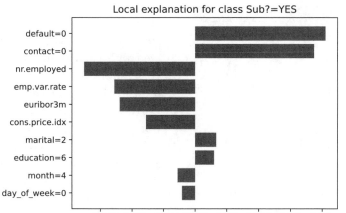

Local explanation for class Sub?=YES

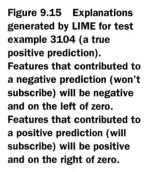

Figure 9.15   Explanations generated by LIME for test example 3104 (a true positive prediction). Features that contributed to a negative prediction (won't subscribe) will be negative and on the left of zero. Features that contributed to a positive prediction (will subscribe) will be positive and on the right of zero.

The features and feature values (of the example being explained) are shown in the y-axis. The x-axis shows LIME feature importances.

Aside from socioeconomic trends, let's look at the personalized features of this customer. The variables with the biggest effect are `contact` (=0), whether they were contacted by cellular or landline (here, 0 = cellular); and `default`, whether they have prior banking defaults in their prior history (here, 0 = they don't have prior defaults).

These interpretations will be intuitive to even non-AI users, such as in sales and marketing, who might further analyze them to fine-tune future marketing campaigns.

9.4.2   *Local interpretability with SHAP*

In this section, we'll cover another widely used local interpretability approach: *SHapley Additive exPlanations* (SHAP). SHAP is another model-agnostic black-box explainer similar to LIME that is used to explain individual predictions (hence, local interpretability) through feature importance.

SHAP is a feature-attribution technique that computes feature importance based on each feature's contribution to the overall prediction. SHAP is built on the concept of Shapley values, which comes from the field of cooperative game theory. In this section, we'll learn what Shapley values are, how they can be applied to computing feature importances, and how we can compute them efficiently in practice.

UNDERSTANDING SHAPLEY VALUES

Let's say a group of four data scientists (Ava, Ben, Cam, and Dev) work collaboratively on a Kaggle Challenge and win first place with total prize money of $20,000. Being a fair-minded group, they decide to split the prize money based on their contributions. They do this by trying to figure out how well they work in various combinations. Since they've worked together a lot in the past, they write down how well they work individually, and also in groups of two and in groups of three. These values representing each combination's effectiveness are shown in figure 9.16.

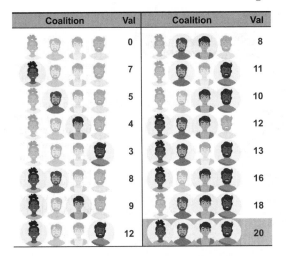

This table lists every possible combination of Ava, Ben, Cam, and Dev, also known as a *coalition*. Associated with each coalition is its value (prize money in $1,000 units), which indicates how much each coalition is worth had they been the only ones working on this project.

For example, the coalition of Ava alone has a value of $7,000, while the coalition of Ava, Ben, and Dev has a value of $13,000. The last coalition of all four of them, called the *grand coalition*, has a value of $20,000, the overall prize money.

The *Shapley value* allows us to attribute the overall prize money to each of these four team members across all the coalitions possible. It essentially helps us determine team member importance to the overall

Figure 9.16   All possible coalitions of Ava, Ben, Cam, and Dev, and their corresponding values (in units of $1,000). The last coalition contains all four friends and has a value of $20,000, the total prize money. There is one coalition of size 0, four coalitions of size 1, six coalitions of size 2, four coalitions of size 3, and one coalition of size 4. This table is called the characteristic function.

collaboration and helps us determine a fair way to split the overall value of the collaboration (in this case, the prize money).

The Shapley value of each team member p (also called player) is computed in a very intuitive manner: we look at how the value *of each coalition changes*, with and without that team member. More formally:

$$\phi_p = \sum_{\substack{S \in \text{ all coalitions} \\ \text{without } p}} \underbrace{\frac{(n - n_s - 1)!n_s!}{n!}}_{\text{weight, } \pi_x} \cdot (val(S \cup p) - \overbrace{val(S)}^{\substack{\text{value of the coalition} \\ S \text{ without } p}})$$

This equation might look intimidating at first, but it's actually quite simple. Figure 9.17 illustrates the components of this equation when computing the Shapley values for Dev (team member 4): (1) coalitions *with* Dev on the first row, (2) corresponding coalitions *without* Dev on the second row, and (3) the weighted difference between the two on the third row.

1 coal. of size 1	3 coalitions of size 2			3 coalitions of size 3			1 coal. of size 4
3	12	11	10	13	16	18	20
0	7	5	4	8	9	8	12
¼ (3–0)	1⁄12 (12–7)	1⁄12 (11–5)	1⁄12 (10–4)	1⁄12 (13–8)	1⁄12 (16–9)	1⁄12 (18–8)	¼ (20–12)

Figure 9.17 Computing the Shapley values for Dev. The top row is all the coalitions with Dev. The middle row shows the corresponding coalitions without Dev. The last row shows the individual weighted differences in the values of the coalitions. Summing across the last row gives us the Shapley values for Dev: $\phi_{Dev} = 6$.

The weights are computed using n, the total number of team members (in this case, four), and n_s, the coalition size. For example, for the coalition $S = \{Ava, Cam\}$, $n_s = 2$. The weights for the coalition without Dev (S) and with Dev ($S \cup Dev$) will both be $\frac{1!2!}{4!} = \frac{1}{12}$. Other weights can be computed similarly.

Summing all the weighted differences in the last row in figure 9.17 gives us the Shapley value for Dev, $\phi_{Dev} = 6$. Similarly, we can also obtain $\phi_{Ava} = 4.667$, $\phi_{Ben} = 4.333$, and $\phi_{Cam} = 5$. This suggests that an equitable way (according to the characteristic function in figure 9.16) to attribute the prize money based on contribution is $4,667, $4,333, $5,000, and $6,000, respectively, between Ava, Ben, Cam, and Dev.

The Shapley value has some interesting theoretical properties. First, observe that $\phi_{Ava} + \phi_{Ben} + \phi_{Cam} + \phi_{Dev} = 20$. That is, the Shapley values sum to the value of the grand coalition:

$$\sum_p \phi_p = val(\{1, 2, \ldots, n\})$$

This property of the Shapley value, called *efficiency*, ensures that the value of the overall collaboration is exactly broken down and attributed to each team member in the collaboration.

Another important property is *additivity*, which ensures that if we have two value functions, the overall Shapley value computed using a joint value function is equal to the sum of the individual Shapley values. This has some important implications for ensemble methods because it allows us to add Shapley values across individual base estimators to obtain the Shapley values across the entire ensemble.

So, what does the Shapley value have to do with explainability? Analogous to the case of the four data scientist friends, features in a machine-learning problem collaborate together to make predictions. The Shapley value allows us to attribute how much each feature contributed to the overall prediction.

SHAPLEY VALUES AS FEATURE IMPORTANCE

Let's say that we want to explain the predictions of a black-box model f on an example x. The Shapley value of a feature j is computed as

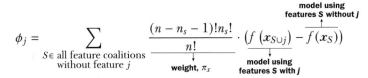

We use the black-box model as the characteristic/value function. As before, we consider all possible coalitions with and without the feature j.

Now, we can compute the Shapley values for all the features. As before, the Shapley value for feature importance estimation is efficient and attributes a part of the overall prediction to each feature:

$$\sum_j \phi_j = f(x)$$

The Shapley value is theoretically well motivated and has some very attractive properties that make it a robust measure of feature importance. There is one significant limitation to using this procedure directly in practice: scalability.

The Shapley computation uses trained models to score feature importance. In fact, it will need to use one trained model for each coalition of features. For example, for our diabetes diagnosis model from earlier with two features—age and glc—we'll have to train three models, one for each coalition: f_1 (age), f_2 (glc), and f_3 (age, glc).

In general, if we have d features, we'll have 2^d total coalitions, and we'll have to train $2^d - 1$ models (we don't train a model for the null coalition). For instance, the Bank Marketing data set has 19 features and will require the training of $2^{19} - 1 = 524{,}287$ models! This is simply absurd in practice.

SHAP

What can we do in the face of such combinatorial infeasibility? What we always do: approximate and sample. Inspired by LIME, the SHAP method aims to learn a linear surrogate function whose parameters are the Shapley values for each feature.

Analogous to LIME, given a black-box model $f_b(x)$, SHAP also trains a surrogate model $f_s(x')$ using a loss function that has a form identical to LIME's. Unlike LIME, however, we have to accommodate the notion of coalitions in the loss function:

$$L\left(f_b(x), f_s(x'|z), \pi_x\right) = \sum_z \underbrace{\pi_x(z)}_{\text{local weight}} \cdot (f_b(x) - f_s(h_x(z)))^2$$

Let's understand this loss function and SHAP by seeing what it does similarly to and differently from LIME (also see figure 9.18). As before, let's say that we're interested in explaining the prediction of the black-box model on an example with five features $x = [x_1, x_2, x_3, x_4, x_5]$:

- LIME creates surrogate examples x' by randomly perturbing the original example x. SHAP uses an involved two-step approach to create surrogate examples:
  - SHAP generates a random coalition vector, z, which is a 0–1 vector indicating if a feature should be in the coalition or not. For example, $z = [1,1,0,0,1]$ represents a coalition of the first, second, and fifth features.
  - SHAP creates a surrogate example from z by using a mapping function $x' = h_x(z)$. Wherever $z_j = 1$, we set $x'_j = x_j$, the original feature value from the example of interest x. Wherever $z_j = 0$, we set $x'_j = x_j^{rand}$, a feature value from another randomly selected example x^{rand}. With the choice of z above, our surrogate example would be $x' = [x_1, x_2, x_3^{rand}, x_4^{rand}, x_5]$.

Thus, each surrogate example is a patchwork of features from the original training example we want to explain and another random training example. The idea is that features belonging to the coalition get feature values from the example of interest, and features not belonging to the coalition get random "realistic feature values" from other examples in the data set.

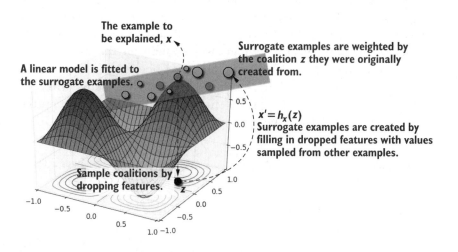

Figure 9.18 SHAP creates a surrogate training set of examples in the locality of the example whose prediction needs to be explained.

- LIME weights surrogate examples x' inversely by their distance from x using the RBF/exponential kernel. SHAP weights surrogate examples x' using the Shapley kernel, which is simply the weight from the Shapley computation, $\pi_x(z) = \frac{(d-n_z-1)!n_z!}{d!}$, where d is the total number of features, and n_z is the coalition size (number of 1s in z). Intuitively, this weight reflects the number of other similar coalitions, with a similar number of zero and nonzero features.

Now that we have a surrogate training set in the locality of the example x, we can train a linear model. A version of SHAP called KernelSHAP uses linear regression for training. The weights of this linear model will be the approximate Shapley values for each feature.

SHAP IN PRACTICE

Like LIME, SHAP is also available as a package available through Python's two most popular package managers: pip and conda. Please see SHAP's GitHub page (https://github.com/slundberg/shap) for documentation and a number of examples illustrating how to use it for classification, regression, and applications for text, image, and even genomic data.

In this section, we'll use a version of SHAP called TreeSHAP that is specifically designed to be used for tree-based models, including individual decision trees and ensembles. TreeSHAP is a special variant of SHAP that exploits the unique structure of decision trees to calculate the Shapley values efficiently.

As mentioned before, Shapley values have a nice property called additivity. For us, this means that if we have a model that is an additive combination of trees, that is, tree ensembles (e.g., bagging, random forests, gradient boosting, and Newton boosting, among others), then the Shapley value of the ensemble is simply the sum of the Shapley values of the individual trees.

Because TreeSHAP can efficiently compute the Shapley values of each feature in each individual tree in an ensemble, we can efficiently get the Shapley values of the entire ensemble. Finally, unlike LIME, TreeSHAP doesn't require us to furnish a surrogate data set because the trees themselves contain all the information (feature splits, leaf values/predictions, example counts, etc.) needed.

TreeSHAP supports many of the ensemble methods discussed in this book, including XGBoost. The following listing shows how to compute and interpret the Shapley values for test example 3104 of the Bank Marketing data set using an XGBoost model.

Listing 9.10   Using TreeSHAP to explain XGBoost predictions

```
import shap

explainer = shap.TreeExplainer(xgb, feature_names=list(Xtrn.columns))

shap_values = explainer(
                Xtst.iloc[3104].values.reshape(1, -1))
```
⊲ **Explains the predictions of test example 3104**

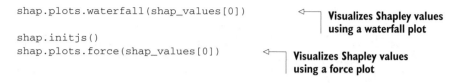

```
shap.plots.waterfall(shap_values[0])
```
⟵ **Visualizes Shapley values using a waterfall plot**

```
shap.initjs()
shap.plots.force(shap_values[0])
```
⟵ **Visualizes Shapley values using a force plot**

This listing visualizes Shapley values in two ways: as a waterfall plot (figure 9.19) and as a force plot (figure 9.20). Keep in mind that SHAP explains classifier models in terms of their prediction probabilities (confidence). For a classifier, the x-axis values will be the log-odds, with 0.0 representing even odds (1:1) of classification, or 50% prediction probability as a positive example.

The waterfall plot in figure 9.19 shows the individual contributions of each feature to the overall prediction for example 3104. As we can see, the individual predictive contributions of each feature add up to the overall final prediction: 0.518. This is a clear visual illustration of the additive nature of SHAP's explanations.

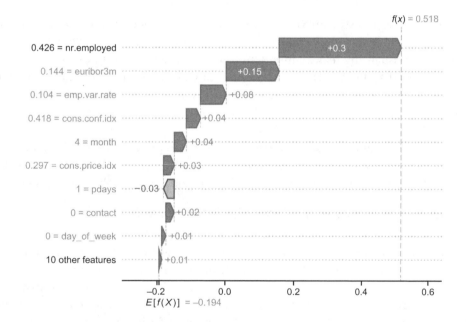

Figure 9.19   A waterfall plot to visualize Shapley values. The values along the left side of the plot show the feature values for test example 3104, while the text in the bars shows their Shapley values.

The force plot in figure 9.20 allows for a more intuitive view of how the features contribute to a prediction. The plot is centered around the prediction (0.518) and visualizes how much the features force the prediction through a positive or negative explanation.

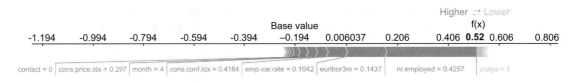

Figure 9.20 A force plot to visualize Shapley values. The features pointing to the right push the prediction on this example (0.52) to be higher than the average prediction (–0.194). The features pointing to the left push the prediction lower and closer to base value. The contributions add up to the overall prediction, which is higher than the base value for this example. The feature values of the example being explained are shown along with the features under the force plot.

> **NOTE** LIME and SHAP are both *additive* local explainability methods. This means that they can be extended to global explainability in a rather straight-forward manner: global feature importances from either method can be obtained by averaging over local feature importances computed with a task-relevant data set.

One drawback of LIME and SHAP is that they are designed only to compute and evaluate individual feature importances, and not feature interactions. SHAP offers some support for visualizing feature interactions in a manner similar to PDPs.

However, like PDPs, SHAP doesn't have any mechanism to automatically identify important interacting feature groups and forces us to visualize all pairs, which can be overwhelming. For example, with 19 features in the Bank Marketing data set, we'll have 171 pairwise feature interactions.

In real-world applications, since many features depend on each other, it's important to also understand how feature interactions come into play in decision making. In the next section, we'll learn about one such method: explainable boosting machines.

9.5 Glass-box ensembles: Training for interpretability

We've learned about model-agnostic explainability methods. These methods can take a model that was already trained (e.g., by an ensemble learner such as XGBoost) and attempt to explain the model itself (global) or its predictions (local).

But instead of treating our ensembles as a black box, can we train an explainable ensemble from scratch? Can this ensemble method still perform well *and* be explainable? These are the types of questions that motivated the development of *explainable boosting machines* (EBMs), a type of glass-box ensemble method. Some key highlights of EBMs are as follows:

- EBMs can be used for both global explainability and local explainability of individual examples!
- EBMs learn a fully factorized model; that is, the model components only depend on individual features or pairs of features. These components provide interpretability directly, and EBMs need no additional computations (like SHAP or LIME) to generate explanations.

- EBMs are a type of *generalized additive model* (GAM), which are nonlinear extensions of GLMs discussed in this chapter and elsewhere in the book. Similar to GLMs, each component of a GAM only depends on one feature.
- EBMs can also detect important *pairwise feature interactions*. Thus, EBMs extend the GAMs to include components of two features.
- EBMs use a *cyclic* training approach, where a very large number of base estimators are trained by repeated passes through all the features. This approach is also parallelizable, which makes EBMs an efficient training approach.

In the next two sections, we'll see how EBMs work conceptually, as well as how we can train and use them in practice.

9.5.1   Explainable boosting machines

EBMs have two key components: they are generalized additive models (GAMs), and they have feature interactions. This allows the model representation to be broken down into smaller components, allowing for better interpretation.

GAMs WITH FEATURE INTERACTIONS

We're familiar with the concept of the GLM, which uses link functions $g(y)$ to relate targets to linear models over features:

$$g(y) = \beta_0 + \beta_1 x_1 + \cdots + \beta_d x_d$$

Each component of the GLM $\beta_j x_j$ only depends on one feature x_j. The GAM extends this nonlinear model over the features:

$$g(y) = \beta_0 + f_1(x_1) + \cdots + f_d(x_d)$$

As with the GLM, each component of a GAM $f(x_j)$ also depends on only one feature x_j. Keep in mind that both GLMs and GAMs can be viewed as ensembles, with each component of the ensemble depending on only one feature! This has important implications for training.

EBMs further extend GAMs to include pairwise components as well. However, since the number of feature pairs can be very large, EBMs only include a small number of important feature pairs:

$$g(y) = \beta_0 + \underbrace{f_1(x_1) + \cdots + f_d(x_d)}_{\text{all individual features}} + \overbrace{f_{ab}(x_a, x_b) + \cdots + f_{uv}(x_u, x_v)}^{\text{important feature pairs}}$$

This is also shown in figure 9.21 for the diabetes diagnosis problem from earlier, but with three variables: `age`, blood glucose level (`glc`), and body mass index (`bmi`). This example EBM contains components for all three features individually, and one pairwise component rather than all three combinations.

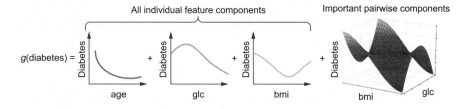

Figure 9.21   An EBM is a generalized additive model consisting of nonlinear components that depend on only one feature as well as nonlinear components that depend on pairs of features. This example shows an EBM for diabetes diagnosis dependent on three variables: `age`, `glc`, and `bmi`. Though there are three pairs of variables (`age-glc`, `glc-bmi`, `age-bmi`), this EBM includes only one of them that it has deemed significant. The explainable boosting model is also an ensemble.

Since each component is a function of only one or two variables, once learned, we can immediately visualize the dependence between each variable (or pair of variables) and the target. In addition, the EBM avoids incorporating all pairwise components, and only selects the most effectual ones. This avoids model bloat and improves explainability. By carefully choosing the structure of the EBM, we can train an explainable ensemble, which makes this a glass-box method.

But what about model performance? Is it possible to train an EBM effectively to perform as well as existing ensemble methods?

TRAINING EBMS

As with GLMs and GAMs, the EBM is also an ensemble of base components over individual features as well as feature pairs. This is important because it allows us to train EBMs sequentially using simple modifications of our favorite ensemble learner: gradient boosting. EBMs are similarly trained using a two-stage procedure:

- In the first stage, the EBM fits components for each feature $f_j(x_j)$. This is done through a cyclical and sequential training process over several thousand iterations, one feature at a time. In iteration t, for feature j, we fit a very shallow $tree_j^t$ using gradient boosting. Once we cycle through all the features within an iteration, we move on to the next iteration. This procedure is illustrated in figure 9.22.
- The partially trained EBM $g(y) = f_1(x_1) + \cdots + f_d(x_d)$ is now frozen and used to evaluate and score all possible feature pairs (x_i, x_j). This enables EBM to determine critically important feature interaction pairs $(x_a, x_b) \cdots (x_u, x_v)$ in the data. A small number of relevant feature pairs are selected.
- In the second stage, the EBM fits shallow trees $tree_{jk}^t$ for each feature pair $f_{jk}(x_j, x_k)$ in a manner identical to the first stage. This produces a fully trained EBM: $g(y) = f_1(x_1) + \cdots + f_d(x_d) + f_{ab}(x_a, x_b) + \cdots + f_{uv}(x_u, x_v)$.

From figure 9.22, we can see that each individual component $f_j(x_j)$ is actually an ensemble of thousands of shallow trees:

$$f_j(x_j) = \text{tree}_j^1(x_j) + \cdots + \text{tree}_j^{5000}(x_j)$$

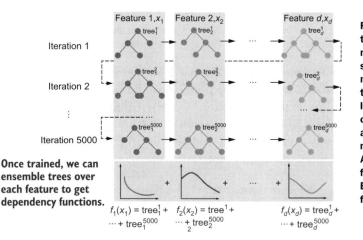

Figure 9.22 **The first stage of the training procedure for EBMs, where models for each feature are trained sequentially and cyclically, with one model per feature per iteration. The trees trained are shallow, and the learning rate is very low. However, over a very large number of iterations, a sufficiently complex nonlinear model for each feature can be learned. A similar procedure is also followed for the second stage of training EBMs, where models for pairwise feature interactions are trained.**

Similarly, each feature interaction component is also an ensemble:

$$f_{jk}\left(x_{jk}\right) = \text{tree}_{jk}^1\left(x_j, x_k\right) + \cdots + \text{tree}_{jk}^{5000}\left(x_j, x_k\right)$$

So how exactly is this EBM a glass box? In three ways:

- *Local interpretability*—For a classification problem, given a specific example, if we want to explain x, we can get the log-odds of prediction from the EBM as $f_1(x_1)$ $+ \cdots + f_d(x_d) + f_{ab}(x_a, x_b) + \cdots + f_{uv}(x_u, x_v)$. By construction, the EBM is already a fully decomposed and additive model, allowing us to simply grab the contribution of each feature $f_j(x_j)$ or feature pair $f_{jk}(x_j, x_k)$. For regression, we can get the contribution to the overall regression value similarly. In both cases, there is no additional procedure like LIME or SHAP, and there is no need to approximate using linear models!
- *Global interpretability*—Since we have each component $f_j(x_j)$ or $f_{jk}(x_j, x_k)$, we can also plot this over the feature ranges of x_j and/or x_k. This will produce a *dependency plot* for the features x_j and/or x_k over all possible values they can take. This tells us how the model behaves in the aggregate.
- *Feature interactions*—Unlike SHAP or LIME, the model also inherently identifies key feature interactions, by design. This provides additional insights into model behavior and helps explain predictions better.

9.5.2 *EBMs in practice*

EBMs are available as part of the InterpretML package. In addition to EBMs, the InterpretML package also provides wrappers for LIME and SHAP, allowing us to use them in one framework. InterpretML also includes some nice functionalities for visualization. In this section, though, we'll only explore how to train, visualize, and interpret EBMs with InterpretML.

NOTE InterpretML can be installed through pip and Anaconda. The package's documentation page (https://interpret.ml/) contains additional information on how to use various glass-box and black-box models.

Listing 9.11 shows how we can train EBMs on the Bank Marketing data set. Like random forests and XGBoost models trained in section 9.2, we'll have to account for the class imbalance in the data. We do this by weighting positive examples by 5.0 and negative examples by 1.0 during training. This listing also creates two visualizations: one for local explainability (of test example 3104) and another for global explainability (using feature importances and dependency plots).

Listing 9.11   Training and visualizing EBMs using InterpretML

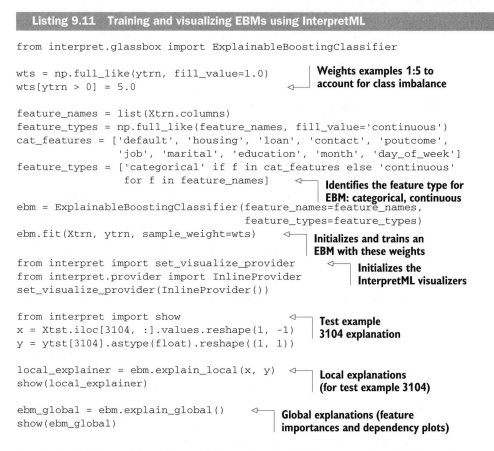

`ExplainableBoostingClassifier` trains for 5,000 rounds by default, with support for early stopping. `ExplainableBoostingClassifier` also limits the number of pairwise interactions to 10 (by default, though this can be set by the user). Since this data set has 19 features, there will be 171 total pairwise interactions, of which the model will pick the top 10.

The trained EBM model has an overall accuracy of 86.69% and balanced accuracy of 74.59%. The XGBoost model trained in section 9.2 has an overall accuracy of

87.24% and balanced accuracy of 74.67%. The EBM model is pretty comparable to the XGBoost model! The key difference is that the XGBoost model is a black box, while the EBM is a glass box.

So, what can we get out of this glass box? Figure 9.23 shows the local explanations of test example 3104. The local explanations show how much each feature and feature interaction pair in the model contributes to the overall positive or negative prediction.

Predicted (1.0): 0.758 | Actual (0.0): 0.242

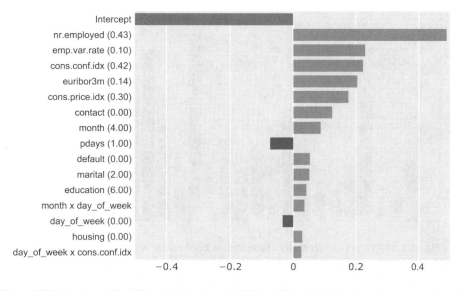

Figure 9.23   Local explainability of test example 3104, with individual features (e.g., `euribor3m` and `poutcome`) and pairwise features (e.g., `month × day_of_week`). The value of each EBM component and their contribution to the overall prediction (Sub? = YES) is shown.

Test example 3104 is a positive example (i.e., `Sub?=YES`, meaning that the customer did subscribe to a fixed-term deposit account). The EBM model has correctly classified this example, with confidence (prediction probability) of 66.1%.

The trained EBM model uses several features such as `nr.employed` that we know are important, similar to other approaches. This trained EBM also uses three pairwise features to make a prediction for 3104: `month × day_of_week`, `day_of_week × cons.conf.idx`, `default × month`. The highest pairwise feature interaction is `month × day_of_week`, which contributes a positive amount to the overall prediction. Contrast this to LIME and SHAP explanations of the XGBoost black box, which could only identify `month` since they don't support feature interactions explicitly. The EBM model is able to learn to use a finer-grained feature and also explain its importance! The takeaway here is that the EBM model is explicitly structured to incorporate feature interactions and to explain them.

EBMs can also provide global interpretability in terms of feature importances. The overall importance is obtained by averaging (the absolute values) of individual feature importances over the entire training set.

The overall model contains 30 components: 19 individual feature components, 10 pairwise feature components, and 1 intercept. The top-15 feature and pairwise feature importances are shown in figure 9.24. These results are in general agreement with previous feature importance measures computed using other methods such as SHAP and LIME.

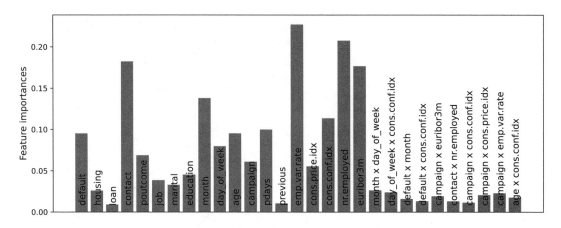

Figure 9.24   Global explainability of the trained EBM model, showing feature importance scores

Finally, we can also obtain dependency plots directly from the EBM (as described earlier in figure 9.22). Figure 9.25 shows the dependency plot for age and how it influences whether someone will subscribe to a fixed-deposit account.

Summary

- Black-box models are typically challenging to understand owing to their complexity. The predictions of such models require specialized tools to be explainable.
- Glass-box models are more intuitive and easier to understand. The structure of such models makes them inherently interpretable.
- Most ensemble methods are typically black-box methods.
- Global methods attempt to generally explain a model's overall decision-making process and the broadly relevant factors.
- Local methods attempt to specifically explain a model's decision-making process with respect to individual examples and predictions.
- Feature importance is an interpretability method that assigns scores to features based on their contribution to correct prediction of a target variable.

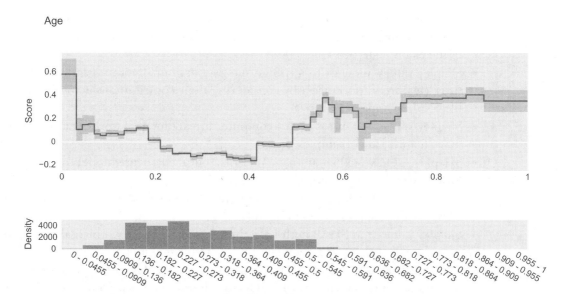

Figure 9.25 Dependency plot for age. The x-axis bins representing age are scaled to the range 0–1 during preprocessing. The raw ages are in the range 17–98. Scores are negative for people in the range 0.2–0.4, which corresponds to ages 33–49. This suggests that absent any other information, people in this age range are typically not likely to subscribe to a fixed-deposit account.

- Decision trees are commonly used glass-box models and can be expressed as a set of decision rules, which are easily interpretable by humans.
- The interpretability of decision trees depends on their complexity (depth and number of leaf nodes). More complex trees are less intuitive and harder to understand.
- Generalized linear models (GLMs) are another commonly used glass-box model. Their feature weights can be interpreted as feature importances as they determine how much each feature contributes to the overall decision.
- Permutation feature importance is a black-box method for global interpretability. It tries to estimate how the model's predictive performance changes from before to after we shuffle/permute features.
- Partial dependence plots (PDPs) comprise another black-box method for global interpretability. Partial dependences are identified using marginalization or summing out of other variables.
- Surrogate models are often used to mimic or approximate the behavior of a black-box model. Surrogate models are glass boxes and inherently explainable.
- Global surrogate models, such as decision trees, train models to optimize the fidelity-interpretability tradeoff.
- Locally Interpretable Model-Agnostic Explanation (LIME) is a local surrogate model that trains a linear model in the neighborhood of the example we want to explain.

- LIME also optimizes the fidelity-interpretability tradeoff and does so with a surrogate training set generated by perturbing features in the local neighborhood of the example to be explained.
- Shapley values allow us to attribute the overall contribution of individual features (feature importances) by considering their contributions across all possible combinations of features.
- Shapley values are infeasible to compute directly for real-world data sets with many features and examples.
- SHapley Additive exPlanations (SHAP) is a local surrogate model that trains a local linear model to approximate Shapley values.
- For tree-based models, a specially designed variant called TreeSHAP is used to compute the Shapley values efficiently.
- Shapley values and SHAP both have the additivity property, which allows us to aggregate Shapley values when ensembling individual models.
- One drawback of LIME and SHAP is that they are fundamentally designed only to compute and evaluate individual feature importances, and not feature interactions.
- The explainable boosting machine (EBM) is a type of glass-box model that can be used for both global explainability and local explainability of individual examples.
- EBMs learn a fully factorized model; that is, the model components only depend on individual features or pairs of features. These components provide interpretability directly, and EBMs need no additional computations (like SHAP or LIME) to generate explanations.
- EBMs are a type of generalized additive model (GAM), which are nonlinear extensions of GLMs.
- EBMs can also detect important pairwise feature interactions. Thus, EBMs extend the GAMs to include components of two features.
- EBMs use a cyclic training approach, where a very large number of base estimators are trained by repeated passes through all the features. This approach is also parallelizable, which makes using EBMs an efficient training approach.

epilogue

You made it! Whether you're a data scientist interested in using ensembles for building enterprise models, an engineer involved in building machine-learning-based applications, a Kaggler looking to gain an extra edge over the competition, a student, or a casual enthusiast, I hope you've learned something new about ensemble methods!

This book was always intended to be more than just a another among hundreds of tutorials that are a simple Google search away. Instead, the goal was to foster intuition and a deeper understanding of what ensembles are, what motivates the design and development of different ensemble methods, and how we can get the best out of them.

We took different ensemble methods apart and put them back together ourselves (in many cases, from scratch!) to really see what makes them tick. We learned about sophisticated off-the-shelf tools and packages for several popular ensemble methods. And, finally, through case studies, we learned how to use ensemble methods in practice to tackle challenging real-world applications.

I hope this immersive approach was helpful in demystifying the technical and algorithmic details conceptually and visually. Armed with this foundation and ensemble mindset, you can now go on to build better applications and create your own ensemble methods. Table E.1 is a flashback to the various ensemble methods we've learned about.

Table E.1   Ensemble methods covered in this book

Chapter	Ensemble methods
Chapter 2	Homogeneous parallel ensembles: bagging, random forests, pasting, random subspaces, random patches, Extra Trees
Chapter 3	Heterogeneous parallel ensembles: majority voting, weighting, Dempster-Shafer ensembling, stacking, and meta-learning
Chapter 4	Sequential adaptive boosting ensembles: AdaBoost, LogitBoost
Chapter 5	Sequential gradient boosting ensembles: gradient boosting (and LightGBM)
Chapter 6	Sequential gradient boosting ensembles: Newton boosting (and XGBoost)

Table E.1 Ensemble methods covered in this book *(continued)*

Chapter	Ensemble methods
Chapter 8	Sequential gradient boosting ensembles: ordered boosting (and CatBoost)
Chapter 9	Explainable ensembles: explainable boosting machines (EBMs)

E.1   Further reading

Ensemble methods are a key part of any data scientist's toolbox, with which we can train ensembles of strong learners, weak learners, and even other ensembles of other ensembles! As you continue to explore this rich and fascinating area, the following resources will help you delve more deeply into specialized subtopics and future directions in the area of ensemble methods.

E.1.1   Practical ensemble methods

- Corey Wade, *Hands-On Gradient Boosting with XGBoost and scikit-learn: Perform accessible machine learning and extreme gradient boosting with Python* (Packt Publishing, 2020)
- Dipayan Sarkar and Vijayalakshmi Natarajan, *Ensemble Machine Learning Cookbook* (Packt Publishing, 2019)

E.1.2   Theory and foundations of ensemble methods

- Robert E. Schapire and Yoav Freund, *Boosting: Foundations and Algorithms* (The MIT Press, 2012)
- Zhi-Hua Zhou, *Ensemble Methods: Foundations and Algorithms, 1st ed.* (Chapman & Hall/CRC, 2012)
- Lior Rokach, *Pattern Classification Using Ensemble Methods* (World Scientific Publishing Co., 2010)

E.2   A few more advanced topics

Before wrapping up, I'll point you toward two other frameworks of machine learning and AI that have seen increased research focus on ensemble methods. The ensemble approaches covered in this book address the "classical machine-learning problems," where data is typically represented as a table. Data, however, is far richer and can have many more modalities and structures than being merely tabular, including object-level representations, images, video, text, audio, graphs, networks, and even multi-modal data with combinations of these!

The framework of relational learning (also known as symbolic machine learning) uses high-level symbolic representations of objects, concepts, and relationships between them. Machine-learning problems can then be framed in this representation and trained using different methods, including ensemble methods. Relational learning is typically well suited for reasoning problems (e.g., link prediction in social networks).

The framework of deep learning (also known as neural machine learning) uses low-level neural connectionist representations of objects and concepts between them. Artificial neural networks and deep learning models are framed in this representation. Deep learning is typically well suited for perception problems (e.g., object detection in video).

Ensemble methods have been employed successfully to various degrees in both of these learning frameworks and are topics of active research in the machine-learning community.

E.2.1 *Ensemble methods for statistical relational learning*

As mentioned earlier, the methods covered in this book are designed for tabular data, where each example is an individual object with several attributes, or features. For example, in diabetes diagnoses, each example is a patient with several attributes such as blood glucose, age, and so on.

However, data is often far more complex and can't be easily squeezed into a table. In diabetes diagnosis, for example, there are many different *types* of objects, such as patients, medical tests, prescriptions, and drugs. Each object has its own set of *attributes*. Different objects have complex *relationships* between them: different patients have varied medical tests, with unique outcomes, specific prescriptions, and so on.

In short, data is often relational. In relational database terms, such data can't always be captured by a single table, but realistically requires multiple tables with complex interactions and cross references between them.

Statistical relational learning (SRL) is a subarea of machine learning that is concerned with training models in such domains. SRL models are effectively probabilistic databases and can answer complex queries beyond simple SQL-like database queries.

SRL models are well suited for modeling tasks such as link prediction, entity resolution, group detection and clustering, collective classification, and other similar graph-based prediction tasks. SRL models have been applied in text mining and natural language processing, social network analytics, bioinformatics, web and document search, and in more complex applications that require reasoning.

SRL is an advanced topic and requires background in first-order logic, graphical models, and probability. The following are good resources to get started on these topics and SRL:

- Lise Getoor and Ben Taskar, eds., *Introduction to Statistical Relational Learning* (The MIT Press, 2009)
- Luc De Raedt, Kristian Kersting, Sriraam Natarajan, and David Poole, *Statistical Relational Artificial Intelligence Logic, Probability, and Computation* (Morgan & Claypool Publishers, 2016)

One prominent ensemble method for SRL is BoostSRL (https://starling.utdallas .edu/software/boostsrl/), which is a gradient-boosting framework for different SRL models. The following reference is a good starting point for delving into ensemble methods for SRL models:

- Sriraam Natarajan, Kristian Kersting, Tushar Khot, and Jude Shavlik, *Boosted Statistical Relational Learners: From Benchmarks to Data-Driven Medicine* (Springer, 2015)

E.2.2 *Ensemble methods for deep learning*

Neural networks have experienced a resurgence and considerable popularity over the past decade, with great success on large-scale learning tasks with text, image, video, and audio. Many ensembling techniques discussed in this book can be applied to create deep learning ensembles by using deep neural networks as base estimators. These include techniques such as bagging, adaptive boosting, and stacking.

The main downside is the computational expense associated with training deep learning ensembles. Individual deep learning models are computationally expensive to train and are data hungry. Because ensemble methods rely on ensemble diversity of multiple base models, an effective deep learning ensemble will require training of many such networks!

Deep learning ensembling techniques typically try to get away with training a single deep neural network and rely on techniques such as *DropOut* (which randomly drops neurons in the network) or *DropConnect* (which randomly drops connections) to create diverse variants from a single pretrained network more efficiently. Here are some helpful references:

- (The original DropOut paper) Geoffrey Hinton, Nitish Srivastava, Alex Krizhevsky, Ilya Sutskever, and Ruslan Salakhutdinov, "Improving neural networks by preventing co-adaptation of feature detectors" (2012)
- (DropOut as a neural ensemble) Pierre Baldi and Peter Sadowski, *Understanding Dropout* (NeurIPS, 2013)

Another approach, called *snapshot ensembling*, saves snapshots of the model's weights during training to create an ensemble without any additional training cost:

- Gao Huang, Yixuan Li, Geoff Pleiss, Zhuang Liu, John E. Hopcroft, and Kilian Q. Weinberger, *Snapshot Ensembles: Train 1, get M for free* (ICLR, 2017)

Yet another approach that specializes deep learning models for tabular data is *neural oblivious decision ensembles* (NODE), which uses differentiable oblivious decision trees (similar to CatBoost) but is trained with backpropagation like a neural network:

- Sergei Popov, Stanislav Morozov, and Artem Babenko, *Neural Oblivious Decision Ensembles for Deep Learning on Tabular Data* (ICLR, 2020)

Deep learning ensembles is an area of active research.

E.3 *Thank You!*

Finally, dear reader, thank you for reading this book and for making it to the very end! I hope that you had fun learning about ensemble methods and that you'll find this book helpful for your projects or perhaps simply as a useful reference. Good luck!

index